Building the Perfect PC

Building the Perfect PC

Third Edition

Robert Bruce Thompson

Barbara Fritchman Thompson

O'REILLY®
Beijing • Cambridge • Farnham • Köln • Sebastopol • Tokyo

Building the Perfect PC, Third Edition

by Robert Bruce Thompson and Barbara Fritchman Thompson

Published by O'Reilly Media, Inc., 1005 Gravenstein Highway North, Sebastopol, CA 95472.

O'Reilly Media books may be purchased for educational, business, or sales promotional use. Online editions are also available for most titles (*http://my.safaribooksonline.com*). For more information, contact our corporate/institutional sales department: 800-998-9938 or *corporate@oreilly.com*.

Editor: Brian Jepson

Production Editor: Rachel Monaghan

Copyeditor: Rachel Head

Proofreader: Rachel Monaghan

Indexer: Angela Howard

Cover Designer: Mark Paglietti

Interior Designer: Ron Bilodeau

Illustrator: Robert Romano

Print History:

August 2004:	First Edition.
December 2006:	Second Edition.
November 2010:	Third Edition.

ISBN: 978-1-449-38824-9

[TI]

To Mark Brokering, who came up with the idea and kept the ball rolling.

Contents

Foreword to the Third Edition

A lot has changed in the computer world since the last edition of this book, and even more since its first edition. Computers have become more powerful: when I wrote the foreword for the first edition, I had over 20 networked desktop computers, far more than I needed, but networking was complex and I needed a full network so that I could understand networking problems. Today, either of the two desktops I use as main machines have more computing power and disk storage than did all my computers put together a few years ago—and if I have a sudden need for a lot more storage or computing power, I have access to "cloud computing" that can supply far more.

There have been other changes since the last edition of *Building the Perfect PC*. Quad- and even hex-core processors (and the chipsets and CPU sockets to support them) have not only become commonplace, but pretty well required. Tiny Mini-ITX systems, formerly niche products, are mainstream. CRT monitors—bottles—have pretty well vanished, replaced by flat-panel LCD displays, some as large as TV sets used to be. Audio and video built in to the motherboard are now good enough for a lot more than they used to be, while some external video cards now do as much computing as the best CPUs did. Audio processing has changed dramatically. Memory has gone through transmogrifications from DDR to DDR2 (now giving way to DDR3). Solid-state drives are available for both laptops and desktops.

If you're contemplating building your own PC, you need to know about all this before you decide what to build. For that matter, you need to know what's going on before you buy a ready-built system, and other than in this book it's hard to find all that information in one place.

The reasons for building your own PC haven't changed a lot in the past decade. You build your own PC so that you will know more about it, how it works, what's probably wrong if something does go wrong, and just for the sheer satisfaction that you've got precisely the machine you want and need. But then, I covered all that in the foreword to the first edition, and those principles haven't changed. If you don't know whether to build or buy, this is still the best book I know of that will help you make that decision; and if you do decide to build your own, you really need this book.

—Jerry Pournelle
Chaos Manor
August 2010

Foreword to the Second Edition

I was asked to revise the foreword I wrote for the first edition of this book, but I found there was no need. A few details have changed, but the principles haven't.

However, the details are important. My main systems at Chaos Manor now mostly run with dual-core (both Intel and AMD) CPU chips. Since the first edition of *Building the Perfect PC*, the video card scene has changed several times. Intel lost its dominance as the maker of the fastest desktop CPUs for the money. AMD took advantage of the Intel stumble and surged ahead to its highest market share yet. AMD and nVidia joined forces, and now AMD has bought ATI. Case designs have changed. We have both DDR and DDR2 RAM to contend with.

If you have the first edition, you know how important the book is, and when you contemplate building a new system, you'll be wise to upgrade. And if you don't have the first edition, this remains the best book you can buy if you're building or planning to build a PC. Now read the foreword to the first edition.

—Jerry Pournelle
Chaos Manor
August 2006

Foreword to the First Edition

I presume you're reading this because you've either just bought this book or you're thinking of buying it, so let's get that out the way now. Should you buy this book, or, having bought it, should you be happy you did? The answer is yes. If the subject of building your own computer interests you—and why in the world are you reading this if it doesn't?—then you need this book.

That out of the way, we can look at the broader question of whether you should build your own computers.

As I look around Chaos Manor (*http://www.jerrypournelle.com*) I see that I have over 20 computers, all networked, and I built nearly every one of them myself. The exceptions are Princess, an ancient Compaq desktop Professional Workstation running Dual Pentium Plus 200 MHz CPUs; a Mac; a TabletPC; and another laptop. No one in his right mind builds his own laptop or Tablet. I keep Princess because I've had her for a decade, and she hasn't been shut down in more than a year, and I haven't the heart to scrap her; besides, she's still useful for doing long web searches. Until fairly recently I had a Compaq Professional Workstation (Dual 750 MHz Pentium III) as my communications system, but I retired it a few months ago in favor of a new 3 GHz built here, and since then every server and workstation added to the Chaos Manor network was built here. Clearly I must like building systems and using them.

It wasn't always this way. Until a few years ago I had at least as many brand-name systems as home-built "white boxes." Then came the consumerization of the PC industry. Manufacturers were forced into cost reduction after cost reduction. Some of those cost reductions were not wise. Some were disasters. Worse, component makers were themselves competing on cost. It became more and more difficult to build a quality line of PCs to sell at any realistic price.

It is still possible to buy quality computers. You'll pay for them, though, and sometimes having paid an arm and a leg, you still won't know what quality you have bought. There are still big companies with mission-critical tasks who are well advised to buy the very best machines from top-of-the-line companies, but most users and small businesses would be better advised to consider building their own, or having them built to specs by a trustworthy local shop—and this book is indispensable when it comes to writing out those specifications.

In general, there are two reasons why you build your own systems. First is if you want the *highest possible performance* using only the latest and greatest components. When new and better components come out, it takes a while for commercial system builders to change over, and the first ones to come out with the latest in high-performance demand and get premium prices; and you can customize your high performance system for your specific needs. If you're interested in building a really screaming machine, you need this book, because building that kind of system is tricky. Components like power supplies, cases, and fans are important, and information about why they are important is often hard to come by. You'll find all the information you need in this book.

The other reason for building your own system is to *get the best performance and quality for your money and to customize your high-performance system for your specific needs*. You probably don't need the very best performance available, and often you can get more than good enough systems at dramatically lower prices. These are known as "sweet spot" systems, and once again, if that's your goal, you need this book, because that too can be tricky. Sometimes saving money isn't a good idea at all. You can fudge on some components, but you're better off paying a premium for others. Bob and Barbara Thompson offer great advice on which is which.

So, if you're thinking of building your own system, you need this book to give you some notion of how difficult it's likely to be, and help you decide if it's a good idea; and if you're determined to build a PC, you need this book because most of us who build PCs have picked up a number of techniques and tricks over the years, and the Thompsons know nearly all of them. Learn from our mistakes. It's a lot easier.

—Jerry Pournelle
Chaos Manor
August 2004

Preface

The more things change, the more they remain the same. When we sat down to write this preface—always the last thing we do when writing a book—it was *déjà vu* all over again. For the second edition, we reused the preface from the 2004 first edition, and for this third edition we'll largely do the same.

In one sense, things have changed a lot over the years. None of the components we used in the second edition are still available. They've been replaced by bigger, faster, better, cheaper parts. But those are mere details. In a fundamental sense, nothing has changed. The reasons for building your own PC are the same. The decisions you need to make differ only in the details. The skills you need to master are the same, and the satisfaction you'll gain from designing and building your own PC is as great as ever.

So, on with the nearly original preface, which needed only slight modifications to update information about the system configurations in the book and other similar details.

Building PCs isn't just for techies anymore.

It used to be, certainly. Only gamers and other geeks actually built their PCs from the ground up. Everyone else just called Dell or Gateway and ordered a system. That started to change around the turn of the century. The first sign was when general merchandisers like Best Buy started stocking upgrade components. If you wanted to expand the memory in your PC or install a larger hard drive or add a CD writer, you could now get the components you needed at the local big-box store.

A year or two later, things changed again. Big-box retailers started carrying PC components like cases and motherboards—parts seldom needed by upgraders, but necessary to build a new PC from scratch. Nowadays, although Best Buy and other local retailers may not carry as broad a range of PC components as some online specialty retailers, you can get everything you need for a new PC with one visit to a big-box store.

Specialty PC component superstores like Fry's carry a full range of components at extremely good prices. We wish we had a Fry's within driving distance. Then again, maybe not. There's too much good stuff there. Our credit cards are smoking already, and a trip to Fry's might be the last straw.

And you can bet that big-box stores don't allocate shelf space to products that aren't selling. Building your own PC has become mainstream. Nowadays, even regular nontechnical people build their own systems and have fun doing it. Instead of settling for a mediocre, cookie-cutter system from Dell or HP, they get

Every project system in this book can be built entirely from components available at your local big-box store. If some of the components we recommend aren't in stock, one or more of the alternative components we recommend almost certainly will be. If you buy this book on a Friday, you can buy your components Saturday morning, assemble the new system Saturday afternoon, test it Sunday, and have it up and running Monday morning.

Brian Jepson Comments

Hell, technically Apple has something to worry about, since a lot of people build PCs to run Mac OS X even though they aren't supposed to.

a PC with exactly the features and components they want, at a good price, and with the pride that comes from knowing they built it themselves. They also get a faster, higher-quality PC with much better reliability than any mass-market system. No small thing, that.

Robert visited Best Buy one day and spent some time hanging out in the PC component aisles. He watched a lot of regular people comparing hard drives, video adapters, DVD writers, and other PC components. Some of them were buying components to upgrade their current systems, but many of them were buying components to build new systems.

Robert watched one grandmotherly woman fill her shopping cart. She chose an Antec case and power supply, a Maxtor hard drive, an Abit motherboard, an AMD Athlon XP processor, an NVIDIA graphics adapter, a couple of sticks of DDR memory, and a LiteOn DVD writer. He approached her, and the conversation went something like this:

Robert: "Looks like you're building a new computer."

Woman: "Yes, I'm building my granddaughter a new PC for her birthday."

Robert: "Are you worried about getting everything to work?"

Woman: "Oh, no. This is the third one I've built. You should try it. It's easy."

Robert: "I may do that."

If she'd had this book, she might have made different choices for one or two of her components. Still, Dell, ASUS, HP Compaq, and Gateway may have something to worry about.

Goals of This Book

This book is your guide to the world of building PCs. Our goal is to teach you—even if you have no training or prior experience—everything you need to know to select the best components and assemble them into a working PC that matches your own requirements and budget.

We present six projects, in as many chapters (Chapters 3 through 8), each of which details design, component selection, and assembly instructions for a particular type of PC. You can build any or all of these systems as presented, or you can modify them to suit your own requirements.

Rather than using a straight cookbook approach, which would simply tell you *how* to build a PC by rote, we spend a lot of time explaining *why* we made particular design decisions or chose certain components or did something a certain way. By "looking over our shoulders" as we design PCs and choose components, you'll learn to make good decisions when it comes to designing and building your own PC. You'll also learn how to build a PC with superior quality, performance, and reliability.

Not that we skimped on the how-to. Each project system chapter provides detailed assembly instructions and dozens of photographs that illustrate the assembly process. Even if you've never seen a hard drive, after reading this book you should be completely comfortable sitting down with a bunch of components to build your own PC.

If you have never built a PC, we hope this book will inspire you to build your first system. If you have some PC-building experience, we hope this book will provide the ideas and advice that you need to make the next PC you build the Perfect PC for your needs.

Audience for This Book

This book is intended for anyone who wants to build a PC for personal or business use. System builders of any experience level will find this book useful because it explains the concepts used to design a PC to fit specific needs and budgets and provides the information needed to choose the best components. First-time system builders will also find this book helpful because it provides detailed step-by-step instructions for building a PC, supplemented by numerous photographs that illustrate each step in detail.

Organization of This Book

The first two chapters of this book are a short but comprehensive course in planning the perfect PC and choosing and buying components for it.

Chapter 1, *Fundamentals*, focuses on things you need to know, things you need to have, and things you need to do before you start to buy components and build your new PC. This chapter explains the advantages of building a PC versus buying one (*you* control the quality, performance, reliability, and quietness of your components), provides design guidelines, and explains the inevitable trade-offs in performance, price, size, and noise level. We list the tools and software you'll need, and we also provide detailed troubleshooting information in this chapter, because it's easier to avoid problems if you know from the beginning what to look out for. After you read this chapter, you'll be prepared for the next step, actually buying the components for your new PC.

Chapter 2, *Choosing and Buying Components*, tells you everything you need to know about how to choose and buy the components you need to build your new PC.

We explain the important characteristics of each component and how to choose among alternatives. We also recommend brands, and provide alternative recommendations for those with different requirements or smaller budgets.

The final six chapters detail project systems, any of which you can build as-is or modify to suit your particular needs. The introductory section of each project chapter is a design guide that explains the choices we made (and why) and how we decided to implement them. Following that is a detailed section on selecting components, with specific products listed by brand name and a bill of materials at the end of the section. In each case, we list alternatives for those with different needs or budgets. The bulk of each chapter is a detailed guide, with numerous photographs, that shows you step-by-step how to build the system.

Chapter 3, *Building a Budget PC*, shows you how to build a fast, reliable PC on a minimum budget. For only $300 or so (not counting external peripherals), you can build a system with high-quality components that matches or exceeds the performance of last year's mainstream models. We designed this budget

When you design and build your own PC, you get something that money can't buy if you purchase a preassembled machine: total control over quality, reliability, performance, and noise level.

We designed all of the project systems in the book to be capable of running Windows 7. We also verified that each system was in fact able to run Windows 7 Ultimate at the performance levels that anyone might reasonably expect. Of course, those performance levels varied by system, from the blazing-fast extreme system to the rather pedestrian appliance system.

system to run the free Linux operating system, but it's also fully capable of running Windows 7. It's ideal as a secondary system—or even a primary system, if your needs are modest—and can be upgraded incrementally to add additional features.

Chapter 4, *Building a Mainstream System*, teaches you how to build a general-purpose PC that is a jack of all trades and a master of…well, quite a few, actually. In the standard configuration, this system combines high performance, top-notch reliability, and moderate cost. Depending on the components you choose—and how much you're willing to spend—you can make this system anything from an inexpensive entry-level box to a do-it-all powerhouse. And it's also quiet, particularly if you build it in a midrange configuration. In a normal office or home environment, you can barely hear it running.

Chapter 5, *Building an Extreme System*, is all about building an extreme-performance PC on a reasonable budget. The project system is optimized for video editing and scientific number crunching but with minimal changes it can easily be morphed into an extreme gaming PC.

Chapter 6, *Building a Media Center System*, shows you how to build a small, quiet, attractive PC to sit in your den or media room to centralize storage and access to your audio and video collection—CDs, DVDs, streaming videos, camcorder footage, digital photographs, and so on. Although we didn't do so for our media center system, you can also enable it to record over-the-air, cable, or satellite television programs by installing one or more tuner cards and a copy of Windows 7 Media Center or a free PVR/DVR package like MythPC. Depending on how you configure it, the media center PC can substitute not only for a commercial DVR unit, but also for an AV receiver, CD player, DVD and/or Blu-ray player, DVD recorder, 5.1 home-theater speaker system, *and* gaming console. Talk about serious bang for the buck.

Chapter 7, *Building an Appliance/Nettop System*, shows you how to build a fully featured PC that is small enough and quiet enough to fit in almost anywhere. Depending on the components you choose, you can make an appliance PC that can serve as an inexpensive secondary system suitable for a dorm room or child's bedroom, a primary general-purpose system, a home theater or PVR system, a barn-burner of a portable gaming system, or a dedicated small server.

Chapter 8, *Building a Home Server*, focuses on building a reliable, high-performance home server. We emphasize reliability and data safety regardless of configuration, because a server failure is as disruptive for a home office as it is for a business. Accordingly, we cover such optional features as redundant disk storage (RAID) and such mandatory features as reliable backup.

> *Each project chapter is full of tips, many of which are useful no matter what type of system you build. Accordingly, we suggest you read the entire book, including all project system chapters, before you start building your new system.*

We'd Like to Hear from You

We have tested and verified the information in this book to the best of our ability, but we don't doubt that some errors have crept in and remained hidden despite our best efforts and those of our editors and technical reviewers to find and eradicate them. Those errors are ours alone. If you find an error or have other comments about the book, you can contact the publisher or the authors.

How to Contact O'Reilly

Please address comments and questions concerning this book to the publisher:

O'Reilly Media, Inc.

1005 Gravenstein Highway North

Sebastopol, CA 95472

(800) 998-9938 (in the United States or Canada)

(707) 829-0515 (international or local)

(707) 829-0104 (fax)

You can also send us email. To be put on our mailing list or to request a catalog, send email to:

info@oreilly.com

To comment on the book, send email to:

bookquestions@oreilly.com

For more information about books, conferences, Resource Centers, and the O'Reilly Network, go to:

http://www.oreilly.com

How to Contact the Authors

To contact one of the authors directly, send mail to:

barbara@hardwareguys.com

robert@hardwareguys.com

We read all mail we receive from readers, but we cannot respond individually. If we did, we'd have no time to do anything else. But we do like to hear from readers.

We each maintain a personal journal page, updated daily, which frequently includes references to new PC hardware we're working with, problems we've discovered, and other things we think are interesting. You can view these journal pages at:

Barbara: *http://www.fritchman.com/diaries/thisweek.html*

Robert: *http://www.ttgnet.com/thisweek.html*

Disclaimer

Much of the information contained in this book is based on personal knowledge and experience. While we believe that the information contained herein is correct, we accept no responsibility for its validity. The hardware designs and descriptive text contained herein are provided for educational purposes only. It is the responsibility of the reader to independently verify all information. Original manufacturer's data should be used at all times when implementing a design.

Warning

Although we tested the configurations we specified for each project system, we did not build and test every permutation with the alternative components we listed. Those alternatives are simply what we might have used if our requirements had been different. That said, we would expect the alternative components we list to work in any combination, and would be very surprised if they didn't. When we are aware of a potential conflict or compatibility issue, we say so.

Safari® Books Online

 Safari Books Online is an on-demand digital library that lets you easily search over 7,500 technology and creative reference books and videos to find the answers you need quickly.

With a subscription, you can read any page and watch any video from our library online. Read books on your cell phone and mobile devices. Access new titles before they are available for print, and get exclusive access to manuscripts in development and post feedback for the authors. Copy and paste code samples, organize your favorites, download chapters, bookmark key sections, create notes, print out pages, and benefit from tons of other time-saving features.

O'Reilly Media has uploaded this book to the Safari Books Online service. To have full digital access to this book and others on similar topics from O'Reilly and other publishers, sign up for free at *http://my.safaribooksonline.com*.

Acknowledgments

The first edition of this book was conceived one day in late 2003, when Robert received a phone call from Mark Brokering, Vice President of Sales and Marketing for O'Reilly Media. Mark had decided to build a new PC rather than buy one, and he'd picked up a copy of Robert and Barbara's book, *PC Hardware in a Nutshell*.

Mark had lots of good questions about which components to choose and, later on, questions about assembling his new system. At some point during the back-and-forth of emails and phone calls, Mark commented, "You know, we really need to do a book about building a PC." And so this book was born.

The working title was *Build Your Own Computer*. None of us thought that was a great title, but none of us could come up with a better one. Then one day Tim O'Reilly weighed in: "Why don't we call it *Building the Perfect PC*?" Duh. It always seems so obvious after the fact.

In addition to Mark, Tim, and the O'Reilly production staff, we want to thank our technical reviewers.

> **Ron Morse** has been an electronics hobbyist for as long as he can remember. "Probably longer. There was that unfortunate incident as a teenager when I removed the back of a then-new color television set…." In the more than 30 years since he was released from the hospital, he has devoted every spare dollar and available credit card balance to pursuing his interests in aviation, photography, and electronics. He bought his first personal computer in 1983 and has been upgrading, modifying, and repairing them (mostly in that order) ever since.

In his spare time Ron served on active duty with the Navy for 26 years, retiring in 2001 with the rank of Captain. He was awarded the Bronze Star medal for his service in Bahrain and Saudi Arabia during Operations Desert Shield and Desert Storm and also holds the Defense Superior Service Medal, the Defense Meritorious Service Medal, the Navy Meritorious Service Medal, and the Army Commendation Medal, among others.

After retiring from the Navy, Ron designed and maintained custom computer systems for small businesses and served as a director of the Rinconada Group, a strategic communications firm specializing in programs for business and elected officials and government agencies at the local, state, and national levels.

He lives with his wife Deborah, three Border Collies, and a Queensland Blue Heeler in Albuquerque, New Mexico.

Brian Bilbrey started working with electronics back when vacuum tubes were still in vogue. In passing, he's built gear with those tubes, and with many forms of digital technology, from wirewrap and PCB design through specifying and assembling desktop and server systems for many companies over the years. Usually Brian's formal role in a firm is some form of system administrator, but he finds several hats to wear as time goes on.

Brian is approaching the end of his fourth decade in pursuit of an actual sheepskin, as life and work always seemed more interesting and, well, educational. But in a couple of years, with optional sleep and an understanding full-time job, that item will get crossed off the bucket list, too.

Brian lives in Bowie, Maryland, with his lovely bride of 12 years, Marcia, and a slowly evolving collection of rescue dogs. Currently those are Molly, a loving but elderly black lab, and Lexi, a tactical nuke disguised as a 15-pound chipuggle.

Both Ron and Brian did yeoman duty in finding mistakes we made and in making numerous useful suggestions, all of which helped make this a better book. We're entirely responsible for any errors that remain.

We also want to thank our contacts at the hardware companies, who provided technical help, evaluation units, and other assistance. There are far too many to list individually, but they know who they are. We also want to thank the readers of our books, websites, and forums, many of whom have taken the time to offer useful suggestions for improvements to this book. Thanks, folks. We couldn't have done it without you.

Finally, we want to thank our editor, Brian Jepson, who contributed numerous useful comments and suggestions.

Thank You

Thank you for buying this new edition of *Building the Perfect PC*. We hope you enjoy reading it as much as we enjoyed writing it.

Fundamentals

1

The idea of building their first PC intimidates many people, but there's really nothing to worry about. Building a PC is no more technically challenging than changing the oil in your car or hooking up a DVD player. Compared to assembling one of those "connect tab A to slot B" toys for the kids, it's a breeze.

PC components connect like building blocks. Component sizes, screw threads, mounting hole positions, cable connectors, and so on are mostly standardized, so you needn't worry about whether something will fit. There are minor exceptions, of course. For example, some small cases accept only microATX motherboards and half-height or half-length expansion cards. There are also some important details to pay attention to. You must verify, for example, that the motherboard you intend to use supports the processor you plan to use. But overall, there are few "gotchas" involved in building a PC. If you follow our advice in the project system chapters, everything will fit and everything will work together.

Nor do you need to worry much about damaging the PC—or it damaging you. Simple precautions such as handling components with reasonable care, grounding yourself before touching static-sensitive components, and verifying cable connections before you apply power are sufficient to prevent damage to all those expensive parts you bought. Other than inside the power supply—which you should *never* open—the highest voltage used inside a modern PC is 12V, which presents no shock hazard.

This chapter doesn't cover the nuts-and-bolts details of assembling a PC, because that's covered exhaustively in text and images in the project system chapters. Instead, this chapter explains the fundamentals—everything you need to prepare yourself properly. It examines the advantages of building your own PC and explains how to design a PC that is perfect for your needs. It tells you what you need to know and do before you start the project, and lists the components, hand tools, and software tools you'll need to build your system. Finally, because the best way to troubleshoot is to avoid problems in the first place, it includes a detailed troubleshooting section.

Let's get started.

Mixing Old and New

Most compatibility issues arise when you mix new components with older ones. For example, an older video card may not fit the video slot in a new motherboard, and a new processor may not be compatible with an older motherboard. If you build a PC from all new components, you are likely to encounter few such issues. Still, it's a good idea to verify compatibility between the motherboard and other major components, particularly the CPU, video adapters, and memory. The configurations in this book have been tested for compatibility.

Why Build a PC?

With entry-level PCs selling for less than $500 and fully equipped mainstream PCs for $1,000, you might wonder why anyone would bother to build a PC. After all, you can't save any money building one, can you? Well, yes, you can. But that's not the only reason to build a PC. There are many incentives:

Lower cost

PC makers aren't in business for charitable reasons. They need to make a profit, so they need to sell computers for more than they pay for the components and the labor to assemble them. Significantly more, in fact, because they also need to support such expensive operations as research and development departments, toll-free support numbers, and so on.

But PC manufacturers get big price breaks because they buy components in huge volume, right? Not really. The market for PC components is extremely efficient, with razor-thin margins whether you buy one unit or 100,000. A volume purchaser gets a price break, certainly, but it's a lot smaller than most people think.

Mass-market PCs are inexpensive not because the makers get huge price breaks on quality components, but because they generally use the cheapest possible components. Cost-cutting is a fact of life in mass-market, consumer-grade PCs. If mass-market PC makers can save a few bucks on the case or the power supply, they do it every time, even though spending a few dollars more (or even a few cents more) would have allowed them to build a noticeably better system. If you compare apples to apples—a home-built system versus a corporate business-class system—you'll find you can build it yourself for less (sometimes a lot less). Our rule of thumb is that, on average and all other things being equal, you can build a midrange PC yourself for about 75% to 85% of what a major manufacturer charges for an equivalent top-quality system.

More choice

When you buy a PC, you get a cookie-cutter computer. You can choose such options as a larger hard drive, more memory, or a better display, but basically you get what the vendor decides to give you. If you want something that few people ask for, like a better power supply or quieter cooling fans or a motherboard with more features, you're out of luck. Those aren't options.

And what you get is a matter of chance. High-volume direct vendors like Dell and HP often use multiple sources for components. Two supposedly identical systems ordered the same day may contain significantly different components, including such important variations as different motherboards or displays with the same model number but made by different manufacturers. When *you* build a PC, you decide exactly what goes into it.

Cheaper by the Dozen?

For example, when AMD or Intel announces new processor models, the news stories often report "Quantity 1000" pricing for the OEM or "tray" versions. This is what a computer maker who buys processors 1,000 at a time pays. A maker who buys 100,000 at a time may pay a few dollars less per processor. If you buy just one OEM processor, you'll typically pay a couple bucks more than the Quantity 1000 pricing. You may even pay less, because PC makers often order more processors than they need to take advantage of price breaks on larger quantities, and then sell the unneeded processors at a slight loss to distributors who then sell them to retailers.

DON'T COMPARE APPLES TO ORANGES

For more than 25 years, Robert's friend Jerry Pournelle wrote the Chaos Manor column for *BYTE*. One month, Jerry decided to build an inexpensive PC as a project system for his column. He wanted to see if he could match the price of a mass-market system he'd seen advertised in the morning paper. So Jerry headed off to Fry's and returned to Chaos Manor with a stack of components.

Shortly afterward, Robert got a phone call from Jerry. Jerry said he'd spent $50 more on components than the mass-market PC would have cost him, "and that doesn't even count the time it'll take me to assemble it." That didn't sound right, so Robert started asking questions. The processor speed, amount of memory, and hard drive size were the same, so Robert started drilling down.

Robert: "What kind of case and power supply did you buy, and how much did they cost you?"

Jerry: "It's an Antec with a 350W power supply. I paid about $70 for it."

Robert: "Was that the cheapest case and power supply Fry's had?"

Jerry: "Well, no. They had a no-name case with a 300W power supply for $14, but I sure wouldn't use something that cheap for any of my systems."

Robert: "How about the motherboard?"

Jerry: "I got an ASUS motherboard for $130. They didn't have that $90 ASUS motherboard you recommended. They had an ECS motherboard for $38, but there was no way I was going to use that."

And so on. Jerry did what most of us would do and what any sensible person would do. He built his "inexpensive" PC using the least expensive high-quality components he could find. But he then compared that top-notch inexpensive system against a mass-market system that was built using the cheapest components available. Would the mass-market system's maker have used a $14 case and power supply and a $38 motherboard? In a heartbeat.

Jerry couldn't bring himself to take the cost-cutting measures that mass-market PC makers take without a second thought, so he ended up comparing apples to oranges. Jerry spent about $150 more on just the case, power supply, and motherboard, and ended up with a system than cost only $50 more than the piece of junk being advertised in the morning paper. If instead he'd compared the cost of his system against a system of equivalent quality, such as an entry-level business-class system, he might have been surprised at just how much he saved.

Flexible design

One of the best things about building your own PC is that you can optimize its design to focus on what is important to you and ignore what isn't. Off-the-shelf commercial PCs are by nature jacks of all trades and masters of none. System vendors have to strike a happy medium that is adequate, if not optimum, for the mythical "average" user.

Want a small, quiet PC for your home theater system? There are three options. You can use a standard PC despite its large size and high noise level, you can pay big bucks for a system from a specialty builder that does just what you want, or you can build your own. Need a system with a ton of redundant hard disk storage for editing video or a professional audio workstation? Good luck finding a commercial system that fits your requirements, at least at a reasonable price. When you build your own PC, you can spend your money on things that matter to you, not things that don't.

Brian Jepson Comments

Regarding home theater systems, there is another option: the Mac Mini is hugely popular here, so you might want to give it a nod. That's probably one reason that it's often at the top of Amazon's desktop PC category.

Better component quality

Most computer vendors cut costs by using cheaper OEM versions of popular components if they're "visible" and no-name components if they're not. By "visible" we mean a component that people might seek out by brand name even in a prebuilt PC, such as an ATI or NVIDIA video adapter. Invisible components are ones that buyers seldom ask about or notice, such as motherboards, optical and hard drives, power supplies, and so on.

OEM components may be identical to retail models, differing only in packaging. But even if the parts are the same, there are often significant differences. Component vendors usually do not support OEM versions directly, for example, instead referring you to the system vendor. If that system vendor goes out of business, you're out of luck, because the component maker provides no warranty to end users. Even if the maker does support OEM products, the warranty is usually much shorter on OEM parts—often as little as 30 to 90 days. The products themselves may also differ significantly between OEM and retail-boxed versions. Major PC vendors often use downgraded versions of popular products, for example, an OEM video adapter that has the same or a very similar name as the retail-boxed product but runs at a lower clock rate than the retail version. This allows PC makers to pay less for components and still gain the cachet from using the name-brand product.

It's worse when it comes to "invisible" components. We've popped the lid on scores of consumer-grade PCs over the years, and it never ceases to surprise us just how cheaply they're built. Not one of them had a power supply that we'd even consider using in one of our own systems, for example. They're packed with no-name motherboards, generic memory, the cheapest optical drives available, and so on. Even the cables are often shoddy. After all, why pay a buck more for a decent cable? In terms of reliability, we consider a consumer-grade PC a disaster waiting to happen.

Quality Costs Money

Not all commercial PCs are poorly built. Business-class systems and gaming systems from "boutique" vendors are well engineered with top-quality components and high build quality. Of course, they also cost a lot more than consumer-grade systems.

No bundled software

Most purchased PCs include Microsoft Windows. If you don't need or want this software, building a PC allows you to avoid paying the "Microsoft tax."

Full, Upgrade, and OEM Windows Licenses

We formerly recommended installing an OEM (System Builder) version of Windows. No more. We used to pay $50 or $60 for an OEM Windows license, but beginning with Windows Vista, Microsoft started increasing the prices of OEM Windows licenses and putting increasingly Draconian restrictions on them.

Buying an individual OEM Windows license is now a sucker bet. Actually, using an OEM Windows license on a system you build for your own use violates and voids the license. An OEM Windows license is technically valid only for a system that you build and subsequently sell to someone else. We suppose you could build a system and sell it to your husband or girlfriend without violating the license agreement, but that's treading a fine line.

Assuming you have a qualifying older version of Windows, a Windows Retail Upgrade license—which costs about the same amount as an OEM license—is a much better deal for most people. Finally, a full retail Windows license is available for those who don't qualify for an upgrade. A full retail license

costs about 50% more than an OEM or Retail Upgrade license, but that license (including upgraded versions of it) can be freely moved from system to system.

Before you buy Windows, make sure you understand all the license alternatives. The best discussion we've seen of the complexities of Windows licensing is Ed Bott's column on the subject (http://www.zdnet.com/blog/bott/what-microsoft-wont-tell-you-about-windows-7-licensing/1514).

Finally, as long as you have a new system with no operating system installed on it, you might as well give Linux a try before you shell out money for Windows. Most people who give Linux a serious trial are very impressed with it, and a significant number of them end up converting to using Linux exclusively. We and many of our friends are among that group. There are many different Linux distributions available, but two of the most newbie-friendly are Ubuntu (http://www.ubuntu.com) and Linux Mint (http://www.linuxmint.com).

Warranty

The retail-boxed components you'll use to build your own PC include full manufacturer warranties that may run from one to five years or more, depending on the component. PC makers use OEM components, which often include no manufacturer warranty to the end user. If something breaks, you're at the mercy of the PC maker to repair or replace it. We've heard from readers who bought PCs from makers who went out of business shortly thereafter. When a hard drive or video card failed six months later, they contacted the maker of the item, only to find that they had OEM components that were not under manufacturer warranty.

Experience

If you buy a computer, your experience with it consists of taking it out of the box and connecting the cables. If you build the computer, you know exactly what went into it, and you're in a much better position to resolve any problems that may occur.

Upgrades

If you design and build your own PC, you can upgrade it later using industry-standard components. That's sometimes not the case with commercial systems, some of which are intentionally designed to be incompatible with industry-standard components (although this is a less common practice today than when we wrote the first edition of this book). PC makers do this because they want to force you to buy upgrade and replacement components from them, at whatever price they want to charge.

Save Those Receipts

Keep receipts together with the "retain this portion" of warranty cards and put them someplace they can be found if required for future warranty service. This goes for software, too. Ron Morse puts all that stuff in an envelope and tapes it to the inside of the case cover, or some other out-of-the-way location. That keeps all the papers in one place and everything associated with that particular computer…well, associated with that particular computer.

Intentional Gotchas

These designed-in incompatibilities may be as trivial as nonstandard screw sizes, or as profound as components that are electrically incompatible with standard components. For example, some Dell PCs have used motherboards and power supplies with standard connectors but nonstandard pin connections. If you replaced a failed Dell power supply with a standard ATX power supply—or if you connected the nonstandard Dell power supply to a standard motherboard—the power supply and motherboard were destroyed as soon as you applied power to the system.

Brian Bilbrey Adds

Another egregious offender in this realm was eMachines, which put proprietary, really terrible power supplies in their systems. For a while there, I was putting compatible quality replacements in those for friends and family…from PC Power & Cooling.

Ron Morse Comments

You missed one of the best reasons to build your own PC, at least if you have children (or grandchildren). Building a PC is one of the best mother/father–daughter/son weekend projects I can imagine.

Brian Bilbrey Adds

I second this, especially since you can't buy a Heathkit tube radio or television anymore.

Designing the Perfect PC

A sign you'll see in many repair shops says, "Good. Cheap. Fast. Pick any two." That's also true of designing a PC. Every choice you make involves a trade-off, and balancing those trade-offs is the key to designing a PC that's perfect for your needs. Each project system chapter has a graphic that looks something like this:

Price	☆ ☆ ☆ ☆ ☆
Reliability	☆ ☆ ☆ ☆ ☆
Size	☆ ☆ ☆ ☆ ☆
Noise level	☆ ☆ ☆ ☆ ☆
Expandability	☆ ☆ ☆ ☆ ☆
Processor performance	☆ ☆ ☆ ☆ ☆
Video performance	☆ ☆ ☆ ☆ ☆
Disk capacity/performance	☆ ☆ ☆ ☆ ☆

Ah, if it were only true. Reality, of course, is different. One can't put the highest priority on everything. Something has to give. As Frederick the Great said of designing military defenses, "He who defends everything defends nothing." The same is true of designing a PC.

If you focus on these elements while designing your PC, you'll soon realize that compromises are inevitable. If small size is essential, for example, you must make compromises in expandability, and you may very well have to compromise in other respects. The trick is to decide, before you start buying components, which elements are essential, which are important, which would be nice to have, and which can be ignored.

Once you have the priority of those elements firmly fixed in your mind, you can make rational resource allocations and good purchasing decisions. It's worth looking at each of these elements in a bit more detail:

Price

> We put price first, because it's the 900-pound gorilla in system design. If low price is essential, you'll be forced to make compromises in most or all of the other elements. Simply put, high performance, reliability, low noise, small size, and other desirable characteristics cost money. We suggest you begin by establishing a ballpark price range for your new system and then play "what-if" with the other elements. If you've set too low a price, it will soon become clear that you'll need to spend more. On the other hand, you may well find that you can get away with spending less and still get everything you want in a system.

Reliability

We consider high reliability essential in any system, even the least expensive entry-level PC. If a system is unreliable, it doesn't matter how feature-laden it is, or how fast, or how cheap. We always aim for 5-star reliability in systems we design for ourselves and others, although sometimes price and other constraints force us to settle for 4-star reliability. The best mass-market systems may have 3-star reliability, but most deserve only a 1- or 2-star rating.

What does reliability mean, and how do you design for it? A reliable system doesn't crash or corrupt data. It runs for years with only an occasional cleaning. We are always amused when people claim Windows is crash-prone. That was true of Windows 9X, of course, but Windows NT/2000/XP/Vista/7 has never blue- or black-screened on us without good reason, and that's going back to the early days of Windows NT 4. We're not Microsoft fanboys—far from it—but the truth is that most system crashes that are blamed on Windows are actually caused by marginal or failing hardware, buggy third-party drivers, or malware.

There are a few simple rules for designing a reliable system. First, use only top-quality parts. They don't have to be the fastest available—in fact, high-performance parts often run hotter and are therefore less reliable than midrange ones—but top-quality components may be a full order of magnitude more reliable than run-of-the-mill ones. Use a motherboard built around a reliable chipset and made by a top-notch manufacturer. For Intel processors, Intel motherboards and chipsets are the standard by which we judge, and for AMD processors the same is true of ASUS and GIGABYTE motherboards and AMD chipsets. Use a first-rate power supply and the best memory available. Avoid cheap cables. Keep the system cool and clean out the dust periodically. That's all there is to it. Following this advice means the system will cost a bit more, but it will also be significantly more reliable.

Size

Most people prefer a small PC to a large one, but it's easy to design a system that's too small. Albert Einstein said, "Everything should be made as simple as possible, but not simpler." In other words, don't oversimplify. Use the same rule when you choose a size for your PC. Don't over-smallify.

Choosing a small case inevitably forces you to make compromises. A small case limits your choice of components, because some components simply won't fit. For example, you may have to use a different optical drive than you'd prefer because your first choice is too long or too tall to fit into the case. A small case also limits the number of components you can install. For example, you may have to choose between installing a card reader and installing a second hard drive. Because a small case can accept fewer (and smaller) fans, it's more difficult to cool the system properly. To move the same amount of air, a smaller fan must spin faster than a larger fan, which generates more noise. The limited case volume makes it much harder to work inside the case, and makes it more difficult to route cables

Determining Quality

Of course, this begs the question, how does one tell great from good from bad? Discriminating among companies and brands is difficult for someone who doesn't know which companies have an established reputation for quality and reliability, which purvey mostly junk, and which are too new to have a track record. All of the components and brands we recommend in this book are safe choices, but the proliferation of brands makes it easy to choose inferior components.

If you must use components other than those we recommend, the best way to avoid inferior components is to do your homework. Visit the manufacturers' websites. A good website doesn't guarantee that the products are also good, but a poor website almost certainly means the products are also poor. Check online reviews of products you are considering, and visit discussion forums for those components. In the end, trust your own judgment. If a component appears cheap, it probably isn't reliable. If the documentation is sparse or isn't written in good English, that tells you something about the likely quality of the component as well. If the component has a much shorter warranty than similar components from other manufacturers, there's probably good reason.

Finally, although price is not a perfect predictor of component quality, it's usually a very good indicator. The PC component business is extremely competitive, so if a product sells for much less than similar competing products, it's almost certainly inferior.

to avoid impeding air flow. All other things being equal, a small PC will cost more, run slower, produce more heat and noise, or be less reliable than a standard-size PC (or possibly all of those).

For most purposes, the best choice is a standard mini- or mid-tower case. A full-tower case is an excellent choice for a server, or for an office system that sits on the floor next to your desk. Choose a microATX or other small form factor case only if size is a high priority.

Noise level

Noise isn't the problem it was a few years ago. Back then, the constant demand for more performance had led to systems with 130W processors and 200W video cards. Better technology has shrunk the die sizes of processors and video GPUs and greatly reduced their power consumption. With that reduction in power consumption comes a reduction in the amount of heat produced and the number and speed of the fans needed to cool the system. Nowadays, most budget and mainstream systems are reasonably quiet, although performance and extreme gaming systems may still sound like leaf blowers.

Still, it's quite possible to build two systems with similar components and have one system twice as loud as the other. Throughout this book, whenever possible we choose the quietest available standard components. Even the loudest system we built—the extreme system—is quiet enough that most people will not find it intrusive, particularly if it's under a desk.

Expandability

Expandability is worth considering when you design a PC. For some systems, expandability is unimportant. You design the system for a particular job, install the components you need to do that job, and never open the case again except for routine cleaning and maintenance. For most general-purpose systems, though, expandability is desirable. For example, if you need more disk space, you might prefer to add a second hard drive rather than replacing the original drive. You can't do that unless there's a vacant drive bay. Similarly, integrated video might suffice at first, but you may later decide that you need faster video. If the motherboard you used has no PCI Express expansion slot available for a video card, you're out of luck. The only option is to replace the motherboard.

Keep expandability in mind when you choose components, so you won't paint yourself into any corners. Unless size constraints forbid it, choose a case that leaves plenty of room for growth. Choose a power supply that has sufficient reserve to support additional drives, memory, and perhaps a faster processor. Choose a motherboard that provides sufficient expansion slots and memory sockets to allow for possible future expansion. Choose less flexible components only if you are certain that you will never need to expand the system.

Brian Bilbrey Comments

Or possibly a jet engine. I have a server-grade tower system at my desk. It's reasonably quiet in operation, but when booting, before the fan regulation kicks in, it does sound a bit like a Boeing spooling up on the ramp. People down the hall have been known to come looking, "What was that?!?"

Processor performance

Most people worry too much about processor performance. Here's the truth. Midrange processors—those that sell for $150 (give or take $25)—are noticeably faster than $50 to $100 entry-level processors. Performance processors—those that sell for $300 (give or take $100)—are noticeably faster than mainstream processors. Not night-and-day different, but it is noticeable. The most expensive "extreme" processors, which sell for up to $1,000, are typically two to four times faster than midrange processors. For casual use—browsing the Web, checking email, word processing, and so on—choose a $60 to $75 "value" processor. For a general-purpose system, choose a processor that sells for $150 to $200 in retail-boxed form. If you want a bit more processor horsepower for extreme gaming or other tasks and are willing to pay the price, a performance processor may be worth buying. It makes little sense to choose an extreme processor unless cost is no object and performance is critical.

Video performance

Video performance, like processor performance, usually gets more attention than it deserves. It's probably no coincidence that processors and video adapters are two of the most heavily promoted PC components. When you design your PC, be careful not to get caught up in the hype. If the PC will be used for intense 3D gaming or similarly demanding video tasks, you need a high-end video adapter (or multiple video adapters). Otherwise, you don't.

Integrated video—a video adapter built into the motherboard—is the least expensive video solution and is perfectly adequate for most uses. The incremental cost of integrated video ranges from $0 to perhaps $10, relative to a similar motherboard without integrated video. The next step up in video performance is a standalone video adapter, which requires the motherboard to have a slot to accept it. Standalone video adapters range in price from $25 or so up to $600 or more. A $75 to $100 video adapter is sufficient to play most 3D games, particularly those that have been available for a year or more.

More expensive video adapters provide incrementally faster 3D video performance and may support more recent versions of Microsoft DirectX, both of which are of interest to serious gamers. A $150 to $200 video adapter suffices to play even recent, demanding 3D games at reasonable resolutions and frame rates.

Only rabid gamers buy the most expensive video adapters, and they get a lot less for their money than you might expect. A $600 video adapter, for example, isn't four times faster than a $150 video adapter. It may be only 25% faster, which for most people isn't worth the extra cost. High-end video adapters also run hot and are generally equipped with dedicated cooling fans, which produce additional noise.

When you design your PC, we recommend using integrated video unless you need the faster 3D performance a standalone video adapter can provide. If you choose integrated video, make sure the motherboard has a PCI Express x16 slot available in case you later decide to upgrade the video.

Disk capacity/performance

A mainstream 7,200 RPM serial ATA (SATA) hard drive is the best choice for nearly any system. Such drives are fast, inexpensive, and reliable. The best models are also relatively quiet and produce little heat. When you design your system, use one of these drives unless you have good reason to do otherwise.

Avoid 5,400 RPM or 5,900 RPM drives, which cost less than 7,200 RPM models but have noticeably poorer performance. The exception to that rule is when performance doesn't matter. For example, you may need to store huge amounts of data that is seldom accessed, in which case performance may be less important than capacity and cost. Similarly, if you're using the drive in an external chassis for doing overnight backups, you probably don't care if the backup takes four hours to complete on a 5,400 RPM drive versus only three hours on a 7,200 RPM drive.

If you need very high disk performance, consider installing a *solid-state drive* (SSD). An SSD replaces the spinning platters of a hard drive with flash memory chips. Because memory chips are much more expensive than disk platters, SSDs cost much more per unit capacity than hard drives. SSDs are also much faster than hard drives, consume little power, produce little heat, and are completely silent. Unless you don't need much storage space, it's impractical to use SSD storage exclusively, but you can get the best of both worlds by using a relatively small SSD to store your operating system, applications, and working data and install one or more hard drives for cheap bulk storage.

See Chapter 2 for specific component recommendations.

Balanced Design

Novice PC builders often ignore the important concept of balanced design. Balanced design means allocating your component budget to avoid bottlenecks. If you're designing a gaming PC, for example, it makes no sense to spend $50 on the processor and $500 on the video card. The resulting system is nonoptimal because the slow processor is a bottleneck that prevents the expensive video adapter from performing to its full potential.

The main enemy of balanced design is the constant hype of manufacturer advertising and enthusiast websites (which sometimes amount to the same thing). It's easy to fixate on the latest "must-have" component, even though its price may be much too high to justify. Many people just can't help themselves. Despite their best intentions, they end up spending $500 for a premium LCD display when a $200 model would have done just as well, or they buy a $400 video adapter when a $150 adapter would suffice. If your budget is unlimited, fine. Go for the latest and best. But if you're building a system to a fixed budget, every dollar you spend needlessly on one component is a dollar less you have to spend somewhere else, where it might make more difference.

Balanced design does not necessarily mean giving equal priority to all system components. For example, we have built servers in which the disk arrays and tape backup drive cost more than $10,000 and the rest of the system components

---

Brian Bilbrey Comments

Don't buy an ATA/IDE (now often called Parallel ATA, or PATA) drive except to replace a drive in an older system that doesn't accept SATA drives. PATA is a dying standard.

totaled less than $2,000. A balanced design is one that takes into account the tasks the system must perform and allocates resources to optimize performance for those tasks.

But balanced design takes into consideration more than simple performance. A truly balanced design accommodates non-performance issues such as physical size, noise level, reliability, and efficient cooling. You might, for example, have to choose a less expensive processor or a smaller hard drive in order to reserve sufficient funds for a quieter case or a more reliable power supply.

The key to achieving a balanced design is to determine your requirements, look dispassionately at the available alternatives, and choose accordingly. That can be tougher than it sounds.

Designing a Quiet PC

The ongoing PC performance race has had the unfortunate side effect of making PCs noisier. Faster processors use more power, which in turn requires larger (and noisier) power supplies. Faster processors also produce more heat, which requires larger (and noisier) CPU coolers. Modern hard drives spin faster than older models, producing still more noise and heat. Fast video adapters have their own cooling fans, which add to the din. While building a reasonably quiet PC that performs well is easier today, fast and powerful machines still need plenty of noisy moving air.

Fortunately, there are steps you can take to reduce the amount of noise your PC produces. No PC with moving parts is completely silent, but significant noise reductions are possible. Depending on your requirements and budget, you can build a PC that is anything from quietly unobtrusive to nearly silent. The key to building a noise-reduced PC is to recognize the sources of noise and to minimize or eliminate noise at the source.

The major sources of noise are typically the power supply, CPU cooler fan, and supplementary case fans. Minor sources of noise include the hard drive, chipset fan, video adapter fan, and optical drive. As you design your PC, focus first on major noise sources that can be minimized inexpensively, then minor noise sources that are cheap to deal with, then major noise sources that are more expensive or difficult to minimize, and finally (if necessary) minor noise sources that are expensive or difficult to fix. Use the following guidelines:

Choose a low-power processor

> The amount of power consumed by the processor has a direct effect on the noise level of the system. The peak power consumption of mainstream processors ranges from about 30W to 140W. That power ends up as waste heat that must be exhausted from the case. Using a lower-power processor produces less waste heat, which in turn allows you to use a quieter CPU cooler, fewer and quieter case fans, and so on. Power consumption isn't necessarily proportional to processor performance. For example, one processor that draws 70W peak power may be faster than another that draws 130W. None of this is to say that there's anything wrong with choosing a high-wattage processor, but doing so complicates cooling and noise issues.

WHAT ARE DBS, ANYWAY?

The following is a gross oversimplification, and we're sure we'll hear about it from people who know more than we do about sound, but here goes.

Sound is measured and specified in deciBels—a tenth of a Bel—which is abbreviated dB. (Some components specify Bels; multiply by 10 to get dB.) Because humans perceive identical sound levels at different frequencies as having different loudness, various weighting schemes are used. The most common, A-weighting, is abbreviated as dB(A). There are also dB(B) and dB(C) scales, but those are not commonly used.

A sound level of 0 dB is defined as the threshold of hearing, a sound level that is just barely perceptible in the absence of any other sound. Here are some reference points:

- 20 dB—a very quiet library or church; rural background noise at night; the quietest possible PC with moving parts
- 25 dB—a whispered conversation; a very quiet PC
- 30 dB—suburban background noise at night; a quiet PC
- 40 dB—a quiet conversation; a standard PC
- 50 dB—normal household noise; a normal conversation at 1 meter; a loud PC
- 60 dB—office conversation; a loud gaming PC or server

The dB scale is logarithmic, which means that an increase of about 3 dB doubles the sound level. For example, if a power supply produces 30 dB and a CPU cooler also produces 30 dB, running both at the same time doubles the sound level to 33 dB (not 60 dB). Doubling the sound level again by running four 30 dB devices simultaneously increases the overall sound level by 3 dB again, to 36 dB. Running 8 such devices doubles the sound level to 39 dB, 16 takes it to 42 dB, and so on.

However, because of the way humans perceive sound, a 1 dB difference is barely perceptible; a 3 dB difference is noticeable, but a sound must be about 10 dB louder to be perceived as "twice as loud." For example, if one computer produces 40 dB and another 30 dB, the first computer actually produces about 10 times the sound level of the second PC, but to human ears it "sounds" only twice as loud.

PC components differ dramatically in sound levels. For example, a very quiet hard drive might produce 25 dB, while another model produces 30 dB or more. At idle, a standard 400W power supply might produce 40 dB, a quieter model 30 dB (half as "loud"), and a specialty quiet model only 20 dB (half as "loud" again). The same differences exist among other noise-producing components, such as CPU coolers, supplemental case fans, optical drives, and so on. Merely by choosing the quietest standard PC components rather than noisier alternatives, you can reduce the noise level of your PC noticeably.

Choose a quiet case

Inexpensive cases are designed with little thought to noise abatement. Better cases incorporate numerous design features that reduce noise, including large, slow-spinning exhaust fans, sound-absorbing composite panels, rubber shock mounts for drives that isolate vibration, and so on. We cover case considerations thoroughly in the next chapter.

Choose a quiet power supply

In most systems, the power supply is potentially the first or second largest noise source, so minimizing power supply noise is critical. Here are a few tips:

- At the first level, choose a noise-reduced power supply, such as the models we recommend in the next chapter. Such power supplies cost little or no more than competing models of equivalent capacity and quality but are noticeably quieter. A system that uses one of these power supplies can be quiet enough to be unobtrusive in a normal residential environment.

- The next step down in noise level is a power supply that is specifically designed to minimize noise. These power supplies cost a bit more than comparable noise-reduced power supplies but produce as little as 18 dB at idle, and not much more under load. A system that uses one of these power supplies (and other similarly quiet components) can be nearly inaudible in a normal residential environment. You won't have any trouble recognizing any of these models, because all of them are advertised and promoted as "Quiet PC" or "Silent" models.

- Finally, some power supplies use huge passive heatsinks rather than cooling fans. These power supplies, such as the FSP ZEN 400 (*http://www.fspgroupusa.com*), have no moving parts, and the only noise they produce is a very slight buzz from the electronic components.

Choose an efficient power supply

Power supply efficiency has a direct bearing on system noise level. Every power supply requires higher input power than the output power it provides, and that power difference is converted to heat within the power supply. For example, if the system actually requires 200W from the power supply, a 67% efficient power supply draws 300W of input power to provide that 200W of output power (200W/0.67 = 300W). That extra 100W is converted to heat within the power supply. An 85% efficient power supply requires only about 235W of input power to provide 200W of output power. The difference between 300W input and 235W input power translates to an extra 65W of heat within your system. The efficiency of mainstream power supply models ranges from about 65% to 90% or higher.

Choose a quiet CPU cooler

As processor speeds have increased over the last few years, manufacturers have gone from using passive heatsinks to using heatsinks with slow, quiet fans to using heatsinks with fast, loud fans. Current processors differ greatly in power consumption from model to model. At the lower end of the range—less than 50W—nearly any decent CPU cooler can do the job with minimal noise, including the stock CPU coolers bundled with retail-boxed processors and inexpensive third-party units. At the middle of the range—50W to 90W—standard CPU coolers begin to produce intrusive noise levels, although specialty quiet CPU coolers can cool a midrange processor with little or no noise. At the upper end of the range, even the quietest fan-based CPU coolers produce some noise. Here are some tips to keep in mind when selecting a CPU cooler:

- For a processor with low to moderate power consumption, try using the stock CPU cooler supplied with the retail-boxed processor. If it produces too much noise, install an inline resistor to reduce the voltage supplied to the fan, which reduces fan speed and noise. Resistor kits are sold by quiet-PC vendors such as FrozenCPU (*http://www.frozencpu.com*), QuietPC USA (*http://www.quietpcusa.com*), and Endpcnoise.com (*http://www.endpcnoise.com*).

The 80 PLUS Initiative

The 80 PLUS initiative sets standards for power supply efficiency. A power supply that meets the basic 80 PLUS requirements must be at least 80% efficient at 20%, 50%, and 100% load, and must have a power factor (PF) of at least 0.9 at 100% load. The 80 PLUS Bronze certification requires the power supply to be at least 85% efficient at 50% load and 82% efficient at 20% and 100% load, with a PF of 0.9 or better at all three load levels. The 80 PLUS Silver and Gold certifications require the power supply to be at least 85%/88%/85% efficient or 87%/90%/87% efficient, respectively, again with a PF of at least 0.9 at all three load levels.

Less than half of the power supplies currently sold have any 80 PLUS certification. Less than 4% have the 80 PLUS Gold certification, and about the same percentage have the 80 Plus Silver certification. Roughly 20% have the 80 PLUS Bronze certification, and another 20% the basic 80 PLUS certification.

- For high-current processors, there are several alternatives. The CPU coolers that AMD and (particularly) Intel bundle with their retail-boxed performance processors are much better than they were a few years ago. Even with a hot processor, a retail-boxed CPU cooler does a reasonably good job of cooling the processor with little noise.

- To minimize noise with any processor, install a Thermalright (*http://www.thermalright.com*) or Zalman (*http://www.zalmanusa.com*) unit. For processors with low to midrange power consumption, some of these premium coolers can be run in silent (fanless) mode, which completely eliminates CPU cooler noise.

MONITORING CPU TEMPERATURE

Modern motherboards provide temperature sensors at important points such as the CPU socket. The motherboard reports the temperatures reported by these sensors to the BIOS. You can view these temperatures by running BIOS Setup and choosing the option for temperature reporting, which can usually be found under Advanced→Hardware Monitoring, or a similar menu option. Alternatively, most motherboards include a monitoring utility—Intel's, for example, is called the *Intel Active Monitor*—that allows you to monitor temperatures from Windows rather than having to run BIOS Setup.

CPU temperature can vary dramatically with changes in load. For example, a CPU that idles at 30° C may reach 50° C or higher when it is running at 100% capacity. A hot-running CPU may reach temperatures of 70° C or higher under load, which is perilously close to the maximum acceptable temperature for that processor, so it is very important to verify that your CPU cooler and system fans are doing their jobs properly.

An idle temperature of 30° C or lower is ideal, but that is not achievable with the hottest processors, which idle at 40° C or higher with any but the most efficient CPU coolers. In general, a CPU cooler that produces an idle temperature of 40° C or lower suffices to cool the CPU properly under load.

If you want to verify temperature under load, run an application that loads the CPU with intense calculations, ideally with lots of floating-point operations. Two such applications we have used are the SETI@home client (*http://setiathome.ssl.berkeley.edu*) and the Mersenne Prime client (*http://mersenne.org*). Run the application for an hour to ensure the CPU has reached a steady-state temperature and then use the temperature monitoring application to view the temperature while the application is still running.

CPU Coolers and Motherboard Compatibility

If you choose an aftermarket CPU cooler, verify that it is physically compatible with your motherboard and case. Quiet CPU coolers often use very large heatsinks, which may conflict with protruding capacitors and other motherboard components. Most premium CPU cooler manufacturers post motherboard compatibility lists on their websites. It's just as important to verify that the CPU cooler fits your case. Some high-end CPU coolers are physically huge. Before you buy one of those, make sure the chassis structure won't prevent it from being installed, and make sure there's sufficient clearance between the motherboard and case cover that you'll be able to reinstall the cover with the CPU cooler in place.

Choose quiet case fans

Most modern systems have at least one supplemental case fan, and some have several. The more loaded the system, the more supplemental cooling you'll need to use. Use the following guidelines when selecting case fans:

- Case fans are available in various sizes, from 60 mm to 200 mm. All other things being equal, a larger fan can move the same amount of air with less noise than a smaller fan, because the larger fan doesn't need to spin as fast. Of course, the fan mounting positions in most cases are of fixed size, so you may have little choice about which size fan(s) to use. If you do have a choice—for example, if the case has two or three fan positions of different size—use the largest fan that fits.

- Case fans vary significantly in noise level, even for the same size and rotation speed. Many factors come into play, including blade design, type of bearings, grill type, and so on. In general, ball bearing fans are noisier but more durable than fans that use needle or sleeve bearings.

- The noise level of a fan can be reduced by running it at a lower speed, as long as it moves enough air to provide proper cooling. The simplest method to reduce fan speed is to install an inline resistor to reduce the supply voltage to 7V. These are available from the sources listed earlier, or you can make your own with a resistor from Radio Shack or another electronics supply store. Some fans include a control panel, which mounts in an available external drive bay and allows you to control fan speed continuously from zero to maximum by adjusting a knob. Finally, some fans are designed to be controlled by the power supply or a motherboard fan connector. These fans vary their speed automatically in response to the ambient temperature, running at high speed when the system is heavily loaded and producing lots of heat, and low speed when the system is idle.

- The mounting method you use makes a difference. Most case fans are secured directly to the chassis with metal screws. This transfers vibration directly to the chassis panels, which act as sounding boards. A better method is to use soft plastic snap-in connectors rather than screws. These connectors isolate vibration to the fan itself. Better still is to use the soft plastic snap-in connectors in conjunction with a foam surround that insulates the fan frame from the chassis entirely.

The preceding six elements are the major steps required to quietize your PC. Once you minimize noise from those major sources, you can also take the following steps to reduce noise from minor sources. Some of these steps cost little or nothing to implement, and all contribute to quieting the PC:

Put the PC on a mat

Rather than putting the PC directly on your desk or the floor, put a sound-deadening mat between it and the surface. You can buy special mats for this purpose, but we've used objects as simple as a couple of mouse pads, front and rear, to accomplish the same thing. The amount of noise reduction from this simple step can be surprisingly large.

Choose a quiet hard drive

Once you've addressed the major noise sources, hard drive noise may become noticeable, particularly during seeks. The best way to reduce hard drive noise is to choose a quiet hard drive in the first place. Seagate Barracuda and Samsung Spinpoint models are the quietest mainstream hard drives. If even those 7,200 RPM models are too noisy for your requirements, use a 5,400 or 5,900 RPM drive. If even those are too loud, install an SSD.

Choose a video card with a passive heatsink

All video adapter chipsets produce significant heat, but some video adapters use a passive heatsink rather than a fan-based cooler. If possible, choose a video adapter with a passive heatsink.

Choose a motherboard with a passive heatsink

The northbridge chip of modern chipsets dissipates significant heat. Most motherboards cool this chip with a large passive heatsink, but some use a fan-based cooler. Again, these coolers typically use small, fast fans that produce significant noise. If possible, pick a motherboard with a passive heatsink.

Silent PC Review

Silent PC Review (http://www.silent-pcreview.com) is an excellent source of information about quiet PC issues. The site includes numerous articles about reducing PC noise, as well as reviews of quiet PC components, a forum, and other resources.

Designing a Small PC

At the beginning of the millennium, some forward-thinking PC builders and manufacturers began to design and build PCs that were smaller and/or more portable than traditional mini-tower systems. Small PCs have become extremely popular, and it's no wonder. These systems are small, light, easily portable, and fit just about anywhere. The two standards for small PCs, largest first, are:

microATX PC

A microATX PC is basically a cut-down version of a standard ATX PC. The microATX case and motherboard are smaller and provide less expandability, but are otherwise comparable in features and functionality to a standard ATX system. microATX cases are available in three styles. Micro-tower cases resemble shrunken versions of standard mini- and mid-tower cases. Slimline cases are about the size and shape of a DVD player. "Cube" cases are typically 8" tall and roughly a foot wide and deep. The relatively small case capacity makes cooling more difficult and puts some restraints on the number and type of hard drives, expansion cards, and other peripherals you can install, but it is possible to build a reliable, high-performance PC in the microATX form factor.

Mini-ITX PC

The Mini-ITX form factor was pioneered by VIA Technologies and remained a niche standard for several years. Over the last year or two, mainstream motherboard and case manufacturers have introduced a wide range of Mini-ITX products—enough that we now consider Mini-ITX a mainstream technology.

Mini-ITX motherboards are 170 mm (6.7") square and are compatible with microATX and full ATX cases and power supplies. Of course, there's usually little point to installing a tiny motherboard in a large case, so most Mini-ITX systems are built in Mini-ITX cases, which accept only Mini-ITX motherboards.

In the past, Mini-ITX systems were low-powered in every sense. They consumed little electricity and used very low-performance processors. Most Mini-ITX systems used passive cooling and "wall-wart" power supplies, which eliminates fan noise and allows the system to be almost totally silent. Mini-ITX was most appropriate for such "appliance" applications as small Linux servers, routers, and satellite DVR playback-only systems.

That's all changed. Although you can still build an inexpensive, quiet, low-power "appliance" Mini-ITX system—in fact, we'll do so as one of the project systems in this book—you can also build a high-performance Mini-ITX system that matches all but the fastest desktop systems. Motherboards like the GIGABYTE GA-H55N-USB3 and the Intel BOXDH57JG use the most recent performance chipsets and accept mainstream and performance processors like the Intel Core i3/i5/i7 models.

The main limitations of Mini-ITX systems all result from the small physical size of Mini-ITX cases. For example, Mini-ITX motherboards may have only one or two memory slots, rather than four or more, and only two SATA connectors, versus four, six, or more on standard motherboards. Mini-ITX motherboards simply aren't large enough to contain all the features and connectors present on standard microATX or full ATX motherboards.

The small volume of Mini-ITX cases also puts strict limits on the size and number of drives you can install. For example, some mini-ITX cases accept only one 2.5" (notebook) hard drive and a slim optical drive. With some Mini-ITX case/motherboard combinations, you're limited to integrated video because there's no room (or slot) for a PCI Express video adapter. The small volume of a Mini-ITX case also limits the size and number of cooling fans. What fans are present must run at high speed to provide sufficient cooling, so a typical high-performance Mini-ITX system will be noticeably louder than an equivalent system built in a larger case. Finally, Mini-ITX motherboards are usually more expensive, sometimes significantly so, than comparable microATX or full ATX motherboards.

If you need to design a small PC, recognize that each step down from a standard mini-tower involves additional compromises in performance, cost, reliability, noise level, and other key criteria. Reducing case size limits the number and type of components you can install and makes it more difficult to cool the system effectively. It also makes it harder to quiet the PC. For example, small cases often use relatively loud power supplies. Because the power supply is proprietary, installing an aftermarket quiet power supply is not an option. Similarly, using a small case forces you to trade off performance against cooling against noise. For example, you may be forced to use a slower processor than you'd like, because the necessary CPU cooler for a faster processor is too large to fit in the available space or is louder than acceptable.

When it comes to designing small full-performance systems, our rule is to use
a standard mini-tower case whenever possible. If that's too large, step down
to a microATX case. If even a microATX system is too large, if and only if you are
certain that the trade-offs are worth it, build a Mini-ITX system.

Things to Know and Do Before You Start

We've built many systems over the years, and we've learned a lot of lessons
the hard way. Here are some things to keep in mind as you begin your project:

Make sure you have everything you need before you start

> Have all of the hardware, software, and tools you'll need lined up and
> waiting. You don't want to have to stop in mid-build to go off in search of
> a small Phillips screwdriver or to drive to the store to buy a cable. If your
> luck is anything like ours, you won't find the screwdriver you need and the
> store will be closed. In addition to tools and components, make sure you
> have the distribution CDs for the operating system, service packs, device
> drivers, diagnostics utilities, and any other software you'll need to com-
> plete the build.

RTFM

> Read the fine manuals, if only the Quick Start sections. Surprisingly, while
> system manuals are notoriously awful, many component manuals are ac-
> tually quite good. You'll find all sorts of hints and tips, from the best way
> to install the component to suggestions on optimizing its performance.

Download the latest drivers

> Although PC component inventories turn over quickly, the CDs included
> with components usually don't contain the most recent drivers. Some
> manufacturers don't update their driver CDs very often, so the bundled
> drivers may be a year or more out of date, even if the component itself
> was made recently. Before you begin building a PC, visit the websites for
> each component and download its most recent driver and BIOS updates.
> (Bookmark the URLs so you can easily find updates later.) Unpack or unzip
> them if necessary, burn them to CD, and label the CD. You may choose to
> install drivers from the bundled CD—in fact, at times it's necessary to do
> so because the downloadable updates do not include everything that's
> on the CD—but you want to have those later drivers available so that you
> can update your system immediately.

Ground yourself before touching components

> Processors, memory modules, and other electronic components—including
> the circuit boards in drives—are sensitive to static shock. Static electricity
> can damage components even if the voltage is too low for you to see or
> feel a static spark. The best way to avoid static damage to components is
> to get in the habit of grounding yourself before you touch any sensitive
> component. You can buy special antistatic wrist straps and similar devices,
> but they're really not necessary. All you need do is touch a metal object
> like the chassis or power supply before you handle components.

Static Guard

To minimize problems with static, wear wool or cotton clothing and avoid rubber-soled shoes. Static problems increase when the air is dry, as is common in winter when central heating systems are in use. You can reduce or eliminate static with a spray bottle filled with water to which you've added a few drops of dishwashing liquid. Spritz your work area thoroughly immediately before you begin working. The goal is not to get anything wet, but simply to increase the humidity of the air. (Whatever you do, avoid wetting the case or components themselves, especially the connectors and slots, which must be kept clean and dry at all times.)

Keep track of the screws and other small parts

Building a PC yields an incredible number of small pieces that need to be kept organized. As you open each component box, your pile of screws, cables, mounting brackets, adapters, and other small parts grows larger. Some of those you'll need, and some you won't. As we can attest, one errant screw left on the floor can destroy a vacuum cleaner. Worse, one unnoticed screw can short out and destroy the motherboard and other components. The best solution we've found is to use an egg carton or old ice cube tray to keep parts organized. The goal is to have all of the small parts accounted for when you finish assembling the PC.

Use force when necessary, but use it cautiously

Many books tell you never to force anything, and that's good advice as far as it goes. If doing something requires excessive force, chances are a part is misaligned, you have not removed a screw, or something similar. But sometimes there is no alternative to applying force judiciously. For example, drive power cables sometimes fit so tightly that the only way to connect them is to grab them with pliers and press hard. (Make sure all the contacts are aligned first.) Likewise, some combinations of expansion card and slot fit so tightly that you must press very hard to seat the card. If you encounter such a situation, verify that everything is lined up and otherwise as it should be (and that there isn't a stray wire obstructing the slot). Then use whatever force it takes to do the job, which may be substantial.

Check and recheck before you apply power

An experienced PC technician building a PC does a quick scan of the new machine before performing the *smoke test* by applying power to the PC (if you don't see any smoke, it passes the test). Don't skip this step, and don't underestimate its importance. Most PCs that fail the smoke test do so because this step was ignored. Until you gain experience, it may take several minutes to verify that all is as it should be—all components secure, all cables connected properly, no tools or other metal parts shorting anything out, and so on. Once you are comfortable working inside PCs, this step takes 15 seconds, but that may be the most important 15 seconds of the whole project.

A Snake in the Woodpile

Some PCs use a variety of screws that look very similar but are in fact threaded differently. For example, the screws used to secure some case covers and those used to mount some disk drives may appear to be identical, but swapping them may result in stripped threads. If in doubt, keep each type of screw in a separate compartment of your organizer.

A Screw Loose Somewhere

After we build a system, we pick it up, shake it gently, and tilt it front-to-back and side-to-side. If something rattles, we know there's a screw loose somewhere.

Start small for the first boot

The moment of greatest danger comes when you power up the PC for the first time. If the system fails catastrophically—which sometimes happens no matter how careful you are—don't smoke more than you have to. For example, the SOHO Server project system we built for this book uses four hard drives and two memory modules. When we built that system, we installed only one drive and one memory module initially. That way, if something shorted out when we first applied power, we'd destroy only one drive and memory module rather than all of them. For that reason, we suggest starting with a minimum configuration—motherboard, processor, one memory stick, video, and one hard drive. Once you're satisfied that all is well, you can add your optical and other drives, additional memory, expansion cards, and so on.

Leave the cover off until you're sure everything works

Experts build and test the PC completely before putting the lid back on and connecting the external cables. Novices build the PC, reassemble the case, reconnect all the cables, and *then* test it.

GOOD ADVICE FOR FIRST-TIME SYSTEM BUILDERS

Ron Morse, one of our technical reviewers, has been building PCs for 20 years. He makes the following suggestions for first-time system builders:

- Try to arrange a couple of hours when you can reasonably expect to be free of interruptions to build your first PC. It's a sequential process and you need to keep track of what you have (and haven't) done.
- Building while this week's NASCAR crashfest or the home team's latest losing effort plays on the TV isn't a good idea, either. While there's nothing difficult about building a PC, it does take a certain level of concentration. I like to play music, but not Mahler or the Squirrel Nut Zippers, both of whom cause me to think too much about the music instead of what I'm supposed to be doing.
- Most pro shops don't allow food or drink in the assembly area. It's a good rule for the home builder, too. In addition to the obvious concerns about spills and crumbs, condensation from the outside of a cold drink container can drip unnoticed into a sensitive area and residue from "finger food" can cause all sorts of problems by contaminating contacts or making small parts hard(er) to grasp and place.

Pace yourself. Building a PC is amazingly simple…after it's finished. Getting there takes concentration and some physical dexterity. Plan to take short breaks at logical points during the build, then take them.

Things You Need to Have

The following sections detail the items you should have at hand before you actually start building your new system. Make a checklist and make sure you check off each item before you begin. There are few things as frustrating as being forced to stop in mid-build when you belatedly realize you're missing a cable or other small component.

Components

Building a PC requires at least the following components. Have all of them available before you start to build the system. Open each component box and verify the contents against the packing list before you actually start the build.

- Case and power supply, with power cord
- Motherboard, with custom I/O shield, if needed
- Processor
- CPU cooler, with thermal compound or pad
- Memory module(s)
- Hard drive(s) and cable(s)
- Optical drive, with data cable
- Video adapter, unless embedded
- Sound adapter, unless embedded
- Network adapter, unless embedded
- Any other expansion cards (if applicable)
- Supplementary case fan(s)
- Keyboard, mouse, display and other external peripherals
- Screws, brackets, drive rails, and other connecting hardware

Hand Tools and Supplies

You really don't need many tools to build a PC. We built one PC using only a Swiss Army Knife, just to prove it could be done. Our basic PC building toolkit is a #1 Phillips screwdriver. It's a bit small for the largest screws and a bit large for the smallest, but we've built dozens of systems using no other tool.

It's helpful to have more tools, of course. Needle-nose pliers are useful for setting jumpers. A flashlight is often useful, even if your work area is well lit. A 5 mm (or, rarely, 6 mm) nut driver makes it faster to install the brass standoffs that support the motherboard. A larger assortment of screwdrivers can also be helpful.

> **Non-Fatal Attraction**
>
> *Don't worry about using magnetized tools. Despite the common warnings about doing so, we've used magnetized screwdrivers for years without any problem. They are quite handy for picking up dropped screws and so on. Use commonsense precautions, though, such as avoiding putting the magnetized tips near the flat surface of a hard drive or other magnetic media.*

You may also find it useful to have some Nylon cable ties (not the paper-covered wire-type twist ties) for dressing cables after you build the system. Canned air and a clean microfiber dust cloth are useful for cleaning components that you are migrating from an older system. A new eraser can be helpful for cleaning contacts if you mistakenly grab an expansion card by the connector tab.

Software Tools

In addition to hand tools, you should have the following software tools available when you build your system. Some are useful when you build the system, others to diagnose problems. We keep copies of our standard software tools with our toolkit. That way, we have everything we need in one place. Here are the software tools we recommend:

Operating system distribution discs

> OS distribution discs are needed when you build a system, and may also be needed later to update system software or install a peripheral. We always burn copies of the distribution discs to CD-R or DVD+R and keep a copy with our toolkit. If you use Windows, remember to record the initialization key, serial number, and other data you'll need to install the software. Use a felt-tip permanent marker to record this data directly onto the disc immediately after you burn it. It also helps to record the same information on a small piece of paper so that you'll have it available while the disc is in the drive.

Service packs and critical updates

> Rather than (or in addition to) updating Windows and Office online, download the latest service packs and critical updates and burn them to CD-R. In addition to giving you more control of the process, having these updates on CD-R means you can apply them even when the system has no Internet connection, such as when you're building it on your kitchen table.

Major applications discs

> If your system runs Microsoft Office or other major applications that are distributed on CDs, keep a copy of those discs with your toolkit. Again, don't forget to record the serial number, initialization keys, and other required data on the disc itself and on a supplementary note (because it's really hard to enter that serial number onscreen while it's spinning in the optical drive).

Driver CDs

> Motherboards, video adapters, sound cards, and many other components include a driver CD in the box. Those drivers may not be essential for installing the component—the Windows or Linux distribution CD may (or may not) include basic drivers for the component—but it's generally a good idea to use the driver CD supplied with the component (or an updated version downloaded from the website) rather than using those supplied with the OS, if any.

Use Some Protection

It's a very bad idea to connect a PC directly to the Internet, and that's especially true for an unpatched system. Several of our readers have reported having a new system infected by a worm almost instantly when they connected to the Internet, intending to download patches and updates. Patch the new system before you connect it to the Internet, and never connect it directly to the Internet. Use a NAT gateway/router between any PC and your broadband modem.

First Things First

Pay close attention to the instructions that come with the driver. Most drivers can be installed with the hardware they support already installed. But some drivers, particularly those for some USB devices, need to be installed before the hardware is installed.

In addition to basic drivers, the driver CD may include supporting applications. For example, a video adapter CD may include a system tray application for managing video properties, while a sound card may include a bundled application for sound recording and editing. We generally use the bundled driver CD for initial installation and then download and install any updated drivers available on the product website. Keep a copy of the original driver CD and a CD-R with updated drivers in your toolkit.

Hard drive installation/diagnostic utility

We're always amazed that so few people use the installation and diagnostic software supplied with hard drives. Perhaps that's because many people buy OEM hard drives, which include only the bare drive. Retail-boxed drives invariably include a utilities CD. Most people ignore it, which is a mistake.

Seagate, for example, provides DiscWizard installation software and SeaTools diagnostic software. If you're building a system, you can use the bootable floppy or bootable CD version of DiscWizard to partition, format, and test the new drive automatically. If you're adding a drive, you can use the Windows version of DiscWizard to install, prepare, and configure the new drive automatically. You can configure the new drive as a secondary drive, keeping the original drive as the boot drive. You can specify that the new drive be the sole drive in the system, and DiscWizard will automatically migrate your programs and data from the old drive. Finally, you can choose to make the new drive the primary (boot) drive and make the old drive the secondary drive. DiscWizard does all of this automatically, saving you considerable manual effort.

Hard Drive Diagnostics

All hard drive makers provide installation and diagnostic utilities. If you buy an OEM hard drive or lose the original CD, you can download the utilities from the manufacturer's website. For obvious reasons, many of these utilities work only if a hard drive made by that manufacturer is installed.

Diagnostic utilities

Catch 22. Diagnostic utilities are of limited use in building a new system, because if the PC works well enough to load and run them, you don't need to diagnose it. Conversely, when you need to diagnose the PC, it's not working well enough to run the diagnostic utility. Duh. (Diagnostic utilities can be helpful on older systems, for example, to detect memory problems or a failing hard drive.) The only diagnostic utility we use routinely when building systems is a Knoppix Live Linux CD (*http://www.knoppix.com*). With Knoppix, you can boot and run Linux completely from the CD, without writing anything to the hard drive. Knoppix has superb hardware detection—better than Windows—and can be useful for diagnosing problems on a newly built system that refuses to load Windows.

Driver Education

Keep original driver CDs stored safely. They may be more valuable than you think. More than once, we've lost track of original driver CDs, thinking we could always just download the latest driver from the manufacturer's website. Alas, a company may go out of business, or its website may be down just when you desperately need a driver. Worse still, some companies may charge for drivers that were originally freely downloadable. That's one reason we don't buy HP products.

Test Your Memory

Many system builders routinely run a memory diagnostic to ensure the system functions before installing the operating system. One excellent utility for this purpose is MEMTEST86 (http://www.memtest86.com). It's free, self-boots from a floppy drive, or can be run in DOS mode from an optical boot disk. Best of all, it does a great job of testing the otherwise difficult-to-diagnose memory subsystem.

Burn-in utilities

PC components generally fail quickly or live a long time. If a component survives the first 24 hours, it's likely to run without problems for years. The vast majority of early failures are immediate, caused by DOA components. Something like 99% of the remaining early failures occur within 24 hours, so it's worth "burning in" a new system before you spend hours installing and configuring the operating system and applications.

Many people simply turn on the system and let it run for a day or two. That's better than nothing, but an idling system doesn't stress all components. A better way is to run software that accesses and exercises all of the components. One good (and free) ad hoc way to burn in a system is to compile the Linux kernel, and we sometimes use that method. We generally use special burn-in software, however. The best product we know of for that purpose is BurnInTest from PassMark Software (*http://www.pass-mark.com*).

Troubleshooting

Many first-time system builders are haunted by the question, "What if it doesn't work?" Or, worse still, "What if it goes up in flames the first time I turn it on?" Set your mind at ease. This isn't rocket surgery. Any reasonably intelligent person can build a system with a high degree of confidence that it will work normally the first time it is turned on. If you use good components and assemble them carefully, you're actually less likely to encounter problems with a home-built system than with a pre-built mail-order system or one off the shelf from your local superstore.

Still, it can happen. So, while it would take a whole book to cover troubleshooting in detail, it's worth taking a few pages to list some of the most likely problems and solutions. Fortunately, it's easier to troubleshoot a newly built system than a system that's been in use for some time. Fewer things can go wrong with a new system. You can be certain that the system is not infected with a virus or malware, for example, and driver problems are much less likely on a new system because you will have all the latest drivers installed.

The best time to troubleshoot is while you build the system. A good carpenter measures twice and cuts once. Take the same approach to building your system, and you're unlikely to need any of this troubleshooting advice. As you build the system, and then again before you apply power for the first time, verify that all cables are oriented and connected correctly. Make sure expansion cards, memory modules, the processor, and so on are fully seated, and that you haven't left a tool in the patient. Each project system chapter includes a final checklist. Verifying the items on that checklist eliminates about 99% of the potential problems.

Possible problems fall into one of four categories, easy versus hard to troubleshoot and likely versus unlikely to occur. Always check the easy/likely problems first. Otherwise, you may find yourself replacing the video card before

---

Contents May Settle During Shipping

Shipping can be tough on a computer. We always pop the cover of PCs that have been shipped, and often find something has been jarred loose. Our editor reports that when he shipped a PC to his parents, it arrived with the video card completely out of its slot. Not good.

Even worse, shipping can cause the CPU cooler to break loose. A heavy heatsink rattling around can do some serious damage to other components. If someone ships a system to you, always open it up and verify that everything is properly connected before you apply power to the system.

you notice that the display isn't plugged in. After you exhaust the easy/likely possibilities, check the easy/unlikely ones, followed by the hard/likely ones and finally the hard/unlikely possibilities.

Other than sheer carelessness—to which experienced system builders are more prone than novices—most problems with new systems result from one or more of the following:

Cable problems

Disconnected, misconnected, and defective cables cause more problems than anything else. The plethora of cables inside a PC makes it very easy to overlook a disconnected data cable or to forget to connect power to a drive. And the cables themselves cannot always be trusted, even if they are new. If you have a problem that seems inexplicable, always suspect a cable problem first.

Configuration errors

Years ago, motherboards required a lot more manual configuration than modern motherboards do. There were many switches and jumpers, all of which had to be set correctly or the system wouldn't boot. Modern motherboards autoconfigure most of their required settings, but they may still require some manual configuration, either by setting physical jumpers on the motherboard or by changing settings in BIOS Setup. Motherboards use silkscreened labels near jumpers and connectors to document their purposes and to list valid configuration settings. These settings are also listed in the motherboard manual. Always check both the motherboard labels and the manual to verify configuration settings. If the motherboard maker posts updated manuals on the Web, check those as well.

Incompatible components

In general, you can mix and match modern PC components without worrying much about compatibility. For example, any SATA hard drive or optical drive works with any SATA interface, and any ATX12V power supply is compatible with any ATX12V motherboard (although a cheap or older power supply may not provide adequate power). Most component compatibility issues are subtle. For example, if you install a 4 GB memory module in your system, when you power it up the system may see only 2 GB because the motherboard doesn't recognize 4 GB memory modules properly. It's worth checking the detailed documentation on the manufacturers' websites to verify compatibility.

Dead-on-arrival components

Modern PC components are extremely reliable, but if you're unlucky one of your components may be DOA. This is the least likely cause of a problem, however. Many novices think they have a DOA component, but the true cause is almost always something else—usually a cable or configuration problem. Before you return a suspect component, go through the detailed troubleshooting steps described next. Chances are the component is just fine.

Here are the problems you are most likely to encounter, and what to do about them:

Cables Are Commonplace

Fortunately, most problems with defective cables involve data cables, and those are pretty easy to come by. For example, when we recently assembled a new PC, the motherboard came with two SATA data cables. The hard drive came with another SATA data cable, and the optical drive with still another SATA data cable. That gave us four SATA data cables, only two of which we needed. The two extra cables went into our spares kit, where they'll be available if we need to swap cables to troubleshoot another system. This, incidentally, is another good reason to buy retail-boxed drives, at least until you accumulate some spare cables.

Troubleshooting

Problem: When you apply power, nothing happens.

- Verify that the power cable is connected to the PC and to the wall receptacle, and that the wall receptacle has power. Don't assume. We have seen receptacles in which one half worked and the other didn't. Use a lamp or other appliance to verify that the receptacle to which you connect the PC actually has power. If the power supply has its own power switch, make sure that switch is turned to the "On" or "1" position. If your local mains voltage is 110/115/120V, verify that the power supply voltage selector switch, if present, is not set for 220/230/240V. (If you need to move this switch, disconnect power before doing so.)

- If you are using an outlet strip or UPS, make sure that its switch (if equipped) is on and that the circuit breaker or fuse hasn't blown.

- If you installed a video adapter, pop the lid and verify that the adapter is fully seated in its slot. Even if you were sure it was seated fully initially—and even if you thought it snapped into place—the adapter may still not be properly seated. Remove the card and reinstall it, making sure it seats completely. If the motherboard has a retention mechanism, make sure the notch on the video card fully engages the retention mechanism. Ironically, one of the most common reasons for a loose video card is that the screw used to secure it to the chassis torques the card, pulling it partially out of its slot. This problem is rare with high-quality cases and video cards but is quite common with cheap components.

- Verify that the 20- or 24-pin main ATX power cable and the 4-pin ATX12V (or 8-pin EPS12V) power cable are securely connected to the motherboard and that all pins are making contact. If necessary, remove the cables and reconnect them. Make sure the latch on each cable plug snaps into place on the motherboard jack. Also, if your video adapter requires supplemental power, make sure the appropriate power cable is connected to it.

- Verify that the front-panel power switch cable is connected properly to the front-panel connector block. Check the silkscreen label on the motherboard and the motherboard manual to verify that you are connecting the cable to the right set of pins. Very rarely, you may encounter a defective power switch. You can eliminate this possibility by temporarily connecting the front-panel reset switch cable to the power switch pins on the front-panel connector block. (Both are merely momentary on switches, so they can be used interchangeably.) Alternatively, you can carefully use a small flat-blade screwdriver to short the power switch pins on the front-panel connector block momentarily. If the system starts with either of these methods, the problem is the case power switch.

- Start eliminating less likely possibilities, the most common of which is a well-concealed short circuit. Begin by disconnecting the power and data cables from the hard, optical, and floppy drives, one at a time. After you disconnect each, try starting the system. If the system starts, the drive you just disconnected is the problem. The drive itself may be defective, but it's far more likely that the cable is defective or was improperly connected. Replace the data cable, and connect the drive to a different power supply cable.

Swapping Power Supplies

If you have a spare power supply—or can borrow one temporarily from another system—you might as well try it as long as you have the cables disconnected. A new power supply being DOA is fairly rare, at least among good brands, but as long as you have the original disconnected, it's not much trouble to try a different one.

Brian Bilbrey Comments

I keep a spare, high-quality, decent-capacity power supply on hand, awaiting the day the unit in the system dies. It would have been handy a couple of months ago if I found I'd replaced that spare the last time I had to use it. The computer stayed offline until I bought a power supply at a local big-box store, for considerably more money than I'd have paid if I'd ordered that spare online, before I needed it. Sigh.

- If you have expansion cards installed, remove them one by one. Remove all but the video adapter. If the motherboard has embedded video, temporarily connect your display to it and remove the video card as well. Attempt to start the system after you remove each card. If the system starts, the card you just removed is causing the problem. Try a different card, or install that card in a different slot.

- Remove and reseat the memory modules, examining them to make sure they are not damaged, and then try to start the system. If you have two memory modules installed, install only one of them initially. Try it in both (or all) memory slots. If that module doesn't work in any slot, the module may be defective. Try the other module, again in every available memory slot. By using this approach, you can determine if one of the memory modules or one of the slots is defective.

- Remove the CPU cooler and the CPU. Check the CPU to make sure there are no bent pins. If there are, you may be able to straighten them using a credit card or a similar thin, stiff object, but in all likelihood you will have to replace the CPU. Check the CPU socket to make sure there are no blocked holes or foreign objects present.

- Remove the motherboard and verify that no extraneous screws or other conductive objects are shorting the motherboard to the chassis. Although shaking the case usually causes such objects to rattle, a screw or other small object may become wedged so tightly between the motherboard and chassis that it will not reveal itself during a shake test.

- If the problem persists, the most likely cause is a defective motherboard.

Problem: The system seems to start normally, but the display remains black.

- Verify that the display has power and the video cable is connected. If the display has a non-captive power cable, make sure the power cord is connected both to the display and to the wall receptacle. If you have a spare power cord, use it to connect the display. Make sure that the correct input is selected. Many displays have VGA, DVI, and/or HDMI connectors on them. Ordinarily, the display detects which input is receiving a video signal and selects it automatically. If that doesn't work, use the manual input-select button on the display to select the active source.

- Verify that the brightness and contrast controls of the display are set to midrange or higher.

- Disconnect the video cable and examine it closely to make sure that no pins are bent or shorted. Note that the video cable on some analog (VGA) displays is missing some pins and may have a short jumper wire connecting other pins, which is normal. Also check the video port on the PC to make sure that all of the holes are clear and that no foreign objects are present.

- If you are using a standalone video adapter in a motherboard that has embedded video, make sure the video cable is connected to the proper video port. Try the other video port just to make sure. Most motherboards with embedded video automatically disable it when they sense a video

> **Use New Thermal Goop Every Time**
>
> *Before you reinstall the CPU, always remove the old thermal compound and apply new compound. You can generally wipe off the old compound with a paper towel, or perhaps by rubbing it gently with your thumb. (Keep the processor in its socket while you remove the compound.) If the compound is difficult to remove, try heating it gently with a hair dryer. Never operate the system without the CPU cooler installed.*

card is installed, but that is not universally true. You may have to connect the display to the embedded video, enter BIOS Setup, and reconfigure the motherboard to use the video card.

- Try using a different display, if you have one available. Alternatively, try using the problem display on another system.

- If you are using a video card, make certain it is fully seated. Many combinations of video card and motherboard make it very difficult to seat the card properly. You may think the card is seated. You may even feel it snap into place. That does not necessarily mean it really is fully seated. Look carefully at the bottom edge of the card and the video slot, and make sure the card is fully in the slot and parallel to it. Verify that installing the screw that secures the video card to the chassis did not torque the card, forcing one end up and out of the slot.

- If your video card requires a supplemental power cable, be sure to connect it and make sure it snaps into place.

- If the system has PCI or PCIe expansion cards installed, remove them one by one. (Be sure to disconnect power from the system before you remove or install a card.) Each time you remove a card, restart the system. If the system displays video after you remove a card, that card either is defective or is conflicting with the video adapter. Try installing the PCI or PCIe card in a different slot. If it still causes the video problem, the card is probably defective. Replace it.

Problem: When you connect power (or turn on the main power switch on the back of the power supply), the power supply starts briefly and then shuts off.

- This is usually normal behavior. When you connect power to the power supply, it senses the power and begins its startup routine. Within a fraction of a second, the power supply notices that the motherboard hasn't ordered it to start, so it shuts itself down immediately. Press the main power switch on the case and the system should start normally.

- If pressing the main power switch doesn't start the system, you have probably forgotten to connect one of the cables from the power supply or front panel to the motherboard. Verify that the power switch cable is connected to the front-panel connector block, and that the 20-pin or 24-pin main ATX power cable and the 4-pin ATX12V power cable are connected to the motherboard. Connect any cables that are not connected, press the main power switch, and the system should start normally.

- If the preceding steps don't solve the problem, the most likely cause is a defective power supply. If you have a spare power supply, or can borrow one temporarily from another system, install it temporarily in the new system. Alternatively, connect the problem power supply to another system to verify that it is bad.

- If the preceding step doesn't solve the problem, the most likely cause is a defective motherboard. Replace it.

Danger, Will Robinson

All of the following steps assume that the power supply is adequate for the system configuration. This symptom may also occur if you use a grossly underpowered power supply. Worse still, doing that may damage the power supply, motherboard, and other components.

Chapter 1

Problem: The display shows BIOS boot text, but the system doesn't boot and displays no error message.

- This may be normal behavior. Restart the system and enter BIOS Setup (usually by pressing Delete or F1 during startup). Choose the menu option to use default CMOS settings, save the changes, exit, and restart the system.

- If the system doesn't accept keyboard input and you are using a USB keyboard and mouse, temporarily swap in a PS/2 keyboard and mouse. If you are using a PS/2 keyboard and mouse, make sure you haven't connected the keyboard to the mouse port and vice versa. Of course, many motherboards no longer incorporate "legacy" PS/2 inputs, so skip this step if it doesn't apply.

- If the system still fails to boot, run BIOS Setup again and verify all settings, particularly CPU speed, FSB speed, and memory timings.

- If the system hangs with a DMI pool error message, restart the system and run BIOS Setup again. Search the menus for an option to reset the configuration data. Enable that option, save the changes, and restart the system.

- If you are using an Intel motherboard, power down the system and reset the configuration jumper from the 1–2 (Normal) position to 2–3 (Configure). Restart the system, and BIOS Setup will appear automatically. Choose the option to use default CMOS settings, save the changes, and power down the system. Move the configuration jumper back to the 1–2 position and restart the system. (Actually, we routinely run the configuration option—when such an option is offered—and reset BIOS values to the defaults every time we first use a new motherboard, regardless of make, model, or chipset. It may not be absolutely required, but we've found that doing this minimizes problems.)

- If you are still unable to access BIOS Setup, power down the system, disconnect all of the drive data cables, and restart the system. If the system displays a Hard Drive Failure or No Boot Device error message, the problem is a defective cable (more likely) or a defective drive. Replace the drive data cable and try again. If the system does not display such an error message, the problem is probably caused by a defective motherboard.

Problem: The monitor displays a Hard Drive Failure or similar error message.

- This is almost always a hardware problem. Verify that the hard drive data cable is connected properly to the drive and the interface and that the drive power cable is connected.

- Use a different drive data cable and connect the drive to a different power cable.

- Connect the drive data cable to a different interface.

- If none of these steps corrects the problem, the most likely cause is a defective drive.

Problem: The display shows a No Boot Device, Missing Operating System, or similar error message.

- This is normal behavior if you have not yet installed an operating system. Error messages like this generally mean that the drive is physically installed and accessible, but the PC cannot boot because it cannot locate the operating system. Install the operating system.

- If the drive is inaccessible, verify that all data and power cables are connected properly. If it is a parallel ATA drive, verify that master/slave jumpers are set correctly and that the drive is connected to the primary interface.

- If you upgrade your motherboard but keep your original hard drive (or use a utility to clone your original), your operating system installation may not have the drivers necessary to function with your new hardware. If you're upgrading your motherboard, chances are good that enough things are different that Windows won't be able to boot. You'll need to reinstall Windows.

Problem: The system refuses to boot from the optical drive.

- All modern motherboards and optical drives support the El Torito specification, which allows the system to boot from an optical disc. If your new system refuses to boot from a CD, you can verify that the CD is bootable by booting it in another system.

- Run BIOS Setup and locate the section where you can define boot sequence. The default sequence is often (1) hard drive, (2) optical drive, (3) USB boot device, and (4) network boot device. Sometimes, by the time the system has decided it can't boot from the hard drive, it "gives up" before attempting to boot from the optical drive. Reset the boot sequence to (1) optical drive, and (2) hard drive. We generally leave the system with that boot sequence. Most systems configured this way prompt you to "Press any key to boot from CD" or something similar. If you don't press a key, they then attempt to boot from the hard drive, so make sure to pay attention during the boot sequence and press a key when prompted.

- Some high-speed optical drives take several seconds to load a CD, spin up, and signal the system that they are ready. In the meantime, the BIOS may have given up on the optical drive and gone on to try other boot devices. If you think this has happened, try pressing the reset button to reboot the system while the optical drive is already spinning and up to speed. If you get a persistent prompt to "press any key to boot from CD," try leaving that prompt up while the optical drive comes up to speed. If that doesn't work, run BIOS Setup and reconfigure the boot sequence to put the USB boot device first and the optical drive second. You can also try putting other boot device options, such as a network drive or boot PROM, ahead of the optical drive in the boot sequence. The goal is to provide sufficient delay for the optical drive to spin up before the motherboard attempts to boot from it.

- If none of these steps solves the problem, verify that all data cable and power cable connections are correct. If the system still fails to boot, replace the optical drive data cable.

- If the system still fails to boot, disconnect all drives except the primary hard drive and the optical drive. If the system still fails to boot, the optical drive is probably defective. Try using a different drive.

Problem: When you first apply power, you hear a continuous high-pitched screech or warble.

- The most likely cause is either that one of the system fans has a defective bearing or that a wire is contacting the spinning fan. Examine all of the system fans—CPU fan, power supply fan, and any supplemental fans—to make sure they haven't been fouled by a wire. Sometimes it's difficult to determine which fan is making the noise. In that case, use a cardboard tube or rolled-up piece of paper as a stethoscope to localize the noise. If the fan is fouled, clear the problem. If the fan is not fouled but still noisy, replace the fan.

- Rarely, a new hard drive may have a manufacturing defect or have been damaged in shipping. If so, the problem is usually obvious from the amount and location of the noise, and possibly because the hard drive is vibrating. If necessary, use your cardboard tube stethoscope to localize the noise. If the hard drive is the source, the only alternative is to replace it.

Problem: You hear a repeating, alternating two-tone "siren" sound after the system has been powered on for a short period.

- The sound is a warning that the CPU temperature is approaching dangerous levels and usually indicates there is not a good thermal bond between the CPU and the heatsink/fan (HSF) assembly. If you hear this warning, shut down the system immediately. Fortunately, the most common causes of this problem are easy to resolve. First, ensure the HSF assembly is properly mounted on the CPU and that all clips, screws, and retaining pins are fully seated and tight. If the warning persists, there may not be enough thermal paste between the CPU and HSF, or the paste may not be evenly distributed over the entire surface where the CPU and HSF meet. If the HSF came with a preapplied thermal pad, the pad may have been damaged prior to assembly or the protective plastic foil that protects the pad during shipment may not have been removed.

We've developed these troubleshooting procedures over many years and hundreds of systems, but if you work carefully while building your own new system, chances are you won't have to use any of them. About 99% of the new systems we build start up normally the first time we apply power. If this is your first build, your odds are probably even better because you'll probably pay even closer attention than we do to the details while you're building the system.

Choosing and Buying Components

2

The components you choose for your system determine its features, performance level, and reliability. How and where you buy those components determines how much the system costs.

Sometimes it is a good idea to spend more for additional features or performance, but often it is not. The trick is to figure out where to draw the line—when to spend extra money for extra features and performance, and when to settle for a less expensive component. Our years of experience have taught us several lessons in that regard:

- Benchmarks lie. Buying PC components based solely on benchmark results is like buying a car based solely on its top speed. It's worse, actually, because no standards exist for how benchmarks measure performance, or what aspect of performance they measure. Using one benchmark, Component A may be the clear winner, with Component B lagging far behind. With another benchmark, the positions may be reversed. When you select components for your new system, we suggest you regard benchmarks with suspicion and use them only as very general guidelines, if at all.

- Performance differences don't matter if it takes a benchmark to show them. Enthusiast websites wax poetic about a processor that's 10% faster than its competitor or a video card that renders frames 5% faster than its predecessor. Who cares? A difference you won't notice isn't worth paying for.

- It's easy to overlook the really important things and focus on trivialities. The emphasis on size and speed means more important issues are often ignored or at best given short shrift. For example, if you compare two hard drives, you might think the faster drive is the better choice. But the faster drive may also run noticeably hotter and be much louder and less reliable. In that situation, the slower drive is probably the better choice.

- Integrated (or embedded) components are often preferable to stand-alone components. Many motherboards include integrated features such as video, audio, and LAN adapters. The integrated video on modern motherboards suffices for most purposes. Only hardcore gamers and others with special video requirements need to buy a separate video adapter.

Ron Morse Comments

Conventional wisdom is that a change in performance has to be on the order of 25% to 30% before it becomes immediately obvious. This doesn't mean that small improvements aren't important, but it does mean you probably won't notice them until you realize that a job that used to take many minutes doesn't take quite as many minutes as it used to.

The best integrated audio—such as that on motherboards that use Intel and NVIDIA chipsets—is good enough for almost anyone. Integrated LAN adapters are more than good enough for nearly any desktop system.

The advantages of integrated components are threefold: cost, reliability, and compatibility. A motherboard with integrated components costs little or no more than a motherboard without such components, which can save you $100 or more by eliminating the cost of inexpensive stand-alone equivalents. Because they are built into the motherboard, integrated components are usually more reliable than standalone components. Finally, because the motherboard maker has complete control over the hardware and drivers, integrated components usually cause fewer compatibility issues and device conflicts.

- Buying at the "sweet spot" is almost always the best decision. The sweet spot is the level at which the price/performance ratio is minimized—that is, where you get the most bang for your buck. For example, Intel sells a broad range of desktop processors, from $50 dual-core Celerons to $1,000 six-core Core i7 processors. Dual-core Celeron processors are cheap, but slow. Six-core Core i7 processors are fast, but hideously expensive. There must be a happy medium. The sweet spot for processors is around $175 (give or take $25) for a retail-boxed CPU. If you spend much less, you get less performance per dollar spent. If you spend much more, you get only a slight performance increase. This sweet spot has stayed the same for years. The same $175 buys you a faster processor every time Intel cuts prices, but that $175 processor has always been the bang-for-the-buck leader.

- It's almost always worth paying more for better quality and reliability. If the specs for two components look very similar but one sells for less than the other, it's a safe bet that someone cut corners to reduce the price of the cheaper component. The cheaper component may use inferior materials, have shoddy build quality or poor quality control, or the manufacturer may provide terrible tech support or a very short warranty. If it's cheaper, there's a reason for it. Count on it. The best way to avoid the trap of poor-quality components is to be willing to pay a bit more for quality. The price difference between a mediocre product and a top-quality one can be surprisingly small. Throughout this book, we recommend only high-quality products. That's not to say that products we don't list are bad, but those we do recommend are good.

- Brand names really do mean something, but not all brands are good ones. Brand names imply certain performance and quality characteristics, and most manufacturers take pains to establish and maintain those links in consumers' minds. Different brand names are often associated with different quality and/or performance levels in a good/better/best hierarchy, in the same way that General Motors sells its inexpensive models as Chevrolets and its expensive models as Cadillacs.

For example, ViewSonic makes several lines of LCD displays, including its high-end Pro Series, its midrange Graphics Series, and its entry-level Value Series. ViewSonic also maintains a separate brand name for its cheapest

Bang for the Buck

To find the sweet spot, just compare the price of a component to its performance or capacity. For example, if one processor costs $175 and the next model up is 10% faster, it should cost at most 10% more. If it costs more than that, you've reached the wrong part of the price/performance curve, and you'll be paying a premium for little additional performance. Similarly, before you buy a hard drive, divide the price by the capacity. At the low end, you may find that a small hard drive costs more per gigabyte than a larger drive. At the high end, a very large drive probably costs significantly more per gigabyte than a medium-capacity model. The sweet spot is in the middle, where the cost per gigabyte is lowest. Make sure, though, that you compare apples to apples. Don't compare a quad-core or six-core processor to a dual-core processor, for example, or a 7,200 RPM hard drive to an SSD model.

Of course, all of that assumes that you care about bang for the buck. If you have the budget and performance is more important to you than cost, by all means buy the $1,000 processor. You'll have the fastest system possible, which for a lot of people is no small thing.

products: OptiQuest. If you buy a Pro Series monitor, you know it's going to cost more than the lower-end models, but you also know it's going to have excellent performance and will likely be quite reliable. Conversely, if you buy an OptiQuest monitor, you know it's going to be cheap and not very good. A few manufacturers also have special high-end brand names, although that practice has declined as margins have eroded throughout the industry.

- If you're on a tight budget, shop by brand name rather than by specifications. For the same price, it's usually better to choose a component that has less impressive specifications but a better brand name rather than a component with better specifications but a poor brand name. For example, if you can't afford a high-end 24" Samsung LCD display, but a 22" Samsung model with similar specifications or a Brand-X 24" display with similar specifications is within your budget, choose the 22" Samsung model. It may be a bit smaller than the Brand-X display, but the Samsung will almost certainly have better display quality and be more reliable. In other words, if you have to choose between better quality and higher performance, choose quality every time.

- Similarly, if you're choosing between two lines offered by a particular manufacturer, choose the better-quality model. For example, if a display manufacturer offers a 24" model from its entry-level line at about the same price as a 22" model from its premium line, choose the latter. You give up a bit of screen size, but display quality will be higher, and possibly reliability as well. Conversely, if the manufacturer offers good/better/best lines, you'll probably get optimum bang for the buck by choosing the midsize "better" model rather than the small "best" model or the large "good" model.

In this chapter, we tell you what we've learned based on more than 20 years of experience buying PC hardware components. By necessity, the project systems in this book are built with specific components. The obvious problem with any such list of specific components is that new products are constantly introduced and older products discontinued. A product that is leading-edge when we proof the final galleys may be midrange by the time the book arrives in bookstores and discontinued by the time you read it. Nor is this problem limited to printed books; even enthusiast websites can't keep up with the flood of new products. So, rather than a detailed discussion of such ephemeral details, this chapter focuses heavily on the important characteristics of hardware components—the things you need to understand to make good decisions.

Fortunately, progress in PC components is generally evolutionary rather than revolutionary, and the quality level you can expect from any particular manufacturer is pretty predictable. If we use, for example, a Seagate Barracuda 7200.12 hard drive in one of the project systems, and that exact drive is no longer available when you start ordering parts for your own system, it's probably safe to assume that a similar 7200.12 model will do the job just as well. And if Seagate has by then introduced a 7200.13 series, it's very likely that those new models will be at least as fast and reliable as the earlier models.

A Rose by Any Other Name

It's not uncommon for several manufacturers to relabel identical or very similar products from the same Pacific Rim factory. For example, the factory that makes many of the cases that Antec sells under its brand names also makes similar cases that are sold under other brand names such as Chieftec and Chenming. Contrary to web wisdom, that doesn't mean those similar products are identical to the Antec cases. Different companies can specify different levels of finish, quality control, and so on. A case with the Antec name on it meets Antec's quality standards. An "identical" case with a different brand name may not be of the same quality.

This practice is also common with power supplies. Many well-regarded brand-name power supplies are in fact manufactured by a company other than the one whose name they bear. For example, many Antec and PC Power & Cooling power supplies are actually made by Seasonic, which also sells power supplies under its own name. Once again, don't assume that two very similar power supplies are of equal quality simply because they were made by the same manufacturer. Seasonic-manufactured power supplies that are branded by Antec, PC Power & Cooling, or Seasonic meet those companies' respective quality control standards. The same is not necessarily true of a similar power supply with a different company's name on it.

With so many alternatives, it's easy to buy the right part from the wrong source. Accordingly, the last part of this chapter distills what we've learned about how and where to buy PC hardware components. When you finish reading this chapter, you'll have all the information you need to make the right buying decisions.

Online Customer Product Reviews

Most online computer product vendors, notably NewEgg, have active user review sections for the products they carry. We suggest you take those reviews with a grain of salt, if not a boatload.

Here's the fundamental problem. Say 1,000 people buy a particular product from NewEgg. Of those 1,000 buyers, 900 are satisfied with the product, 90 are delighted, and 10 are unhappy. As any marketing executive will tell you, when someone loves a product, he'll tell a friend; when someone hates a product, he'll tell the whole Internet.

And that's exactly what happens. All 10 unhappy buyers write one-star reviews. Maybe a tenth of the delighted buyers write four- or five-star reviews. And maybe 1% of the satisfied buyers write reviews, which are typically three, four, or five stars. A product that satisfied 99% of buyers ends up with 28 reviews, averaging a mediocre three stars.

To make matters worse, some or all of those one-star reviews may not be the product's fault at all. A rebate company may have been lax in fulfilling rebate requests, and many of the buyers who didn't get their rebate checks will take it out on the product. It's also common for buyers to blame a product for their own errors. For example, probably 99% of the motherboards returned to online vendors as defective are actually perfectly good. The buyer simply made a mistake such as forgetting to connect a cable or installing an incompatible processor or memory.

So, our advice about online component reviews is not to take them too seriously. If a product has hundreds of reviews and a very high average rating, it's probably safe to assume that it's a good product. Conversely, if a product has hundreds of reviews and a bad to mediocre rating, it may indeed be a bad product, but it may also be a good product that's simply suffering from "piling on." (Believe it or not, many bad reviews are written by people who've never actually used the product; the same is true, but to a much lesser extent, for good reviews.) Finally, if a product has relatively few reviews (say, less than 50), the average rating, good or bad, is statistically meaningless.

Enthusiast Website Product Reviews

Conversely, some of the top-tier enthusiast websites are excellent sources of reliable product reviews, particularly for gaming-related components such as fast video adapters, high-end processors, premium memory, solid-state drives, and so on. They may tell you more than you ever wanted to know about the technical details of a product, and they may get excited about performance differences that are immaterial to you, but their reviews are generally unbiased and reliable.

Two sites we trust are AnandTech (http://www.anandtech.com) and Tom's Hardware (http://www.tomshardware.com).

Choosing Components

The biggest advantage of building your own PC is that you can choose which components to use. If you buy a cookie-cutter system from Dell or HP, most of the decisions are made for you. You can specify a larger hard drive, more memory, or a different monitor, but the range of options is quite limited. Want a better power supply, a quieter CPU cooler, or a motherboard with built-in FireWire and enhanced RAID support? Tough luck. Those options aren't on the table.

When you build from scratch, you get to choose every component that goes into your system. You can spend a bit more here and a bit less there to get exactly the features and functions you want at the best price. It's therefore worth devoting some time and effort to component selection, but there are so many competing products available that it's difficult to separate the marketing hype from reality.

The reality is that you get what you pay for—or perhaps we should say, you get no more than you pay for. If you're not careful, you can get much less than you pay for, whether by choosing the wrong components, or the wrong vendor, or both. To avoid that problem, you need to educate yourself about what's important and what's not when it comes to choosing components.

Still, we understand that many people will want specifics, so we'll do our best to provide them by naming names and offering advice. We don't doubt that some people will take issue with some of our recommendations and advice. We don't claim that the products we recommend are "the best" in any absolute sense, because we haven't tested every product on the market and because what's "best" is inherently subjective. What's "best" for us may be just "very good" from your point of view; however, it almost certainly won't be "terrible."

So, keeping all of that in mind, the following sections describe the manufacturers we recommend for the various components you'll need to build your own PC.

Case

The case (or chassis) is the foundation of any system. Its obvious purpose is to support the power supply, motherboard, drives, and other components. Its less-obvious purposes are to contain the radio-frequency (RF) interference produced by internal components, to ensure proper system cooling, and to subdue the noise produced by the power supply, drives, fans, and other components with moving parts.

A good case performs all of these tasks well and is a joy to work with. It is strongly built and rigid. Adding or removing components is quick and easy. All the holes line up. There are no sharp edges or burrs. A bad case is painful to work with, sometimes literally. It may have numerous exposed razor-sharp edges and burrs that cut you even if you're careful. It is cheaply constructed of flimsy material that flexes excessively. Tolerances are very loose, sometimes so much so that you have to bend sheet metal to get a component to fit, if that is even possible. Using a cheap case is a sure way to make your system-building experience miserable.

Depending on the case size and type, expect to pay at least $50 for a good basic case without a power supply, and $100 or more for that case with a good power supply. Case and power supply quality is one of the major areas for cost-cutting in mass-market systems, many of which use a case and power supply combo that would retail for half the price of decent components, or less. If you must economize on these components, we strongly recommend that you buy an inexpensive case without a power supply and install a good power supply. Using a cheap power supply almost guarantees problems—if not initially, then certainly as the system ages.

Here are some important considerations when choosing a case:

Build quality and price

Build quality correlates closely to price. Better and more expensive cases are heavier, stiffer, and have no dangerous sharp edges or burrs. Panels are heavy-gauge and fit to tight tolerances, often with captive screws, and supplemental case fans are of good quality. One exception to the heavier-is-better rule is portable gaming cases, which are often made from aluminum or a light alloy but are engineered to provide stiffness and tight tolerances.

Size and type

Mainstream cases are generally categorized as server, full-tower, mid-tower, mini-tower, microtower, desktop, or slimline. There are also various special-purpose cases available that are optimized for specific purposes, such as media center/home theater cases and gaming cases. For maximum flexibility and expandability as well as better cooling, choose a large case. If size is a major consideration, choose the smallest case that will accept the motherboard that you want to use and has sufficient drive bays for all of the drives you want to install.

Motherboard form factor compatibility

Motherboards are available in numerous form factors, which differ in size and (sometimes) mounting hole positions. Fortunately, only three of those form factors are commonly used for desktop motherboards. From largest to smallest, these include: ATX (305 mm × 244 mm board size), microATX or µATX (244 mm × 244 mm) and Mini-ITX (170 mm × 170 mm).

With very few exceptions, cases built to accept these form factors are backward-compatible. An ATX case can accept an ATX, µATX, or Mini-ITX motherboard. A µATX case can accept a µATX or Mini-ITX motherboard, and a Mini-ITX case can accept only a Mini-ITX motherboard.

A few motherboards designed for gaming systems or servers use the Extended ATX (EATX) form factor, which has a board size of 305 mm × 330 mm. These motherboards fit only EATX cases, which can also accept motherboards in any of the three most common form factors.

Bundled power supply

Many mainstream cases include a power supply, which may or may not be suitable for your purposes. Case quality and power supply quality generally go hand-in-hand. We've never seen a cheap case that included anything other than a junk power supply, and we've seldom seen a high-quality case that included anything less than a midrange power supply.

Expensive and special-purpose cases—particularly server and gaming cases—often do not include a power supply, on the assumption that you'll want to choose a power supply to fit your particular needs. Media center/home theater cases may or may not include a power supply. Unless you just happen to love a case that comes only with a bundled power supply, we recommend that you buy the case and power supply separately. You may pay a few bucks more than you would for a case with a bundled power supply, but you'll also probably get a better power supply.

Be wary of very small cases and bare-bones systems like those sold by Shuttle, Foxconn, MSI, and others that come with a bundled power supply. Some of these cases use power supplies with proprietary physical form factors, which means the only source for a replacement power supply is the original vendor. These proprietary power supplies may be extremely expensive or no longer available when your original power supply needs to be replaced. If you buy such a case, either make sure that it accepts industry-standard replacement power supplies or resign yourself to paying through the nose to replace the power supply when it inevitably fails.

Front-panel connectors

Most cases provide front-panel connectors for USB and audio. Some also provide connectors for FireWire and/or eSATA, which are used to connect external hard drives, camcorders, and similar devices. A few cases include a built-in front-panel card reader, which is useful for transferring files from a digital camera or camcorder. If a case you otherwise like lacks one or more front-panel connectors that you want, you can purchase a port extender that fits in an open external drive bay and provides the connectors you need.

Case material

Nearly all cases use some plastic, particularly for the front panel, but the frame should be of stiff, heavy-gauge steel or aluminum, as should the side and top panels. Steel is rigid but heavy. Aluminum frames can be as rigid as steel, but are much lighter. In fact, the first time UPS showed up with an aluminum case without a power supply installed, we picked up the shipping box and thought they'd forgotten to put the case in the box. All other things being equal, an aluminum case costs more than a similar steel case but provides similar rigidity. Some sources claim that aluminum cases provide superior cooling, but we've never been able to confirm these claims. We suggest that you choose a steel case unless system weight is a major concern, such as for a LAN party gaming system or when building a stackable media center/home theater system.

Cooling

Inexpensive cases often make no special provisions for better cooling, and may even lack mounting positions for supplemental cooling fans. What fans and mounting positions they do include are often small—60 mm to 80 mm. (Of course, small cases are limited in both the number and size of fan positions.) Better cases have multiple fan-mounting positions, usually of larger size—typically 90 mm up to 250 mm (!), depending on the size of the case—and may have fans already installed in some or all positions. Midrange cases usually include inexpensive fans, which are not the quietest or most durable models available. Premium cases are often supplied without fans, on the theory that you'll want to choose your own fans, but those that have fans installed usually include midrange or better fans. Some high-end gaming cases include provisions for installing liquid cooling, and a few of those have a radiator and tubing preinstalled.

Because larger fans move more air at slower (and quieter) rotation speeds, we recommend that you choose a case with as many and as large fan mounting positions as possible. If you'll be running hot components, such as a gaming video card (or two) or an extreme processor, look for a case that includes ductwork designed to exhaust hot air from those components directly to the outside of the case.

Quiet PC technology

Many premium cases include various quiet PC technologies, such as sound-deadening panels, vibration isolators in the drive bays, thermally controlled case fans, and so on. Although some of these features can be added via third-party products, if noise level is a major consideration we suggest that you purchase a case that's designed from the ground up to minimize noise.

Recommended case brands

There are many good case brands, but **Antec** (*http://www.antec.com*) stands out from the crowd. Antec offers a huge range of cases, from inexpensive basic cases to premium special-purpose cases, with or without bundled power supplies. The bundled power supplies, most of which are actually made by Seasonic, are generally excellent. Over the last decade, we've used Antec cases for probably 95% of the systems we've built, and we've never been disappointed.

Cooler Master (*http://www.coolermaster.com*) is Antec's major competitor in the PC case segment. It's a well-respected brand that's particularly popular amongst gamers. Cooler Master offers a broad selection of case types and styles, although not quite as broad as Antec. The Cooler Master cases we've seen are similar to Antec cases in quality and features, although we generally prefer Antec's bundled power supplies.

Lian Li (*http://www.lian-li.com*) makes one or two entry-level cases but is primarily known for its high-end cases, most of which use aluminum construction and sell for premium prices. Construction quality is excellent on every Lian Li case we've seen, and they're particularly popular for portable gaming systems and media center/home theater systems. Most Lian Li cases are sold without a power supply.

Silverstone (*http://www.silverstonetek.com*) was originally best known for its media center/home theater cases but has since branched out to become a full-line case supplier, selling an extremely broad range of cases—everything from entry-level mini-tower cases to cube-style small form factor cases to super-premium media center/home theater cases. We have limited experience with Silverstone cases, but all of those we've seen have been of excellent quality. Most Silverstone cases are sold without a power supply.

Thermaltake (*http://www.thermaltakeusa.com*) cases are particularly popular among extreme gamers—including those who want a case designed from the ground up for liquid cooling—but Thermaltake also offers a complete range of general-purpose cases, including small form factor and media center/home theater cases. Construction quality is generally excellent. Most Thermaltake cases are sold without a power supply.

Power Supply

The power supply is one of the most important components in a PC, yet most people give it little consideration. In addition to providing reliable, stable, closely regulated power to all system components, the power supply draws air through the system to cool it. A marginal or failing power supply can cause many problems, some of which may be very subtle and difficult to track down. Most problems are not subtle, however. A poor or marginal power supply is likely to cause system crashes, memory errors, and data corruption and may fail catastrophically, taking other system components with it.

Here are some important considerations when choosing a power supply:

Form factor

Unless you buy a case with a bundled power supply, the first thing to determine is which power supply form factor(s) will fit the case you've chosen. Full-tower cases and most mid- and mini-tower cases accept ATX12V or ATX12V/EPS12V power supplies. Smaller cases, including most µATX cases, may accept only smaller power supplies that use the SFX12V, TFX12V, or a proprietary form factor. Mini-ITX cases accept Mini-ITX power supplies.

Wattage rating

Wattage ratings are not standardized, so you can't simply compare numbers. High-quality power supplies have wattage ratings speci-fied at 40° C or 50° C. Cheap power supplies are often rated at 25° C or even 20° C, which unrealistically inflates their capabilities. For example, a power supply rated for 500W output at 20 °C may actually be able to deliver only 300W at the higher temperatures actually present in a working power supply.

Size your power supply according to the system configuration, taking into account the wattage required by the processor and video adapter. The power draw of mainstream processors ranges from less than 30W to more than 130W. Video power draw ranges from just a few watts for most integrated video adapters to 150W or more for some high-end gaming video adapters, and 400W or more for extreme gaming systems with dual or quad video adapters.

Main power connector

The original ATX specification and the ATX12V 1.X specifications defined a 20-pin main power connector, which provides power to the motherboard. The ATX12V 2.0 specification (and later versions) expanded the main power connector to a 24-pin version that is a superset of the original 20-pin connector. That is, the 20 original pins remain the same, and 4 additional pins have been added to one end of the connector.

Most (but not all) current motherboards and power supplies have the 24-pin connector. Many 24-pin power supplies use a split connector, which allows them to function as a 20-pin or 24-pin power supply, depending on which type your motherboard requires. Most 20-pin motherboards can accept the 24-pin connector directly simply by allowing the extra 4 pins to overhang the motherboard connector, but some motherboards have capacitors or other components that prevent a 24-pin plug from being inserted completely into the 20-pin socket. Sometimes it's possible to bend the interfering component slightly to provide clearance for the 24-pin power supply plug, but 24-to-20 pin adapter cables are readily available and a much safer solution.

Even if you use a 20-pin motherboard, we recommend buying a 24-pin power supply.

Supplemental power connectors

Early PCs required only the main power connector to power the motherboard and peripheral power connectors to power drives and other peripherals. As the power requirements of newer and faster processors and video adapters continued to climb, supplemental power connectors were added to power supplies to meet these larger power requirements. Modern power supplies provide the following supplemental connectors:

+12V power connector

All current ATX12V power supplies provide a four-pin (2×2) +12V power connector, which connects directly to the motherboard near the processor and provides power to the processor.

Power supplies that meet both the current ATX12V and EPS12V standards provide at least one eight-pin (4×2) secondary +12V power connector and, optionally, a tertiary +12V power connector that uses the same four-pin arrangement as the connector on a standard ATX12V 2.X power supply. To ensure backward compatibility with ATX12V motherboards, most EPS12V power supplies implement the secondary eight-pin connector or connectors as a splittable pair of four-pin 2×2 connectors, either of which may be used to provide processor power on an ATX12V motherboard.

Most standard motherboards require only a single four-pin +12V power connector, which is provided by any current ATX12V power supply. You need concern yourself with this issue only if the motherboard you use requires additional +12V power connectors, which very few desktop boards do.

PCIe power connector

Most entry-level and midrange video adapters can be powered by the PCIe slot itself, but the very fast video adapters used in some gaming systems may require much more power than the PCIe slot can provide. ATX12V 2.1 and later power supplies include one or more PCIe power connectors to provide additional power to the video adapter(s). These connectors plug directly into the video card, supplying supplemental power beyond the power that is provided by the PCIe slot itself.

The original PCIe power connector, defined in the ATX12 2.1 specification, is a six-pin (3×2) connector that must be capable of providing up to 75W of supplemental power to a video adapter. ATX12V 2.2 defined an eight-pin PCIe power connector, which is capable of supplying another 150W to a video adapter. The eight-pin adapter is backward-compatible with the six-pin adapter, so a video adapter that requires a six-pin PCIe power connector can be powered by an eight-pin PCIe power connector. The converse is not true, because a video adapter that accepts an eight-pin PCIe power connector may draw more current than the six-pin PCIe power connector can supply.

Current ATX12V power supplies provide at least one six-pin PCIe power connector. High-wattage power supplies may provide several PCIe power connectors (six-pin, eight-pin, or some combination thereof). For example, the PC Power & Cooling TurboCool 1200, a power supply popular among extreme gamers, provides three six-pin PCIe power connectors and three six/eight-pin PCIe power connectors.

Other than gaming systems, very few systems require the PCIe power connector at all, so most builders need not concern themselves with the number or type of PCIe power connectors present on the power supply. If you are building an extreme gaming system, pay close attention to the number and type of PCIe power connectors, particularly if you plan to install two or more video cards.

Peripheral power connectors

All power supplies provide some or all of the following peripheral power connectors:

Berg power connector

Some current power supplies no longer include the obsolete four-pin Berg power connector. This connector was used to power floppy disk drives, which are now nearly extinct. (Of the few floppy disk drives still available, most of them, including internal models, are USB-powered.)

Absence of Berg connectors is no reason to reject a power supply. If for some reason you actually need a Berg connector, you can buy an inexpensive Molex-Berg adapter cable. Some power supplies that do not include Berg connectors include such an adapter cable in the box.

Molex power connector

All current power supplies still include the obsolescent Molex power connector. The Molex power connector was originally used to power ATA/IDE and earlier types of hard drives and is still used today to power case fans, front-panel lights, and some internal peripherals.

SATA power connector

The SATA power connector is the current standard for powering internal peripherals, primarily hard drives and optical drives. There are actually three types of SATA power connector. The 15-pin *Standard* SATA power connector is used for powering optical drives and 3.5" hard drives in desktop systems and is the type you'll find on any current desktop power supply.

The six-pin *Slimline* SATA power connector is used to power optical drives and 2.5" hard drives in notebook systems and some Mini-ITX and other small form factor systems. The nine-pin *Micro* SATA power connector is used to power 1.8" hard drives in notebook systems. If you need to install a peripheral that requires a Slimline or Micro SATA power connector in a desktop system, you can purchase a Standard-to-Slimline or Standard-to-Micro SATA power adapter cable.

For mainstream systems, nearly any current power supply provides enough SATA power connectors to power all of the drives. If you are building a server that will have many hard drives installed, make sure you have sufficient SATA power connectors for all of the hard drives and optical drives you plan to install. (We once built a tower system that contained 12 internal drives; we ran out of drive bays and SATA power connectors at the same time.) The length of the SATA power cables is seldom an issue unless you are building a full-tower system populated with a lot of drives. In that situation, pay careful attention to the lengths of the SATA power cables and the positions of the connectors on the cables.

Manufacturer

Many power supply vendors don't actually manufacture power supplies, but simply relabel power supplies made by other companies. That's not necessarily a bad thing. For example, two of the most reputable power supply vendors, Antec and PC Power & Cooling, purchase most or all of their power supplies from other companies and rebrand them. Some first-rate companies, notably Seasonic, manufacture and sell power supplies under their own name and also distribute power supplies to other companies for relabeling. Still other companies do all three: manufacture and sell power supplies under their own brand names, manufacture power supplies for relabeling by other companies, and buy power supplies from other manufacturers and put their own brand names on them.

> **Ron Morse Comments**
>
> *Always check the box. Most of the time a product requiring a particular power connector or two will come with converter cables. The converter cables have Molex sockets on one end (Molex being sort of the Rosetta Stone of PC power connectors) and a plug for whatever the product needs on the other.*
>
> *If for some reason you encounter a device that needs a power connector that isn't already on your power supply or doesn't come with a converter, your local RadioShack store will almost certainly have what you need in stock.*

About the only way to determine which company actually made a particular power supply is to check the UL label and look up the manufacturer in a database. Here's one website that maintains such a list:

http://www.jonnyguru.com/modules.php?name=NDArticles&file=print&nd ar_id=24

Some power supply manufacturers produce only cheap power supplies. Some produce a wide range of models, from cheap to first-rate units. A few produce only high-quality power supplies. Among the manufacturers (as opposed to brand names) we've found to be consistently reliable are Channel Well (USA), FSP/Sparkle, Seasonic, and Win-Tact.

Here are some less important things to consider when choosing a power supply:

Modular power supply cables

Many power supplies have fixed power cables. If you're building a system in a relatively large case, that's not a problem; there are plenty of places to tuck unused power cables out of the way. But in smaller systems, space is at a premium. The last thing you want is unused power cables cluttering up the available space, blocking air flow and interfering with fans. That's why some power supplies use modular cables. The cables that are always required—the main power cable, the +12V motherboard power cable, and perhaps one peripheral power cable—are permanently affixed to the power supply. You can connect optional cables, such as the PCIe power cable and additional peripheral power cables, only if you need them. There are several jacks on the power supply body that accept PCIe power cable(s) and additional peripheral power cables, allowing you to install only those cables you actually need. Most modular power supplies come with a good selection of optional cables, but if you need extra cables of a particular type you can usually buy them separately from the company that makes the power supply.

All other things being equal, a power supply that provides modular cables is usually a bit more expensive than one that does not. More importantly, it is also a bit less reliable, at least in theory, because it uses plugs and jacks rather than soldered connections. On balance, we tend to use a modular power supply when we build a small system and a standard power supply when we build a full-size system, but the difference is not enough either way to make it a major decision factor. Treat modular power cables as a tiebreaker if you're choosing between two otherwise similar power supplies. Otherwise, don't worry about them.

Efficiency

Typical power supplies of a few years ago had efficiencies around 70%, which meant that 100W of AC input was required to provide 70W of DC output, with the remaining 30W simply producing waste heat inside the power supply. Most current power supplies are rated at 80% or higher efficiency, and the most efficient exceed 90%. The issue is not simply wasted power and higher electricity bills; it's that waste heat. Heat is the enemy of PCs, and it's worthwhile to reduce waste heat whenever possible.

The efficiency of any power supply varies with load. Efficiency is maximum at somewhere near the middle of its range. For example, a power supply that is accurately rated for 400W maximum wattage will be most efficient somewhere near 200W output, with efficiency gradually decreasing as the load approaches either 0% or 100%. That's why it's a mistake to buy too much power supply for your system. If your power supply is routinely operating at, say, 25% of rated wattage, the good news is that it'll probably last forever, but the bad news is that it's operating inefficiently. Conversely, it's a mistake to buy too little power supply. If your power supply routinely operates at 90% of rated capacity, it's also operating very inefficiently and will probably die an early death.

Small differences in power supply efficiency may be significant if you're a corporation with a fleet of thousands of desktop or server PCs. Otherwise, give preference to the more efficient unit, but don't make it a deciding factor.

Power-factor correction

Power supplies of a few years ago typically had power factors of 67% or so. In essence, that means those power supplies drew 150% of their nominal maximum input power two-thirds of the time and zero power one-third of the time. For example, a power supply with a rated input of 300W and operating at full capacity would actually draw 450W for two out of every three cycles of the 60 Hz AC current, and 0W for the third cycle. In other words, it would draw 450W for 1/30th of a second and then no power for the following 1/60th of a second. That may seem a small difference from drawing 300W continuously, but it has major implications for businesses that must size their computer rooms' electrical infrastructure and UPSs for the maximum current draw rather than an average draw.

Some years ago, power supplies with power-factor correction (PFC) started becoming more common. Most of these early PFC power supplies used passive PFC, which amounts to a simple coil that helps smooth out current draw. These units were able to improve power factors to 75% or more. A few current PFC power supplies use passive PFC, but most use active PFC, which uses live electronic components to smooth current draw. A typical active PFC power supply improves the power factor to 90% or more, and the best reach 99%. For home use, PFC efficiency is a minor issue, but it's still worth choosing a power supply with a high PFC factor, if only because such power supplies are generally better-made than units with lower PFC factors.

Use the following guidelines to choose a power supply appropriate for your system:

- Above all, make sure the power supply you buy fits your case and has the proper connectors for your motherboard and, if applicable, your video card(s).

- Assuming honest wattage ratings (like those from the vendors we recommend), for a typical entry-level system, install a 300W or larger power supply. For a mainstream system, install a 400W or larger power supply. For a high-performance system, install a 500W or larger power supply (possibly much larger). If you're installing multiple video adapters in an NVIDIA SLI (Scalable Link Interface) or AMD/ATI CrossFireX configuration, make sure to use a power supply that is certified for such use.

Recommended power supply brands

There are many good power supply brands, but **Antec** (*http://www.antec.com*), **PC Power & Cooling** (*http://www.pcpower.com*), and **Seasonic** (*http://www.seasonicusa.com*) stand out from the crowd. All three companies offer a wide range of power supplies to fit various needs.

Processor

A few years ago, if we checked an online PC component vendor for desktop processors, there would have been maybe eight or nine Intel processors on offer and about the same number of AMD processors. When we started working on this section, we checked the NewEgg desktop processor page. There were 44 AMD processors available, ranging in price from $36 to $296, and 42 Intel processors, ranging in price from $41 to $1,000. That's a lot of options. How can AMD and Intel possibly make that many different processors? And how can anyone make the best choice among 86 processors ranging in price from $36 to $1,000?

The short answer is that AMD and Intel really don't make all that many different processors. They each make only a few significantly different models, but offer those models in various speeds and with different combinations of minor features. It's like buying a car. The base model may have a dozen options available, and by the time you total up all the available permutations, that base model can be ordered in thousands of different configurations.

A particular processor series may be available in numerous models that vary in speed, number of cores, number of threads per core, amount of L3 cache, power consumption, and so on. There is also frequently pricing overlap between models from different processor series. For example, the day we checked, no less than four different Intel processors were selling for exactly the same price, $199.99. Table 2-1 lists them.

Table 2-1. Four $200 Intel processor models

Model	Cores	Threads	Speed	L3 cache	Process	Socket	Power
Core 2 Quad Q9300	4	4 (1/core)	2.5 GHz	6 MB	45 nm	LGA 775	95W
Core i5-660	2	4 (2/core)	3.33 GHz	4 MB	32 nm	LGA 1156	73W
Core i5-661	2	4 (2/core)	3.33 GHz	4 MB	32 nm	LGA 1156	87W
Core i5-750	4	4 (1/core)	2.66 GHz	8 MB	45 nm	LGA 1156	95W

As Intel was fully aware when it set the prices for these four processors, their overall performance is very similar. Will a quad-core processor with a slower clock speed but more L3 cache outperform a dual-core processor with a faster clock speed and less L3 cache, or vice versa? Will a dual-core processor that runs two threads per core outperform a quad-core processor that runs only one thread per core, or vice versa? The answer to all of those questions is both yes and no, because the winner will be different for different applications. Some applications are clock speed–bound, while others are core-bound, thread-bound, or L3 cache–bound—or some combination of those factors. The upshot is that on average you get $200 worth of performance, whichever of these $200 processors you use.

But what about the Core i5-660 and -661 models? They appear to be identical other than in power consumption. Why would anyone pick the -661 for the same price as the -660, when the only difference appears to be that the -661 draws more power? Here's where we get into really minor differences:

- The -660 and -661 both include integrated Intel HD Graphics, but the -660 uses a basic graphics frequency of 733 MHz, while the -661 boosts that to 900 MHz for faster video performance.

- The -660 supports Intel Virtualization Technology for Directed I/O (VT-d), a memory-mapping technique that has both advantages and disadvantages. The -661 does not support VT-d.

- The -660 supports Intel Trusted Execution Technology, which is essentially hardware support for Digital Restrictions Management (DRM). The -661 has no such support.

As it happens, we wanted to use a processor in this price range for our mainstream system. So which one did we choose, and how did we choose it? All four are excellent processors, but…

- We first eliminated the Core 2 Quad Q9300 from consideration. It's based on older technology, but that's not necessarily a problem. We ruled out the Core 2 Quad because it uses the obsolescent Socket LGA 775, which would have limited our choice of motherboards and future upgrade/repair options.

- We next eliminated the Core i5-750. It's an excellent processor, and for some people would be the best choice of the four. However, it has the highest power consumption of the remaining candidates, and lacks integrated video.

- With the choice down to the Core i5-660 and -661, the decision becomes almost a toss-up. In return for its somewhat higher power consumption, the -661 provides faster integrated graphics. The -661 lacks VT-d (which we'd kind of like to have just on general principles), but it also lacks hardware DRM, which we'd definitely prefer not to have.

On that basis, we chose the Intel Core i5-661, but the truth is that any of the other three would have done nearly as well.

Most people spend too much time dithering about which processor to install. The only really important decision is how much to spend. After you make that decision, it really comes down to the minor details. Here are the considerations for each of the processor price ranges:

Embedded ($60 to $150, including motherboard)

Although tiny motherboards with embedded processors have been available for years, they didn't really become mainstream items until Intel introduced its Atom series of low-power processors. Although the Atom is certainly no speed demon, it is fast enough for appliance systems, and even as the foundation for small, quiet, low-power general-purpose systems, such as a bedroom, kitchen, or kids' room PC. Atom processors aren't available separately at retail vendors. Intel sells them in bulk to OEMs and systems integrators, who build motherboards or complete systems around them.

Purchasing an Intel Atom processor means also buying the motherboard it's soldered onto. Most such motherboards include "integrated everything," including video, audio, LAN, and often WiFi. Such motherboards sell for $60 to $150 or more, depending on their features, their quality, and the Atom model they include. A very small minority of those motherboards are µATX, and there are even one or two full ATX models available, but the vast majority are Mini-ITX boards, designed to fit the smallest cases.

The Atom is available in single- and dual-core models at various clock speeds. The slowest single-core models are appropriate for an appliance system such as a network-attached storage (NAS) box or a Linux router. The faster dual-core Atom processors are fast enough that most people consider them suitable for light general use, such as checking email or browsing the Web. (Robert's den system is a passively cooled and nearly silent dual-core Atom Mini-ITX box running Linux, which he uses for checking web mail and looking up details on IMDb while we're watching videos.)

Entry level (under $100)

Our praise of the Intel Atom aside, these are the least expensive processors that are really suitable for a general-purpose PC. At the bottom of this range—sub-$60 processors—are the least expensive socketed AMD Sempron and Intel Celeron models. These processors are low-power in both senses, providing limited CPU performance while consuming 65W or less. They are single-core or very low-end dual-core, and are suitable if you need more performance than the fastest Atom processors can provide but don't need the performance of a more expensive processor.

The $60 to $100 price range is the realm of low-end dual- and triple-core processors and a few of the least expensive quad-core units. AMD owns this market segment with its Athlon II and Phenom II series of two-, three-, and four-core processors. In this price range, AMD processors offer more cores, more threads, and more general bang for the buck than similarly priced Intel processors. Any of these processors is an excellent choice for an entry-level general-purpose system.

Mainstream ($100 to $200)

Although AMD offers many processors in this price range, Intel owns this market segment. Intel processors simply provide more bang for the buck than AMD processors in this price range—sometimes dramatically so.

In the lower half of this price range, dual-core Intel Core i3-series processors consistently edge out comparably priced dual- and triple-core AMD Phenom and Athlon II processors for most applications. In the upper half of this price range, dual- and quad-core Intel Core i5-series processors outperform comparably priced quad- and hex-core AMD processors.

Mainstream processors, particular those from the upper half of the price range, are the best choice for most systems. They are noticeably faster than entry-level processors and cost only a little more, while at the same time they are only a bit slower than performance processors.

Performance ($200 to $400)

With the exception of its fastest hex-core model, AMD no longer offers desktop processors in the $200 and higher price range. This is the realm of fast Core 2 Quad and Core i5 processors and midrange Core i7 processors. Performance processors are popular primarily among serious gamers, who are willing to spend extra money in return for the slight competitive edge that one of these faster processors provides.

Extreme ($400+)

This rarefied range is thinly populated by a few of the fastest Intel Core i7 processors, up to and including $1,000+ processors. Extreme processors are favored by well-heeled gamers and by business users like real-time commodity traders, to whom literally a fraction of a second may mean the difference between a huge profit and a huge loss. These processors are faster than mainstream and performance processors (sometimes noticeably so). If performance is the top priority and cost is not an issue, choose an extreme processor. Otherwise, spend that extra money on extra memory, a better display, a faster video card, or a larger hard drive. Or just keep the money in your bank account.

Also consider the following issues when you choose a processor:

- Even a $75 processor is fast enough for typical general-purpose computing, such as reading email, browsing the Web, running office productivity applications, burning DVDs, watching YouTube videos, and so on. If you never load the system heavily, you won't notice much difference between that $75 processor and a more expensive model.

- Budget processors are hampered not just by their lower clock speeds and smaller number of cores and threads, but by small caches, which cripple performance, particularly if you work with large data sets (e.g., rendering video). In such situations, the performance difference between a budget processor and even a mainstream processor (let alone a performance or extreme processor) can be like the difference between night and day. For example, Robert uses a fast quad-core processor to render video much faster than real-time. (That is, rendering a 10-minute video takes only a couple of minutes.) Rendering that same 10-minute raw video segment on a budget processor might take 10 or 15 minutes, which is a huge difference when you're actually sitting staring at the screen waiting for the render to finish.

- Processors in the "sweet spot" range—$150 to $200 for a retail-boxed processor—usually represent the best bang for the buck. They're noticeably faster than budget processors for even moderately demanding applications, and are fast enough even for CPU-intensive tasks like casual video rendering.

- Buy the processor you need initially, rather than buying a slower processor now and planning to upgrade later. Processor upgrades, both AMD and Intel, are a minefield of compatibility issues.

Recommended processors

For appliance systems, the **Intel Atom** is hard to beat. Intel, ASUS, and GIGABYTE all offer very good Mini-ITX motherboards with embedded Atom processors. Zotec offers excellent Atom motherboards, but they're very pricey (too much so, we think).

For budget systems, dual-, triple-, or quad-core **AMD Athlon II** or **Phenom** processors in the sub-$100 range offer more cores, threads, and overall performance than similarly priced Intel processors, although Intel sells a lot of Pentium E- and G-series processors in this price range due to its reputation for quality, compatibility, and reliability.

For mainstream and higher systems, it's all Intel. We recommend choosing your processor according to your budget from among the broad range of **Intel Core i3**, **Core i5**, and **Core i7** processors.

Heatsink/Fan Units (CPU Coolers)

Modern processors may consume from 25W to 130W or more. Nearly all systems deal with the resulting heat by placing a massive metal heatsink in close contact with the processor and using a fan to draw air through the heatsink fins. This device is called a *heatsink/fan* (HSF) or *CPU cooler*.

Most AMD and Intel processors are available with or without a bundled CPU cooler. The bulk, OEM, or white-box form includes just the processor. The retail-boxed form costs a few bucks more and includes the same processor with a bundled CPU cooler (and, usually, a longer warranty).

Bundled CPU coolers have gotten much better over the years. Although aftermarket units may provide better cooling and lower noise levels, the bundled CPU cooler is generally more than good enough to cool the CPU while keeping noise down to an acceptable level. Gamers, overclockers, and others who run their processors hot may find an aftermarket CPU cooler worth the extra money, as may those who want to build the quietest possible system. For most other people, a retail-boxed processor with bundled CPU cooler is the best choice.

Use the following guidelines when choosing an HSF:

- Make certain the HSF is rated for the exact processor you use. An HSF that physically fits a processor may not be sufficient to cool it properly. By definition, a bundled HSF is rated for the processor it comes with.

- Make sure the HSF is usable with your motherboard and case. Some HSFs are incompatible with some motherboards because clamping the HSF into position may crush capacitors or other components near the processor socket. Good third-party CPU coolers often list compatibility with specific motherboard models. Check the website. Premium CPU coolers are usually physically large. If you intend to purchase such a cooler, make sure your case has enough clearance between the motherboard and cover panel for the cooler to fit.

- Pay attention to noise ratings. Some high-efficiency HSFs designed for use by overclockers and other enthusiasts have very noisy fans. Other HSFs are nearly silent. The best (and most expensive) third-party CPU coolers are both highly efficient and very quiet. Note that these coolers are often supplied without a fan, which you must purchase separately from among the models recommended for that specific cooler.

- Use the proper thermal compound. When you install an HSF, and each time you remove and replace it, use fresh thermal compound to ensure proper heat transfer. Thermal compound is available in the form of viscous thermal "goop" and as phase-change thermal pads, which melt as the processor heats up and solidify as it cools down. Make sure that the thermal compound you use is approved by the processor maker and, if applicable, the cooler maker.

Recommended CPU cooler brands

Unless you have good reason to do otherwise, buy a retail-boxed CPU with a bundled cooler. If you need high-performance cooling or an extremely quiet cooler, purchase a CPU cooler made by **Arctic Cooling** (*http://www.arctic-cooling.com*), **Scythe** (*http://www.scythe-usa.com*), **Thermaltake** (*http://www.thermaltakeusa.com*), or **Zalman** (*http://www.zalmanusa.com*).

Motherboard

The motherboard is the main logic board around which a PC is built. It is the center of the PC, in the sense that every system component connects to the motherboard, directly or indirectly. The motherboard you choose determines which processors are supported, how much and what type of memory the system can use, what type of video adapters can be installed, the speed of communication ports, and many other key system characteristics.

Here are some important considerations when choosing a motherboard:

CPU socket

The fundamental characteristic of a motherboard is the CPU socket, because it determines which processors physically fit that motherboard. There are two types of sockets:

Intel sockets

The oldest of the current Intel sockets is the obsolescent *Socket LGA 775*, also known as *Socket T*. Socket LGA 775 processors and motherboards are still widely available, and are likely to remain so through at least 2011 and into 2012. It's not necessarily a bad idea to build a new system around an obsolescent socket—prices on older gear are often excellent—as long as you're aware that it may be difficult or impossible to find a replacement motherboard or processor two or three years down the road. At worst, you may need to replace both the motherboard and the processor if one or the other fails. Socket LGA 775 motherboards accept dual-core Pentium processors, single- and dual-core Celeron processors, and Core 2 Duo and Core 2 Quad processors.

Intel's current entry-level/mainstream socket is *LGA 1156*, also known as *Socket H*. With this socket, Intel moved functions formerly performed by the separate northbridge section of the chipset onto the processor chip itself, which accounts for the need for almost 400 more pins than LGA 775. The high-speed Direct Media Interface (DMI) link formerly used to link the northbridge and southbridge sections of the chipset is now implemented within the processor package, as are the QuickPath Interconnect (QPI) formerly used to connect the processor to the I/O hub (southbridge), a PCI Express 2.0 x16 link for communication with a graphics adapter, and a dual-channel DDR3 memory controller. In effect, LGA 1156 moves all of the high-bandwidth functions formerly performed by a separate northbridge onto the processor itself and leaves only the former southbridge chipset functions on the separate southbridge chip, now called the *Platform Controller Hub* (PCH). Socket LGA 1156 motherboards accept Core i3, Core i5, and Core i7 processors. LGA 1156 processors and motherboards are likely to remain Intel's mainstream desktop solution for the next few years.

Intel's current performance socket is *Socket LGA 1366*, also known as *Socket B*. Like LGA 1156, LGA 1366 uses an external southbridge chip for USB and other communications functions, and incorporates a DDR3 memory controller on the processor (triple-channel DDR3, in this case). The major difference between LGA 1156 and LGA 1366 is that the latter moves PCI Express off the processor chip, using a QPI link to communicate with a separate partial northbridge chip that supports video and other PCI Express communications. Socket LGA 1366 motherboards currently accept only Core i7 and Xeon (workstation/ server) processors. LGA 1366 processors and motherboards are likely to remain Intel's performance desktop solution for the next few years.

AMD sockets

Like Intel, AMD has three current processor sockets, but in AMD's case the three sockets are actually just very minor variations of one socket. In fact, the 940-pin Sockets AM2 and AM2+ and the 941-pin Socket

AM3 are pin-compatible physically, although a processor designed for one of those sockets will not necessarily operate in one of the other sockets.

Socket AM2 dates from May 2006, when it replaced Sockets 754 and 939 for Sempron and Athlon processors. Socket AM2 is characterized by its support for DDR2 memory, HyperTransport 2.0 operating at 1.0 GHz, and one power plane to drive both cores and the Integrated Memory Controller (IMC).

Although Socket AM2 processors have been discontinued, Socket AM2 motherboards are physically and electrically compatible with current Socket AM2+ and AM3 processors. Note, however, that using a later processor in an AM2 motherboard requires a BIOS update that may or may not be available from the manufacturer, and the old motherboard will not be able to take advantage of additional features supported by the newer processor. Although Socket AM2 motherboards may be available new for some time to come, don't buy one.

Socket AM2+ is a transitional socket. The two major upgrades from Socket AM2 are the addition of HyperTransport 3.0 operating at 2.6 GHz and split power planes, one of which powers the CPU cores and the other the IMC. Socket AM2+ motherboards can use AM2, AM2+, or AM3 processors, assuming that a suitable BIOS is available, and are often promoted as "Socket AM3-Ready," although they are limited to using DDR2 memory. Socket AM2+ motherboards are widely available and likely to remain so for some time to come.

Socket AM3 is AMD's current mainstream socket. Socket AM3 differs from AM2+ in that it supports processors that use either DDR2 or DDR3 memory.

If you intend to build an AMD-based system, buy a Socket AM2+ or (preferably) a Socket AM3 motherboard.

Supported CPU types

Just because a CPU physically fits the socket on a motherboard doesn't mean that CPU is compatible with that motherboard. Two issues affect compatibility:

VRM support

Voltage Regulator Modules (VRMs) on a motherboard supply power to the processor. VRMs are rated to deliver specific maximum current. If a particular processor draws more current than the VRMs can provide, that processor cannot be used on that motherboard.

BIOS compatibility

Even if a particular motherboard is compatible in every respect with a particular processor, that processor cannot be used in that motherboard if the BIOS does not support that specific processor model. Even an apparently trivial difference between a supported processor and a new model may be enough to make that new model unusable without a BIOS update.

Catch 22!

Motherboards sold at retail may not have the most recent BIOS version. This is not usually a problem, because you can download and install the most recent BIOS update once you have your new system up and running.

It becomes a major problem, though, if the processor you buy for that motherboard is not supported by the older BIOS. Your system won't boot because the old BIOS doesn't recognize the processor, and you can't update the BIOS to recognize the processor because your system won't boot. Arrrrrghhhh!

You might think you could avoid this problem by checking the motherboard web page for a detailed list of supported processors. The problem with this is that the product page almost always lists supported processors for a motherboard with the latest BIOS update installed. The best way to avoid this problem is to buy your motherboard from a high-volume dealer so that you'll get fresh stock.

Chapter 2

Form factor

Like cases, motherboards are available in numerous form factors, the most popular of which are full ATX, µATX, and Mini-ITX. Although Mini-ITX motherboards are physically compatible with µATX and ATX cases and µATX motherboards with ATX cases, it seldom makes sense to install a smaller form factor motherboard in a larger case. A µATX motherboard generally costs about as much as a similar full ATX motherboard, and Mini-ITX motherboards are often actually more expensive than similar µATX and ATX boards. Using a smaller motherboard than the case can accept simply gives up memory and expansion slots, communications ports, and other potentially valuable features for no reason. It may also cause problems with cables that are too short to reach the smaller motherboard.

Memory slots

Every motherboard includes one or more memory slots, but the number and type of these slots differ, as follows:

Number

Typical ATX motherboards provide slots for four memory modules. µATX boards usually provide two or four slots. Mini-ITX boards provide one or two slots. All other things being equal, it's better to have more memory slots than fewer, for three reasons. First, the number of memory slots (and the maximum capacity of each) puts a hard limit on the amount of memory that can be installed. Second, it may be less expensive—sometimes much less expensive—to install a given amount of memory using more smaller modules rather than fewer larger modules. For example, if you intend to install a total of 8 GB of memory, the price of four 2 GB memory modules may be much less than the price of two 4 GB modules. Third, if you decide to upgrade your system in mid-life, it's easier and cheaper to add memory modules than to remove and discard the current modules and replace them with all new modules.

Type and capacity of modules supported

Current desktop motherboards use one of four types of memory modules: 240-pin DDR2-SDRAM DIMM, 240-pin DDR3-SDRAM DIMM, 200-pin DDR2-SDRAM SO-DIMM, or 240-pin DDR3-SDRAM SO-DIMM. The SO-DIMM modules are actually notebook memory, but they are used by a few Mini-ITX motherboards. Mainstream ATX, µATX, and Mini-ITX motherboards accept either 240-pin DDR2 or DDR3 DIMMs. A few hybrid Socket AM2+/AM3 motherboards accept *either* 240-pin DDR2 *or* DDR3 DIMMs, but only one type at a time.

Just because a memory slot physically accepts a memory module doesn't mean that module is compatible with that motherboard. The chipset and/or BIOS may limit the module capacity. For example, although a 4 GB DDR2-SDRAM module may be physically identical to a 2 GB module, a particular motherboard may support 2 GB modules, but not 4 GB modules. If you install the 4 GB module, the results are unpredictable. The system may fail to boot. More likely, it will boot normally, but will recognize the 4 GB module as only 2 GB. If the BIOS is limiting module capacity, updating the BIOS may allow the system to recognize the larger memory modules. If the chipset is limiting module capacity, there's no fix.

Note that the maximum memory module capacity (and the maximum overall memory) supported by a motherboard may depend on the number of memory slots occupied and/or the speed of that memory. For example, a particular motherboard may support 8 GB of total memory in the form of two 4 GB modules, but not in the form of four 2 GB modules. Similarly, a motherboard may allow all four of its memory slots to be populated with slower memory, but only two slots with faster memory.

Before you purchase a motherboard, make sure it supports the specific memory configuration you want to use. Check the detailed motherboard specifications web page and also use one or more of the memory configurator pages provided by Crucial, Kingston, and other memory vendors.

Expansion slots

Most motherboards include expansion slots, which you can populate with expansion cards to provide functions that the motherboard does not. For example, if you purchase a motherboard that provides only USB 2.0 communication ports, you can later upgrade your system by installing a USB 3.0 expansion card. Most current motherboards provide some mix of PCI and PCI Express (PCIe) slots.

PCI

The older PCI standard defines one specific set of physical and electronic requirements for a PCI expansion slot, so any current PCI expansion card can be used in any current PCI slot (assuming that the case puts no constraints on the physical height or length of the card). In June 2010, Intel announced that it was retiring the PCI specification in favor of PCI Express. PCI expansion cards and motherboards with PCI slots are likely to remain available for some time to come, but development of new PCI products has now largely ended, and future products will all be PCI Express.

PCI Express

The newer PCIe standard defines the physical and electronic characteristics of a connector that may be used individually (called PCIe 1x) or may be concatenated into a single combined 4x, 8x, or 16x PCIe connector to provide correspondingly higher bandwidth.

PCI Express is now used universally for video adapter cards, but as of mid-2010 PCI expansion cards still greatly outnumber PCI Express expansion cards, despite the fact that PCI Express is superior and has been available for years. Until now, most expansion card makers have adopted an if-it-ain't-broke-don't-fix-it attitude. With Intel's deprecation of the PCI standard, we expect that to change, with more and more PCI Express expansion cards becoming available over the coming months and years and PCI expansion cards becoming increasingly hard to find.

Communications ports

All motherboards provide various communications ports. Most still provide at least one legacy serial port and parallel port, although these ports are now often present only as header-pin sets on the motherboard rather than as physical connectors on the rear I/O panel. If you need to use them, you'll need to install a cliffhanger bracket (usually supplied with the retail-boxed motherboard) to extend the ports out to an expansion slot cover. Beyond these legacy ports, current motherboards may provide some or all of the following communication ports:

USB 2.0

All current motherboards provide multiple USB 2.0 ports, both as physical connectors on the rear I/O panel and as header-pin sets that can be extended to the front-panel connectors. Most current peripherals—from keyboards and mice to speakers, printers, scanners, and digital cameras—use the USB 2.0 interface, so it's important to have enough for your needs. (Of course, you can always add a USB hub, but that increases costs and desktop clutter.) Look for a motherboard with at least six USB 2.0 ports; eight or more is better.

USB 3.0

The most recent USB standard, USB 3.0, will eventually replace USB 2.0, just as USB 2.0 eventually replaced USB 1.0 and USB 1.1. The *raison d'être* for USB 3.0 is speed. USB 2.0 has a nominal data rate of 480 Mb/s (60 MB/s) and typical real-world throughput (after protocol overhead) of 25 MB/s. For most peripherals, that's more than fast enough, but it's marginal for such high-speed peripherals as external hard drives.

USB 3.0 has a nominal raw data rate of 4 Gb/s (500 MB/s) and real-world throughput of about 400 MB/s, fast enough even for external hard drives and solid-state drives. USB 3.0 is also backward-compatible with devices that use earlier USB standards, although those devices still run at the lower data rates for which they were designed.

Eventually, USB 3.0 ports will be ubiquitous, but for now most motherboards do not provide any USB 3.0 ports at all. Those that do generally provide only one or two, in combination with several USB 2.0 ports. As devices that need the higher speed of USB 3.0 and chipsets that support USB 3.0 become more common, more motherboards will start including USB 3.0 ports. For now, we consider USB 3.0 support a nonissue. If you later need USB 3.0, it will be easy enough to buy an inexpensive USB 3.0 PCI Express adapter card and install it in your system.

eSATA

Many current motherboards provide eSATA ports, sometimes as internal connectors, sometimes on the rear I/O panel, and sometimes both. These ports are used primarily to connect external hard drives

DIY eSATA

You can use eSATA even if your motherboard doesn't explicitly support it. The only real differences between an eSATA port and a standard internal SATA port are the physical connectors and the signal voltage.

If you need to connect an eSATA device and you have no eSATA ports, you can "convert" a standard internal SATA port by buying an eSATA cliffhanger bracket. The bracket installs in place of an expansion slot cover and has a cable that you connect to one of the standard SATA ports on your motherboard. The jack on the cliffhanger bracket accepts a standard eSATA cable to connect the external device.

The only difference between this DIY eSATA and a real eSATA port is the lower signaling voltage on the DIY eSATA port, which limits the total cable length to one meter (about 40 inches), versus two meters with a real eSATA port.

and hard drive docking stations, both of which are common backup devices. If you use or plan to use eSATA devices, you'll want at least one or two eSATA ports available on the motherboard you choose.

IEEE-1394 (FireWire)

Some motherboards—particularly "media" series models—include one or two IEEE-1394 (FireWire) ports, usually as a physical connector on the rear I/O panel and perhaps a second port as header pins on the motherboard. These ports may be IEEE-1394a (FireWire 400), which has a maximum data rate of 400 MB/s, or IEEE-1394b (FireWire 800), which has a maximum data rate of 800 MB/s.

FireWire is a declining standard. It's still widely used in some specialty markets (notably, camcorders), but it is being displaced by eSATA and USB 3.0. If you need FireWire to support your camcorder or other device, look for a motherboard that provides one or two FireWire ports. If a motherboard you otherwise like has no FireWire ports, you can add them easily by installing an inexpensive PCI or PCI Express FireWire expansion card.

Use the following guidelines when choosing a motherboard:

- For a general-purpose system, choose a µATX motherboard, unless you need the additional expansion slots available on a full ATX model. For a small system, use a µATX motherboard. For a really small system, use a Mini-ITX motherboard. (Note that Mini-ITX motherboards often cost significantly more than µATX models with similar features and quality, so use Mini-ITX only if you really need it.)

- For an Intel-based system, choose a Socket LGA 1156 or a Socket LGA 1366 motherboard that is compatible with your choice of processor. Avoid Socket 775 (Socket T) motherboards, which are obsolescent. For an AMD-based system, choose a Socket AM3 motherboard if it is compatible with your chosen processor; otherwise, choose a hybrid Socket AM2+/AM3 model. Avoid Socket AM2 and Socket AM2/AM2+ models.

- Make sure the motherboard supports the exact processor you plan to use. Just because a motherboard supports a particular processor family doesn't mean it supports all members of that family. You can find this information on the motherboard maker's website or in the release notes to the BIOS updates. It's also important to know exactly what revision of the motherboard you have, because processor support may vary by motherboard revision level.

- Make sure the motherboard supports the type and amount of memory you need. Do not make assumptions about how much memory a motherboard supports. Check the documentation to find out what specific memory configurations are supported.

- Before you choose a motherboard, check the documentation and support that's available for it, as well as the BIOS and driver updates available. Frequent updates indicate that the manufacturer takes support seriously.

Recommended motherboard brands

For systems with Intel processors, we recommend **Intel** (*http://www.intel.com*), **GIGABYTE** (*http://www.gigabyte-usa.com*), and **ASUS** (*http://usa.asus.com*) motherboards. For AMD processors, we prefer GIGABYTE and ASUS. All three of these companies offer top-notch motherboards, in everything from basic vanilla units to feature-laden, high-performance boards. Intel tends to be a bit "stodgier" than the other two, emphasizing stability over performance and features, but the differences are small in any case. (If it's any indication, most of our own systems use Intel motherboards.)

If cost is a major consideration, we recommend **ASRock** (*http://www.asrock. com*) motherboards. Originally spun off from ASUS in 2002 to compete with low-end motherboard makers, ASRock has developed a reputation for inexpensive motherboards with very good quality, stability, and feature sets. Recently, ASRock has introduced higher-end motherboards as well.

Memory

The only real decisions are how much memory to install, what size and type of modules to use, and what brand to buy. Consider the following factors when choosing memory modules (DIMMs):

- For budget systems, install no less than 512 MB per core, and at least 1 GB total. (For a single-core budget system, install 1 GB or more; for a dual-core system, 1 GB or more; for a triple-core budget system, 1.5 GB or more; and for a quad-core budget system, 2 GB or more.) For mainstream systems, install 2 GB or 4 GB, with a minimum of 512 MB/thread and 1 GB per core. For performance systems, workstations, and multimedia/graphics systems, install 4 GB or more, with a minimum of 512 MB/thread and 1 GB per core. If you're running a 64-bit operating system, increase these recommended amounts by 50% to 100%.

- Memory manufacturers such as Crucial (*http://www.crucial.com*), Kingston (*http://www.kingston.com*), Corsair (*http://www.corsairmemory.com*), and Mushkin (*http://www.mushkin.com*) provide online memory *configurators* that allow you to enter the brand and model of your motherboard and return a list of compatible memory modules. Before you buy memory, use these configurators to make sure the memory you order is compatible with your particular motherboard.

- For motherboards that use 240-pin DDR2 memory, buy DDR2 memory modules of at least the speed required by your motherboard/processor combination. DDR2 memory is available in PC2 3200, PC2 4200, PC2 5300, PC2 6400, and PC2 8000 variants. Choose the fastest modules that do not sell at a significant price premium over slower modules. Once again, choose modules that support fast CAS latency timings only if they cost little or no more than modules with standard timings.

- For higher performance, install DIMMs in matched pairs or triplets to enable dual- or triple-channel memory operation.

DDR2 Versus DDR3

If your motherboard supports both DDR2 and DDR3 memory modules, install DDR3 for higher performance and ease of future memory upgrades.

- It's generally less expensive to buy a given amount of memory in fewer modules. For example, if you are installing 4 GB of memory, two 2 GB DIMMs will probably cost less than four 1 GB DIMMs. Using fewer but larger DIMMs also preserves memory slots for future expansion. However, the largest-capacity modules often sell at a substantial premium. For example, a 4 GB DIMM may cost five times as much as a 2 GB DIMM, rather than only twice as much.

- Verify the memory configurations supported by your motherboard. For example, a particular motherboard may support 2 GB DIMMs, but not 4 GB DIMMs. Similarly, one motherboard may support 2 GB DIMMs in all four of its memory slots, but another may support 2 GB DIMMs in only two of its four slots. Check the motherboard documentation to determine the memory configurations your chosen motherboard supports.

- Non-parity memory modules provide no error detection or correction. ECC modules detect and correct most memory errors but are slower and more expensive than non-parity modules. Use ECC memory if you install more than 8 GB of memory and the motherboard supports ECC memory. For 8 GB or less, use non-parity modules.

> **Ron Morse Comments**
>
> *This needs to be emphasized. With the trend toward 64-bit operating systems and more than 4 GB of installed RAM, problems related to this are becoming more common.*

Recommended memory brands

There are many good memory vendors. Some, such as Corsair, Mushkin, OCZ, and Patriot, are well-known names among extreme gamers and other enthusiasts. But **Crucial** (*http://www.crucial.com*) and **Kingston** (*http://www.kingston.com*) are the two top-tier desktop memory vendors whose products we've used almost exclusively for the last decade or more. Both offer a broad line of memory and memory-related products at competitive prices, from budget modules to high-performance premium modules. Other than from lightning strikes, catastrophically blown power supplies, and similar misfortunes, we don't recall ever having a memory module from either company fail in use.

Kingston is a packager: it buys memory chips from other companies and builds modules with those chips. Crucial (actually, Micron Technology) is fully vertically integrated. Sand goes in one side of its plants, and finished memory modules come out the other side. Because we have found Crucial memory to be utterly reliable and competitively priced, and because we like the idea of a company building (and controlling) its products from start to finish, we order Crucial memory whenever possible.

Floppy Disk Drive (FDD)

You probably don't need an FDD in your new system. Few current motherboards provide the traditional FDD interface, so old-style FDDs are no longer usable. If you need FDD support to transfer data from old floppies, buy an inexpensive external USB floppy drive. If for some reason you want an internal FDD, buy an internal USB model, which connects to a set of USB header pins on the motherboard. If you need to boot from the FDD—for example, to run a classic computer game—configure the boot sequence section of BIOS Setup to put the FDD first, where it will be listed as a USB Mass Storage Device.

Recommended FDD brands

If you need an FDD, any brand is fine.

Hard Drive

It's easy to choose a good hard drive. Hitachi, Samsung, Seagate, Toshiba (notebook drives only), and Western Digital produce drives at similar price points for any given size and type of drive.

Compatibility is not an issue for hard drives. Hard drives are plug-and-play devices. Any recent hard drive will coexist peacefully with any other recent hard drive or optical drive, regardless of manufacturer.

Use the following guidelines when you choose a hard disk:

- Hard drives are available in standard ATA (*Parallel ATA* or *PATA*) and *Serial ATA* (*SATA*) interfaces. PATA drives are obsolescent and are suitable only for upgrading older systems that lack SATA interfaces. For a new system, choose a drive that supports the SATA 3.0 Gb/s interface. A few newer premium models support the more recent SATA 6.0 Gb/s interface, but even the fastest hard drives are incapable of saturating a SATA 3.0 Gb/s interface, so the SATA 6.0 Gb/s interface is really just marketing hype.

- Although it's tempting to buy the highest-capacity drive available, high-capacity drives often cost more per gigabyte than midrange drives, and the highest-capacity drives are often slower than midrange models. Decide what performance level and capacity you need, and then buy a drive that meets those requirements. Typically, you can choose the model based on cost per gigabyte. However, you may need to buy the largest drive available despite its higher cost per gigabyte and slower performance, simply to conserve drive bays and SATA ports.

- Choose a 7,200 RPM SATA drive for a general-purpose system. 10,000 RPM drives cost more than 7,200 RPM models, are not all that much faster, and are much noisier and hotter-running than 7,200 RPM models.

- Get a model with larger buffer/cache if it doesn't cost much more. Some drives are available in two versions that differ only in buffer size. One might have a 16 MB buffer and the other a 32 MB buffer. It's worth paying a few extra dollars for the larger buffer.

Recommended hard drive brands

We've used many desktop hard drives from all four companies that currently make them, not to mention drives from another dozen or two companies that have fallen by the wayside over the years. We usually install **Seagate** (*http://www.seagate.com*) drives, because they are fast, quiet, cool-running, reliable, and competitively priced. **Western Digital** (*http://www.wdc.com*) went through a very bad patch a few years ago, with high out-of-the-box and in-use failure rates. For years, we wouldn't even consider installing a Western Digital drive. Fortunately, Western Digital has since addressed its quality problems and now produces reliable models across the full range of capacities and performance levels. We still seldom use Western Digital drives, though, because they generally cost more than comparable Seagate models. **Samsung** (*http://www.samsung.com*) produces a much narrower range of drives than Seagate or Western Digital, but the drives Samsung does offer are competitive with comparable units from Seagate and Western Digital. Like Samsung, the last member of the Big Four, **Hitachi** (*http://www.hitachi.com*), produces a relatively narrow range of models. After being burned by the fiasco several years ago when Deskstar drives were dropping like proverbial flies, we never installed another Hitachi drive, so we can't comment on their current quality.

Enterprise- Versus Consumer-Grade Drives

If you peruse the hard drive section of an online vendor's store, you may be puzzled to find two similar drives from the same manufacturer selling for very different prices. For example, we just checked NewEgg and found a 1 TB Seagate Barracuda 7200.12 for $75 and a 1 TB Seagate Barracuda ES.2 for $160. The capacities are identical, as are the rotation rates and cache sizes. So why the huge difference in price?

The 7200.12 is a "consumer-grade" drive and the ES.2 is an "enterprise-grade" drive. Obviously, the ES.2 must be a better drive, right? Well, it depends on how you define better. The ES.2 isn't faster or more durable than the 7200.12. The ES.2 does have a longer warranty—five years versus three—but it really isn't any less likely to fail than the 7200.12.

The real difference is in the firmware. Consumer-grade drives like the 7200.12 have firmware designed on the assumption that they're the only hard drive in the computer. Accordingly, their firmware has very aggressive error-recovery routines, which may cause the drive to time out for anything from a few milliseconds to (in extreme cases) a minute or more. Enterprise-grade drives like the ES.2 have firmware designed on the assumption that the drive will be running in a RAID, with parity data available on other physical drives in the system. Accordingly, the ES.2 has much less aggressive error-recovery routines, because it can assume it will have help from other drives in recovering errors.

Basically, then, the consumer-grade drive is much better at recovering errors without assistance, but is therefore more likely to time out, which is a Very Bad Thing for a drive that's operating as part of an array. The enterprise-grade drive needs a little help from its friends to recover from errors, but is therefore very unlikely to time out during error recovery. In an enterprise RAID setup, having a drive time out is very nearly as bad as having a drive fail completely, so the higher price of enterprise-grade drives is well worth paying. For a home or small-office system, including one with a RAID, we think the consumer-grade drives are the better choice.

Solid-State Drive (SSD)

Solid-state drives serve the same purpose as hard drives—mass storage—but are purely electronic devices. Rather than storing data on spinning disk platters, an SSD stores data in flash memory. All but the least expensive SSDs are faster than the fastest hard drives—sometimes much faster. (In fact, the fastest SSDs can saturate a SATA 3.0 Gb/s interface, which is the real reason that motherboard makers are beginning to introduce models with SATA 6.0 Gb/s ports.)

SSDs are simultaneously reliable and unreliable: reliable in the sense that they have no moving parts and are much less subject to shock damage than rotating drives, and unreliable in the sense that SSDs are inherently consumable items. We know the idea of "using up" an SSD sounds odd, but that is in fact what happens. The nature of flash memory is that the individual cells used to store data survive for only so many write cycles. Once a cell exceeds that number of writes, it is no longer usable.

Manufacturers implement various firmware schemes to load-level their drives, and recent operating systems (such as current Linux distributions and Windows 7) include support for TRIM, a technology that maximizes the usable life of an SSD.

But, inevitably, a heavily used SSD begins to lose both capacity and performance as time passes. Used improperly, an SSD may begin to show performance degradation after only a few weeks or even days of use. With TRIM enabled, that same drive will provide excellent performance for months or even years of use.

It's difficult for us to write authoritatively about SSDs, because right now the entire market segment is in a state of flux. Better drives are released literally every month, and strides are being made in improving both performance and sustainability. If you buy an SSD now, just be aware that you're buying into a rapidly developing technology. Anything you buy now will inevitably be replaced by a better, larger, faster, and more durable model for the same price soon after you buy it.

So, is buying an SSD now a sucker bet? Not at all. The best current models are blazingly fast and quite durable, assuming they're not abused. Although an SSD is often the only drive in a notebook system, we think the best way to use SSDs in a desktop system is as a boot/system/working data drive in a system that also has one or more standard hard drives for bulk data storage.

If you browse the SSD section of an online component vendor's site, the first thing you'll notice is that SSDs have small capacities and high prices. At a time when 1 TB desktop hard drives are midrange in capacity and sell for well under $100, a typical SSD stores from 32 GB to 256 GB and sells for anywhere from 4 to 10 times as much.

Other than price, there are several considerations when choosing an SSD:

Capacity

All other things being equal, SSDs typically sell for about the same amount per GB across the line. For example, if a particular model of SSD is available in 32, 64, 128, and 256 GB capacities, each step up typically doubles the price. That's because the vast bulk of the cost of an SSD is in the flash memory. Doubling capacity requires twice as much flash memory, and so doubles the price.

We think the best strategy is first to determine how much space you need for your operating system, applications, and working data, then to add a bit extra for growth and buy an SSD of that capacity. When we did that, we settled on a 128 GB model for Robert's primary system, mainly because he does a lot of video editing, which involves manipulating many multi-gigabyte files. For most people, a 32 GB SSD will suffice.

> ### Read, but Don't Write
>
> *Reading from an SSD does nothing to degrade it. Read all you want. But every write to the drive causes very slight degradation, which adds up over time. Does that mean an SSD is essentially a read-only device? Of course not. Write to your SSD when you need to, but avoid unnecessary writes. The biggest offenders in that regard are the Windows paging file and the Linux swap area. Always put these on a hard drive, not on your SSD.*

> ### Ron Morse Comments
>
> *Windows users installing the 64-bit version of either Vista or Windows 7 will probably want to use a 64 GB or larger SSD for their system drives.*

Cell type

Two types of flash memory are used in SSDs. *Single-level cell* (SLC) memory is faster and can sustain many more write cycles than *multi-level cell* (MLC) memory, but it also costs much more. SLC memory is widely used in enterprise-class SSDs, some of which can store 1 TB or more and cost as much as a good used car. A few premium consumer-grade SSDs also use SLC memory. They are generally of very low capacity, and cost about four times as much per GB as drives of comparable capacity that use MLC memory. For most people, the additional speed of an SLC drive will be much less important than the higher price. A good MLC drive is so much faster than any hard drive that the faster-still SLC drive will seem a minor improvement.

Memory speed

There are large differences in speed between the least expensive and most expensive MLC SSDs, because fast flash memory chips cost more than slow ones. The least expensive SSDs use very slow flash memory chips, and may have read and write data transfer rates that are slower than a standard desktop hard drive. A similar SSD that uses the fastest available flash memory chips may have data transfer rates two or three times higher than the fastest hard drives.

Recommended SSD brands

SSDs have been available for years as niche products in the laptop/notebook market, so as they become increasingly mainstream there's some history to judge them by. It would be useless for us to recommend specific models, because that information would be out of date long before you saw it. We can, however, recommend two vendors who have a history of producing SSDs that have been very competitive on price, quality, and performance. The first, unsurprisingly, is **Intel** (*http://www.intel.com*), which over the years has produced a series of excellent SSDs. We have no doubt that whichever models Intel offers when you're ready to buy your own SSD will be equally competitive. Our second recommended manufacturer is **Crucial** (*http://www.crucial.com*), a company that knows as much about memory as any other on the planet. We suggest you start your search with what those two companies have to offer and use them as standards to which to compare competing offerings.

Optical Drive

With the exception of Blu-ray drives, optical drives are a mature product category and have become commoditized. Hobbyists continue to debate their finer points, but the truth is that one $20 DVD-ROM drive or $30 DVD writer is much like any other.

Every system needs at least one optical drive, if only for loading software, but for most desktop systems the only decisions you need to make are whether you need Blu-ray support and whether to buy a read-only drive or a writer (burner). For some small systems, the physical dimensions of the drive may

Ron Morse Comments

SSDs are available from an astonishing number of vendors. Once you've identified the device you want, a little careful shopping can save you a pile. When checking the prices of SSDs, however, be sure you're comparing the same model. A retailer may advertise, for example, a "Kingston SSD," but without checking you won't know if it's offering the better-performing "V+" model at an attractive price or one of the mainstream "V" models at a higher price than you would pay for the same device elsewhere.

The state of the art for SSDs is changing rapidly, and it is not uncommon to find a manufacturer or vendor slashing prices on its current offerings in preparation for the arrival of new models. A new-stock but "discontinued" device can be an exceedingly good buy. If you shop large e-tailers like NewEgg, Amazon.com, and Frys.com, be sure to check the "specials" on their websites before going on to the main SSD section.

be critical. Many small cases accept standard optical drives, but Mini-ITX and other very small cases may require a slimline optical drive and may limit the depth of the drive.

Unless there's good reason to do otherwise, install a DVD writer in any system you build. Saving $10 by installing a read-only DVD-ROM drive instead of a DVD writer often turns out to be a poor economy, given the additional flexibility the writer provides.

If you need Blu-ray support, you can choose among three types of drives:

Blu-ray writers

Blu-ray writers can read and write Blu-ray discs, DVDs, and CDs. Write speeds for CD-R/RW and DVD±R/RW discs are typically a bit slower than those of standard DVD writers. Blu-ray writers can write to single-layer (25 GB) or dual-layer (50 GB) write-once (BD-R) or rewritable (BD-RE) discs. Write speeds for BD-R discs are typically 8X, 10X, or 12X, which means it takes about 8 to 12 minutes to write a full BD-R/SL disc and twice that for a BD-R/DL disc. BD-RE discs are written at 2X, which means it may take about 50 minutes to write a full BD-RE/SL disc, and twice that for a BD-RE/DL disc.

Blu-ray writers are still niche products, primarily because the drives and discs are expensive relative to DVD writers and media. On a per-byte basis, BD-R discs are nearing price parity with DVD±R discs, which is to say that a BD-R/SL disc has roughly six times the capacity of a DVD±R/SL disc and costs roughly six times as much. BD-RE/SL discs are considerably more expensive, but may make sense in some applications. BD-R/DL and BD-RE/DL discs are extraordinarily expensive and should be used only if there is no alternative.

If you install a Blu-ray writer, we recommend that you also install a standard DVD writer. Use the expensive Blu-ray writer only to read or write Blu-ray discs, and use the cheap DVD writer for reading and writing standard DVDs and CDs, to save wear and tear on the expensive drive. In fact, we might go further and install three drives in the system: a Blu-ray writer that we'd use only for burning BD-R/RE discs; a Blu-ray reader that we'd use for reading Blu-ray discs; and a standard DVD writer that we'd use for everything else.

Blu-ray combo drives

Blu-ray combo drives read Blu-ray discs, DVDs, and CDs, and can write DVDs and CDs (but not Blu-ray discs). Installing a Blu-ray combo drive makes no sense unless you happen to need this particular combination of features in a system that has room for only one optical drive, or you're short of ports. Otherwise, install two drives: a standard DVD writer and a read-only BD-ROM drive. The total cost will be the same or less, the individual drives are likely to have better specifications than the combo drive, and if the reader outlives the writer (as is likely) you can replace just the $30 writer when it fails instead of replacing the $100 combo drive.

BD-ROM drives

BD-ROM drives read Blu-ray discs and standard DVDs, but cannot write discs. Because of higher component costs and licensing fees, BD-ROM drives typically cost three to four times as much as DVD-ROM drives. The least expensive models typically have 4X BD-ROM read speeds and 2 MB caches, which suffices for watching or ripping movies. More expensive models typically offer 8X, 10X, or 12X BD-ROM reads and 4 MB or larger caches, but unless you need additional read speed there's little reason to spend more money.

Burnout

If you write a lot of discs, expect to replace the burner frequently. Drives that are used primarily or solely to read discs often last for years, even under fairly heavy use. Burning discs frequently is hard on DVD writers, which in our experience seldom last for more than 1,000 to 1,500 burns. (We've never tested a Blu-ray writer to destruction because we can't afford that many discs.)

Furthermore, although this sounds very odd and we have no explanation for the phenomenon, burners seem to age even sitting unused on the shelf. Several times, we've installed a new burner that had been sitting unused in the box for a year or more, only to find that it died an early death.

Ron Morse Comments

Cheap capacitors degrade when not charged.

Finally, a word about interfaces. Every type of optical drive is available in external form. All external optical drives provide a USB 2.0 interface, and some also provide an IEEE 1394 (FireWire) and/or eSATA interface. Internal optical drives are available in old-style ATAPI and SATA interfaces, with the exception of Blu-ray drives, which are nearly all SATA.

Ordinarily, this isn't an issue. ATAPI is obsolescent going on obsolete, so it's usually a no-brainer to choose a SATA optical drive. The one exception is if you're building a system around a tiny motherboard that has a limited number of SATA interfaces and an ATA interface that would otherwise go unused. In that case, you may need all of the SATA ports for hard drives, so you may have no choice but to install an ATAPI optical drive. If you do that, make sure to use a UDMA ATA cable rather than a standard cable.

Recommended optical drive brands

Years ago, we recommended Plextor optical drives. They were built like tanks and (given high-quality blanks) produced perfect burns every time. As an experiment, we once burned through an entire spindle of 100 DVD+R discs, one after the other, and scanned the resulting discs. The first disc we burned was nearly perfect, as we expected. But the hundredth disc—written when the Plextor drive had been burning discs continuously for hours—was also nearly perfect, which we didn't expect.

No other drive we torture-tested this way came even close to the Plextor. Most started producing bad discs after they'd burned only a few discs at this 100% duty cycle. More than a few simply died partway into the spindle.

Alas, those days are long gone. Plextor still sells competent optical drives, but the optical drive market has changed dramatically. When Plextor sold $200+ DVD burners in competition with lesser brands that sold for a third of that, there was room in the budget to build those drives to an extremely high standard. Nowadays, no one would buy a $200 DVD burner. Plextor now has to compete with $25 units and price its drives at $40 or $50, so there's simply no longer anything but mediocre DVD burners available.

For standard optical drives, we recommend **ASUS** (*http://usa.asus.com*), **Lite-On** (*http://us.liteonit.com*), and **Samsung** (*http://www.samsung.com*). For Blu-ray burners, we recommend **Pioneer** (*http://www.pioneerelectronics.com*).

Backup Hardware

With typical desktop hard drives storing 1 TB or more, the thought of backing up a computer can be pretty intimidating. Maintaining proper backups is not quick, easy, or cheap. Nor is it optional, at least if you care at all about your data. Because it's so much trouble to maintain proper backups, most people's solution to protecting their data is simply to ignore the problem and hope nothing bad ever happens. Inevitably, they're disappointed.

Like anything with moving parts, any hard drive will eventually fail. If you're lucky, you'll get at least some warning when your hard drive is about to fail. But don't count on that. All too often, hard drives fail like light bulbs—fine one moment and dead the next. If all of your data is on that hard drive and you have no backups, you might as well kiss your data goodbye. Yes, it's possible that some of your data may be recoverable, but—as many people have learned to their regret—that recovery may come at a cost of hundreds or even thousands of dollars.

The only solution is to back up your system regularly and maintain multiple copies of your data, including at least one off-site copy. Then, when the worst happens, you'll have lost only the data you created or modified since your last backup.

Developing and implementing a backup strategy is beyond the scope of this book, but whatever backup procedure you use will obviously require hardware to make the copies. Disregarding tape drives, which are too expensive for a home or small office system, there are several practical alternatives.

Optical discs

A DVD+R disc stores about 4.4 GB, which for many people is sufficient for routine backups, and requires only a few minutes to write and verify. The disc costs only $0.25 or so and is small, light, and portable. Disc wallets that hold from 16 to 100 or more discs are readily available, and you can carry the wallet with you when you leave the house.

Obviously DVD+R isn't a workable solution for a full backup of a large hard drive, which might require hundreds of discs, but it offers more than enough capacity to store most people's primary working data, such as email, documents, digital photographs, and so on. We use DVD+R discs as a supplement, writing all of our working data to one every Sunday.

Discs Matter

Although it's impossible to burn good discs with a poor burner, it's very possible to burn poor discs with a good burner. All you need to do is feed low-quality blank discs to the good burner, and you'll get rotten results. We could write an entire book (well, at least an entire chapter) about disc quality.

Fortunately, we don't have to write all that, and you don't need to read it. If you want top-quality burns, use top-quality discs. The best discs available are made by Taiyo-Yuden (http://www.t-yuden.com). They cost more than inferior discs, but they're worth it if what you're burning to the disc matters to you. If you can't get TY discs, buy Verbatim (http://www.verbatim.com) discs.

Incidentally, although the practice isn't as widespread as it was a few years ago, TY discs are sometimes counterfeited. You can avoid that risk by buying from a reputable authorized TY dealer. If you find spindles of "Taiyo Yuden" discs on eBay selling at a discount, it's a pretty safe bet that they're fakes.

USB flash drives

USB flash drives are another popular choice for backing up data. Their primary advantages are small size and—because they have no moving parts—high durability. Robert once overlooked a USB flash drive in the watch pocket of his jeans. After being run through the washing machine and dryer, it worked as well as ever. In an even more extreme case, one of our readers reported accidentally running over a USB flash drive with his car. The case was crushed, but he was able to plug in the drive and read the data from it. True grit.

You have to make a trade-off when you choose a USB flash drive: capacity versus speed versus cost. Pick any two. Current models range from 1 GB to 256 GB in capacity. The fastest USB flash drives use memory fast enough to sustain USB 2.0 transfer rates (about 25 to 30 MB/s) for both reads and writes. The slowest have real-world write speeds of only 2 or 3 MB/s. And the price of a USB flash drive correlates directly to both capacity and speed.

Ideally, you'd probably like a USB flash drive with huge capacity and stunning speed. Alas, the price of such a drive would be more than you're likely to want to pay. For example, Kingston offers a 256 GB flash drive (rated at only 12 MB/s for writes) that sells for $850. Economic realities mandate that the fastest flash drives are available only in small capacities—typically 1 to 4 GB—while the largest flash drives are available only with pedestrian write speeds.

We find the lower write speeds of high-capacity flash drives acceptable, because we use flash drives in the same way we use DVD+R discs: for quick daily or weekly backups of our working data sets. For example, it takes 6 or 7 minutes to write and verify a 4 GB backup set to a DVD, which corresponds closely to a USB flash drive with a write speed of about 10 MB/s. In effect, the USB flash drive is equivalent to a miniature stack of DVDs.

Several manufacturers offer USB flash drives that are specifically designed to back up Windows (and, usually, Mac) systems. These drives contain special backup software that backs up changed files automatically. You just plug the drive into a USB port, and it automatically runs the backup.

Among those, our favorite is the new **Lexar Echo SE Backup Drive** (*http://www.lexar.com/echo/echo_se.html*), which is available in 16, 32, 64, and 128 GB models. Lexar rates these drives as supporting "up to" 10 MB/s writes, which raised a red flag for us. Ordinarily, the rated write speed of a USB flash drive is unrealistically high because it's achievable only when writing a single large file. When writing many small files, the actual write speed plummets, often to half or less the rated speed.

We tested a 32 GB Lexar Echo SE by writing a data set of 1,363 files and directories totaling 4,100 MB. The write completed in 6:42 (402 seconds), for a sustained data transfer rate of about 10.2 MB/s, better than advertised. We next wrote a single 4,100 MB compressed archive file, expecting even faster results. For the first few hundred MB, the Echo SE indeed ran faster, at about 13 MB/s. However, it completed the 4,100 MB write in 6:39 (399 seconds), just three seconds faster than the same-sized collection of small files, and with an identical write speed. Lexar has obviously done something effective to optimize this drive for real-world backups of many smaller files, and we recommend the Lexar Echo SE Backup drive without qualification.

External hard drives

As useful as DVD+R discs and USB flash drives are for routine partial backups, they have neither the capacity nor the speed for full backups of a system with a large hard drive or drives. For that, the only practical solution is to back up to another hard drive.

The mainstream solution is to use external hard drives, which are available from numerous manufacturers—including drive manufacturers Hitachi, Samsung, Seagate, Toshiba, and Western Digital, as well as many other vendors—in capacities from 20 GB to 3 TB. The smallest units use 2.5" 5,400 RPM notebook hard drives, are powered by the USB cable, and fit in your shirt pocket. The highest-capacity units use 5,400 or 7,200 RPM desktop hard drives, and are still small enough to be easily portable.

If you decide to use an external hard drive (or, better, multiple drives) for backing up, pay close attention to the interface(s) it offers. Units are available for USB 2.0, USB 3.0, FireWire, eSATA, and various combinations thereof. The vast majority of external hard drives currently in use are connected to USB 2.0 ports, which is fine if you have only a few GB to back up but is much too slow for doing routine backups of large data sets. If you routinely do backups of 100 GB or more, an eSATA or USB 3.0 model is a much better choice because the data-transfer rate is limited only by the speed of the hard drives.

Most external hard drives include backup software for Windows. The first time you use the drive, you simply plug it in, power it up, and allow the software to install on Windows. The software does a full backup of your Windows system. (If you're using USB 2.0, this initial backup may well take overnight to finish.) When the backup completes, you can shut down the drive, disconnect it, and take it with you when you leave the house. When you reconnect the drive to your system, it automatically scans for new and changed files and does a quick differential backup of only those files. Most external drives can be used with more than one computer to maintain separate backups for each.

Among the many USB 2.0 external drives available, we recommend the **Seagate Free Agent** series (*http://www.seagate.com*). They're available in capacities from 240 GB to 3 TB, and the bundled software is excellent. If you have a USB 3.0 port available and need a fast, high-capacity external drive, choose one of the **Western Digital My Book** models (*http://www.wdc.com*).

But, before you buy an external drive, read on.

Removable hard drive bays

External hard drives are convenient, but the problem is that you really need at least two or three of them to maintain an adequate set of backups. Each time you buy an external hard drive, you're paying for the external enclosure and the backup software. If you can get along with only two or three external drives, that cost premium is not outrageous. But if you need more, the cost starts to mount up. (Robert, for example, routinely uses more than a dozen external drives, both for backups and for archiving data off our disk arrays and into deep storage.)

One good solution to this problem is to install a removable hard drive bay in your system. Such bays fit into an external 5.25" drive bay and are connected to a standard SATA data cable and power cable. The front of the removable drive bay has an opening that accepts a standard 3.5" desktop hard drive, which you can just slide in and out as needed. (You will have to enable AHCI in your BIOS and operating system if you want to hot-swap drives.)

Removable hard drive bays have several advantages. They accept standard desktop hard drives, which are inexpensive (relative to external drives) and appear to the computer as just another hard drive. Because the drives use the SATA interface, they are as fast as an internal drive. Because the removable drive bay accepts any standard SATA hard drive, you can recycle older hard drives that you've retired when upgrading a system. And, when you leave home, it's much easier to carry a bare hard drive in a plastic shell or wallet than it is to disconnect and haul an external hard drive around with you. (Be careful when removing a hard drive; depending on how hot-running the drive is and how long it's been running, it may be too hot to touch.)

We've used several models of removable drive bays, but our favorite is the **Antec Easy SATA** (*http://www.antec.com*). It just works, and at $20 or so, there's no reason not to install one.

Hard drive docking stations

Hard drive docking stations are similar conceptually to removable hard drive bays, but they are external devices rather than internal. Like removable drive bays, docking stations use the SATA/eSATA interface, and so support hot-swapping.

A typical hard drive docking station holds one or two 3.5" desktop hard drives or 2.5" notebook hard drives vertically in a plastic or metal base, is powered by a wall wart, and connects to the computer with an eSATA cable(s). The hard drives are exposed and can be inserted or removed simply by sliding them into or out of the docking station. (Once again, for hot-swapping you'll need to enable AHCI in your BIOS and operating system.)

The disadvantage of a hard drive docking station versus a removable drive bay is that the docking station adds desktop clutter. The advantage is that the docking station is the most cost-efficient way of using removable hard drives. For example, the hard drive docking station we recommend, the **SYBA SD-ENC50020** (*http://www.syba.com*), sells for about $25 and holds two hard drives simultaneously.

Video Adapters

The *video adapter*, also called a *graphics adapter*, renders video data provided by the processor into a form that the monitor can display. Many motherboards include embedded (integrated) video adapters. You can also install a stand-alone video adapter, also called a *video card* or *graphics card*, in a PCI Express expansion slot. Keep the following in mind when choosing a video adapter:

- Unless you run graphics-intensive games, 3D graphics performance is unimportant. Any recent video adapter is more than fast enough for business applications and casual gaming. Even integrated video, let alone any current standalone video adapter, is fast enough to support the 3D requirements of the Windows Aero Glass interface.

- Choose integrated video unless there is good reason not to. Integrated video adds little or nothing to the price of a motherboard, and generally suffices for anyone except hardcore gamers or those with other special video requirements. Make sure any motherboard you buy allows integrated video to be disabled and provides a PCI Express slot, though. That way, you can upgrade the video later if you need to by installing a separate video card.

- Make sure that the video adapter you choose (or the integrated video on your motherboard) provides the type of video output connector you need. Nearly all displays provide a 15-pin analog (DSUB) VGA connector. All but the least expensive displays also provide a DVI connector, which may be analog, digital, or hybrid. Some displays provide an HDMI connector, which may or may not be HDCP-enabled.

- If you plan to use dual displays, make sure that your integrated video or video adapter supports dual displays, and that it provides the type of video connectors you need for both displays. Note that some video adapters provide one analog and one digital video connector, but allow only one of those to operate at a time. The most flexible choice is a card with dual DVI-I hybrid video connectors, which support both analog and digital displays, or dual HDMI connectors.

- If you need a 3D graphics adapter, don't overbuy. A $400 video adapter is faster than a $100 adapter, but nowhere near four times faster. As with other PC components, the bang-for-the-buck ratio drops quickly as the price climbs. If you need better 3D graphics performance than integrated video provides but you don't have much in the budget for a video adapter, look at "obsolescent" 3D video adapters—those a generation or two out of date. If you buy an older adapter, make sure the level of DirectX it supports is high enough to support the games you play.

- Make sure that the adapter you choose has drivers available for the operating system you intend to use. This is particularly important if you run Linux, BSD, or another OS with limited driver support.

- In any case, but particularly if you will use a large, high-resolution display, make certain the video adapter and its drivers support the native resolution of the display. For example, if the highest resolution supported by your video adapter is 1920×1080, you will not be pleased with the image quality from that adapter on your expensive new 30" 2560×1600 display.

- If you want to use dual displays, it simplifies matters to install a video card that has two identical video outputs (preferably digital) and connect it to two identical displays. It's often possible to configure a mixed environment—for example, one integrated video output and one video output from a separate video adapter driving two dissimilar displays—but doing so makes configuring the system more complex.

Recommended video adapter brands

Our first recommendation is to use integrated video unless you have good reason to do otherwise. ATI, Intel, and NVIDIA integrated video are all excellent, and more than sufficient for most purposes.

If you need a standalone video adapter, consider models from **ASUS** (*http://usa.asus.com*), **EVGA** (*http://www.evga.com*), **GIGABYTE** (*http://www.gigabyte-usa.com*), **Sapphire** (*http://www.sapphiretech.com*), **VisionTek** (*http://www.visiontek.com*), or **XFX** (*http://www.xfxforce.com*). All of those companies build video adapters around chipsets produced by ATI or NVIDIA, or both. The video adapter market is extremely competitive, so price is usually an excellent guideline to performance, features, and quality.

If you simply need a bit more 3D horsepower than integrated video provides, look for an adapter in the $25 to $50 range from any of these manufacturers, using either an ATI or NVIDIA chipset. The $50 to $100 range covers entry-level 3D gaming adapters, the fastest of which are sufficient for all but the most intense 3D games. If you're seriously interested in 3D gaming, you probably know more than we do about gaming graphics adapters. If not, spend some time on AnandTech (*http://www.anandtech.com*) and Tom's Hardware (*http://www.tomshardware.com*) before you plunk down money for a video adapter.

Display

The good news is that nowadays buying a bad display takes some serious effort. If you stick to good brand names, the chances that you'll get a bad display are very close to zero. The display business is extremely competitive, and bad vendors simply don't stay in business for long. The competitive nature of the business also means you don't have to worry much about over-paying for a display. Doing a bit of price shopping for the models you're interested in just about guarantees you'll get a good display at a good price.

Here's what to look for when you shop for a display:

Resolution

Resolution is the number of pixels (dots) that make up the image, specified as the number of columns by the number of rows. For example, a display whose resolution is listed as 1920×1080 uses a rectangular matrix of 1,920 columns in 1,080 rows. Such a display has a total of 1,920×1,080 pixels, or 2,073,600 pixels. Resolution of current desktop displays ranges from 1024×768 to 2560×1600. All other things being equal, higher resolution is better because at any given screen size it produces a sharper image and finer detail.

> **Blu-ray/HDTV**
>
> *If you intend to watch Blu-ray discs or other 1080P HDTV material on your system, choose a display with at least 1920x1080 resolution.*

> **Ron Morse Comments**
>
> *But note that screen elements, especially text, displayed on a high-resolution display will be smaller than the same elements on a lower-resolution display. This isn't a problem for applications that let you adjust the size of things within the application window, but applications that depend upon system fonts can be rendered unusable because the text is too small to read comfortably, especially if you're older or have less-than-perfect vision.*
>
> *Both Windows and Linux let you compensate to a certain degree with settings that make everything larger by a given percentage (I use 115% on my 1920x1200 display, but that isn't a perfect solution. I can now read the text and the application menus, but some applications just can't cope with the altered system settings and don't draw the contents of their own windows properly anymore.)*
>
> *Yet another trade-off.*

Aspect ratio

The aspect ratio of a display is calculated simply by dividing the number of columns by the number of rows. For example, a 1024×768 display has an aspect ratio of 1024/768 = 1.33:1 and a 2560×1600 display has an aspect ratio of 2560/1600 = 1.6:1. Rather than using such fractional numbers, aspect ratios are usually converted to whole numbers by multiplying both sides by an appropriate factor. For example, the 1.33:1 aspect ratio is normally multiplied by 3 to give a stated aspect ratio of 4:3, and the 1.6:1 aspect ratio is normally multiplied by 10 to give a stated aspect ratio of 16:10. (Of course, it could also be stated as 8:5 with equal accuracy, but apparently marketers like larger numbers.)

Until a few years ago, most computer displays used aspect ratios similar to those of older television sets, typically 4:3 or 5:4. Such displays are often referred to as "square," even though they're really not. However, they are nearly as tall as they are wide, in contrast to modern widescreen displays, most of which are, like modern televisions, much wider than they are tall. Although some people prefer "square" displays, the market is shifting quickly to widescreen models. As of mid-2009, the number of widescreen displays available outnumbered square displays by about two to one, and as of mid-2010 that ratio had increased to about three to one. "Square" displays are a dying breed.

Screen size

Screen size is simply the diagonal measurement of the screen. Current desktop displays range from 17" to 30" diagonally. There are two schools of thought about screen size. One argues that you should buy the largest, highest-quality display that you can afford and have space for. The other argues that two or more smaller displays are more useful than a single larger display. If you choose the latter route, make sure that your video adapter and drives support multiple displays.

All three of these characteristics are interrelated in real-world displays. Various standards—official, unofficial, and semi-official—exist that tie these characteristics together. Table 2-2 lists important desktop display standards in order of increasing total display resolution.

Table 2-2. *Desktop display standards*

Name	Display size and type	Resolution	AR	Megapixels
WXGA+	17" and 19" widescreen	1440×900	16:10	1.296
SXGA	17" and 19" square	1280×1024	5:4	1.310
"900P"	20" widescreen	1600×900	16:9	1.440
WSXGA+	22" widescreen	1680×1050	16:10	1.764
UXGA	20" and 21" square	1600×1200	4:3	1.920
1080P	21" through 27" widescreen	1920×1080	16:9	2.073
WUXGA	23" through 28" widescreen	1920×1200	16:10	2.304
WQXGA	30" widescreen	2560×1600	16:10	4.096

Beyond the basics, here are some other factors to consider:

Interface(s)

> Displays may provide one or several interfaces. A few inexpensive models provide only a DB-15 analog (VGA) connector. Most displays provide both a DB-15 and a *Digital Visual Interface* (DVI) connector, which may be analog-only (DVI-A), digital-only (DVI-D), or hybrid analog/digital (DVI-I).

> Some displays provide a *High-Definition Multimedia Interface* (HDMI), which is compatible with DVI-D but also includes the audio signal on the same connector. If your video adapter has a DVI-D or DVI-I connector and your display has an HDMI connector, or vice versa, you can purchase an adapter cable that will allow the two to function together.

> If you intend to watch copy-protected content (such as Blu-ray movies) on your display, make sure at least one of the DVI or HDMI connectors includes *High-bandwidth Digital Content Protection* (HDCP) support.

Brightness and contrast

> A bright display is important, particularly if your viewing environment is well lit, and also to give you some reserve as the display backlighting gradually dims with usage. Brightness is specified in *nits* (candellas/square meter, or cd/m²). The least-expensive displays may be rated at only 200 nits. Better displays are generally rated at 250 to 300 nits, and a few high-end or specialty displays may be rated at 400 nits or more. We consider a display rated at 250 nits or more to be sufficient.

> Contrast specifies the ratio between the luminances of the brightest white and darkest black the monitor can display, and is determined by panel type and quality as well as backlight intensity. A monitor with high contrast can display very dark shadows and very bright highlights simultaneously and shows gradation in both the shadows and the highlights. Inexpensive displays have contrast ratios as small as 300:1, and some high-end or specialty displays are rated as high as 10,000,000:1.

> Unfortunately, contrast specifications are essentially useless. Different display makers use different methods to calculate them. Two comparable displays from different makers may have identical actual contrasts, and yet one manufacturer may rate its display at 500:1 and the other at 1,000:1. As far as we know, each manufacturer is consistent. For example, if one ASUS display is rated at 500:1 and another at 1,000:1, it's safe to assume that the latter display has superior contrast.

Response time

> Fast response time is important to avoid smearing and other artifacts during fast-motion video segments, particularly with 3D computer games. Typical displays have 4 millisecond (ms) or 5 ms response times, which are sufficient for anything other than extreme gaming. Premium models and those targeted at gamers typically have 2 ms to 3 ms response times, with a few models at less than 2 ms. Inexpensive displays and very large displays may have slower response times, typically 6 ms to 10 ms, but sometimes 20 ms or more. For general use, we consider a response time of 10

ms or less adequate. If you watch a lot of HD video, look for a model rated at 5 ms or less. If you're heavily into extreme gaming, look for a model rated at 3 ms or less.

Backlighting

LCD displays backlight the image one of two ways:

CCRT

Most displays use *cold cathode ray tube* (CCRT) illumination. CCRTs are similar to fluorescent tubes and are subject to failure and to gradual dimming over time.

LED

Some premium displays substitute white LEDs for the CCRTs. Entry-level LED models—which are still more expensive than CCRT models—are *edge-lit*, with LEDs along the edges of the panel. More expensive *full-field* LED displays use a large numbers of LEDs behind the entire surface of the panel.

LED backlighting has several advantages. First, LEDs do not burn out or dim noticeably over time (a typical LED might dim to 50% of its original brightness after 50 years of constant use). Second, LEDs can be significantly brighter than CCRTs, which allows higher contrast and a brighter image. Third, full-field LED displays can greatly increase the dynamic contrast range of the image by selectively illuminating only some of the LEDs in the array. In brighter image areas, all LEDs are lit; in dimmer areas, only a fraction of the LEDs are lit.

We consider CCRT displays acceptable for almost any purpose. Rather than spending money on LED backlighting, we'd spend it on a larger or higher-resolution CCRT display—for now, at least. Currently, about 10% of all LCD displays use LED backlighting. As the technology becomes less expensive, we expect it to replace CCRTs entirely.

Minor features

We suggest you choose your display based on the factors we've already discussed. If those aren't sufficient to narrow down your choice to one display, it's time to start looking at less important factors. Taken individually, all of these "extra" features may be minor, but taken as a group they may be enough to swing your decision to one particular model.

Some displays include built-in speakers, which are at best mediocre but may be good enough for your purposes (if only to reduce desktop clutter). Some displays also include a built-in microphone that's useful for Skype and similar VoIP services. Although it is less common than it was a few years ago, a few displays include a built-in webcam, which is useful for Skype or recording YouTube videos. Finally, to reduce desktop clutter, a few displays include a built-in USB 2.0 hub. Note that some of these are passive hubs, and may not have sufficient power for many USB devices. Others are powered USB hubs and work just the same as any other USB hub.

Recommended display brands

Our opinion, confirmed by our readers and colleagues, is that **ASUS** (*http://usa.asus.com*), **NEC** (*http://www.necdisplay.com*), **Samsung** (*http://www.samsung.com*), and **ViewSonic** (*http://www.viewsonic.com*) make the best displays available. Their displays, particularly midrange and better models, provide excellent image quality and are quite reliable. You're likely to be happy with a display from any of these first-tier manufacturers. One up-and-coming display manufacturer that we've heard lots of good things about is **Hanns.G** (*http://www.hannsg.com/us*). Its displays are generally a bit less expensive than comparable models from the top-tier makers, but have competitive specifications. Most Hanns-G owners we've spoken with are extremely pleased with their displays.

Audio Adapter

> **Brian Bilbrey Comments**
>
> *I continue to use my Creative PCI audio card, because often the newest motherboard has good support in Linux for everything but the audio. When PCI is gone, whatever shall I do?*

Audio adapters, also called *sound cards*, are almost a dead breed. Integrated audio is more than good enough for nearly any purpose. Consider buying a separate audio adapter only if you are building an extreme gaming rig, a media center/home theater system that will connect to a professional-level sound system, or a professional audio/video-production system. Even for those purposes, chances are you'll find integrated audio sufficient, so try it before you buy a separate audio adapter.

Internal audio adapters are available to fit PCI slots or PCI Express slots. Before you buy an internal audio adapter, make sure you have an available slot of the proper type. External audio adapters, intended primarily for notebook systems, connect to the computer via USB.

Recommended audio adapter brands

Unless you have good reason to do otherwise, use the integrated motherboard audio. For extreme gaming, choose a **Creative Labs** (*http://us.creative.com*) Xi-Fi card or an **Auzentech** (*http://www.auzentech.com*) Xi-Fi card with the features and specifications you need. Some gamers and media center/home theater system–builders prefer **ASUS** (*http://usa.asus.com*) Xonar series sound cards. If you're an audiophile or do serious audio/video production, choose an **M-AUDIO** (*http://www.m-audio.com*) adapter with the features and specifications you need.

Speakers

Computer speakers span the range from $10 pairs of small satellites to $500+ sets of five speakers that are suitable for home theater systems. Personal preference is the most important factor in choosing speakers.

Speakers that render a Bach concerto superbly are often not the best choice for playing a first-person shooter game. For that matter, speakers that one person considers perfect for the Bach concerto (or the game), another person may consider mediocre at best. For that reason, we strongly suggest that you attempt to listen to speakers before you buy them, particularly if you're buying an expensive set.

Speaker sets are designated by the total number of satellite speakers, followed by a period and a "1" if the set includes a subwoofer (also called a low-frequency emitter, or LFE). Speaker sets are available in 2.0 (front left/right satellites), 2.1 (front left/right satellites and a subwoofer), and 5.1 (front/back and left/right satellites, a front-center satellite, and a subwoofer) configurations.

Other than configuration, the main specification for a speaker set is the wattage of the various speakers. That value should be provided as RMS wattage but is sometimes specified as the much higher peak wattage value. Don't fall prey to wattage overkill. Just a few watts per satellite is sufficient to produce uncomfortably loud sound, and a 100W subwoofer can literally rattle the walls.

The advantage of high wattage ratings is that such speakers have a wide dynamic range with full sound quality. A high-wattage speaker may typically actually use only a few watts, but when a very loud transient (such as a gunshot in a game or a crescendo in a concert) occurs, the high-power amplifier has sufficient power to accurately reproduce that sound at the proper high volume. A less expensive speaker with a lower-power amplifier has to strain to reproduce such transients, and will do so at lower sound quality and volume than the more capable speaker.

The price of a speaker set doesn't necessarily correspond to the number of speakers in the set or their wattage. Both speaker (driver) quality and amplifier quality are important. There are inexpensive 5.1 speaker sets with relatively high wattage—which use cheap drivers and cheap amplifiers—and some low-wattage 2.0 or 2.1 sets that cost a bundle but provide top-notch sound.

We recommend that you decide on the number of speakers according to your needs and your budget. Buy a 5.1 set only for serious gaming or media center/home theater use; otherwise, buy the best 2.0 or 2.1 set you can afford. If you have $75 to spend, for example, you're better off buying a good 2.1 speaker set than a cheesy 5.1 set. (Barbara uses a 2.0 M-AUDIO studio monitor set on her primary computer; Robert uses a 2.1 Logitech Z-series set on his.)

Recommended speaker brands

Altec-Lansing (*http://www.alteclansing.com*), **Creative** (*http://us.creative.com*), and **Logitech** (*http://www.logitech.com*) all offer speaker sets in all three configurations in a range of prices, from $15 2.0 sets to 5.1 sets that cost several hundred dollars. All of them offer excellent value in their price ranges, although we admit to a preference for Logitech. At the high end, **M-AUDIO** (*http://www.m-audio.com*) offers premium-quality 2.0 and 2.1 sets and has an excellent reputation with audiophiles.

Keyboards

The best keyboard is a matter of personal preference. A keyboard we really like, you may dislike intensely, and vice versa. Ultimately, your own preferences are the only guide.

Keyboards vary in obvious ways—layout, size, and style—and in subtle ways like key spacing, angle, dishing, travel, pressure required, and tactile feedback. People's sensitivity to these differences varies. Some are keyboard agnostics who can sit down in front of a new keyboard and, regardless of layout or tactile response, be up to speed in a few minutes. Others have strong preferences about layout and feel. If you've never met a keyboard you didn't like, you can disregard these issues and choose a keyboard based on other factors. If love and hate are words you apply to keyboards, use an identical keyboard for at least an hour before you buy one for yourself.

That said, here are several important characteristics to consider when you choose a keyboard:

- Keyboards are available in two styles, the older straight keyboard and the modern ergonomic style. Some people strongly prefer one or the other. Others don't care. If you've never used an ergonomic keyboard, give one a try before you buy your next keyboard. You may hate it—everyone does at first—but then again, after you've used it for an hour or so you may decide you love it.

- The position of the alphanumeric keys is standard on all keyboards other than those that use the oddball Dvorak layout. What varies, sometimes dramatically, is the placement, size, and shape of other keys, such as shift keys (Shift, Ctrl, and Alt), function keys (which may be across the top, down the left side, or both), and cursor control and numeric keypad keys. If you are used to a particular layout, purchasing a keyboard with a similar layout makes it easier to adapt to the new keyboard.

- Most current keyboards use the USB interface natively and are supplied with an adapter for those who need to connect them to a PS/2 keyboard port. We use mostly USB keyboards, but it's a good idea to have at least one PS/2 keyboard available (or a PS/2 adapter) for those times when Windows shoots craps and won't recognize USB devices.

- Some keyboards provide dedicated and/or programmable function keys to automate such things as firing up your browser or email client, or to allow you to define custom macros that can be invoked with a single keystroke. These functions are typically not built into the keyboard itself, but require loading a driver. To take advantage of those functions, make sure a driver is available for the OS you use.

- The weight of a keyboard can be a significant issue for some people. The lightest keyboard we've seen weighed just over a pound, and the heaviest nearly eight pounds. If your keyboard stays on your desktop, a heavy keyboard is less likely to slide around. Conversely, a heavy keyboard may be uncomfortable if you work with the keyboard in your lap.

- Some manufacturers produce keyboards with speakers, scanners, and other entirely unrelated functions built in. These functions are often clumsy to use, fragile, and have limited features. If you want speakers or a scanner, buy speakers or a scanner. Don't get a keyboard with them built in.

- Wireless keyboards are ideal for presentations, TV-based web browsing, or just for working with the keyboard in your lap. Wireless keyboards use a receiver module that connects to a USB port or the PS/2 keyboard port on the PC. The keyboard and receiver communicate using either radio frequency (RF) or infrared (IR). IR keyboards require a direct line of sight between the keyboard and receiver, while RF keyboards do not. Most IR keyboards and many RF keyboards provide limited range—as little as five feet or so—which limits their utility to working around a desk without cables tangling. Any wireless keyboard you buy should use standard AA, AAA, or 9V alkaline or NiMH batteries rather than a proprietary battery pack.

Recommended keyboard brands

Logitech (*http://www.logitech.com*) and **Microsoft** (*http://www.microsoft.com*) both produce a wide range of excellent keyboards, one of which is almost certainly right for you. Even their basic models are well built and reliable. The more expensive models add features such as RF or Bluetooth wireless connectivity, programmable function keys, and so on.

Mice

Choosing a mouse is much like choosing a keyboard. Personal preference is by far the most important consideration. If possible, try a mouse before you buy it.

Use the following guidelines when choosing a mouse:

- Mice are available in various sizes and shapes, including small mice intended for children, notebook-sized mice, the formerly standard "Dove bar" size, the mainstream ergonomic mouse, and some oversized mice that have many buttons and extra features. Most people find standard-sized mice comfortable to use for short periods, but if you use a mouse for longer periods small differences in size and shape often make a big difference in comfort and usability. Although oversized mice provide attractive features and functions, people with small hands may find such mice too large to use comfortably. Pay particular attention to mouse shape if you are left-handed. Although asymmetric ergonomic mice are often claimed to be equally usable by left- and right-handers, many lefties find them uncomfortable and resort to right-handed mousing. Some manufacturers, including Logitech, produce symmetric ergonomic mice.

Small Hands, Big Mouse

Don't assume that hand size and mouse size are necessarily related. For example, Barbara, who has small hands, prefers the Microsoft IntelliMouse Explorer, which is an oversized mouse. She found that using a standard or small mouse for long periods caused her hand to hurt. Changing to a large mouse solved the problem.

- Get a wheel mouse. Although some applications do not support the wheel, those that do are the ones most people are likely to use a great deal—Microsoft Office, Internet Explorer, Firefox, and so on. Using the wheel greatly improves mouse functionality by reducing the amount of mouse movement needed to navigate web pages and documents. Mice with a tilt-wheel allow you to scroll vertically and horizontally.

Ron Morse Comments

*I have to put in a plug for the guys at Unicomp, who still make the classic IBM Model "M" keyboards to IBM's original design and specifications (*http://pckeyboards.stores.yahoo.net/keyboards.html*).*

They're heavy so they don't move around and have the same key spacing and "touch" as the IBM Selectric typewriter. They're built like tanks (mine has been in daily use since 1994).

No other keyboard has the glorious tactile response of the Model "M," and there is absolutely no ambiguity about whether a keystroke has registered or not. Not to mention the wonderful clicky noise that tells everyone in the room you're gettin' 'er done.

Unicomp sells a number of styles and sizes starting at about $70, including customized models for point of sale or other special purposes. There's even a Linux model (no, you don't have to build it yourself). They also sell the same keyboards with quiet, rubber dome key switches instead of the traditional "buckling spring" design for use in quiet environments. Unicomp keyboards can be ordered with either the mini-DIN (PS/2) or USB interface.

- Standard two-button mice (three, counting the wheel) suffice for most purposes. However, five-button mice are ideally suited to some applications, such as games and web browsing. For example, the two extra buttons can be mapped to the Back and Forward browser buttons, eliminating a great deal of extraneous mouse movement.

- Mice have cords ranging in length from less than 4 feet to about 9 feet. A short mouse cord may be too short to reach the system, particularly if it is on the floor. If you need a longer mouse cord, purchase a PS/2 keyboard or USB extension cable, available in nearly any computer store.

- Consider buying a cordless mouse. The absence of a cord can make a surprising difference.

Recommended mouse brands

Logitech (*http://www.logitech.com*) and **Microsoft** (*http://www.microsoft.com*) both produce a wide range of excellent optical mice, in corded and cordless models. One of them is almost certainly right for you. Even their basic models are well built and reliable. The more expensive models have more features, are more precise, and are probably more durable. We use both Logitech and Microsoft mice on our personal systems.

> **Mouse Alternatives**
>
> *Consider using a trackball or touchpad, particularly if you experience hand pain when using a mouse.*

Buying Components

We've bought a boatload of PC components over the last 25 years, for ourselves and on behalf of employers and clients. In the following sections, we'll tell you what we learned along the way.

Buying Guidelines

Until the early 1990s, most computer products were bought in computer specialty stores. Retail sales still make up a significant chunk of computer product sales—although the emphasis has shifted from computer specialty stores to local "big-box" retailers like Best Buy, Fry's, Walmart, and Costco—but online resellers now account for a large percentage of PC component sales.

Should you buy from a local brick-and-mortar retailer or an online reseller? We do both, because each has advantages and disadvantages.

Local retailers offer the inestimable advantage of instant gratification. Unless you're more patient than we are, when you want something, you want it Right Now. Buying from a local retailer puts the product in your hands instantly, instead of making you wait for FedEx to show up. You can also hold the product in your hands, something that's not possible if you buy from an online reseller. Additionally, local retailers have a big advantage if you need to return or exchange a product: if something doesn't work right, or if you simply change your mind, you can just drive back to the store rather than dealing with the hassles and cost of returning a product to an online reseller.

Online resellers have the advantage in breadth and depth of product selection. If you want the less expensive OEM version of a product, for example, chances are you won't find it at local retailers, most of which stock only retail-boxed products. If an online reseller stocks a particular manufacturer's products, it will tend to stock the entire product line, whereas local retailers often pick and choose only the most popular items in a product line. Of course, the popular products are usually popular for good reasons. Online resellers are also more likely to stock niche products and products from smaller manufacturers. Sometimes, if you must have a particular product, the only option is to buy it online.

Online resellers usually advertise lower prices than local retailers, but it's a mistake to compare only nominal prices. When you buy from a local retailer, you pay only the advertised price plus any applicable sales tax. When you buy from an online retailer, you pay the advertised price plus shipping, which may end up costing you more than buying locally.

Although online resellers *may* have a lower overall price on a given component, it's a mistake to assume that this is always the case. Local retailers frequently run sales and rebate promotions that cut the price of a component below the lowest online price. For example, we bought a spindle of 100 discs on sale from a local retailer for $19.95 with a $10 instant rebate and a $20 mail-in rebate. After the cost of the stamp to mail in the rebate form, they *paid* us $9.68 to carry away those 100 discs, which is pretty tough for an online reseller to match.

In particular, local retailers are usually the best place to buy heavy, bulky, or fragile items, such as monitors, cases, UPSs, and so on. Local retailers receive these items in pallet loads, which makes the cost of shipping an individual item almost nothing. Conversely, online resellers have to charge you, directly or indirectly, for the cost of getting that heavy item to your door.

Whether your purchase your PC components from a local brick-and-mortar store or a web-based retailer, here are some guidelines to keep in mind:

- Make sure you know exactly what you're buying. For example, a hard drive may be available in two versions, each with the same or a similar model number but with an added letter or number to designate different amounts of cache. Or a hard drive maker may produce two models of the same size that differ in price and performance. Always compare using the exact manufacturer model numbers. Before you buy a product, research it on the manufacturer's website and on the numerous independent websites devoted to reviews. We usually search Google with the product name and "review" in the search string.

- Vendors vary greatly. Some we trust implicitly, and others we wouldn't order from on a bet. Some are always reliable, others always unreliable, and still others seem to vary with the phases of the moon. We check *http:// www.resellerratings.com*, which maintains a database of customer-reported experiences with hundreds of vendors.

- The list price or *suggested retail price* (SRP) is meaningless. Most computer products sell for a fraction of the SRP, others sell for near the SRP, and for still others the manufacturer has no SRP but instead publishes an *estimated selling price* (ESP). To do meaningful comparisons, you need to know what different vendors charge for the product. Fortunately, there

Use Tax

Ah, but you don't have to pay sales tax when you buy online, right? Well, maybe. In most jurisdictions, you're required by law to pay a use tax in lieu of sales tax on out-of-state purchases. Most people evade use taxes, of course, but that free ride is coming to an end. States faced with increasing budget problems, which is to say all of them, are starting to clamp down on people who buy from online resellers and don't pay use tax. States are using data-mining techniques to coordinate with one another and with credit card companies and online retailers to uncover unpaid use taxes. If you don't pay use taxes, one day soon you're likely to hear from the audit division of your state department of revenue, asking what those credit card charges were for and why you didn't report the use taxes due on them. Count on it.

are many services that list what various vendors charge. We use *http://www.pricescan.com*, *http://www.pricewatch.com*, *http://www.pricegrabber.com*, and *http://www.froogle.com*. These services may list 20 or more different vendors, and the prices for a particular item may vary dramatically. We discard the top 25% and the bottom 25% and average the middle 50% to decide a reasonable price for the item.

- Many components are sold in retail-boxed and OEM forms. The core component is likely to be similar or identical in either case, but important details may vary. For example, processors are available in retail-boxed versions that include a CPU cooler and a three-year warranty. They are also available as OEM components (also called *tray packaging* or *white box*) that do not include the CPU cooler and have only a 90-day warranty. OEM items are not intended for retail distribution, so some manufacturers provide no warranty to individual purchasers. OEM components are fine, as long as you understand the differences and do not attempt to compare prices between retail-boxed and OEM.

- The market for PCs and components is incredibly competitive and margins are razor-thin. If a vendor advertises a component for much less than other vendors, it may be a "loss leader." More likely, though, particularly if its prices on other items are similarly low, that vendor is cutting corners, whether by using your money to float inventory, by shipping returned products as new, by charging excessive shipping fees, or, in the ultimate case, by taking your money and not shipping the product. If you always buy from the vendor with the rock-bottom price, chances are you'll waste a lot of time hassling with returns of defective, used, or discontinued items and dealing with your credit card company when the vendor fails to deliver at all. Ultimately, you're likely to spend more money than you would have by buying from a reputable vendor in the first place.

- The actual price you pay may vary significantly from the advertised price. When you compare prices, include all charges, particularly shipping charges. Reputable vendors tell you exactly how much the total charges will be. Less reputable vendors may forget to mention shipping charges, which could be very high. Some vendors break out the full manufacturer pack into individual items. For example, if a retail-boxed hard drive includes mounting hardware, some vendors will quote a price for the bare drive without making it clear that they have removed the mounting hardware and charge separately for it. Also be careful when buying products that include a rebate from the maker. Some vendors quote the net price after the rebate without making it clear that they are doing so.

- Some vendors charge more for an item ordered via their 800 number than they do for the same item ordered directly from their website. Some others add a fixed processing fee to phone orders. These charges reflect the fact that taking orders on the Web is much cheaper than doing it by phone, so this practice has become common. In contrast, some of our favorite vendors do not even provide telephone order lines.

- It can be very expensive to ship heavy items such as UPSs and printers individually. This is one situation in which local big-box stores like Best Buy have an advantage over online vendors. The online vendor has to charge you for the cost of shipping, directly or indirectly, and that cost can amount to $50 or more for a heavy item that you need quickly. Conversely, the big-box stores receive inventory items by the truckload or even via railcar shipments, so the cost to them to have a single item delivered is quite small. They can pass that reduced cost on to buyers. If you're buying a heavy item, don't assume that it will be cheaper online. Check your local Best Buy or other big-box store: you may find that it actually costs less there, even after you pay sales tax. And you can carry it away with you instead of waiting for FedEx to show up with it.

- Most direct resellers are willing to sell for less than the price they advertise. All you need to do is tell your chosen vendor that you'd really rather buy from them, but not at the price they're quoting. Use lower prices you find with the price comparison services as a wedge to get a better price. But remember that reputable vendors must charge more than the fly-by-night operations if they are to make a profit and stay in business. If we're ordering by phone, we generally try to beat down our chosen vendor a bit on price, but we don't expect them to match the rock-bottom prices that turn up on web searches. Of course, if you're ordering from a web-only vendor, dickering is not an option, which is one reason why web-only vendors generally have better prices.

- Using a credit card puts the credit card company on your side if there is a problem with your order. If the vendor ships the wrong product, a defective product, or no product at all, you can invoke chargeback procedures to have the credit card company refund your money. Vendors who live and die on credit card orders cannot afford to annoy credit card companies, so they tend to resolve such problems quickly. Even your threat to request a chargeback may cause a recalcitrant vendor to see reason.

- Some vendors add a surcharge, typically 3%, to their advertised prices if you pay by credit card. Surcharges violate credit card company contracts, so some vendors instead offer a similar discount for paying cash, which amounts to the same thing. Processing credit card transactions costs money, and we're sure that some such vendors are quite reputable, but our own experience with vendors that surcharge has not been good. We always suspect that they discourage using credit cards because their business practices result in a relatively high percentage of chargeback requests.

- Good vendors allow you to return a defective product for replacement or a full refund (often less shipping charges) within a stated period, typically 30 days. Buy only from such vendors. Nearly all vendors exclude some product categories, such as notebook computers, monitors, printers, and opened software, either because their contracts with the manufacturer require them to do so or because some buyers commonly abuse return periods for these items, treating them as "30-day free rentals." Beware of the phrase "All sales are final." That means exactly what it says.

> **A Cunning Plan**
>
> *Nearly all retailers refuse to refund your money on opened software, DVDs, etc. and will only exchange the open product for a new, sealed copy of the same title. One of our readers told us how he gets around that common policy: he returns the open software in exchange for a new, sealed copy of the same product, keeping his original receipt. He then returns the new, sealed copy for a refund. That's probably unethical and may be illegal for all we know, but it does work. Recently, though, some stores, including Best Buy, have begun annotating the original receipt when you make an exchange. Oh, well. It was too good to last.*

- Check carefully for any mention of restocking fees. Many vendors who trumpet a "No questions asked money-back guarantee" mention only in the fine print that they won't refund all your money—they charge a restocking fee on returns. We've seen fees as high as 30% of the purchase price. These vendors love returns, because they make a lot more money if you return the product than if you keep it. Do not buy from a vendor that charges restocking fees on exchanges (as opposed to refunds). For refunds, accept no restocking fee higher than 10% to 15%, depending on the price of the item.

- If you order by phone, don't accept verbal promises. Insist that the reseller confirm your order in writing, including any special terms or conditions, before charging your credit card or shipping the product. If a reseller balks at providing written confirmation of its policies, terms, and conditions, find another vendor. Most are happy to do so. If you're ordering from a vendor that uses web-based ordering exclusively, use a screen-capture program or your browser's save function to grab copies of each screen as you complete the order. Most vendors send a confirming email, which we file in our "Never Delete" folder.

- File everything related to an order, including a copy of the original advertisement, the email (or faxed or written) confirmation provided by the reseller, copies of your credit card receipt, a copy of the packing list and invoice, and so on. We also jot down notes in our PIM regarding telephone conversations, including the date, time, telephone number and extension, person spoken to, purpose of the call, and so on. We print a copy of those to add to the folder for that order.

- Make it clear to the reseller that you expect them to ship the exact item you have ordered, not what they consider to be an "equivalent substitute." Require that they confirm the exact items they will ship, including manufacturer part numbers. For example, if you order an EVGA 512-P3-N871-AR GeForce 9800 GTX+ graphics card with 512 MB of RAM, make sure the order confirmation specifies that item by name, full description, and EVGA product number. Don't accept a less detailed description such as "graphics card," "EVGA graphics card," or even "EVGA 9800 GTX graphics card." Otherwise, you may get less than you paid for—a lesser GeForce card, a card with a slower processor or less memory, or even a card with a GeForce processor made by another manufacturer.

- Verify warranty terms. Some manufacturers warrant only items purchased from authorized dealers in full retail packaging. For some items, the warranty begins when the manufacturer ships the product to the distributor, which may be long before you receive it. OEM products typically have much shorter warranties than retail-boxed products—sometimes as short as 90 days—and may be warranted only to the original distributor rather than to the final buyer. Better resellers may "endorse the manufacturer warranty" for some period on some products, often 30 to 90 days. That means that if the product fails, you can return the item to the reseller, who will ship you a replacement and take care of dealing with the manufacturer. Some resellers disclaim the manufacturer warranty, claiming that once they ship the item dealing with warranty claims is your problem, even if the product arrives DOA. We've encountered that problem a couple of times. Usually, mentioning phrases like "merchantability and fitness for a particular purpose" and "revocation of acceptance" leads them to see reason quickly. We usually demand that the reseller ship us a new replacement product immediately and include a prepaid return shipping label if they want the dead item back. We don't accept or pay for dead merchandise under any circumstances, and neither should you.

- Direct resellers are required by law to ship products within the time period they promise. But that time period may be precise (e.g., "ships within 24 hours") or vague (e.g., "ships within three to six weeks"). If the vendor cannot ship by the originally promised date, it must notify you in writing and specify another date by which the item will ship. If that occurs, you have the right to cancel your order without penalty. Make sure to make clear to the reseller that you expect the item to be delivered in a timely manner. Reputable vendors ship what they say they're going to ship when they say they're going to ship it. Unfortunately, some vendors have a nasty habit of taking your money and shipping whenever they get around to it. In a practice that borders on fraud, some vendors routinely report items as "in stock" when in fact they are not. Make it clear to the vendor that you do not authorize them to charge your credit card until the item actually ships, and that if you do not receive the item when promised you will cancel the order.

Even if you follow all of these guidelines, things may go wrong. Even the best resellers sometimes drop the ball. If that happens, don't expect the problem to go away by itself. If you encounter a problem, remain calm and notify the reseller first. Good resellers are anxious to resolve problems. Find out how the reseller wants to proceed, and follow their procedures, particularly for labeling returned merchandise with an RMA number.

If you seem to have reached a dead end with the vendor, explain one last time why you are dissatisfied and ask them to resolve the problem. Tell them that unless they resolve the matter you will request a chargeback from your credit card company. Mail-order and Internet vendors live and die on credit card revenue, so maintaining a good relationship with the credit card companies is critically important to them. Finally, but only as a last resort, contact your bank or credit card issuer and request a chargeback. Be prepared to provide a full explanation of the problem with documentation.

Recommended Sources

The question we hear more often than any other is, "What company should I buy from?" When someone asks us that question, we run away, screaming in terror. Well, not really, but we'd like to. Answering that question is a no-win proposition for us, you see. If we recommend a vendor and that vendor treats the buyer properly, well that's no more than was expected. But Thor forbid that we recommend a vendor who turns around and screws the buyer.

So, which online resellers do we buy from? Over the years, we've bought from scores of online vendors, and our favorites have changed. For the last decade or so, our favorite has been **NewEgg** (*http://www.newegg.com*). NewEgg offers an

> ### Loot, Pillage, and Burn
>
> *Thor? Yes, it's true. Robert the Red is of Viking extraction. On government forms, he describes himself as "Viking-American." And no, he doesn't wear a funny helmet. Except among friends. And he hasn't pillaged anything in months. Years, maybe. In fact, he's not absolutely certain what pillaging is, although it does sound like fun.*

extraordinarily good combination of competitive prices, wide product selection, good customer support, timely shipping, and fair return or replacement policies. We know of no other direct vendor that even comes close.

NewEgg's prices aren't always rock-bottom, but they generally match those of any other vendor we're willing to deal with. NewEgg runs daily specials that are often real bargains, so if you're willing to consider alternatives and to accumulate components over the course of a few weeks, you can save a fair amount of money. NewEgg ships what it says it's going to ship, when it says it's going to ship it, and at the price it agreed to ship it for. If there's a problem, it's rectified. It's hard to do better than that.

In the last year or two, we've started ordering some computer components from **Amazon** (*http://www.amazon.com*). Amazon's selection is not as wide as NewEgg's for most items, but its prices are excellent. Amazon generally ships quickly, and we consider it on a par with NewEgg for hassle-free ordering. Packaging is one area where Amazon has an advantage over NewEgg. Although NewEgg has recently taken steps to improve its packaging, in the past we have received components from NewEgg that were damaged in shipping. Conversely, Amazon's attitude is apparently that nothing succeeds like excess. In the past, Amazon over-packaged, to put it mildly. So much so that it's received complaints about all the packaging material that needs to be recycled. Fortunately, Amazon has responded to these complaints and now uses sane packaging.

All of that said, if you buy from NewEgg or Amazon and subsequently your goldfish dies and all your teeth fall out, don't blame us. All we can say is that NewEgg and Amazon have always treated us right. Things can change overnight in this industry and, while we don't expect NewEgg or Amazon to take a sudden turn for the worse, it could happen.

As for local retailers, we buy from—in no particular order—Best Buy, Target, Office Depot, OfficeMax, and our local computer specialty stores, depending on what we need and who happens to have advertised the best prices and rebates in the Sunday ad supplements. Walmart, which used to sell only assembled PCs, has recently started stocking PC components such as ATI video adapters, so we'll add Walmart to our list as well.

Russian Dolls

One of our readers told us the story of ordering a USB thumb drive from Amazon. It arrived in its retail blister-packed card, which was wrapped in bubble-wrap, which was inserted in a padded envelope, which was placed in a box filled with packing peanuts, which was placed in a larger box, also filled with packing peanuts. By the time our reader actually found the thumb drive, he'd forgotten why he ordered it.

Another Cunning Plan

If you buy from a local retailer, open the box from the bottom rather than the top. If you need to return a non-defective item, that makes it easier to repackage the product with the manufacturer's seals intact, which keeps the retailer happy and can help you avoid restocking fees.

Final Words

We've done our best in this chapter to tell you how to choose components for your new system and where and how to buy them. The specific components you need differ according to the type of system you plan to build. We describe how to make component-specific decisions in the "project system" chapters later in the book. So, before you actually start ordering components, you might want to read some (or all) of those chapters.

When the components arrive, restrain yourself. Don't start building your system before the FedEx truck even pulls out of your driveway, particularly if this is your first system build. Read or re-read the relevant project chapter first.

One thing you should do immediately, though, is check the contents of the boxes that were just delivered. Verify what you ordered against the packing list and invoice, and verify what's actually in the box against those documents. Usually everything will be right, but if you have components coming from different sources, you don't want to wait a week or two before finding out that an early shipment was wrong or incomplete.

Take it a step further. Once you've verified that everything is correct with the order, start opening the individual component boxes. Look for a packing list in the front of the manual, and make sure that you actually received everything that was supposed to be in the box. It's not uncommon for small parts—mounting hardware, cables, driver CDs, and so on—to be missing. If that happens, call the vendor immediately and tell them what's missing from your order.

At this point, you should have everything you need to start building your new PC. It's kind of like being a kid again, on Christmas morning.

Building a Budget PC

3

Inexpensive doesn't have to mean cheap. The myth persists that you can't save money building your own PC, particularly a budget system. In fact, it's easy to match the price of a mass-market commercial system with a home-built system that uses higher-quality components. Of course, you could instead match the quality level of a mass-market commercial system by buying the cheapest components available and save a few bucks by doing so, but we don't recommend doing that. We think there are good reasons to build inexpensive systems, but no reasons at all to build cheap systems.

We define a budget system as one that seeks the maximum bang for the minimum buck, offering good component quality, reasonable performance, and high reliability. A budget PC uses good-quality components throughout, but those components fall on the low end of the performance range. They may even be a generation or two out of date. That's not necessarily a bad thing, though: last year's models are every bit as good this year as they were 12 months ago, and you can save a lot of money if you don't insist on the very latest components.

In pursuit of low prices, we don't hesitate to buy components that are discontinued and on sale. There are few disadvantages to doing so. Discontinued products nearly always carry the full manufacturer warranty and function as well as they did when they were the latest and greatest products available. Judicious shopping can easily knock $50 or more off the total cost of a budget system. That's nothing to sneeze at when your total budget is only a few hundred dollars.

In this chapter, we'll design and build the perfect budget PC.

Determining Functional Requirements

We began by sitting down to think through our own requirements for a budget PC. Here's the list of functional requirements we came up with:

Reliability

Reliability is important for a budget PC, just as it is for any computer. Although our limited budget may force us to make minor compromises in reliability—such as using a lower-capacity power supply than we might otherwise choose—we'll still keep reliability firmly in mind as we select components. When we're forced to choose—as we inevitably will be—among performance, capacity, or features versus reliability, we'll always favor the latter.

Adequate performance

In order to be useful, a budget PC must perform adequately. Cheap consumer-grade PCs are often obsolete the day they're unpacked. Most of them have slow processors, insufficient memory, small hard drives, and very poor integrated video. That's simply not good enough. For our budget PC, we'll aim for a performance level that matches that of a mainstream or performance PC manufactured a year to 18 months earlier. That means we'll need a processor in the 2.5+ GHz class (or a slightly slower dual-core model), at least 2 GB of memory, a 7,200 RPM hard drive of reasonable capacity, and either fast integrated video or an inexpensive standalone video adapter.

Usable peripherals

Cheap consumer-grade PCs always scrimp on peripherals. A typical cheap mass-market system is bundled with a $2 mouse, a $3 keyboard, a $3 set of speakers, a $20 DVD drive, and a $75 monitor, none of which are good for anything but the trash bin. We can do better than that, even within the constraints of our tight budget. We'll have to spend an extra $5 here and $20 there, but we'll end up with solid, usable peripherals that are likely to last for the life of the system.

Noise level

There's little room in the budget for special quiet components, but that doesn't mean a budget PC must necessarily be noisy. We'll choose the quietest components available in our price range, always giving price and reliability high priority, but keeping noise level in mind as well. For example, two hard drives may be priced identically, but one may be literally twice as loud as the other. The same is true of other components, such as cases and power supplies. By choosing carefully, we can build a budget PC that is much quieter than a similar but noisier configuration that costs the same.

Hardware Design Criteria

With the functional requirements determined, the next step was to establish design criteria for the budget PC hardware. Here are the relative priorities we assigned for our budget PC. Your priorities may, of course, differ.

Price	★★★★☆
Reliability	★★★★☆
Size	★☆☆☆☆
Noise level	★★☆☆☆
Expandability	★☆☆☆☆
Processor performance	★★★☆☆
Video performance	★★☆☆☆
Disk capacity/performance	★★★☆☆

As you can see, this is a well-balanced system. Price and reliability are our top concerns, with everything else secondary. Here's the breakdown:

Price

Price is the 900-pound gorilla for a budget system. We set our target cost for this system at $350 excluding external peripherals and software ($500 with the keyboard, mouse, speakers, and display), and we'll try very hard to stay within that budget. That's the same budget figure we used in the previous editions, but this time we'll get a lot more computer for our money. With a $350 budget, we plan to spend roughly 50%—split about equally—on the motherboard, processor, and memory, 25% on the case and power supply, and 25% on the optical and hard drives.

Reliability

Reliability is as important as price. An unreliable system is not worth having. To get that reliability, we'll use good brand-name components throughout.

Size

Size is unimportant, so we'll pay it no mind. As it turns out, the best case for our purposes is a standard mid-tower unit.

Noise level

We'd like a quiet system, but we don't have any extra money to spend to reduce noise. We'll do what we can to choose the quietest possible inexpensive components, but otherwise we'll let the chips fall where they may.

Expandability

Expandability is unimportant. If we do upgrade this system, say three years down the road, chances are we'll be swapping components out rather than adding them.

Processor performance

Processor performance is moderately important for our budget PC, both initially and to ensure that the system will have enough horsepower to run new software versions without requiring a processor upgrade. We'd have loved to use a quad-core processor in this system, but there's simply no room in the budget. We can only afford to spend perhaps $60 on the processor, which limits our choices to AMD or Intel single- or dual-core budget processors.

Video performance

2D video quality is important for our budget system, because it determines display clarity and sharpness for the browsers, office suites, and similar applications that this system will run. A budget system is not intended for serious gaming, so 3D video performance is relatively unimportant. Still, we'd like enough video horsepower for at least casual 3D gaming, so we'll choose a motherboard with fast integrated video, such as the NVIDIA GeForce 8200. Just to keep our options open, we'll make sure our motherboard provides a PCI Express x16 video slot. That way, if after a couple of years we need faster video, we can install a $50 PCI-E video adapter, which by then will be as fast or faster than the fastest video cards available today.

Disk capacity/performance

Disk capacity and performance are moderately important for the budget system. A small, slow hard drive can noticeably degrade system performance. Fortunately, fast hard drives of reasonably large capacity are relatively inexpensive. Rather than spending $30 on a small, slow hard drive, we'll spend an extra $15 or $20 for a mainstream 7,200 RPM drive with midrange capacity.

Component Considerations

With our design criteria in mind, we set out to choose the best components for the budget PC system. The following sections describe the components we chose, and why we chose them.

Case and Power Supply

Antec NSK-4482 Mid-Tower Case (*http://www.antec.com*)

It's easy to spend too little on the case and power supply for a budget system. When we searched NewEgg for computer cases with power supplies, we found more than 100 products for $50 or less. We wouldn't use any of those on a bet. Cheap cases are bad enough: things don't fit properly, and they're full of burrs and sharp edges that make working on them dangerous. But cheap power supplies are worse. It's simply not possible to build a reliable system using a cheap power supply. Even a budget system deserves a top-quality power supply, although a low-wattage unit—something in the 350W range—is sufficient.

Unfortunately, the price of a decent case and power supply has risen significantly over the last few years, probably because of the financial crisis and the decline of the U.S. dollar relative to Pacific Rim currencies. A couple of years ago, models suitable for a budget system sold in the $65 to $75 range. Equivalent cases now sell in the $90 to $100 range, which takes a larger bite out of our budget.

In that price range, we think the Antec NSK-4482 is the best choice. It's very attractive, and the bundled EarthWatts 380 power supply is perfectly acceptable. Other suitable cases in that price range are the ThermalTake Element T and the Antec NSK-3480.

> **Shipping Coal to Newcastle**
>
> *Incidentally, shipping cases is expensive. You can often save $20 or more if you can find a suitable case locally or a model online that includes free shipping.*

Processor and CPU Cooler

AMD Athlon II X2 240 (*http://www.amd.com*)

We'd like a triple- or quad-core processor, but with only about $60 allocated to the processor, our choices are realistically limited to single- and dual-core "value" processors. Intel sells several models in this price range, but dollar-for-dollar in value processors, AMD models offer more bang for the buck than Intel models. At the time we purchased the processor for this system, the $60 retail-boxed AMD Athlon II X2 240 Regor dual-core processor was clearly the best processor for the money. Built on the 45 nm process, with two cores running at 2.8 GHz and maximum power consumption of 65W, this was the ideal processor for our budget system. Of course, by the time you order your $60 processor it'll almost certainly be a faster model, but even this $60 value processor is no slouch in terms of performance.

We could actually have bought the 240 Regor processor for $53 rather than $60, but that would have been an OEM model rather than a retail-boxed model. That extra $7 bought us both a 3-year warranty (versus a 30-day warranty on the OEM model) and a reasonably quiet and effective CPU cooler. Given the choice, it's almost always better to buy a retail-boxed processor than an OEM model.

Even though it's a budget processor, the performance of the 240 Regor is reasonably good. Table 3-1 shows the overall performance of our budget processor compared to the processors used in the other project systems in this book, and, for reference, benchmarks for several processors in older but still useful systems we have around the house (RBT indicates systems used by Robert, and BFT indicates Barbara's system). For comparison, we've also included the three primary desktop systems we were using when we wrote this book.

> **Figures Lie and Liars Figure**
>
> *There's really no way to assign a single number to quantify the overall performance of a processor. Two different processors with very similar benchmark scores may have noticeably different performance, depending on what you test. One may, for example, excel in rendering video but lag badly on another type of task, while the other is exactly opposite. We always take benchmark numbers with a (very large) grain of salt. That said, the Passmark CPU Mark score is a widely accepted metric for overall processor performance, so we include those one-number scores to give you an idea of how the budget processor holds up against the competition.*

Table 3-1. Relative processor performance

System	Processor	CPU Mark score
Extreme system	Intel Core i7 X 980	10,140
Current office desktop system (RBT)	Intel Core2 Quad Q9650	4,583
Mainstream system	Intel Core i5 661	3,170
Media center system	Intel Core i3 530	2,714
Current den system (RBT)	Intel Core2 Duo E6750	1,663
Budget and home server systems	AMD Athlon II X2 240	1,640
Current office desktop system (BFT)	Intel Core2 Duo E6400	1,263
Appliance/nettop system	Intel Atom D510	666
(Older system)	Intel Pentium 4 3.80 GHz	638
(Older system)	AMD Athlon 64 4000+	628
(Older system)	Intel Celeron 540	493
(Older system)	Intel Pentium 4 3.00 GHz	488
(Older system)	AMD Sempron 3100+	449

Although the Core i7 processor we're using in the extreme system is more than six times faster than our budget processor, the performance of the budget processor holds up very well in comparison to that of two of our current primary systems, both of which were high-performance systems when they were built. (We were stunned to see just how well that Core2 Quad held up; we built that system almost two years earlier as an Extreme System and, with a CPU Mark score considerably higher than some current Core i7 processors, the Core2 Quad still nearly qualifies for that designation.)

The Core i3, which qualifies as a low-mainstream processor, is nearly twice as fast as our budget processor, but it also costs twice as much. And the 240 Regor budget processor is more than twice as fast as the Intel Atom D510, which itself is faster than processors like the Intel Pentium 4 and Celeron and the AMD Athlon 64 and Sempron, all of which are still in use in tens of millions of systems.

If you can afford to spend a bit more for the processor, consider something like the triple-core AMD Athlon II X3 435 Rana. An extra $15 or so buys you a 50% performance boost in processor performance over the 240 Regor, taking you into the low-mainstream processor class. (Of course, other than for processor-bound tasks, 50% faster *processor* performance doesn't translate into 50% faster *system* performance, but it does provide noticeably snappier response times.)

Motherboard

ASRock K10N78M-PRO (*http://www.asrock.com*)

The 240 Regor is a Socket AM3 processor, so the first selection criterion for a motherboard in the $60 range was Socket AM3 compatibility, which either a hybrid Socket AM2+/AM3 model or a pure Socket AM3 model provides. (A hybrid motherboard can use either a Socket AM2+ or a Socket AM3 processor; an AM3 motherboard can use only a Socket AM3 processor.) Note that socket compatibility is only a first-cut criterion. Just because a motherboard supports Socket AM3 processors doesn't necessarily mean it supports the specific Socket AM3 processor you want to use.

We'd prefer to use a first-tier motherboard from GIGABYTE or ASUS, both of which offer Socket AM3 motherboards in this price range. Unfortunately, budget motherboards from first-tier makers are feature-light. For example, they may offer only 100BaseT (100 megabit/second) networking rather than 1000BaseT (1,000 Mb/s, or *gigabit*), and their integrated video is several generations out of date. So we narrowed things down by looking for a suitable motherboard made by ASRock, a second-tier motherboard manufacturer that is famed for its first-tier quality. We found several ASRock candidates in the $55 to $65 range.

Narrowing things further, we wanted integrated video in the NVIDIA GeForce 8200 or ATI RADEON HD 3200 class, either of which provides excellent 2D display quality and has enough 3D horsepower to use for casual gaming. (Boards with integrated RADEON HD 4200 sell for a few dollars more, and you might expect they'd outperform the GeForce 8200/RADEON 3200 boards, but they don't.

The next real step up from the 8200/3200 boards are ones with integrated RADEON HD 3300, and those were selling for $85 or so when we bought our motherboard.) We also want a PCI Express x16 slot in case we want to upgrade the graphics at some point.

We would prefer DDR3 memory for its faster transfers, but in practical terms overall system performance will be very similar with DDR2 memory. At the time we ordered components for this system, DDR2 and DDR3 memory modules of the same capacity were selling for about the same price, but DDR3 motherboards were still selling for a $15 or more premium over comparable DDR2 motherboards, so we decided that a DDR2 motherboard was the better choice.

Among the motherboards that met our requirements and sold for about $60, the best choice was the ASRock K10N78M-Pro. Although it lacks bells and whistles, it has exactly the feature set we wanted: NVIDIA GeForce 8200 integrated video with support for DX10 (gaming graphics), a PCI Express x16 slot for future video upgrades, four SATA 3.0 Gb/s ports (with software RAID 0/1/5/10 support), good 5.1 audio, an integrated 1000BaseT network adapter, six USB 2.0 ports, and so on. At about $60, the ASRock K10N78M-Pro was a perfect fit for our budget system.

The final step, which you ignore at your peril, is to verify that the selected motherboard is compatible with your processor. We visited the ASRock K10N78M-Pro web page and located the processor compatibility list. We had a bad moment when we didn't find our 240 Regor retail-boxed processor (model ADX240OCGQBOX) in the motherboard compatibility list, so we visited the AMD web page for the ADX240OCGQBOX and found that the OEM version of that product had a significantly different product code, ADX240OCK23GQ. That product code *did* appear in the compatibility list. Since the OEM and retail-boxed versions of that processor are actually identical, we knew the retail-boxed 240 Regor would be compatible with our K10N78M-Pro motherboard. Furthermore, the compatibility list said the 240 Regor was compatible with all BIOS versions, so we knew we wouldn't get stuck with an earlier BIOS that wouldn't boot with our processor.

Memory

Crucial CT2KIT12864AA667 2 GB Kit (1 GB x 2) (*http://www.crucial.com*)

The budget system in the preceding edition was equipped with a single-core processor and 512 MB of RAM. Although that was sufficient for snappy performance with Linux or Windows XP, it was marginal for Vista. Windows 7 resource requirements are at least as high as those of Vista, so if you plan to run Windows 7 on your budget system, you'll want at least 1 GB per core, for a total of 2 GB. That's assuming you're running 32-bit Windows 7. If you plan to run the 64-bit version, double the memory requirements.

When we ordered the parts for this system, we found that our $60 budget for memory was sufficient to buy 2 GB, either as two 1 GB DIMMs or as one 2 GB DIMM. We'd have preferred to install 4 GB, but, at $95 or so, a pair of 2 GB

Family Matters

We actually ended up installing 4 GB of memory in this system. Just as we were about to build the system, Barbara's sister, Frances, called to say her desktop PC was having problems. We originally thought it would require only a power supply replacement, but when we popped the lid we realized that the system was four years old. That's getting perilously close to the design life of a PC, so we decided to turn our budget system into a new system for Frances. Chances are she'll use the new system for another four years, so we decided it made sense to install 4 GB of memory and be done with it.

DIMMs would have busted our budget. We plan to run Linux, which will be happy with 2 GB, but if we planned to run Windows 7 we'd try very hard to come up with an extra $40 or so to expand the memory to 4 GB.

Which brings up another issue. The ASRock K10N78M-Pro motherboard supports dual-channel memory operation but has only two DIMM slots. For best memory performance, both of those slots need to be occupied, but of course that leaves no free slots for future upgrades. If we were installing 4 GB of memory there wouldn't be any real decision, as one 4 GB DIMM costs more than twice as much as two 2 GB DIMMs. But installing only 2 GB of memory gives us the option of installing just one 2 GB DIMM (about $50 when we were ordering parts) and thereby sacrificing some memory performance, or installing two 1 GB DIMMs (about $25 each) and thereby giving up a free memory slot for future expansion. You pays your money and you takes your choice.

Video Adapter

Integrated NVIDIA GeForce 8200

The NVIDIA GeForce 8200 video integrated on the ASRock motherboard provides excellent 2D display quality and reasonably good 3D performance for casual gaming and similar tasks. The ASRock motherboard includes a PCI Express x16 video adapter slot, so if necessary we can upgrade the video down the road by installing an inexpensive PCIe video adapter. We don't expect that to be necessary, but if we decide we need more video horsepower than the GeForce 8200 provides, even a $30 standalone video adapter is likely to be more than sufficient.

Hard Disk Drive

Seagate Barracuda 7200.12 ST3500418AS 500GB
(*http://www.seagate.com*)

If we were attempting to cut costs to the bone, we might have chosen a low-capacity hard drive. But when we bought our components, 80 GB drives were selling for $30, versus $45 for the 500 GB Seagate. We decided it made sense to spend the extra $15 to jump from 80 GB to 500 GB. That additional cost is significant for a system with a base budget of $350, but the extra $15 buys us more than six times as much disk space. Even on a budget system, we'd soon be cramped with only 80 GB of disk space.

We've been using Seagate hard drives almost exclusively for many years and have always found them to be fast, quiet, cool-running, reliable, and competitively priced. (Our contacts at data recovery firms also run Seagate drives in their personal systems, which we think speaks volumes.) If for some reason you prefer another brand, Samsung and Western Digital would be our second choices.

Chapter 3

Optical Drive

ASUS DRW-24B1ST DVD writer (*http://www.asus.com*)

DVD burners are so inexpensive nowadays that it makes little sense to save $5 by installing a read-only DVD-ROM drive. If nothing else, you'll want the writer to back up your system. Among the many inexpensive DVD writers available, we chose the ASUS DRW-24B1ST for its combination of features, performance, reliability, and price. Similar models from LiteOn or Samsung are also good choices.

Keyboard and Mouse

Logitech Deluxe 250 Desktop (*http://www.logitech.com*)

Personal preference outweighs all else when choosing a keyboard and mouse. So many personal factors determine usability that no one can choose the "best" keyboard and mouse for someone else.

That said, we had to pick a "budget" keyboard and mouse for our budget system. We wanted something in the sub-$20 range that included a decent keyboard and a reliable optical mouse. Our favorite among inexpensive keyboard/mouse combos is the Logitech Deluxe 250 Desktop, for which we paid $17. If you prefer Microsoft keyboards and mice, the Microsoft Basic White Value Pack 2.0 or the Microsoft Wired Desktop 400 is also a good sub-$20 choice.

Speakers

Logitech LS11 (*http://www.logitech.com*)

Even a budget system needs a decent set of speakers, but we can realistically spend no more than $15 on speakers. In that price range, we recommend the Logitech LS 11 2.0 speaker set. Note, however, that many LCD displays include built-in speakers, which adds little or nothing to their price and can eliminate some desktop clutter. Display speakers are generally small and produce only 0.5W to 1W per channel. That's acceptable for most uses, including watching videos and so on. The $15 standalone units provide somewhat better sound but about the same wattage. We opted for speakers embedded in the display for our budget system.

> **Rachel Head Comments**
>
> *Neatly recouping the extra $15 spent on the hard drive!*

Display

19":

ASUS VW193TR (*http://www.asus.com*)

ASUS VH196T

ASUS VH198T

Hanns.G HW191APB (*http://www.hannsg.com*)

20":

ASUS VH202T-P

Hanns.G HZ201HPB

Samsung P2050 (*http://www.samsung.com*)

ViewSonic VX2033wm (*http://www.viewsonic.com*)

In the preceding edition, we allocated $120 to the display and recommended three 17" CRT models from NEC, Samsung, and ViewSonic. Nowadays, $120 buys you a lot more display. The entry level for LCD displays is now a 19" 1440×900 model. (There are smaller displays available, but they generally cost the same as a 19" model, if not more.) Basic models suitable for a budget system cost $110 to $130. In the $130 to $160 range, you can buy a 20" model with 1600×900 resolution, a nice step up. You're likely to be happy with any of the models listed above, or their successors. Note that some models include speakers and others do not.

Matching Displays to Video Adapters

In the past, gamers tended to choose only those LCD displays that had the fastest response times, because many mainstream displays had response times too slow to provide high-quality gaming video. That's less of an issue nowadays, because all but the least expensive LCD displays are fast enough to provide at least reasonable gaming response.

Serious gamers also choose displays with native resolutions that match the optimum video adapter settings for their systems. For example, a gaming rig may be able to display 3D games at 2560x1600 resolution, but only at unacceptably slow frame rates. Rather than use such a high-resolution display, a gamer might use a 1600x1050 display, at which resolution the frame rates are acceptably fast.

The ASRock K10N78M-PRO motherboard's integrated NVIDIA GeForce 8200 video supports resolutions up to 1920x1200 on

the DVI video output and is more than fast enough to provide excellent 2D video quality at its highest resolution. But if you plan to do any 3D gaming with your budget system, be aware that for many 3D games the GeForce 8200 will not be fast enough to drive a high-resolution display at anything near full resolution with usable frame rates.

If you don't want to install a faster video adapter—and perhaps a faster processor as well—the alternatives are to use less demanding game settings, accept lower frame rates, or run at lower than nominal resolution, which may cause blockiness and other video artifacts. With resource-intensive 3D games, you may have to make all three of these compromises, and even then performance may be unacceptable. Still, a budget system isn't designed for serious 3D gaming, and this system as configured can play many less demanding 3D games with acceptable performance.

Component Summary

Table 3-2 summarizes our component choices for the budget system. Not counting shipping, sales tax, or software, the total for the budget system came to $351. With display, the budget system cost $475, give or take. Not bad for a fully equipped system. We could have made small economies here and there to reduce the price further. For example, we might have saved $25 by buying a really cheap case (although we'd still have installed a $40 Antec Earth-Watts 380 power supply, or something similar). We could have saved $10 on the motherboard by accepting less capable integrated video and another $20 by using a slow single-core processor. Substituting a smaller hard drive might have saved us another $15, and we could have cut maybe $5 from the total by using a DVD-ROM drive rather than a DVD writer. All told, we might have gotten the cost of our budget system down into the $300 range, but we feel that would have been a false economy.

Table 3-2. *Bill of materials for budget*

Component	Product
Case	Antec NSK-4482 Mid-Tower Case
Power supply	Antec EarthWatts 380W (bundled)
Motherboard	ASRock K10N78M-PRO
Processor	AMD Athlon II X2 240
CPU cooler	(Bundled)
Memory	Crucial CT2KIT12864AA667 2 GB Kit (1 GB x 2)
Video adapter	(Integrated NVIDIA GeForce 8200)
Hard disk drive	Seagate Barracuda 7200.12 ST3500418AS (500GB)
Optical drive	ASUS DRW-24B1ST DVD writer
Keyboard and mouse	Logitech Deluxe 250 Desktop
Speakers	Logitech LS11 (or embedded display speakers)
Display	(See text)

Reality Check

When Barbara's sister Frances's system—the budget system from the preceding edition of this book—failed after more than four years of heavy use, it caught us at a bad time. We could have fixed her system, but at four years old it was nearing the end of its design life anyway. We didn't have any suitable spare systems sitting around, and we weren't quite ready to build this budget system. Frances needed a system quickly, so she asked us to look at the systems Costco had on offer and pick one out for her.

The least expensive desktop system on the Costco website was a Dell Inspiron 570, for $499.99 plus tax and shipping. For $150 more, the Inspiron 570's general specifications matched those of our budget configuration almost exactly, except that it had 4 GB of RAM rather than 2 GB and included a Windows 7 license.

Making those two changes would have increased our total cost by about $130, just $20 short of the Dell price. So why bother?

Because the two systems are only superficially similar. Granted, both have exactly the same processor and the same or similar hard drives, but otherwise the Dell system has lower-quality components. Our system has a better case and power supply, a higher-quality motherboard, top-notch memory, a faster optical drive, and a better keyboard, mouse, and speakers.

Also, paying $90 or so for a Windows 7 license would be a waste. Frances has been using Linux for years and has no desire to use (or pay for) Windows. So, our system costs about $110 less and is built with higher-quality components. That's a no-brainer.

Building the Budget System

Figure 3-1 shows the major components of our budget system. The Antec NSK-4482B case is at the upper left, with the ASRock K10N78M Pro motherboard to its right. In the foreground, left to right, are the Crucial 4 GB memory kit, the ASUS DRW-24B1ST DVD writer, the 500 GB Seagate Barracuda hard drive, and the AMD Athlon II X2 240 Regor processor.

Figure 3-1. *Budget system components, awaiting construction*

It's As Easy As 2, 1, 3

Although by necessity we describe building the system in a particular order, you don't need to follow that exact sequence when you build your own system. Some steps—for example, installing the processor and memory before installing the motherboard in the case—should be taken in the sequence we describe, because doing otherwise makes the task more difficult or risks damaging a component. But the exact sequence doesn't matter for most steps. As you build your system, it will be obvious when sequence matters.

Before you proceed, make sure you have everything you need. Open each box and verify the contents against the packing list. Once you're sure everything is present and accounted for, it's time to get started.

Preparing the Case and Installing Drives

The first step in building any system is always to make sure that the power supply is set to the correct input voltage. Some power supplies, including the Antec EarthWatts 380, set themselves automatically. Others must be set manually using a slide switch to select the proper input voltage. Bundled power supplies are nearly always set properly by default, if applicable, but there are rare exceptions, so it's always a good idea to verify the input voltage setting before you proceed.

Avoid Fireworks

If you connect a power supply set for 230V to a 115V receptacle, no harm is done. The PC components will receive only half the voltage they require, and the system won't boot. But if you connect a power supply set for 115V to a 230V receptacle, the PC components will receive twice the voltage they're designed to use. If you plug in the system, that overvoltage will destroy it instantly in clouds of smoke and showers of sparks.

Figure 3-2. *Remove the two thumbscrews that secure the top panel*

To begin preparing the case, remove the two thumbscrews that secure the top panel, as shown in Figure 3-2.

After you remove both thumbscrews, slide the top panel slightly toward the rear, as shown in Figure 3-3, and then lift it off.

With the top panel removed, lift the left side panel straight up and remove it, as shown in Figure 3-4. Remove the right side panel in the same manner. Put the top panel and both side panels safely aside, where they won't be scratched while you are building the system.

Figure 3-3. *Slide the top panel to the rear to release it*

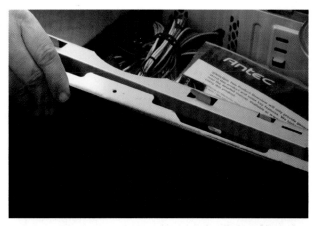

Figure 3-4. *Remove the side panels and set them safely aside*

The next step is to remove the internal 3.5" drive bay, which is secured by three screws. One screw, shown in Figure 3-5, secures the internal 3.5" drive bay to the 5.25" drive bay above it. Two other screws, one visible in Figure 3-6, secure the bottom front of the internal 3.5" drive bay to the inside front of the chassis. Remove all three of those screws. (You may find it easier to remove the two lower screws if you turn the case on its side temporarily.)

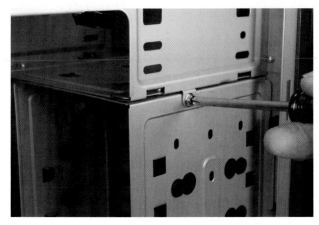

Figure 3-5. *Remove the screw that secures the side of the 3.5" internal drive bay to the 5.25" drive bay above it*

Figure 3-6. *Remove the two screws that secure the bottom of the 3.5" internal drive bay to the front of the chassis*

Figure 3-7. *Slide the 3.5" internal drive bay slightly toward the rear of the case and lift it out*

After you remove all three screws, slide the drive bay slightly toward the rear of the chassis to free the locking tabs and lift the drive bay clear of the chassis, as shown in Figure 3-7.

Fragile Connectors

Be extremely careful when you remove and replace the internal 3.5" drive bay. When this bay is removed, the panel ends of the front-panel connector wires are visible, including those for the power switch. The fine-gauge wires connect to tiny pins on the backs of the switches, and somehow we managed to pull the power switch wire loose from the power switch.

We didn't discover that until we were connecting the power switch wires to the motherboard, so we had to remove the internal 3.5" drive bay to repair the connection. The pins on the power and reset switches are tiny and fragile, so it would be quite possible to snap them off entirely by putting tension on the wires connected to them. You have been warned.

Place the drive bay on a flat surface, right-side up. Slide your hard drive into the drive bay, with the rear (data and power connector side) of the hard drive toward the rear of the drive bay. Slide the drive forward and backward until two of the screw holes in the hard drive align with the holes in the rubber grommets on the drive bay. When the drive is correctly aligned, the rear of the drive should protrude slightly from the rear of the drive bay, as shown in Figure 3-8.

Figure 3-8. *Slide the hard drive into the internal drive bay and secure it with four hard drive mounting screws*

Chapter 3

The parts bag includes special screws designed to mount hard drives in this bay. These screws (two of them fully visible in Figure 3-8) are threaded for only part of their length. The unthreaded portion is supported by the silicone grommet, which isolates the drives to reduce noise and vibration. Insert four of these screws, two per side, and tighten them finger-tight plus a quarter turn or so. Do not overtighten the screws, or you'll eliminate the benefits of the grommets.

If you have more than one hard drive to install, repeat these steps for the other drives. If you're installing two drives, leave at least one unoccupied mounting slot between them to improve ventilation.

After you install the hard drive or drives in the bay, slide the drive bay back into position, as shown in Figure 3-9. Make sure the locking tabs and slots on the two drive bays latch into position as you slide the bay into place. Also note the slot on the center-front edge of the drive bay (visible at the bottom of Figure 3-9), which mates with a corresponding metal tab on the chassis.

Once the drive bay is correctly positioned, maintain slight pressure on it toward the front of the case to force the side screw holes into alignment. Reinsert and tighten the screw that secures the internal 3.5" drive bay to the 5.25" drive bay above it. Then reinstall the two screws that secure the bottom of the internal 3.5" drive bay to the chassis.

The next step is to install the optical drive. To begin, use your fingers from inside the case to press outward on the top plastic bezel cover until it snaps free, as shown in Figure 3-10.

If you have a second 5.25" device to install (such as the Antec Easy SATA hard drive docking station), you'll need to prepare a second 5.25" drive bay. To do so, use a screwdriver to twist the metal RF shield (behind the plastic bezel cover) back and forth until it snaps free.

Using both thumbs, slide the optical drive into the drive bay, as shown in Figure 3-11. If it binds, pull the drive out slightly and reseat it. Press the drive bezel flush with the case bezel.

Figure 3-9. *Slide the internal drive bay back into place and secure it with the three screws you removed earlier*

Sharp Edges

Be careful when removing the metal RF shield, and be careful working in that drive bay later. Snapping the metal RF shield free leaves a sharp burr on the top edge of the remaining RF shield.

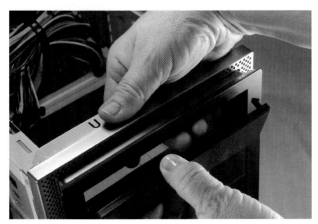

Figure 3-10. *Working from inside the case, press the top plastic drive bay bezel until it snaps out*

Figure 3-11. *Slide the optical drive into the drive bay until its bezel is flush with the case bezel*

Locate the optical drive mounting screws in the parts bag. These screws are the most finely threaded in the bag. Use at least four screws (two per side) to secure the optical drive to the chassis, as shown in Figure 3-12. Tighten the screws finger-tight plus maybe a quarter turn. (It's difficult to overtorque these screws because their heads are quite shallow. Your screwdriver will lose its grip before you can overtighten them.)

Note the shorter screw slot at the top-front position in Figure 3-12. Using a screw in that position prevents the drive from sliding back into the case more than a tiny fraction of an inch. We actually used six screws—one at the rear on each side and two at the front on each side—but if you use only one front screw per side, install it in that shorter slot position.

Nearly every case we've ever used, including the Antec NSK-4482, comes with a generic I/O shield. The generic shield never matches the motherboard I/O panel, so you'll need to remove the stock I/O shield and replace it with the one supplied with the motherboard.

To remove the I/O shield, use a tool handle to press from outside the case until the I/O shield pops loose, as shown in Figure 3-13. Be careful with your fingers: I/O shields are made of thin metal and may have edges sharp enough to cut you. Don't worry about damaging the generic I/O shield supplied with the case. You can discard or recycle it.

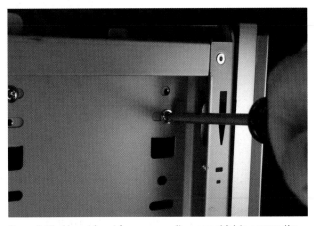

Figure 3-12. *Use at least four screws (two per side) to secure the optical drive to the chassis*

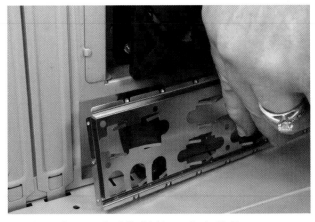

Figure 3-13. *Remove the I/O shield supplied with the case*

Avoid Brute Force

Be careful not to bend the I/O shield while seating it. The template holes need to line up with the external port connectors on the motherboard I/O panel. If the template is even slightly bent, it may be difficult to seat the motherboard properly.

Like all motherboards, the ASRock K10N78M-PRO comes with a custom I/O shield that matches the motherboard I/O panel. Before you install the custom I/O shield, compare it to the motherboard I/O panel to make sure the holes in the I/O shield correspond to the connectors on the motherboard.

Once you've done that, press the custom I/O shield into place. Working from inside the case, align the bottom, right, and left edges of the I/O shield with the matching case cutout. When the I/O shield is positioned properly, press gently along the edges to seat it in the cutout, as shown in Figure 3-14. It should snap into place, although getting it to seat properly sometimes requires several attempts. It's often helpful to press gently against the edge of the template with the handle of a screwdriver or nut driver.

Chapter 3

After you install the I/O shield, carefully slide the motherboard into place, making sure that the back panel connectors on the motherboard are firmly in contact with the corresponding holes on the I/O shield. Compare the positions of the motherboard mounting holes with the standoff mounting positions in the case. One easy method is to place the motherboard in position and insert a felt-tip pen through each motherboard mounting hole to mark the corresponding standoff position beneath it. Alternatively, you can simply look down through the motherboard mounting holes to determine which chassis positions need to have standoffs installed and then mark those positions with a felt-tip pen, as shown in Figure 3-15.

Figure 3-14. *Install the I/O shield supplied with the motherboard*

Figure 3-15. *Locate and mark the proper positions for standoffs to be installed*

The ASRock K10N78M-PRO motherboard has six mounting holes. Some cases are shipped with several standoffs already installed, but the Antec NSK-4482 has no standoffs preinstalled. So, we need to install standoffs in all six of the positions required by the motherboard.

Install brass standoffs for each motherboard mounting hole. Although you can screw in the standoffs using your fingers or needlenose pliers, it's much easier and faster to use a 5 mm nut driver, as shown in Figure 3-16. Tighten the standoffs finger-tight, but do not overtighten them. It's easy to strip the threads by applying too much torque with a nut driver.

Avoid Grounding Problems

If your case comes with preinstalled brass standoffs, make absolutely certain that each standoff matches a motherboard mounting hole. If you find one that doesn't, remove it. Leaving an "extra" standoff in place may cause a short circuit that may damage the motherboard and/or other components, or at least cause a boot failure.

Also, if you use a case that uses stamped raised areas in the motherboard tray instead of standoffs, be aware that some motherboards may fail to boot in such cases because the raised areas ground parts of the motherboard that were not intended to be grounded.

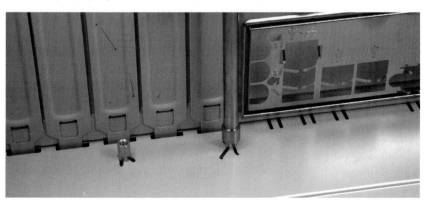

Figure 3-16. *Install a brass standoff at each marked position*

Once you've installed all the standoffs, do a final check to verify that (a) each motherboard mounting hole has a corresponding standoff, and (b) no standoffs are installed that don't correspond to a motherboard mounting hole. As a final check, we usually hold the motherboard in position above the case and look down through each motherboard mounting hole to make sure there's a standoff installed below it.

Populating the Motherboard

With the case prepared, the next step is to populate the motherboard by installing the processor, CPU cooler, and memory. To begin, place the motherboard on a firm, flat surface. Place the pink antistatic foam supplied with the motherboard between it and the work surface to protect the motherboard against physical or static electricity damage.

Locate the metal cam lever on the side of the processor socket. In its closed position, along the edge of the processor socket, this lever applies pressure to lock the processor pins into the socket. In its open position, with the lever vertical relative to the socket, that pressure is released, allowing a processor to be inserted or removed without damaging the pins. Press the cam lever slightly outward (away from the socket) to release it from the plastic latches that secure it, and then lift the lever, as shown in Figure 3-17, to the full vertical position.

Open the processor box and remove the hard plastic shell that contains the processor. Touch the chassis or power supply to ground yourself before you open that plastic shell and touch the processor itself. Be careful when opening the inner packaging. More than once, we've had the plastic shell give way suddenly and ended up with the processor dropping into our laps (or flying across the room…).

Open the inner package carefully and remove the processor from the antistatic foam bed upon which it rests. Orient and align the processor with the processor socket. The socket has an arrow on one corner that corresponds to an arrow on one corner of the processor. Make sure these arrows are aligned, and then simply drop the processor into the socket, as shown in Figure 3-18.

Figure 3-17. *Release the cam lever from the processor socket and lift it up*

Figure 3-18. *Orient and align the processor properly with the socket and then drop it into place*

The processor should seat flush with the socket without any pressure being applied. **Never press down on the processor, or you may bend the processor pins and ruin it.** If the processor doesn't drop into the socket freely, it's not aligned properly. Realign it and try again until it drops easily into the socket and seats completely.

Once the processor is seated properly, press the metal cam lever downward toward the socket and snap it into position under the plastic locking tab on the socket, as shown in Figure 3-19. You should feel some resistance on the lever as the cam clamps the processor pins into the socket. If you feel any more than very slight resistance, release the pressure, verify that the processor is correctly seated, and try again.

After you install the processor, the next step is to install the CPU cooler. Before you install the cooler, examine the bottom of the heatsink to verify that the patch of thermal compound is present and undamaged.

The CPU cooler clamps to the processor socket with two metal brackets that fit over plastic tabs on opposite sides of the processor socket. One of the brackets is free-floating. The other has a latching lever that cams the CPU cooler into tight contact with the processor. You can place either bracket over either tab, but it's easier to use the latching bracket on the tab nearest the edge of the motherboard, where there's more room to maneuver.

Locate the latching bracket on one side of the CPU cooler. Tilt that side of the CPU cooler slightly up from the processor surface, and hook the free-floating bracket over the black plastic tab on the edge of the processor socket, as shown in Figure 3-20. Make sure the hole in the bracket catches the tab, and then lower the other side of the CPU cooler until its base is in full contact with the processor. (You may have to use your finger to hold the bracket in place.)

> **A Penny Saved Is a Hundred Dollars Wasted**
>
> *If you ever remove and replace the processor, don't attempt to reuse the thermal compound. Rub off any compound present on the processor surface and the heatsink base—if it's tenacious you can warm it slightly with a hair dryer—and then polish both the processor surface and the heatsink base with a clean paper towel to remove all traces of the old compound. Apply new thermal compound according to the instructions supplied with it. (We generally use Antec Silver thermal compound, which is inexpensive and effective.)*

Figure 3-19. *Press the cam lever down and snap it into place under the plastic locking tab on the processor socket*

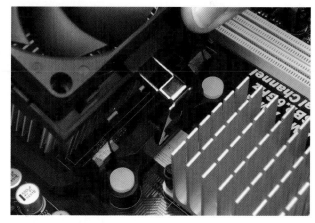

Figure 3-20. *Hook the free-floating metal bracket over the black plastic tab on the processor socket*

Making sure that the first bracket remains connected and maintaining finger pressure to keep the CPU cooler in position, press the second (cammed) bracket into position over the second tab, as shown in Figure 3-21.

Verify that both brackets are secured over both tabs, and then press the black plastic cam lever down until it latches to lock the CPU cooler to the processor socket, as shown in Figure 3-22.

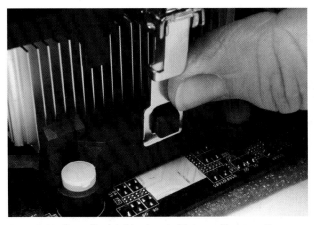

Figure 3-21. *Press the latching bracket into position over the second tab*

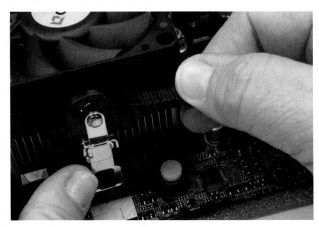

Figure 3-22. *Press the black plastic cam lever on the CPU cooler down until it latches to secure the CPU cooler to the processor socket*

Ordinarily, we make a point of connecting the CPU cooler fan to the motherboard fan power header pins immediately after installing the CPU cooler, lest we forget to do so. With this motherboard and CPU cooler, though, there's a slight problem. The length of the CPU fan cable and the location of the CPU fan power connector on the motherboard make it easier to install the memory modules before connecting the fan.

To install the memory modules, open the DIMM locking brackets on both sides of both memory sockets, as shown in Figure 3-23.

Touch the chassis or power supply to ground yourself before you handle the memory modules. Align one DIMM with the memory slot nearest the processor, as shown in Figure 3-24. Make sure the keying notch on the contact edge of the memory module aligns with the keying tab in the socket and that the two sides of the memory module fit into the slots on the vertical sides of the memory slot.

Align the memory module and the slot, with the DIMM vertical relative to the slot and both sides of the DIMM aligned with the vertical slots in the socket. Using both thumbs, press straight down on the memory module until it seats, as shown in Figure 3-25.

Before you install the second memory module, make sure the first module is fully seated and latched. The metal contacts on the base of the memory module should be concealed by the memory socket, and the plastic latching tabs on the memory socket should snap into place to latch the module into position, as shown in Figure 3-26. If the metal contacts on the base of the memory module are visible, the DIMM is not fully seated. Remove it, realign it, and reseat it. If the latching tabs are not seated in the notches on the memory module, it's possible that the module is not seated completely, but sometimes those latching tabs don't snap into position even if the module is seated properly.

If the metal contacts on the base of the module are not visible and the DIMM otherwise appears to be fully seated, simply use finger pressure to snap the latching tabs into position.

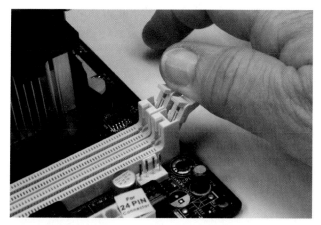

Figure 3-23. *Open the DIMM locking tabs on both sides of both memory sockets*

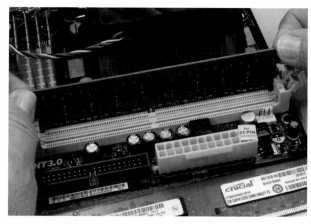

Figure 3-24. *Align the memory module with the socket*

Figure 3-25. *Press straight down on both sides of the memory module until it seats completely in the socket*

Figure 3-26. *Verify that the memory module is latched into position*

With the memory installed, you can now connect power to the CPU fan. This connector is keyed by plastic tabs on the cable connector and the motherboard header-pin set to prevent it from being connected incorrectly. Align the cable connector with the header pins and press the cable connector onto the header pins, as shown in Figure 3-27.

The motherboard is now prepared. Place it aside for now. Use the antistatic foam under the motherboard to make sure it's not damaged by static electricity.

Figure 3-27. *Connect the CPU fan power cable to the CPU fan header pins*

Installing the Motherboard

Installing the motherboard is the most time-consuming step in building the system because there are so many cables to connect. It's important to get all of them connected right, so take your time and verify each connection before and after you make it.

Seating and securing the motherboard

To begin, slide the motherboard into the case, as shown in Figure 3-28. Carefully align the back panel I/O connectors with the corresponding holes in the I/O shield, and slide the motherboard toward the rear of the case until the motherboard mounting holes line up with the standoffs you installed earlier.

Before you secure the motherboard, verify that the back panel I/O connectors mate properly with the I/O shield, as shown in Figure 3-29. The I/O shield has metal tabs that ground the back panel I/O connectors. Make sure none of these tabs intrude into a port connector. An errant tab at best blocks the port, rendering it unusable, and at worst may short out the motherboard. Use a flashlight or other bright light to make sure you can see any problem clearly.

Figure 3-28. *Slide the motherboard into position*

Figure 3-29. *Verify that the back panel connectors mate cleanly with the I/O shield*

After you position the motherboard and verify that the back panel I/O connectors mate cleanly with the I/O shield, insert a screw through one mounting hole into the corresponding standoff, as shown in Figure 3-30. You may need to apply some pressure to align the motherboard mounting holes with the standoffs until you have inserted two or three screws.

If you have trouble getting all the holes and standoffs aligned, insert two screws in opposite corners but don't tighten them completely. Use one hand to press the motherboard into alignment, with all holes matching the standoffs. Then insert one or two more screws and tighten them completely. Finish mounting the motherboard by inserting screws into all standoffs and tightening them.

Chapter 3

Figure 3-30. *Install screws in all six mounting holes to secure the motherboard*

With high-quality products like the Antec case and the ASRock motherboard, all the holes usually line up perfectly. With cheap products, that's often not true. At times, we've been forced to use only a few screws to secure the motherboard. We prefer to use all of them, both to physically support the motherboard and to make sure all of the grounding points are in fact grounded, but if you simply can't get all of the holes lined up, just install as many screws as you can.

Connecting power to the motherboard

With the motherboard installed and secured, the next step is to connect power to the motherboard. In the bundle of cables coming from the power supply, locate the ATX12V cable. Depending on the power supply, this cable may be labeled ATX12V, CPU Power, or something similar. It uses a four-pin (2×2) keyed connector with two 12VDC wires (yellow) and two ground wires (black) diagonally opposite in the connector body. (The Antec power supply actually provides two of these connectors; use one and tuck the other aside.)

Align the ATX12V cable connector with the motherboard ATX12V jack. One side of the cable connector has a plastic latch that snaps over a protruding ledge on the motherboard connector. Make sure those are oriented properly relative to each other and then press the cable connector into the motherboard socket, as shown in Figure 3-31. Make sure the connectors mate and latch.

The next step is to connect the 24-pin ATX main power connector to the motherboard. Locate the main power cable from the bundle coming out of the power supply and route that cable to the front edge of the motherboard. Like the ATX12V connector, the ATX main power connector is keyed and has a latch. Orient the cable connector properly relative to the motherboard socket and press the connector into place, as shown in Figure 3-32. Make absolutely sure that the connectors mate and latch.

Figure 3-31. *Connect the ATX12V power cable (CPU power) to the motherboard*

Figure 3-32. *Connect the 24-pin ATX main power connector to the motherboard*

Connecting front-panel I/O ports

The next step is to connect the front-panel audio and USB ports. Locate the front-panel audio cable. This cable has two connectors, one labeled HD AUDIO and the other AC'97. This motherboard provides an HD audio connector, so we'll leave the AC'97 connector unused. The audio header pin set is located at the far back corner of the motherboard, colored lime. This connector is keyed with a missing pin on the motherboard header-pin set and a blocked hole on the cable connector. Orient the HD audio cable connector properly, making sure that the missing pin corresponds to the blocked hole, and press the cable connector onto the header-pin set, as shown in Figure 3-33.

The front-panel USB cable supports two front-panel USB ports. This cable connects to either of the two sets of USB header pins (color-coded blue) located in the front corner of the motherboard near the expansion slots. Like the audio connector, the USB connector is keyed with a missing pin on the motherboard header-pin set and a corresponding blocked hole on the cable connector. Align and orient the USB cable connector properly relative to the motherboard USB header-pin set, and press the cable connector onto the header pins, as shown in Figure 3-34.

Figure 3-33. *Connect the front-panel HD audio cable to the motherboard*

Figure 3-34. *Connect the front-panel USB cable to the motherboard*

Connecting front-panel switch and indicator cables

The next step is to connect the front-panel switch and indicator cables to the motherboard. Before you begin connecting front-panel cables, examine the cables. Each is labeled to indicate its purpose. Match those labels with the front-panel connector pins on the motherboard to make sure you connect the correct cable to the appropriate pins. Once you determine the proper orientation for each cable, connect it as shown in Figure 3-35.

Figure 3-35. *Connect the front-panel switch and indicator cables*

Keep the following guidelines in mind as you connect the front-panel cables:

- Although Intel has defined a standard front-panel connector block and uses that standard for its own motherboards, few other motherboard makers adhere to that standard. Accordingly, rather than providing an Intel-standard monolithic connector block that would be useless for motherboards that do not follow the Intel standard, most case makers, including Antec, provide individual one-, two-, or three-pin connectors for each switch and indicator.

- Not all cases have cables for every connector on the motherboard, and not all motherboards have connectors for all cables provided by the case.

- The power switch and reset switch connectors are not polarized and can be connected in either orientation.

- LED connectors are polarized and should be connected with the ground wire and the signal wire oriented correctly. Most cases use a common wire color—usually black, although sometimes white or green—for ground, and a colored wire for signal.

- The power LED connector is often problematic, as it is for this system. There are two types of power LED connector. The first has two pins. The second has three pins, but only two wires, with the middle pin unused.

A motherboard may provide either or both types of power LED connector, and a case may provide either or both types of power LED cable. The ASRock K10N78M-PRO motherboard provides only a two-pin power LED connector. The Antec NSK-4482 case provides only a three-pin power LED cable. That leaves us with two options. We took the easy way out by simply leaving the power LED disconnected. If you want your power LED to function, use a sharp knife or diagonal cutters to carefully cut the power LED cable connector lengthwise, dividing it into two single-wire connectors. Connect each of those separately to the two power LED pins on the motherboard.

- The power LED connectors on some motherboards are dual-polarized and can support a single-color (usually green) power LED or a dual-color (usually green/yellow) LED. The Antec NSK-4482 case and the ASRock K10N78M-PRO motherboard both support only a single-color power LED. If you are using a different case and motherboard that support a dual-color power LED, check the case and motherboard documentation to determine where and how to connect the power LED cable.

When you're connecting front-panel cables, try to get it right the first time, but don't worry too much about getting it wrong. Other than the power switch cable, which must be connected properly for the system to start, none of the other front-panel switch and indicator cables is essential, and connecting them wrong won't damage the system.

Connecting drive power and data cables

We're in the final stretch now. All that remains is to connect a few cables. To begin, connect two SATA data cables to SATA ports 0 and 1 on the motherboard, as shown in Figure 3-36. We'll use one of these cables for the optical drive and the other for the hard drive.

Locate an available SATA power cable in the cable bundle coming from the power supply and connect it to the power connector on the optical drive. SATA power (and data) cables use an L-shaped key on the connector body to prevent installing the cables backward. Make sure the L is oriented properly on the cable and drive, and then press the connector into place, as shown in Figure 3-37. Press the connector firmly straight in until you're sure the connector is fully seated. Do not apply any sideways pressure or torque to the connector.

Locate the free end of SATA data cable 1 and press the connector onto the optical drive data connector, as shown in Figure 3-38. Once again, make sure the L key is oriented properly on the cable and drive, and then press the connector firmly straight in until the connector is fully seated.

Locate a SATA power cable in the cable bundle coming from the power supply. You can use a second SATA power connector on the same cable you connected to the optical drive or one of the separate cables with a SATA power connector. Make sure the L key is oriented properly on the cable and hard drive, and then press the SATA power connector into place, as shown in Figure 3-39. Press the connector straight in without applying any sideways pressure, and make sure the cable connector mates firmly with the drive connector.

Locate the free end of SATA data cable 0 and press the connector onto the hard drive data connector, as shown in Figure 3-40.

Figure 3-36. *Connect the SATA data cables for the hard drive and optical drive to motherboard SATA ports 0 and 1*

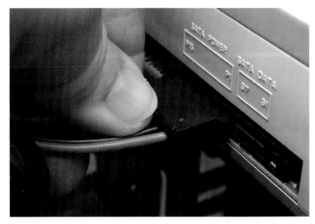

Figure 3-37. *Connect a SATA power cable to the optical drive*

Figure 3-38. *Connect SATA data cable 1 to the optical drive*

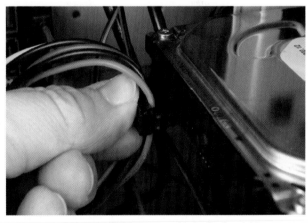

Figure 3-39. *Connect a SATA power cable to the hard drive*

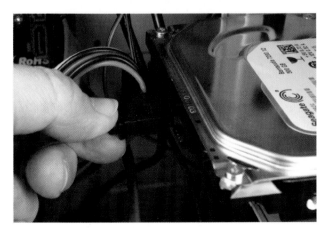

Figure 3-40. *Connect SATA data cable 0 to the hard drive*

Final Assembly Steps

Congratulations! You're almost finished building the system. Only a couple of final steps remain to be done, and these won't take long.

First, connect the supplemental case fan.

The Antec NSK-4482 has one rear-mounted 120 mm supplemental fan. To enable it, connect a four-pin Molex connector from the power supply to the connector on the fan, as shown in Figure 3-41.

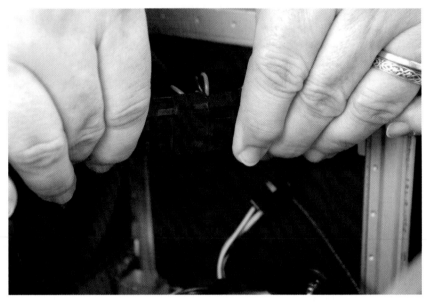

Figure 3-41. *Connect power to the rear case fan*

The final step in assembling the system is to dress the cables. That simply means routing the cables away from the motherboard and other components and tying them off so they don't flop around inside the case. Chances are that no one but you will ever see the inside of your system, but dressing the cables has several advantages other than making the system appear neater. First and foremost, it improves cooling by keeping the cables from impeding air flow. It can also improve system reliability. More than once, we've seen a system overheat and crash because a loose cable jammed the CPU fan or case fan.

After you've completed these steps, take a few minutes to double-check everything. Verify that all cables are connected properly, that all drives are secured, and that there's nothing loose inside the case. It's a good idea to pick up the system and tilt it gently from side to side to make sure there are no loose screws or other items that could cause a short. Also, check one last time that the power supply is set for the correct input voltage. Use the following checklist:

☐ Power supply set to proper input voltage (if applicable)

☐ No loose tools or screws (tilt and shake the case gently)

☐ Heatsink/fan unit properly mounted; CPU fan connected

☐ Memory module(s) fully seated and latched

☐ Front-panel switch and indicator cables connected properly

☐ Front-panel USB cable connected properly

☐ Hard drive data cable connected to drive and motherboard

☐ Hard drive power cable connected

☐ Optical drive data cable connected to drive and motherboard

☐ Optical drive power cable connected

☐ All drives secured to drive bay or chassis, as applicable

☐ Expansion cards (if any) fully seated and secured to chassis

☐ Main ATX power cable and ATX12V power cable connected

☐ Case fan(s) installed and connected (if applicable)

☐ All cables dressed and tucked

Once you're certain that all is as it should be, it's time for the smoke test. Leave the cover off for now. Unlike many power supplies, the Antec EarthWatts has a separate rocker switch on the back that controls power to the power supply. By default, it's in the "0" or off position, which means the power supply is not receiving power from the wall receptacle. Ensure the rocker switch is off, then connect the power cable to the wall receptacle and then to the system unit. Next, flip the power supply switch to the "1" or on position. Press the main power button on the front of the case, and the system should start up. Check to make sure that the power supply fan, CPU fan, and case fan are spinning. You should also hear the hard drive spin up. At that point, everything should be working properly.

> **False Starts**
>
> *When you turn on the rear power switch, the system will come to life momentarily and then die. That's normal behavior. When the power supply receives power, it begins to start up. It quickly notices that the motherboard hasn't told it to start, though, so it shuts down again. All you need to do is press the front-panel power switch and the system will start normally.*

Final Words

This system assembled easily and quickly. If we hadn't had to shoot images, it probably would have taken us about 20 minutes to build. A first-time system builder should be able to assemble this system in an hour or so, and certainly over the course of an evening.

We're extremely happy with this system, or perhaps we should say that Barbara's sister is extremely happy with it. Although it cost only $350 excluding the display and software, many people would be happy with this system as their only system. It's slower than the fastest current systems, but it's more than fast enough for casual use, including even light gaming. It's also quiet enough that we wouldn't hesitate to use it in our den, living room, or bedroom.

Although we didn't think about it until we'd already given the system to Barbara's sister, with some minor additions such as a larger hard drive or drives this would also make an excellent poor man's media center system. The system is quiet enough to be unobtrusive in a typical den or home-theater room, and the black micro-tower case won't clash visually with most AV setups. The processor and video are both fast enough to deal with full 1080p HD video via the DVI output, and the system has slots available if you want to add a tuner card or cards.

All in all, this turned out to be a perfect budget PC.

Chapter 3

Building a Mainstream System

A mainstream system is one that seeks balance at a reasonable price point. A mainstream system uses top-quality (but midrange in terms of performance) components throughout, because that is where you find the best value for your dollar. What differentiates a mainstream system from a budget PC is that the former makes fewer compromises. Whereas price is always a very high priority for a budget PC, it is less important for a mainstream system. If spending more money yields better performance or reliability, or adds desirable features, a mainstream system gets those extra dollars, whereas a budget PC probably doesn't.

Relative to the budget PC, the mainstream system gets more expensive components, particularly where they pay off in additional performance, convenience, or data safety. Typically, it will have a better motherboard, a faster processor, more memory, more disk storage, better external peripherals, and additional features. Considered individually, the incremental cost of better components is usually quite small. But taken collectively, the difference adds up fast. Depending on which components you choose, a mainstream system may cost 50% to 100% more than a budget system. That extra money buys you higher performance now and later, and extends the period between upgrades. If a budget PC will meet your needs for 12 to 18 months without upgrades, a mainstream system may suffice for 24 to 36 months or longer, depending on the demands you put on it.

In this chapter, we'll design and build the perfect mainstream system.

A Sheep in Wolf's Clothing

Many consumer-grade systems, particularly those sold in office superstores and big-box stores and by some large OEMs, masquerade as mainstream systems but are really budget PCs with a few extra bells and whistles. These PCs have faster CPUs, more memory, and larger hard drives—components whose specifications are easily visible—but use the same low-end motherboards, cheap cases, and marginal power supplies found in their less expensive budget lines.

And the "upgrades" those systems include are often less significant than you might expect from the description. For example, that larger hard drive may be available in two models, one with an 8 MB buffer and the other with a 32 MB buffer. The latter model may cost $8 more. Guess which model you'll find in that consumer-grade system? Or a system may be advertised as

having a RADEON HD 5570 video adapter. What isn't advertised is that that adapter uses slower memory and runs at a lower clock speed than the retail-boxed model you can buy.

True mainstream systems, at least as we define them, are a vanishing breed. Marketers believe that spending $5 more on a better power supply or $10 more on a better motherboard will only boost the price of their systems, making them uncompetitive with other brands, without increasing sales volume or profit. From their point of view, buyers are too ignorant to appreciate the difference between cheap components and good components that cost only slightly more. Unfortunately, they're usually right. Of course, the best answer to that is to build your own mainstream system from top-notch components.

Determining Functional Requirements

First, we sat down to think through our own requirements for a mainstream system. Here's the list of functional requirements we came up with:

Reliability

> First and foremost, the mainstream system must be reliable. We expect it to run it all day, every day, for years, without complaint. The key to reliability is choosing top-quality components: particularly the motherboard, memory, hard drive, and power supply. These components don't need to be the largest or fastest available, but they do need to be of high quality.

Balanced performance

> A mainstream system is a jack of all trades and master of none. We expect it to perform any task we might give it at least competently, if not better. But, because this is not a cost-no-object system, we need to balance component performance against price. For example, we expect this system to be capable of serious number crunching, but the fastest processors cost more than we can justify for this system. Accordingly, we'll aim for a balanced design that allows the system to do most things very well and everything else at least acceptably well.

Noise level

> Most mainstream systems are used in environments where noise is an issue. Accordingly, we'll design this system for quiet operation, but we won't spend much extra money to do so. That means, for example, that we'll choose the hard drive, case, and power supply based on noise level, but we won't spend $50 extra to replace the stock CPU cooling fan with a silent unit or $100 extra for a fanless power supply. Our goal is a quiet PC, not a silent PC (if there can truly be such a thing).

Hardware Design Criteria

With the functional requirements determined, the next step was to establish design criteria for the mainstream system hardware. Here are the relative priorities we assigned for our mainstream system. Your priorities may, of course, differ.

As you can see, this is a well-balanced system. Other than expandability and video performance, which are relatively unimportant, all of the other criteria are of similar priority. Here's the breakdown:

Price

> Price is moderately important for this system, but value is more so. We won't attempt to match the low price of commercial systems built with low-end components, but we won't waste money, either. If spending a bit more noticeably improves performance, reliability, or usability, or if it adds features we want, we won't begrudge the extra cost.

Price	★★★☆☆
Reliability	★★★★☆
Size	★★★☆☆
Noise level	★★★★☆
Expandability	★★☆☆☆
Processor performance	★★★☆☆
Video performance	★★☆☆☆
Disk capacity/performance	★★★☆☆

Reliability

Reliability is very important. A mainstream system that is not built for reliability is not worth building. We'll also allocate some of the budget to a top-notch UPS to protect the system from power glitches and outright failures.

Size

Size is important because this system must fit in Barbara's already crowded office, so we don't want the system to be any larger than it needs to be to do its job. So, although we will not compromise other criteria in exchange for smaller size, we will choose the smallest case that meets other system requirements.

Noise level

Noise level is at least moderately important for nearly any mainstream system, and is very important for this particular mainstream system. Our goal is to build a quiet PC at little or no incremental cost rather than to build a "silent" PC using expensive special components. Accordingly, when we choose components we'll keep noise level in mind, but we won't pay much extra for a marginally quieter component. We'll choose the quietest possible standard case and power supply, use large, slow-moving fans, use silicone-grommet hard drive mounts, and so on.

Expandability

Expandability is relatively unimportant for most mainstream systems, including this one. Fewer than 5% of commercial mainstream systems are ever upgraded, and those upgrades are usually of a minor nature, such as adding memory or replacing a video card or hard drive. Self-built mainstream systems are more likely to be upgraded, but even with these the upgrades are unlikely to require more than perhaps a spare drive bay or two, an expansion slot, or a couple of available memory sockets. We'll choose a case, power supply, and motherboard that are adequate to support such minor upgrades.

Processor performance

Processor performance is important for a mainstream system, both initially and to ensure that the system can run new software versions without requiring a processor upgrade. Mainstream dual- and quad-core processors—which is to say $150 to $175 Intel Core i5 models and AMD Phenom II X4 models—are the "sweet spot" in price/performance ratio, so that's what we'll use. These will give us roughly twice the performance of a budget system, but without getting into the performance price range.

Video performance

3D graphics performance is important for a mainstream system only if you intend to use it to run 3D games. Otherwise, integrated video suffices. In particular, current-generation integrated video is good enough even for casual gaming. 2D video quality is important for any mainstream system, because it determines display clarity and sharpness for browsers, office suites, and similar 2D applications. AMD and Intel integrated video both provide excellent 2D quality and reasonably good 3D performance.

To future-proof the system, we'll choose a motherboard that provides a PCI Express x16 video card slot. That way, we can always add an inexpensive or midrange video adapter if we need better 3D performance or other features not supported by the integrated video.

Disk capacity/performance

Even though it will connect to a network that has several terabytes of available storage, disk capacity and performance are relatively important for this system because Barbara prefers to work locally, using network drives only for backing up. Fortunately, with fast 1 TB and larger hard drives currently selling for $100 or less, it's easy and inexpensive to accommodate any reasonable disk storage requirements. We'll start by installing a 1 TB drive, with the intention of adding drives from time to time as necessary to extend the life of the system.

Component Considerations

With our design criteria in mind, we set out to choose the best components for the mainstream system. The following sections describe the components we chose, and why we chose them.

Case and Power Supply

Antec Mini P180 µATX case (*http://www.antec.com*)

With a mainstream budget, we can afford a nice case and a premium power supply. There are literally scores of mainstream cases available, so it might seem that choosing just one would be an overwhelming task. As it turned out, though, we were able to narrow down the choices dramatically based on some non-negotiable spousal requirements. This mainstream system would become Barbara's new main office system, and she had some very firm ideas about what constituted an acceptable case.

First and foremost, Barbara's office is directly across the hall from the master bedroom. She has very sharp hearing and is a light sleeper, so even slight computer noise coming from the next room can keep her awake. We decided to consider only cases that incorporated Quiet PC technology, such as silicone-grommet hard drive mounts, sound-deadening panels, large (and quiet) cooling fans, and so on.

The available space limited us to a mini-tower µATX case, which narrowed the selection significantly. Because the system will reside under her desk, Barbara insisted on front-panel USB (for her MP3 players), audio (for her headphones and headset), and eSATA (for her external hard drives) ports. Nearly all mainstream cases provide front-panel USB and audio ports, of course, but relatively few provide a front-panel eSATA port. Although we'll install only a DVD writer initially, Barbara wanted at least two 5.25" external drive bays because she may later decide to install a Blu-ray BD-ROM drive. Finally, Barbara specified one subjective requirement: this system will reside in her office, and she insisted that it be attractive.

Your Mileage May Vary

Although we tested the configuration we used to build our own mainstream system, we did not test permutations with the listed alternatives. Those alternatives are simply the components we would have chosen had our requirements been different. That said, we know of no reason the alternatives we list should not work perfectly.

Taken together, the objective requirements narrowed the field from hundreds of cases to a handful. Applying Barbara's subjective attractiveness requirement narrowed the candidates to only one case, the Antec Mini P180.

The Mini P180 ships sans power supply, which means we can install any power supply that fits our needs and budget. We wanted a reliable, high-quality power supply rated at 450W to 550W, with high energy efficiency, active power-factor correction, and low noise. We'd budgeted $65 to $85 for the power supply. We found several units that met those requirements, including the Antec Earth-Watts EA-500D Green, the Corsair CMPSU-450VX and CMPSU-550VX, and the Seasonic SS-500ET. Any of those models would be an excellent choice, but our familiarity and comfort level with Antec power supplies led us to choose the Antec EarthWatts EA-500D Green.

Motherboard

Intel DH55TC (*http://www.intel.com*)

Intel motherboards set the standards by which we judge all other motherboards for construction quality, stability, and reliability. For our mainstream system, we chose the rock-solid Intel DH55TC, which is a Socket LGA 1156 board that's based on Intel's mainstream H55 chipset. In fact, we liked this board so much that we ended up also using it for our media center system. (As Barbara commented, you know you're a True Geek when you have a list of favorite motherboards.)

It's not that the DH55TC has more features or better performance than its competition. In this class of motherboards, feature sets are similar and performance differences from board to board are too small to matter. It's that the DH55TC Just Works. For example, unlike some competing boards, the DH55TC works flawlessly with the integrated video that actually resides on the Core i5 processor. And although an attractive motherboard isn't necessarily a good one, this motherboard exhibits Intel's traditional high construction quality and close attention to fit and finish. That gives us some confidence that the things we can't see were also done right.

We settled on the DH55TC by our usual process of elimination. We needed a μATX (or Mini-ITX) board to fit the Antec Mini P180 case. We'd already decided to use an Intel Core i5 processor, so we needed a Socket LGA 1156 board. Although we plan to install only a 4 GB memory kit initially, we'd like at least two spare memory slots to allow easy future expansion, and we'd like the motherboard to support at least 8 GB of memory.

In terms of I/O ports, we need at least one 1000BaseT Ethernet port to connect to our network. Barbara has lots of USB devices, so we wanted at least six or eight USB ports. We needed at least one eSATA port—preferably front-panel for Barbara's external hard drives—and two would be better. Although we intend to use integrated video, we wanted at least one PCI Express x16 2.x slot in case we later decide to install a standalone video adapter. Finally, we wanted a board that cost less than $100.

Other excellent alternatives among the Intel-based boards we looked at include the ASRock H55M Pro, the ASUS P7H55-M, and the GIGABYTE GA-H55M-UD2H. If you intend to use an AMD processor, consider an ASRock 880GM-series board, an ASUS M4A785T-series board, or a GIGABYTE GA-880GM-series board.

Processor

Intel Core i5-661 (*http://www.intel.com*)

Intel Core i3-550

When Intel introduced the Core i5-6xx series processors in January 2010, our first impression was that they were superb mainstream processors, but significantly overpriced. At $200, the Core i5-66x processors were not competitive with the less costly AMD Phenom II x4 quad-core models, let alone the $200 Phenom II x6 1055T hex-core processor.

Priced at $150 or so, the dual-core, quad-thread Core i5-6xx series processors might well have knocked AMD out of the mainstream processor market. But $200 was simply too high a price. That's nothing new for Intel, which often prices new processor models well behind AMD on the price/performance curve. Unfortunately for AMD, Intel traditionally also reduces processor prices significantly as production ramps up. Because these new Intel models are produced with a 32-nanometer process, die sizes (and production costs) are accordingly much lower than those of AMD's older-technology processors. That gives Intel lots of headroom to reduce prices and put the squeeze on AMD, making this series of processors one to watch.

Then, in late May 2010, Intel introduced the fastest model to date of its Core i3 series, the $150 Core i3-550, which is only slightly slower than the Core i5-6xx series processors and offers significantly more bang for the buck. With the Core i3-550 selling for $150, it made no sense at all to pay $200 for the Core i5-661. However, if one thing is always true about processor pricing, it's that both Intel and AMD will adjust their prices to whatever level is required to maximize their profits while staying competitive both with each other and within their own product lines. By the time this book is available in bookstores, we expect the Core i3-550 to sell in the $125 range and the Core i5-660/661 in the $150 range, which will make either of them a good choice.

On that basis, we actually installed an Intel Core i5-661 processor in our mainstream system. We chose the Core i5-661 in particular rather than another Core i5 model because we think the -661 has the best combination of features for a general-purpose mainstream system. In particular, the -661 has the best integrated video performance of any current Core i5 model. (Conversely, if we had been building a mainstream corporate system, we'd probably have chosen the Core i5-660, which gives up some video performance but has security and management features that the -661 lacks.)

There are obviously alternatives to the Core i5-661. For the same price, you can buy the Core i5-750, which is based on the older 45-nanometer process but has twice as many cores as the -661 (although each of those cores is single-threaded, versus dual-threaded in the -661) and twice as much L3 cache (although the -750 does not include integrated video). For some applications—notably video encoding, Photoshop, and other heavily threaded applications—the quad-core -750 is faster than the dual-core 6xx series processors. For many productivity applications, the multithreading and Turbo Boost mode of the -661 makes it as fast as or faster than a comparably priced quad-core single-threaded processor. If you prefer an AMD processor, choose whichever AMD Phenom II X4 model is selling for about $150 when you order the parts for your system.

Whichever processor you choose, order the retail-boxed model rather than the OEM model. The retail-boxed models cost a few bucks more than the OEM models, but they have a longer warranty and also bundle a CPU cooler. Bundled CPU coolers have improved dramatically over the last few years. Both AMD and Intel bundled coolers are efficient and very quiet. Unless you're an extreme gamer or overclocker, or if you're trying to build the quietest possible system, we see no reason to install an aftermarket CPU cooler.

Memory

Crucial CT2KIT25664BA1339 PC3-10600 4 GB Memory Kit (2 GB×2)
(*http://www.crucial.com*)

We normally install 1 GB of memory per core for multicore processors, or 512 MB to 1 GB per thread for multithreaded processors. The Intel Core i5-661 processor has two cores, each of which runs two threads, so we decided to install 4 GB of system memory. (Barbara will run 32-bit Ubuntu on this system, which like all 32-bit operating systems recognizes only 3 to 3.5 GB of memory, so there's no point to installing more than 4 GB.)

The Intel DH55TC motherboard has four memory slots and supports dual-channel memory operation, which requires memory modules to be installed in pairs for best performance. Installing a pair of 2 GB modules, for a total of 4 GB, leaves two memory slots available for future expansion. If Barbara later decides to install 64-bit Ubuntu (or another 64-bit OS), we can populate those two free memory slots with a pair of 4 GB modules, boosting total system memory to 12 GB. That should suffice for the expected lifetime of this system.

The Intel DH55TC supports DDR3-1066 (PC3-8500) and DDR3-1333 (PC3-10600) memory. Although faster memory improves overall system performance slightly, it's not worth paying a big premium for it. However, on the day we ordered memory for this system, the PC3-10600 4 GB memory kit was actually selling for a couple bucks less than the PC3-8500 4 GB kit. Hmmm.

There are dozens of memory brands available, although all of them actually use memory chips produced by a small number of manufacturers, of which Micron/Crucial is one. Some of those brands—such as Corsair, OCZ, and Patriot—specialize in high-performance memory and have good reputations among gamers and other extreme PC enthusiasts. But for more than 20 years, we've used Crucial and Kingston memory almost exclusively, and have never had cause to regret that decision.

Brian Jepson Comments

Oddly, Mac OS X can address quite a bit more of RAM even with the 32-bit kernel. But even the 32-bit kernel supports 64-bit binaries, so it's possible that userspace apps are the only ones that will have access to all that memory. I think there's a bit more to this story, but I don't know enough about it to say for sure (I have 8 GB in my Mac running a 32-bit kernel).

Video and Sound Adapters

Integrated Intel HD Graphics and Intel High-Definition Audio

Intel integrated video has always provided excellent 2D image quality, but its 3D graphics performance has always, to put it politely, been rather anemic. Of course, no serious gamer would even consider using integrated video of any type, but integrated ATI or NVIDIA video was at least fast enough to play undemanding 3D games with minimum settings at reasonable frame rates. Under similar circumstances, Intel integrated video often provided only single-digit frame rates and was totally unsuited to playing any but the least demanding 3D games.

Intel addressed the performance problems when it introduced the Core i5 processors, which integrated video on the processor rather than using a separate video chipset on the motherboard. The 2D display quality remained top-notch, but Intel integrated 3D graphics performance went from also-ran to leading the pack. You still won't find any serious gamers using integrated graphics, but the new Intel HD graphics provide at least playable performance for many current 3D games, assuming reasonable resolution and other settings.

Because the integrated graphics are now on-processor (although not on-die), the actual 3D graphics performance varies from model to model. One of the major reasons we chose the Intel Core i5-661 processor rather than one of the other Core i5-6xx models is that the -661 integrated graphics, running at 900 MHz, are the fastest available in the Core i5 lineup. In conjunction with the Intel DH55TC motherboard, the Core i5-661 processor provides resolution up to 1600×1200 and support for analog, DVI-D, and HDMI displays, including dual displays. That's an excellent fit for our mainstream system, providing all the capabilities we might need.

The DH55TC motherboard also includes the Intel High Definition Audio subsystem, with support for eight-channel sound (5.1 plus two independent multistreaming audio channels). Barbara will use either her current M-AUDIO 2.0 speaker set or a Logitech 2.1 speaker set on this system, for either of which the integrated audio is more than sufficient.

Hard Disk Drive

Seagate Barracuda 7200.12 ST31000528AS (1TB) (*http://www.seagate.com*)

A mainstream system needs a mainstream hard drive, and you can't get much more mainstream than a Seagate Barracuda 7200.12 SATA drive. Although the 7200.12 is available in capacities as low as 160 GB, with the 1 TB model selling for $70 you can't save much money by choosing a smaller model. All of the 7200.12 models are reliable, fast, cool-running, and quiet.

The Samsung Spinpoint F3 and the Hitachi Deskstar are other good choices in this price and capacity range. The Western Digital Caviar Black is also an excellent drive. The only reasons we don't recommend it are that it sells for about a 25% premium over the other three drives, and is also louder and hotter-running.

The 7200.11 Firmware Issue

Although Seagate drives through the years have been remarkably reliable, Seagate did run into a major problem with its 7200.11 series. That problem, caused by a firmware bug, was initially reported as affecting only the 1.5 TB 7200.11 model but ultimately was found to affect all 7200.11 models. Seagate responded quickly with a firmware update, but unfortunately the fix came too late for some people, who ended up with bricked drives.

The resulting mess caused a firestorm. As the saying goes, "Make a customer happy and he'll tell a friend; make a customer unhappy and he'll tell the whole Internet." And that's exactly what happened. Although only a small percentage of 7200.11 users actually experienced the problem, the 7200.11 drives—particularly the 1.5 TB models—ended up with a bad reputation, far worse than they actually deserved. Unfortunately, some of that mud stuck to other, perfectly innocent, Seagate models, including the 7200.12.

For what it's worth, Robert runs four 1.5 TB Barracuda 7200.11 drives in his current main system—and has done so since before those drives were officially available for purchase—with no problems whatsoever.

Optical Drive

ASUS DRW-24B1ST DVD writer (*http://www.asus.com*)

Most mainstream systems need only a DVD writer. Among the many inexpensive DVD writers available, we chose the ASUS DRW-24B1ST. Similar models from LiteOn or Samsung are also good choices.

If you need to read Blu-ray discs and you have two external 5.25" drive bays, install a separate BD-ROM drive. The ASUS BR-04B2T is a good choice, as is the LiteOn iHOS104-08. If you have only one external 5.25" drive bay and need a combo DVD writer and Blu-ray reader, install the ASUS BC-08B1ST, the LiteOn iHES208-08, or the Samsung SH-B083L/BSBP. If you need to write BD-R/RE discs, install the Pioneer BDR-205BKS.

Backup Hardware

Antec Easy SATA hard drive docking station (*http://www.antec.com*)

The only practical way to back up systems with a terabyte or more of disk storage is to use external or removable hard drives. Optical discs simply hold too little and are much too slow. Tape drives are simply too expensive.

We have used and continue to use external hard drives, but many of those use slow 5,400 or 5,900 RPM drives, and having multiple units means paying repeatedly for the enclosure. Better is something that uses bare 7,200 RPM hard drives, which are inexpensive and fast. That means a hard drive docking station, either internal or external.

The type of interface is also an issue. USB 2.0 has real-world throughput of 25 to 30 MB/s, which means it can take 10 hours or more to transfer 1 TB. An eSATA interface is bound only by the sustained data transfer rates of the hard drives themselves. In our testing, we were able to transfer data from our internal 7,200 RPM Seagate Barracuda to an eSATA docking station using a similar drive at sustained rates of about 100 MB/s, three to four times faster than a USB external drive. At that speed, routine daily partial backups take only a few minutes to complete.

We've used and can recommend both the Antec Easy SATA hard drive docking station and the SYBA SD-ENC50020. The Antec unit fits into an external 5.25" drive bay and allows you to slide standard 3.5" SATA hard drives in and out. The SYBA unit is an external stand that holds two 2.5" or 3.5" hard drives, which connect via two supplied SATA cables to eSATA ports on your system. The SYBA unit is rare in that it supports faster native SATA transfers rather than the slower bridged transfers more common with external eSATA docking stations. Either unit costs about $25, and both provide very fast transfers.

We chose the Antec Easy SATA hard drive docking station for this system, but the SYBA SD-ENC50020 would be an equally good choice. Either of these units is a good way to recycle older SATA hard drives (run tests first to make sure they're not on their last legs). These units are an inexpensive way to maintain good backups even if you don't have any spare hard drives sitting around gathering dust, though. Hard drives are inexpensive enough now that it's no

Ron Morse Comments

Here's the question: Is your data worth $200?

great hardship to purchase three or four mid-capacity drives and devote them to backup. When your main hard drive fails, or a virus/malware takes over your system, you'll be glad you did.

Keyboard and Mouse

Logitech Cordless Desktop S520 Keyboard/Mouse Combo (*http://www. logitech.com*)

Personal preference outweighs all else when choosing a keyboard and mouse. So many personal factors determine the usability of a keyboard—straight versus ergonomic, layout, key size, cup depth, angle, stroke length, corded versus cordless, and so on—that no one can choose the "best" keyboard for someone else. The same is true, to a lesser extent, for a mouse.

That said, we had to pick a "mainstream" keyboard and mouse for our mainstream system. This will be Barbara's new main office desktop system. She wanted a cordless mouse, and didn't care if the keyboard was wired or cordless. (Barbara doesn't do online banking or other high-security tasks on this system; otherwise, she would have insisted on a wired keyboard.) She generally prefers the feel of Logitech keyboards and mice to similar models from Microsoft, but was willing to consider Microsoft. We decided something in the $50 range would be suitable.

She ended up choosing the Logitech Cordless Desktop S520 Keyboard/Mouse Combo, but the Microsoft Wireless Media Desktop 3000 came in a close second. Of course, there are literally hundreds of keyboard and mouse models available, priced from under $10 to several hundred dollars, so your choice will likely be different than Barbara's.

We've used literally hundreds of different keyboards and mice over the years, from dozens of manufacturers, and we keep coming back to Logitech and Microsoft models. Both companies produces dozens of models, one of which is almost certainly suitable for you. Even the least expensive Logitech and Microsoft models are of reasonably good quality, but you'll probably be happier if you limit your selection to models that cost at least $30 or $35.

Speakers

Logitech Z523 2.1 speaker system (*http://www.logitech.com*)

M-AUDIO Studiophile AV 30 2.0 speaker system (*http://www.m-audio.com*)

A mainstream system deserves a good set of speakers, but we can realistically spend no more than $100 on ours. In the preceding edition, we chose the Logitech Z-2300 2.1 speaker system, which then sold for about $100. The Z-2300 was head-and-shoulders above similarly priced competitors, both in sound quality and in output power. Alas, Logitech apparently realized it was leaving money on the table, because the Z-2300 currently sells for $150 or more.

We think the best current choices in the under-$100 range are the Logitech Z523 if you want a 2.1 speaker system and the M-AUDIO Studiophile AV 30 if you prefer a 2.0 speaker system. The Z523 is an excellent general-purpose set, suitable for anything from listening to music or watching videos to gaming. With 9.5W per channel on the satellites and 21W to the subwoofer, it's much less powerful than the 200W Z-2300 (40W per channel plus a 120W subwoofer), but the Z523 is still powerful enough to produce uncomfortably loud sound. The two-way AV 30 set offers 15W per channel and a flatter frequency response curve from low base to high treble, with sufficient dynamic range to produce accurate sound even for classical music. Gamers will probably prefer the Z523, while anyone who mostly listens to music or watches videos will probably prefer the AV 30.

Of course, if your budget extends to the $150 Z-2300 2.1 set, you can have the best of both worlds. At 120W RMS for the subwoofer and 40W RMS for each satellite, the Z-2300 can rattle the walls when you're gaming, but at lower volume it's also fine for listening to anything from classical music to DVD soundtracks. The satellites do a good job on the midrange and highs, and the subwoofer provides excellent bass response for this price level.

The THX-certified Z-2300 speakers are solidly built, and are attractive enough to use in your living room or den. The subwoofer includes an 8" long-throw woofer and the built-in amplifier. The satellites each use one 2.5" midrange/tweeter driver and are brushed aluminum with removable grilles. The Z-2300 includes a wired remote with volume control, mute button, and headphone jack.

Display

ASUS VW246H (*http://www.asus.com*)

ASUS MS228H

Samsung 2494SW (*http://www.samsung.com*)

Samsung EX2220X

ViewSonic VX2433wm (*http://www.viewsonic.com*)

ViewSonic VX2250wm-LED

With a higher budget for the mainstream system, we can spend half again as much on the display as we did for the budget system. The sweet spot for mainstream displays is $200, give or take $25 or $30, which is likely to remain true for some time to come. There are literally dozens of displays available in that price range, including many models from top-tier manufacturers such as ASUS, Samsung, and ViewSonic.

That price buys you a 24" fluorescent-backlit display with 1920×1080 (Full HD) resolution, fast response, and excellent image quality. If you're willing to step down to a 22" display, you can choose from among several models with LED backlighting, which provides even better display quality and has an essentially unlimited lifetime. (LEDs don't burn out; after 50 years or so, they dim to about half their original brightness.)

With so many good models at similar prices, it's difficult to narrow things down to just one. For a standard display, we think you'll be happy with the ASUS VW246H, the Samsung 2494SW, or the ViewSonic VX2433wm (which was Robert's actual choice). For an LED-backlit display, we recommend the ASUS MS228H, the Samsung EX2220X, or the ViewSonic VX2250wm-LED.

Component Summary

Table 4-1 summarizes our component choices for the mainstream system.

Table 4-1. Bill of materials for mainstream system

Component	Product
Case	Antec Mini P180 micro-tower case
Power supply	Antec EarthWatts EA-500D Green
Motherboard	Intel DH55TC
Processor	Intel Core i5-661 or Intel Core i3-550
CPU cooler	(Bundled with retail-boxed CPU)
Memory	Crucial CT2KIT25664BA1339 PC3-10600 4 GB Memory Kit
Video adapter	(Integrated)
Sound adapter	(Integrated)
Hard disk drive	Seagate Barracuda 7200.12 ST31000528AS (1TB)
Optical drive	ASUS DRW-24B1ST DVD writer
Backup hardware	Antec Easy SATA hard drive docking station
Keyboard and mouse	Logitech Cordless Desktop S520 Keyboard and Mouse Combo
Speakers	Logitech Z523 2.1 speaker system M-AUDIO Studiophile AV 30 2.0 speaker system
Display	(See text)

Assembly Order

Although by necessity we describe building the system in a particular order, you don't need to follow that exact sequence when you build your own system. Some steps—for example, installing the processor and memory before installing the motherboard in the case—should be taken in the sequence we describe, because doing otherwise makes the task more difficult or risks damaging a component. Other steps, such as installing the CPU cooler after you install the motherboard in the case, must be taken in the order we describe, because completing one step is a prerequisite for completing another. But the exact sequence doesn't matter for most steps. As you build your system, it will be obvious when sequence matters.

Building the Mainstream System

Figure 4-1 shows the major components of the mainstream system. The Antec EarthWatts EA-500D Green power supply is to the right of the Antec Mini P180 case, sitting atop the Intel DH55TC motherboard, with the Core i3-550 processor. The Antec Easy SATA hard drive docking station is to the far left, with Crucial 4 GB memory kit to its right. Front and center is the Sony/Optiarc DVD writer, with the Seagate Barracuda hard drive atop it.

Before you proceed, make sure you have everything you need. Open each box and verify the contents against the packing list.

Figure 4-1. *Mainstream system components, awaiting construction*

Preparing the Case

Among the scores of models of computer cases we've used over the years, the Antec Mini P180, along with other members of the P180 family, is our favorite. Despite (or, more probably, because of) the 120 mm rear fan and the 200 mm (!) top fan, the Mini P180 is also one of the quietest cases we've ever used.

But if you've never used anything other than standard computer cases, the Antec P180-series cases take some getting used to. The first thing you'll notice is the dual-chamber setup, with the power supply located in a separate chamber at the bottom of the case. Rather than having the various cables from the power supply simply hanging loose down into the main chamber, where you can route, connect, and dress them as needed, with the P180 you have to make some decisions about which cables you want to run where.

There are two options, which will become obvious when you look inside the open case. First, you can route cables from the power supply up through the bulkhead that separates the two chambers. Second, you can route power supply cables along the outside of the motherboard tray (below the motherboard, once it's installed) and route them back into the main chamber through various cutouts.

The advantage to this more complex cable-routing setup is that you end up with a very clean build, with much less cable clutter, which in turn means better cooling and easier upgrades and repairs. The disadvantage is that you have to think things through beforehand, and you may end up having to go back and reroute one or more cables that you overlooked the need for initially before you finally get it right. On balance, we prefer this cable-routing method, but there's no question that it takes some getting used to.

The exact cable routing you end up with will depend on the specific motherboard, power supply, and drives you use. For example, one power supply may have a main ATX power cable that's long enough to route outside the main chamber and bring back in through a cutout, while a different power supply with a shorter main ATX power cable may require you to run that cable up through the bulkhead that divides the chambers.

Similarly, although the Mini P180 has three external 5.25" drive bays, one is located at the top of the case (in the main chamber) and the other two at the bottom (in the power supply chamber). But the top 5.25" drive bay is depth-constrained (by the body of the top 200 mm fan) to accept drives no deeper than 170 mm.

The upshot is that most current optical drives will fit the top bay, but some (notably some Blu-ray drives) must be mounted in one of the bottom bays. That may seem odd at first, but this system is most likely to be sitting on a desk, where having the optical drive in the lower part of the case is actually more convenient.

To get started preparing the case, remove the top and bottom thumbscrews from the right side panel, as shown in Figure 4-2. (Note the protective plastic film on the side panel; to prevent scratches, leave this film in place until you finish the build.)

Slide the right side panel back about an inch and lift it free of the chassis, as shown in Figure 4-3. Set the panel aside in a safe place.

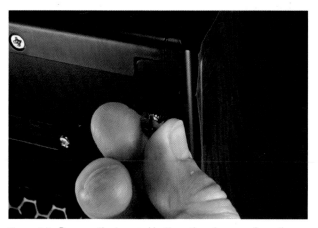

Figure 4-2. *Remove the top and bottom thumbscrews from the right side panel*

Figure 4-3. *Slide the right side panel back an inch or so and remove it*

Remove the two screws that secure the left side panel to the chassis, as shown in Figure 4-4. Lift the side panel free and put it aside in a safe place.

As with most cases, the Antec Mini P180 comes with an I/O shield installed, which fits no motherboard known to man. Press in on the outside of the I/O shield, as shown in Figure 4-5, until it snaps free. Discard the I/O shield.

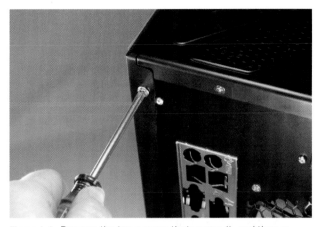

Figure 4-4. *Remove the two screws that secure it, and then re-move the left side panel*

Figure 4-5. *Remove and discard the I/O shield supplied with the case*

Installing the Power Supply

The next step is to install the power supply in the lower chamber. To begin, remove the parts box, as shown in Figure 4-6, and set it aside. This box contains screws, spare cable ties, drive rails for the 5.25" drive bays, an adapter to secure a 3.5" drive in a 5.25" bay, and a bezel for a 3.5" drive that requires external access.

Release the cable wraps that secure the power supply cables into bundles. Extend and sort out the various cables, and leave them hanging loose for now. Working from inside the case, slide the power supply into position, as shown in Figure 4-7.

Figure 4-6. *Remove the parts box and set it aside*

Figure 4-7. *Slide the power supply into position*

Building the Mainstream System

Autosensing Versus Accident-Waiting-to-Happen

The Antec EarthWatts EA-500D is autosensing, which means it adjusts itself automatically to accommodate 115VAC or 230VAC utility power. Many power supplies must be set manually using a slide switch to select the proper input voltage. Before you proceed further, check the back of your power supply for an input voltage selector switch. If one is present, make certain it's set for the correct input voltage.

If you connect a power supply set for 230V to a 115V receptacle, no harm is done. The PC components will receive only half the voltage they require, and the system won't boot. But if you connect a power supply set for 115V to a 230V receptacle, the PC components will receive twice the voltage they're designed to use. If you power up the system, that overvoltage will destroy it instantly in clouds of smoke and showers of sparks.

Bottoms Up

The Antec EarthWatts EA-500D power supply we used has a fan at the back of the unit and a grill at the front of the unit, with the top and the bottom solid sheet metal. Some power supplies have a fan on the bottom of the unit. If your power supply is like that, mount it inverted, with the fan facing up. When the power supply is installed, the bottom is nearly in contact with the bottom of the case, with only thin antivibration/sound-deadening pads separating the power supply case from the bottom of the case.

Installing a bottom-vented power supply oriented normally will cause it to overheat. Inverting it allows the fan/vent to vent upward (where there is clearance), and will have no effect on the power supply. However, mounting the power supply inverted may make it awkward to insert the AC power cable or use the rear switch.

Arrange the power supply cables neatly outside the right side of the case for the moment. Make sure none of the cables are trapped between the power supply and the chassis. Slide the power supply around until the four screw holes in the power supply align with the corresponding holes in the case. Drive the four provided screws to secure the power supply to the case, as shown in Figure 4-8.

You may want to preroute some of the power supply cables at this point, just to get them out of the way. If so, decide which power cables you want to route on the outer right side of the chassis, and which cutouts you want to route them through. (These cables will, of course, be covered when you reinstall the case cover.) Run those cables through the captive cable wrappers and the appropriate cutouts into the upper chamber, as shown in Figure 4-9. For now, don't tighten the cable wrappers.

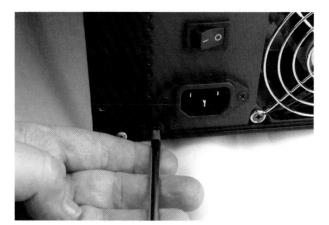

Figure 4-8. *Secure the power supply to the case with four screws*

Figure 4-9. *Route cables along the outer right side of the chassis and through the cutouts*

134 Chapter 4

For the time being, we won't route the cables through the bulkhead that separates the upper and lower chambers. It's easy to do that last, after the motherboard is installed, and keeping those cables out of the upper chamber makes it much easier to complete the motherboard installation.

Mounting the Optical Drive and Hard Drive

The Antec Mini P180 has two removable hard drive cages. The upper cage can hold three hard drives, mounted vertically and secured directly to the cage via screws driven through soft bushings. The lower cage can hold two hard drives, mounted with screws through soft bushings to removable drive trays.

Even if you intend to install only one hard drive in your system, remove both drive cages. Like most µATX cases, the Antec Mini P180 has very limited working room. It's easier to install the motherboard and make connections to it with both drive cages removed. To begin removing the drive cages, remove the thumbscrews, as shown in Figure 4-10.

Use a flat-blade screwdriver or similar tool to snap the pull rings free of their retaining clips and use the pull-rings to pull the drive cages straight out of the chassis, as shown in Figure 4-11.

Figure 4-10. *Remove the thumbscrews that secure the drive cages*

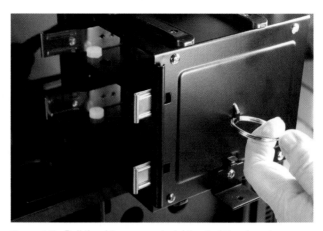

Figure 4-11. *Pull the drive cages straight out of the chassis*

The Antec Mini P180 manual claims that the parts box concealed on the right side of the upper 3.5" drive cage contains screws, spare grommets, standoffs, and so on. We'd already located those in the white cardboard box in the lower chamber, so we wondered what we'd find in that parts box. Figure 4-12 shows its contents. Yep, absolutely nothing.

Still, keep that parts box in mind. Once you finish assembling the system, you'll have lots of leftover screws and other parts that you might need later. Ordinarily, we store those in a plastic bag taped to the floor of the case. The parts box is a neater way to store small spare parts.

Now, decide which drive cage you want to use. Directions follow for using either.

To install a hard drive in the lower drive cage, place the cage on a flat surface and remove one of the drive trays by squeezing both spring clips and sliding the drive tray out of the cage, as shown in Figure 4-13.

Figure 4-12. *The parts box on the upper drive cage is a good place to store excess small parts*

Figure 4-13. *Squeeze both spring clips and slide the drive tray out of the lower drive cage*

Place your hard drive inverted (circuit-board side up) on your work surface. Place the drive tray inverted on top of the drive, with the spring clip ends of the drive tray toward the data and power connector end of the hard drive. Align the drive tray so that the mounting holes in the hard drive are visible through the grommets in the drive tray. Locate the special hard drive mounting screws in the parts box. (One of these screws is visible at the lower center of Figure 4-14.) Drive four of these screws through the grommets and into the drive, as shown in Figure 4-14. Tighten the screws only finger-tight plus perhaps a quarter turn. Overtightening the screws reduces the isolation benefits of the grommets.

Orient the drive tray so that the solid base of the tray will be on the bottom when the drive cage is reinstalled. Slide the drive tray into the drive cage and press straight in until both spring clips snap into place, as shown in Figure 4-15.

Figure 4-14. *Secure the hard drive to the drive tray by driving four of the special hard drive mounting screws through the grommets*

Figure 4-15. *Slide the drive tray into the drive cage until the spring clips snap into place*

We're running neither a hot video adapter nor a hot processor, so we decided to leave both drive cages installed. We're only installing one hard drive, at least for now, so we decided to install it in the upper removable drive cage, leaving the more accessible lower cage available for easier later upgrades. If you decide to use the upper hard drive cage, you'll find it a bit harder to install the drive(s) because they're unsupported and more difficult to keep aligned until you drive in a couple of screws to secure them.

Place the drive cage on its side and use one hand to support the drive and line up the top two screw holes in the drive with the holes in the grommets. Drive in two of the special screws (visible in Figure 4-16) to keep the drive in position. Invert the drive cage to place the unsecured side of the drive on top, as shown in Figure 4-16. Nudge the drive back and forth until one of the screw holes aligns with a grommet hole and drive in that screw. Repeat that process with the fourth screw.

Once the hard drive is installed in the drive cage, set both drive cages aside for now. We'll reinstall the drive cages after we install and connect the motherboard.

The next step is to install the optical drive. Antec recommends installing it, if possible, in the top 5.25" external drive bay. To begin, use your index fingers to grasp the sides of the plastic drive bezel and twist it until it snaps out, as shown in Figure 4-17.

Figure 4-16. *Use four of the special hard drive screws to secure the hard drive directly to the upper drive cage*

Insert the tip of a flat-blade or Phillips screwdriver in the hole in the center of the steel RF shield inside the drive bay and twist it back and forth, as shown in Figure 4-18, until the metal plate snaps free.

Figure 4-17. *Snap out the top 5.25" drive bay bezel*

Figure 4-18. *Twist the metal RF shielding plate until it snaps free*

Locate two drive rails and four optical drive mounting screws in the parts box. Stand the optical drive on its side on your work surface, and align one of the drive rails with the mounting holes in the side of the optical drive. Position the drive rail so that it is about centered vertically on the side of the optical drive, with the front of the metal spring tab flush with the front bezel of the drive. Insert two screws to secure the drive rail to the optical drive, as shown in Figure 4-19. Repeat this procedure to install the second drive rail.

Position the optical drive in the drive bay and slide it into the drive bay, as shown in Figure 4-20, until the spring clips on both drive rails snap into place. Verify that the front bezel of the drive is seated flush with the front bezel of the case.

Figure 4-19. *Use two screws to secure the drive rail to the optical drive*

Figure 4-20. *Slide the optical drive into the bay and press until both spring clips on the drive rails snap into place*

Chapter 4

If the drive refuses to slide all the way into the bay, verify that the top fan assembly isn't preventing it from doing so, as shown in Figure 4-21. The top external 5.25" drive bay accepts drives with a maximum depth of 170 mm (about 6.7"). The Sony Opticarc DVD writer shown in the image clears by about 5 mm. Even if your drive seats completely, check out the back of the drive to make sure the fan doesn't interfere with the data or power connectors on the back of the drive.

Figure 4-21. *Verify that the top fan assembly doesn't interfere with the optical drive*

If your drive does not seat completely, or if the top fan structure interferes with the power or data connectors on the drive, your only options are to use a different optical drive or to mount that drive in one of the lower 5.25" external drive bays.

Note the cutout in the motherboard tray, visible in Figure 4-21 just below the top fan and to the left of the drive connectors. We'll use that cutout to route the SATA power cable and data cable to the optical drive.

Preparing the Motherboard

The next step is to prepare the motherboard by installing the processor, CPU cooler, and memory. Despite the fact that some case and motherboard manuals suggest installing these components after the motherboard has been installed in the case, it's easier and often safer for the motherboard to mount the processor, cooler, and memory first.

To begin, locate the processor socket. Ground yourself by touching the power supply, and then release the chrome metal socket lever by pressing it down and away from the socket body. Once it's free of the catch on the socket body, lift the lever to the straight vertical position, which also raises the load plate to its fully open position, exposing the socket. Snap out the black plastic socket cover and store it with the other small parts in the parts box. If you ever remove the processor from the socket, replace the socket cover to protect the fragile socket contacts.

Open the processor package. Once again, ground yourself to the power supply or chassis frame before you touch the processor itself. Snap off the black plastic processor cover and set it aside. Store the processor cover later for possible future use.

Pin 1 on the processor is indicated by the gold triangle visible on the lower-left corner of the processor in Figure 4-22. Pin 1 on the socket is indicated by a beveled corner on the socket body. The processor and socket are further keyed by two notches on the outer edge of the processor to accommodate the two corresponding posts on the inside edge of the socket. Make sure pin 1 on the processor and the socket are aligned and that both keying notches are aligned with the corresponding posts, and then drop the processor straight into the socket, as shown in Figure 4-22.

Leave the socket lever in the fully open (vertical) position as you lower the load plate into the closed position, as shown in Figure 4-23.

Lower the processor lever slightly, which cams the load plate into locked position. Make sure that the notch on the front of the load plate mates with the shoulder screw cap, as shown in Figure 4-24.

Continue lowering the processor lever (which takes noticeable pressure) and snap it into place under the latch on the load plate, as shown in Figure 4-25.

Examine the surface of the processor carefully. If there are any fingerprints, dust, or other contaminants present, use a clean paper towel to polish the surface of the processor, as shown in Figure 4-26.

Remove the CPU cooler from the processor box and examine the bottom of the cooler. The gray patches visible in Figure 4-27 on the copper bearing surface of the cooler are phase-change thermal compound. (Phase-change is just a fancy way to say that the stuff melts each time the processor heats up and solidifies when the processor cools down.) The thermal compound ensures good heat transfer between the surface of the processor and the base of the heatsink.

If any of those patches are missing or damaged, carefully rub the remaining patches off the copper surface and replace them with an approved thermal paste. If you ever have to remove and replace the processor, don't reuse the existing thermal compound. Rub off any remaining residue from both the processor surface and the heatsink base, and replace it with new thermal compound. (We keep a tube of Antec Silver thermal compound on hand for just this purpose.)

The CPU cooler mounts to the motherboard using four push-posts with twist locks. The tips of the posts protrude a few millimeters on the back side of the motherboard, so you can't install the CPU cooler with the motherboard on a hard surface. We simply tilted the motherboard slightly while mounting the cooler to give clearance for the posts.

Figure 4-22. *Align the processor with the socket and then drop the processor into the socket*

Figure 4-23. *Lower the load plate into the closed position*

Figure 4-24. *Lower the processor lever to cam the load plate into locked position*

Figure 4-25. *Close the processor lever completely and snap it into the latch on the load plate*

Figure 4-26. *If necessary, polish the surface of the processor with a clean paper towel*

Figure 4-27. *Verify that the thermal compound is present and undamaged on the base of the heatsink*

To install the CPU cooler, align the tips of its four posts with the four mounting holes in the motherboard. The four mounting posts/holes form a square, so you can orient the CPU cooler in any of the four possible positions and still mount it successfully. We recommend positioning the CPU cooler so that the power cable for the CPU fan reaches the connector on the motherboard with minimum cable slack. Once you have the four posts and holes aligned, press down firmly on one post, as shown in Figure 4-28, until you feel it snap into place.

After you have snapped all four posts into place, you need to lock them. The top of each CPU cooler post has an arrow to indicate which direction to turn it to lock the post into place. Figure 4-28 shows the cap of a CPU post before it has been twisted to the locked position. You can use your fingers to turn the posts to the locked position, but it's easier to use a flat-blade screwdriver, as shown in Figure 4-29. Lock all four of the posts. Figure 4-30 shows a cap in locked position.

The final step in installing the CPU cooler is to connect the CPU fan power cable to the CPU fan power header pins on the edge of the motherboard, as shown in Figure 4-31. Make sure the keys on the connector bodies match, and then slide the connector onto the pins until it seats.

Ron Morse Comments

The Intel-supplied CPU cooler uses a variable-speed fan with a four-pin power connector. The system controls the fan's operating speed (and the amount of noise it makes) in concert with the operating temperature of the CPU. Make sure you connect the CPU fan to the four-pin header on the motherboard labeled "CPU FAN."

Figure 4-28. *Align the CPU cooler posts with the motherboard mounting holes and press down on the tops of the posts until they snap into position*

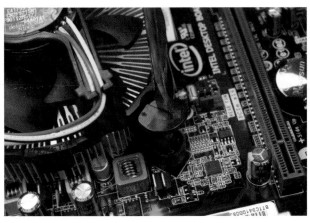

Figure 4-29. *Turn the cap of each CPU cooler post in the direction of the arrow to lock it into place*

Figure 4-30. *A CPU cooler post cap in locked position*

Figure 4-31. *Connect the CPU fan power cable to the CPU fan power header pins*

With the processor and CPU cooler installed, the next step is to install the memory modules. To begin, open all eight of the memory slot latches by pivoting them outward and down, away from the memory slots, as shown in Figure 4-32.

The DH55TC motherboard has four memory slots that accept 240-pin DDR3 memory modules. These slots are arranged in two channels, each of which accepts two DIMMs. Channel A is the pair of slots nearest the processor, and Channel B the two slots nearest the main ATX power connector (visible at the bottom left of Figure 4-33). The blue slot is DIMM 0 for each channel, and the black slot is DIMM 1.

If you are installing a matched pair of memory modules, install them in the two blue (DIMM 0) slots. If you are installing four DIMMs in two matched pairs that differ from each other, install the larger matched pair in the two blue (DIMM 0) slots and the smaller matched pair in the black (DIMM 1) slots. (Obviously, if all four DIMMs are identical it doesn't matter which DIMM goes in which slot.) If you are installing three DIMMs comprising a matched pair and one odd DIMM, install the matched pair in the two blue (DIMM 0) slots, and the third DIMM in either black (DIMM 1) slot.

In any case, install the DIMMs that will occupy the slots nearest the processor first and work forward toward the edge of the board. Before touching a DIMM, ground yourself by touching the power supply or chassis frame. Hold the first DIMM vertically over the appropriate slot. Align both edges of the DIMM with the slots in the vertical posts on the sides of the DIMM slot. DDR3 DIMMs are keyed with an off-center notch on the bottom (contact) edge of the DIMM. Make sure this notch aligns with the corresponding post in the slot, and then slide the DIMM into position, as shown in Figure 4-33.

Figure 4-32. *Open the memory slot latches*

Figure 4-33. *Holding the DIMM vertically, align it with the slot and key and slide it into position*

Once the DIMM is aligned properly, seat it by placing one thumb on each side of the DIMM and pressing down firmly until you feel it snap into place, as shown in Figure 4-34. Although it's better to seat the DIMM by pressing on both ends simultaneously, if you can't get the DIMM to snap into place this way, you can press down first on one end and then the other until it seats completely. Repeat this procedure to install any remaining DIMMs.

Verify that the DIMM is fully seated, as shown in Figure 4-35. If the DIMM is seated properly, none of the contacts on the bottom edge of the module should be visible, and the DIMM latching posts should snap up into the latched position. (If the module is fully seated but the DIMM latching posts remain open, manually close them to engage the notches on the edges of the DIMMs.)

Figure 4-34. *Use both thumbs to press down firmly until the DIMM snaps into place*

Figure 4-35. *Verify that the DIMMs are fully seated and the latching posts are in the latched position*

Installing the Motherboard

With the motherboard populated, the next step is to install it in the case.

Ordinarily, we'd have already compared the I/O shield with the motherboard's back-panel I/O port to make sure they matched and then installed the I/O shield in the case.

We started to do it that way for this system, but we immediately ran into a problem. There is so little clearance for the DH55TC motherboard that we simply couldn't fit the motherboard into the case with the I/O shield installed. Well, we suppose we could have, but doing that would have required removing and reinstalling the rear case fan. That we could have done at the cost of a few extra minutes' work, but it also appeared that we'd have to remove and replace the shelf that supports the two internal hard drive cages, and that shelf is riveted.

Figure 4-36. *Leaving out the I/O shield doesn't greatly increase the open area of the Antec Mini P180 case*

As we sat there considering our alternatives, our gaze settled on the rear of the Mini P180 case, shown in Figure 4-36 with the motherboard already installed. Hmmm. Four expansion slot covers that are mostly holes, and a good-sized grill to ventilate the expansion slots. A 120 mm fan grill. And that's not even counting the honking huge 200 mm fan grill at the top rear of the case. This area of the Antec Mini P180 is mostly open to the air anyway, and we concluded that the small additional gap produced by leaving out the I/O shield wouldn't noticeably affect air flow, cooling, or noise level. So, for the first time since Intel introduced the ATX form factor in 1995, we decided to build a system without installing the I/O shield. (Later testing showed that both the processor and hard drive were running very cool, so we have no concerns about omitting the I/O shield.)

With that decision made, building the system suddenly became a lot easier. Of course, if you use a different case or motherboard, you may have sufficient clearance with the I/O shield in place. Or you may not.

The Intel DH55TC motherboard has eight mounting holes. The Antec Mini P180 case comes with six standoffs preinstalled, so the first step in installing the motherboard is to determine which, if any, of the standoffs are incorrectly positioned and which motherboard mounting holes need additional standoffs installed. To answer those questions, temporarily lower the motherboard into position, as shown in Figure 4-37, and note the locations that require standoffs.

As it turns out, all six of the preinstalled standoffs in the Antec Mini P180 correspond to mounting holes in the Intel DH55TC motherboard. Two motherboard mounting holes have no corresponding standoffs, so we installed standoffs in both of those positions, as shown in Figure 4-38.

Figure 4-37. *Place the motherboard in position to determine the locations where standoffs need to be installed*

Figure 4-38. *Install any missing standoffs needed to support the motherboard*

Once all standoffs are installed, again lower the motherboard into position and make a final check that a standoff is installed for each motherboard mounting hole and that no extra standoffs are present. From the parts box, locate the small plastic bag labeled "Motherboard only" and remove eight motherboard mounting screws. Position the motherboard so that at least one standoff is visible through a mounting hole and partially drive a motherboard mounting screw into that standoff. Realign the motherboard as needed to line up the other mounting holes with their corresponding standoffs, and drive screws into each standoff, as shown in Figure 4-39. Tighten all screws finger-tight plus about a quarter turn. Do not overtighten the screws, or you risk cracking the motherboard.

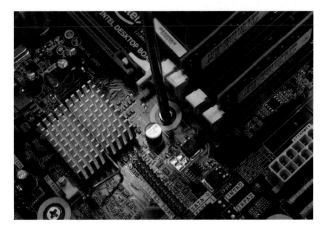

Figure 4-39. *Drive screws into all eight standoffs to secure the motherboard*

Connecting power to the motherboard

The next step is to connect the ATX12V power cable to the motherboard. This cable has a 2×2 keyed connector with two black (ground) wires and two yellow (+12V) wires, and includes a latch. The Antec EarthWatts EA-500D power supply labels these connectors "P2," but other power supplies may label them "CPU" or "ATX12V."

Locate the ATX12V cable bundle coming out of the power supply and route that cable up the outside of the case on the righthand side to the cutout at the top of the motherboard tray. Pass one of the ATX12V connectors into the top chamber of the case and connect it to the motherboard, as shown in Figure 4-40. Make sure the keying on the plug and socket match properly, and then press the connector down until the latch snaps into place.

If you haven't already done so, locate the 24-pin main ATX power connector cable coming out of the power supply, and route it up the outside of the case (on the right) to the cutout nearest the main ATX power connector at the front edge of the motherboard. Align the plug with the socket, making sure the keying matches. Press down firmly on the plug, as shown in Figure 4-41, until you feel it seat completely in the socket and the latch engages.

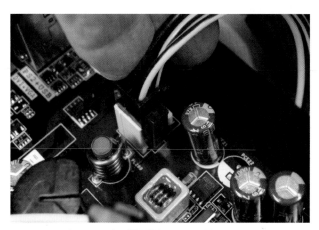

Figure 4-40. *Connect the ATX12V power cable to the motherboard*

Figure 4-41. *Connect the main ATX power cable to the motherboard*

Connecting front-panel ports, switches, and indicators

The Antec Mini P180 case provides front-panel ports for USB, HD or AC'97 audio, and eSATA. Oddly, neither the Mini P180 case nor the Intel Media Series motherboard provides an IEEE 1394/FireWire port—or perhaps those are simply indications of the declining importance of FireWire for desktop systems in an environment where eSATA is commonplace and USB 3.0 will soon become so. It wouldn't surprise us at all if the next HD camcorder we buy has eSATA and/or USB 3.0 ports instead of FireWire.

To begin connecting the front-panel ports, locate the front-panel audio cable. This cable has two connectors—one for HD audio and one for AC'97 audio—to accommodate motherboards with either type of audio connector. Our motherboard provides an HD audio connector, so that's what we'll use. Locate the front-panel HD audio header-pin set, toward the rear corner of the motherboard, near the expansion slots. The header-pin set is keyed with a missing pin that corresponds to a blocked hole on the cable connector. Orient the cable connector and header pins so that the keying matches, and then press the cable connector onto the header pins, as shown in Figure 4-42.

In addition to six rear-panel USB ports, the Intel DH55TC motherboard includes three sets of header pins that each provide two USB ports, for a total of 12 USB ports. The center USB header-pin set also includes special support for an internal *embedded USB* (eUSB) solid-state drive.

We don't expect to install an SSD in this system, and if we did it would be one that uses a standard SATA interface. Even so, with more USB ports on the motherboard than we have places to connect them, we decided to use one of the remaining two USB header-pin sets. One of those sets is located near the front corner of the motherboard, in close proximity to the front-panel switch and indicator pins. To make it easier to install the latter, we decided to use the second USB header-pin set, located just to the rear of that first set.

Like the front-panel audio connectors, the USB cable connector and header-pin set are keyed with a blocked hole and missing pin, respectively. (The USB key pin is different from the audio key pin, to make sure you can't accidentally connect a USB port to the audio header pins, or vice versa.)

To make the connection, orient the front-panel USB cable plug to align its blocked hole with the missing pin on the USB header-pin set. Slide the cable connector down onto the header pins, as shown in Figure 4-43, until it seats completely.

> **eUSB?**
>
> *Embedded USB SSDs are not used in general-purpose PCs. They were designed to replace 1.8" hard drives in embedded, ruggedized, and mil-spec systems, where they serve as the only mass storage device. eUSB SSDs generally use expensive SLC memory and have capacities in the 500 MB to 16 GB range. A 1 GB eUSB SSD may cost $35, a 4 GB model $125, and a 16 GB model $500.*

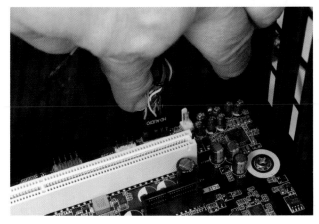

Figure 4-42. *Connect the front-panel audio cable HD audio connector to the FP audio header-pin set*

Figure 4-43. *Connect the front-panel USB cable connector to the USB header-pin set*

Next up are the front-panel switch and indicator cables: namely, the power and reset switches, the hard drive activity LED, and the power LED. Figure 4-44 shows the pinouts for these switches and indicators on the Intel DH55TC motherboard. (Actually, this is an Intel standard, used by all recent Intel motherboards and most motherboards from other makers.)

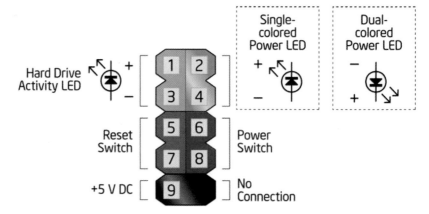

Figure 4-44. *Intel DH55TC front-panel switch and indicator pinouts (image courtesy of Intel Corporation)*

We'll connect three of those cables to the monolithic connector block mapped in Figure 4-44. The one exception is the power LED, because Intel provides two adjacent pins for that connection, while the Antec Mini P180 case provides a three-position/two-pin power LED cable that does not fit this block. Fortunately, the Intel DH55TC motherboard provides an alternative three-position/two-pin motherboard connector that the Antec cable fits. That connection is shown at the bottom center of Figure 4-45 as a blue/white cable connected to the pin set labeled PWR LED. Connect the power switch cable and reset switch cable to the monolithic connector block, as shown in Figure 4-45. Polarity doesn't matter for switches, so you can install the cable connector in either direction. Connect the HDD LED cable to the appropriate pins, making sure to observe polarity. (The red wire is positive and the white wire is ground.) If you connect this cable backward, no harm is done, but the HDD LED won't function.

Locate the black front-panel eSATA cable, and connect it to one of the red eSATA motherboard ports as shown in Figure 4-46. It doesn't matter which one. Make sure the L-shaped key in the cable connector and motherboard connector mate, and then press the cable connector down firmly until it seats.

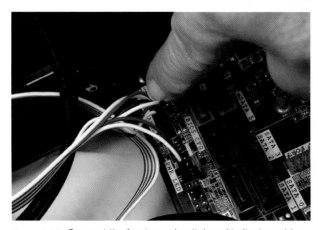

Figure 4-45. *Connect the front-panel switch and indicator cables*

Figure 4-46. *Connect the front-panel eSATA cable*

Installing the Antec Easy SATA Docking Station

The next step is to install the Antec Easy SATA hard drive docking station. At first glance, it might seem that installing the Easy SATA presents a resource-allocation conflict. The Intel DH55TC motherboard provides two eSATA-enabled ports. The front-panel eSATA port that we just connected uses one of those eSATA motherboard ports, leaving us with only one available.

But the Antec Easy SATA unit requires two more motherboard SATA connectors. One of those connects to the Easy SATA using a standard SATA data cable. The second connects via the captive cable (shown in Figure 4-47) to the external eSATA port on the front bezel of the Easy SATA unit. So it appears that we need a total of three eSATA motherboard ports, one more than we have.

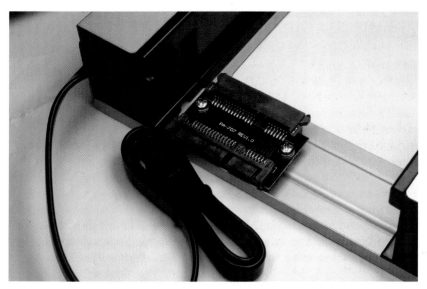

Figure 4-47. *Power and data connectors on the rear of the Antec Easy SATA hard drive docking station*

At this point, we wondered exactly what the difference was between the red eSATA motherboard ports and the black standard SATA motherboard ports. The connectors appear identical except for color, and they accept the same cables. We examined the ports closely to see if there were any physical differences—for example, different pin lengths to support hot-plugging—but could see no differences at all.

So we asked one of our technical contacts at Intel, who explained it all to us. The only difference between the red eSATA motherboard connectors and the black standard SATA motherboard connectors is the signal level. The red connectors use a slightly higher signaling voltage to allow using the longer cables supported by the eSATA specification. The higher voltage on the red ports won't harm standard SATA devices, and eSATA devices work properly on the black ports if the cable lengths are kept short. So, as it turned out, we didn't have a problem at all. We connected the two red eSATA motherboard ports to the eSATA jacks on the Mini P180 case and the front bezel of the Antec Easy SATA unit. We then used a standard black SATA motherboard port to connect the removable drive bay portion of the Easy SATA.

To install the Antec Easy SATA hard drive docking station, follow the same procedure described in the section about mounting the optical drive to remove the plastic bezel and steel RF shielding plate from one of the lower 5.25" drive bays. Attach drive rails to each side of the Easy SATA frame, as shown in Figure 4-48. Both rails should be positioned as shown, using the upper set of screw holes in the Easy SATA frame and with the front edge of the spring clips flush with the front bezel.

Locate one of the SATA power cables from the power supply cable bundle, and feed it through the lower 5.25" external drive bay and out the front of the case. Match the L-shaped keys on the power cable connector and the Easy SATA power connector, and press the power cable connector onto the Easy SATA power connector, as shown in Figure 4-49.

Figure 4-48. *Attach drive rails to both sides of the Antec Easy SATA hard drive docking station*

Figure 4-49. *Connect power to the Easy SATA unit*

Feed a standard SATA data cable through the lower drive bay and connect it to the data connector on the Easy SATA unit, as shown in Figure 4-50.

Make sure the SATA power cable and both SATA data cables will feed through the drive bay opening and into the lower interior chamber, and then slide the Antec Easy SATA unit into the drive bay, as shown in Figure 4-51.

Figure 4-50. *Connect a standard SATA data cable to the Easy SATA data connector*

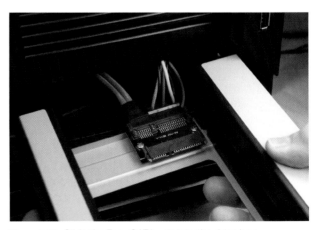

Figure 4-51. *Slide the Easy SATA unit into the drive bay*

Although the Easy SATA frame slides in and out of the bay easily, you may have to use some pressure to force the frame rails to snap into the latched position. Note in Figure 4-52 that the spring clips are still in the unlatched position, tight against the side of the Easy SATA frame rather than projecting out into the thumb holes. To get the frame to seat and latch, we had to withdraw it an inch or two and then slide it quickly into place. Make sure these spring clips latch, or the first time you attempt to remove a hard drive from the frame the whole frame will slide out of the case.

Locate the two SATA data cables in the lower chamber at the rear of the Easy SATA and feed them up through the hole in the sliding door of the interior bulkhead, as shown in Figure 4-53. (The thumbscrew can be loosened if you need to slide that door aside temporarily to route cables.)

Figure 4-52. *Press the Easy SATA frame into the drive bay until the spring clips snap into place*

Figure 4-53. *Route the two SATA data cables from the Easy SATA through the bulkhead and into the upper chamber*

The black captive SATA data cable from the Easy SATA unit feeds the eSATA port on the front of the unit. Because that port may be used to connect an external eSATA device with a long cable, we want to connect the black captive cable to our one remaining motherboard eSATA port, as shown in Figure 4-54. (Yes, it's bass-ackwards that we've now connected two black SATA cables to our two red motherboard SATA ports and we're about to connect red SATA cables to our black motherboard SATA ports. Oh, well.)

The standard SATA data cable from the Easy SATA unit feeds the removable drive bay, which in terms of required signal strength is the same as any internal SATA device. That means we can connect it to any of the four standard SATA ports on the motherboard. We reserved SATA 0 and SATA 1 ports for our hard drive and optical drive, so we decided to connect the Easy SATA data cable to the next available SATA port, SATA 2.

Match the L-shaped keys on the cable connector and motherboard connector, and then press the cable connector into place, as shown in Figure 4-55. Make sure the cable connector seats fully, and that the cables you connected previously are still seated.

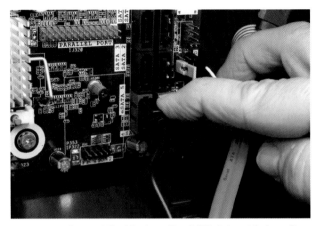

Figure 4-54. *Connect the black captive SATA data cable from the Easy SATA unit to the one remaining motherboard eSATA port*

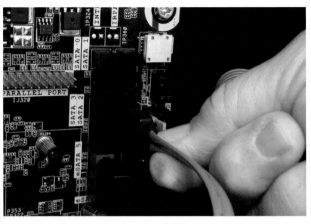

Figure 4-55. *Connect the standard SATA data cable from the Easy SATA unit to one of the standard SATA motherboard ports*

Connecting Power and Data Cables to the Optical Drive and Hard Drive

We're in the home stretch now. All that remains is to connect the power and data cables to the optical drive and hard drive, and do a bit of neatening up. To begin, locate a SATA power cable that also includes a Molex connector. Route that cable up the exterior right side of the case, and pass a SATA power connector through the cutout at the top of the case, nearest the optical drive. Make sure the keying on the cable connector and optical drive connector match up, and then press the SATA power cable connector firmly onto the optical drive power connector, as shown in Figure 4-56.

Pass a standard SATA data cable through the same cutout you used for the power cable, and then connect the SATA data cable to the optical drive, as shown in Figure 4-57.

Run the SATA data cable down the outside of the case on the right, and pass it through the cutout nearest the motherboard SATA connectors. Make sure the keying on the cable and motherboard connector match, and then press the cable connector onto the motherboard connector, as shown in Figure 4-58. Make sure the cable connector seats completely.

Slide the hard drive cage back into the chassis and secure it by reinstalling the thumbscrew. Route a SATA power cable to the hard drive, and connect it, as shown in Figure 4-59.

Connect a standard SATA data cable to the hard drive, as shown in Figure 4-60.

Route the hard drive data cable to the motherboard SATA port area and connect the SATA data cable to a motherboard SATA port, as shown in Figure 4-61. (Yes, we got tired of using all black and red SATA data cables, so we fished out a silver one for the hard drive.)

Chapter 4

Figure 4-56. *Connect a SATA power cable to the optical drive*

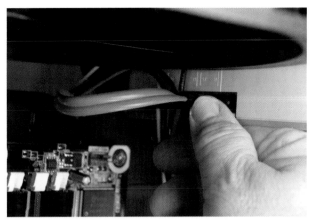

Figure 4-57. *Connect a standard SATA data cable to the optical drive*

Figure 4-58. *Connect the SATA data cable from the optical drive to a motherboard SATA port*

Figure 4-59. *Connect a SATA power cable to the hard drive*

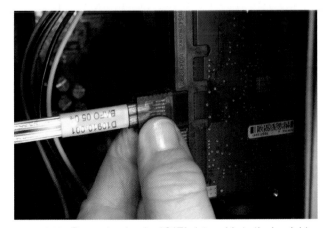

Figure 4-60. *Connect a standard SATA data cable to the hard drive*

Figure 4-61. *Connect the hard drive SATA data cable to a motherboard SATA port*

Finally, route a SATA power cable to the hard drive and connect it, as shown in Figure 4-62. At this point, the system is complete except for some minor cleanup.

Even though we've built several systems with Antec P180-series cases, we're always surprised when we finish one and see how neat the cabling is. Figure 4-63 shows the finished mainstream system, with almost no cable mess. Well, we do plan to do something about that CPU fan power cable and perhaps tuck the SATA power cables to the optical drive and hard drive into the hard drive cage, but otherwise there's no cable dressing remaining to be done inside the main chamber.

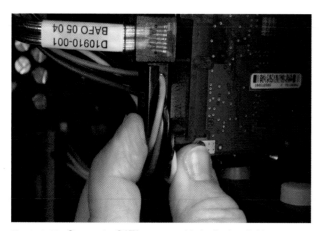

Figure 4-62. *Connect a SATA power cable to the hard drive*

Figure 4-63. *The interior of the mainstream system, seconds after we finished connecting cables*

Chapter 4

Of course, when Robert was a teenager, he tried to fool his mother, who had told him to clean up his room. He simply piled everything in the closet, which worked well until she opened the closet door. Figure 4-64 shows that bedroom closet for our mainstream system—the rats' nest of cabling on the exterior right side of the case. Fortunately, it's not as bad as it looks.

Note that unused Molex power connector hanging loose near the QA PASS label. We left that there to remind us to connect power to the case fans. Do so now, as shown in Figure 4-65.

To dress the messy side of the motherboard tray, first feed any excess cabling back from the main chamber to this side of the tray. Gather and bundle the cables, and secure them using the captive cable ties and the spare cable ties from the parts box.

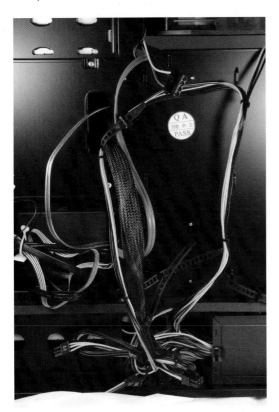

Figure 4-64. *The hidden rats' nest of cables*

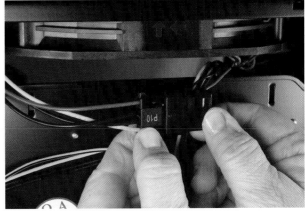

Figure 4-65. *Connect power to the case fans*

Final Assembly Steps

Congratulations! You're almost ready to put the side panels back on the case and declare the system finished.

Before you do that, take a few minutes to double-check everything. Verify that all cables are connected properly, that all drives are secured, and that there's nothing loose inside the case. If your power supply is not autosensing, check one last time to verify that it is set to the correct input voltage. It's a good idea to pick up the system and tilt it gently from side to side to make sure there are no loose screws or other items that could cause a short. Use the following checklist:

- ☐ Power supply set to proper input voltage (if applicable)
- ☐ No loose tools or screws (shake the case gently)
- ☐ CPU cooler properly mounted; CPU fan connected
- ☐ Memory modules fully seated and latched
- ☐ Front-panel switch and indicator cables connected properly
- ☐ Front-panel I/O cables connected properly
- ☐ Hard drive data cable(s) connected to drive(s) and motherboard
- ☐ Hard drive power cable(s) connected
- ☐ Optical drive data cable connected to drive and motherboard
- ☐ Optical drive power cable connected
- ☐ All drives secured to drive bay or chassis, as applicable
- ☐ Expansion card(s) (if any) fully seated and secured to chassis
- ☐ Main ATX power cable and ATX12V power cable connected
- ☐ Top and rear case fans connected
- ☐ All cables dressed and tucked

False Starts

When you turn on the rear power switch, the system will come to life momentarily and then die. That's normal behavior. When the power supply receives power, it begins to start up. It quickly notices that the motherboard hasn't told it to start, though, so it shuts down again. All you need to do is press the front-panel power switch and the system will start normally.

Once you're certain that all is as it should be, it's time for the smoke test. Leave the cover off for now. Connect the power cable to the wall receptacle and then to the system unit. Unlike many power supplies, the Antec unit has a separate rocker switch on the back that controls power to the power supply. By default, it's in the "0" or off position, which means the power supply is not receiving power from the wall receptacle. Move that switch to the "1" or on position. Press the main power button on the front of the case, and the system should start up. Check to make sure that all fans are spinning. You should also hear the hard drive spin up. At that point, everything should be working properly.

At this point, the system is ready to roll. Turn it off, replace the side panels, and strip off any remaining protective plastic film. Move the system to where you plan to use it, connect the display and other external peripherals, fire it up, install your operating system and applications, and restore your data to the new system.

Final Words

Other than the minor issue with the I/O shield and a couple of false starts routing cables, this system went together easily. Not counting the time needed to shoot the images, it took us about 30 minutes from start to finish. A first-time system builder should be able to assemble this system in an evening with luck, and certainly over a weekend.

We're very pleased with our new mainstream system. Despite the numerous large vents and fan grills, the system is extremely quiet—enough so that it's inaudible in a normal room when we're sitting only a couple of feet away. We set both the top and rear fans to slow initially, using the fan switches on the rear of the case. At that speed, we can't hear them at all, and they seem to provide sufficient cooling. After running for more than an hour, the CPU temperature and hard drive temperature were both under 40° C, which speaks well of both the Antec case and the stock Intel CPU cooler.

We installed Windows 7 and Ubuntu Linux 10.04, both of which installed and ran with no problems. Performance-wise, this system "feels" fast (noticeably faster than the budget system, which itself is no slouch). It's also rock-solid stable, as we proved by running the Passmark burn-in utility for 72 hours without a single glitch. We can't ask for much more.

Building an Extreme System

5

In the first two editions of this book, we built systems designed to provide top performance for 3D games. We were planning on doing the same for this new edition, until we talked with several friends who are heavily into gaming. They all told us that, although gaming PCs are still used by many gamers, they are rapidly declining in popularity, with most gamers shifting to gaming consoles.

So, for this edition we decided that rather than building yet another dedicated gaming system, we'd instead build an extreme system. An extreme system is one in which one or more functions—processor and memory performance, video performance, hard disk performance or capacity, noise level, and so on—are optimized for top performance, sometimes at the expense of other functions.

A gaming system is, of course, one form of extreme system, but there are others. For gamers, 3D graphics performance is critical, but for some extreme systems they don't matter much, if at all. Robert, for example, is doing increasingly more video production, which can place extreme demands on a system. For that purpose, processor performance and hard drive capacity and performance are critical, but even integrated video is perfectly acceptable.

One of our correspondents provides an even more striking example of an unusual extreme system. He produces high-resolution CGI graphics videos as a hobby(!), and he's built his own small render farm of several extreme systems configured in a Beowulf cluster. Those systems run headless, so video is literally zero priority. They have small standard hard drives, are built in ordinary mini-tower cases, and look like nothing special. But they're extreme systems, all the same. Each has a high-performance processor and dual high-end video adapters (which function as floating-point operations accelerators), and each spends all its time rendering individual CGI frames. (When his wife commented about how much he was spending on PC components, he told her she should be thankful he hadn't bought a cabin cruiser, as one of their friends had just done.)

We had to pick one extreme system configuration to build for this chapter, and we figured we might as well make it actually useful to us, so we elected to build an extreme video production and scientific number-crunching system for Robert, one with a very powerful processor, fast memory, and a ton of hard disk storage. Along the way, we'll point out alternatives you might choose to configure your own extreme system for your own purposes.

Determining Functional Requirements

We began by sitting down to think through the project. Here's the list of functional requirements we came up with:

Extreme processor/memory performance

> Video editing/rendering and scientific number crunching are both largely processor-bound operations, so raw processor performance is critical. That means we'll want a processor with as many cores and threads as possible, running at the highest possible clock speed. For both of these primary applications, memory performance is also critical. In fact, within reason, the amount of main memory is less important than its performance, so we'll want the fastest memory we can get, with the lowest possible latency.

High-performance, high-capacity mass storage

> Scientific number crunching, at least of the sort Robert does, is not disk-intensive, but serious video editing and rendering requires not just extreme disk capacity but extreme performance as well. The fastest current high-capacity SATA hard drives have sustained transfer rates of about 100 MB/s, so reading or writing a 3 GB video file might take 30 seconds, a significant amount of time when you're working interactively. We need something better than individual hard drives.

Top-notch 2D video

> Although 3D graphics performance is a nonissue, we'll need a large, high-resolution display—at least full 1080p for viewing and editing HD video, and 1920×1200 or higher would be better. We also need a video adapter capable of driving that display.

Hardware Design Criteria

Price	★★☆☆☆
Reliability	★★★★☆
Size	★☆☆☆☆
Noise level	★☆☆☆☆
Expandability	★★★☆☆
Processor performance	★★★★★
Video performance	★☆☆☆☆
Disk capacity/performance	★★★★★

With the broad-brush functional requirements determined, the next step was to establish design criteria for the extreme system hardware. Here are the relative priorities we assigned for the extreme system.

Here's the breakdown:

Price

> Price is important for this system only in the sense that we don't want to spend money needlessly. Our goal is to build, within reason, the fastest system possible without getting into workstation-class components (and prices). We'd like to keep the cost of this system to $3,500 or so, excluding software and external peripherals, but we'll go higher if necessary.

Reliability

> Reliability and stability are very important for this system, but we don't need to do anything special to guarantee them, since no extreme system is built with cheap components. We'll use only top-quality components—particularly for the motherboard, memory, and power supply—which together will ensure high reliability. We'll also make sure the case we use is

very well ventilated and has sufficient fans to ensure the system will be cool-running. We'll also install a professional-grade online uninterruptible power supply, which will protect the system from power glitches.

Size

Size is unimportant. All that matters is that the system fits on or under Robert's desk.

Noise level

Noise level is unimportant, although we neither want nor expect this system to sound like a chainsaw. The system will sit in Robert's office, very close to an actively cooled 2 kVA true UPS, whose cooling fans are louder than any noise this system could produce.

Expandability

Expandability is relatively important. Although this system will be loaded to start with, we definitely want room to grow. In particular, we want room for additional hard drives. We'll start with four 2 TB hard drives, but we'd like enough drive bays to enable us to add several more drives. Also, we may decide at some point to install a high-performance video adapter (or two), not because we'll use this system for 3D gaming, but as math coprocessors. For that reason, we'll use a motherboard that provides two PCI Express video slots.

Processor performance

Processor (and memory) performance ties with disk capacity/performance for top priority in this system. Robert will use this system to edit and render video interactively, which demands high processor performance, and to run scientific software that operates on relatively small data sets but is calculation-intensive. (When Robert starts a run around dinnertime on his current Intel Core2 Quad extreme system, that run sometimes is not complete when he sits down at his desk first thing the next morning.)

We actually thought about building a multiprocessor Xeon workstation system, but a quick check of prices quickly disabused us of that notion. Comparing processor benchmarks, we learned that the fastest current Intel Extreme processor was more than twice as fast as Robert's current Core2 Quad, which means that a run that currently takes 12 hours or more should complete in 5 or 6 hours on a new system built around an Intel Core i7 Extreme processor. That's certainly fast enough, and allows us to keep the system cost within reason.

Video performance

Video performance, in the sense of 3D graphics speed, is completely unimportant for our extreme system. We don't game, and all of our real work is 2D only, so any video adapter that provides sharp, clear 2D display will be perfectly suitable for our needs. Even integrated video would suffice, although we'd still want a PCI Express x16 slot for a possible future upgrade. In fact, we want two such slots, just to cover us in the unlikely event that we'll ever want to install a pair of high-performance video adapters.

If that statement sounds strange, it's not that we think it even remotely possible that we'll suddenly become PC gaming enthusiasts. We want those slots because fast video adapters can be used for more than just rendering 3D graphics at blazing speed. They can also be used as very high-performance math coprocessors, with the main CPU offloading heavy-duty number crunching to them. For now, the main CPU of this system will do the number crunching, but we wanted to leave the dual video adapter option open as a possible future alternative to a very expensive processor upgrade.

Disk capacity/performance

Disk capacity and performance tie with processor performance for top priority in this system. Capacity is crucial, because video editing and rendering simply eats disk space. Even a relatively small project may consume 100 GB or more of disk space, counting the original digital video files, edited clips, various work files, rendered clips in various formats, and so on. Disk performance is also critical, because digital video files (particularly HD files) are *big*. When we're working interactively with multi-gigabyte files, the time required to read and write those files becomes significant, so the faster the disk subsystem is, the better.

Our first thought was to use RAID 10 to increase disk subsystem performance. The obvious problem with RAID 10 is that only half the actual disk space is available to the system, so four 2 TB drives would provide only 4 TB of available disk space. The less obvious problem with RAID 10 is that while it's faster than a single drive, it's not all that much faster. Instead of waiting 30 seconds for that file to load, we might have to wait 25 seconds. That's not much of an improvement in exchange for giving up half our disk space.

The obvious solution would be to use solid-state drives. Unfortunately, we wanted at least 8 TB of disk space. Installing 8 TB of SSDs would have cost at least $25,000, and that's if we bought the cheap ones. We decided that a hybrid disk subsystem made sense, with a single, fast SSD as the boot/ system/working-data drive, and several 2 TB hard drives to provide mass storage. Installing an SSD large enough to hold our working data sets will give us the best of both worlds.

Component Considerations

With our design criteria in mind, we set out to choose the best components for our extreme system. The following sections describe the components we chose, and why we chose them.

Case and Power Supply

Antec Dark Fleet DF-85 (*http://www.antec.com*)

Antec CP-850 850W power supply

The extreme system is destined to become Robert's new main office desktop system, and our first requirement for the case was that it have lots of drive bays. Initially, the system will have six drives—an SSD boot drive, four 2 TB data drives, and an optical drive—but for future expansion we wanted a case that provided room for at least four more hard drives. Obviously, cooling efficiency is important for such a heavily loaded system, so we also wanted a case that made provision for lots and lots of fans.

There were literally a dozen or more cases available from Antec, Cooler Master, ThermalTake, and other good companies that met our broad requirements, most of them server and gaming cases. So, we decided we could give more weight than usual to appearance. Based on how Robert wanted his new system to look, we quickly narrowed down the candidates to two finalists: the Antec Twelve Hundred, shown in Figure 5-1, and the Cooler Master HAF X, shown in Figure 5-2. Both have the pseudo-Victorian mechanical "steampunk" styling that appeals to Robert. Their features are similar and the Twelve Hundred was $30 cheaper, but Robert preferred the styling and red illumination of the HAF X.

It was a close call, but Robert finally decided on the Cooler Master HAF X. He was literally in the process of ordering a HAF X from NewEgg when he received an email from our contact at Antec announcing the launch of the Dark Fleet DF-85 case, shown in Figure 5-3. Now *that's* steampunk. The DF-85 wasn't yet available in retail channels when we started building this system, but Antec was kind enough to send us an evaluation sample that we suspect was literally from the first pallet off the boat.

Figure 5-1. *Antec Twelve Hundred*

Figure 5-2. *Cooler Master HAF X*

Figure 5-3. *Antec Dark Fleet DF-85*

Feature-wise, the DF-85 is easily a match for the Twelve Hundred or the HAF X. With no less than 14 drive bays and 7 standard fans, expandability and cooling are not issues. Four of the nine 3.5" hard drive bays are hot-swappable, as is the 2.5" SSD bay at the top of the case. That makes it very easy for us to remove those drives and take them along with us when we leave the house for an extended period. Instant offsite backup.

The DF-85 is one of several Antec case models that accepts Antec's proprietary oversize CPX form factor power supplies. Why would we want a power supply that's too large physically to fit in any but a few Antec case models? Because it costs more to make something smaller without reducing its functionality. Although Antec produces standard ATX power supplies with high wattage ratings, they're more expensive than a CPX power supply with a similar wattage rating and other specifications. For example, the Antec CP-850 CPX power supply we chose for this system sells for about $110. Standard ATX form factor power supplies of comparable quality and wattage, including Antec models, sell for $150 to $300. By making CPX power supplies physically larger, Antec is able to produce them at lower cost for the same quality.

An 850W power supply is probably overkill, even for a system with a 130W processor and six drives, but this system may in the future have anything up to a dozen drives, so we wanted enough power in reserve. Some power supplies are very inefficient below 50% load, so they waste electricity when lightly loaded. Fortunately, the CP-850 is rated at 80%+ efficiency from a 25% load to 100% load, so we're not giving up any efficiency by running it with a lighter load initially.

Motherboard

Intel Extreme Series DX58SO (*http://www.intel.com*)

An extreme system requires an extreme motherboard. AMD no longer produces extreme processors, so we knew we'd use a high-end Intel Core i7 processor for this system. The fastest chipset available for Core i7 processors is the Intel X58, so we immediately narrowed our motherboard search to models based on that chipset.

There's no getting around it: X58 motherboards are expensive, not least because the X58 chipset itself is expensive. And, just as a Cadillac that sells for twice the price of a Chevy costs a lot less than twice as much to produce, manufacturers price high-end motherboards at a premium larger than the cost difference justifies. Still, if you want the best possible performance, there's no alternative to paying the price for an X58 motherboard.

Well, within reason. Although this is an extreme system, the budget wasn't unlimited. On that basis we ruled out the most expensive models, many of which were priced at $300 or more—for a bare motherboard—and one of which sold for $700! And that one wasn't even gold-plated. We also ruled out the cheesy models from second- and third-tier manufacturers, some of which were priced at $150 or less. A junk motherboard with a premium chipset is still a junk motherboard.

We decided to look for motherboards priced in the $200 to $300 range. We found more than a dozen models from first-tier manufacturers including ASUS, GIGABYTE, and Intel, most of which were near the upper end of our price range. We spent hours studying and comparing the detailed specifications of each of these boards on the manufacturers' websites, and concluded that most of the boards in the upper part of our price range had justified their higher prices by adding generally useless bells and whistles, such as USB 3.0 or SATA 6 Gb/s support.

Assuming all essential features are present, what matters to us—and what should matter to you—is performance, construction quality, and reliability. Performance is a given with any decent X58 motherboard: differences among these boards are so small that they can be ignored. The construction quality and reliability of any first-tier motherboard should be excellent, although Intel-branded boards have always had the edge in those respects.

At first glance, we almost ruled out the Intel DX58SO. That would have been a big mistake. Although it was on the low end of our price range, at first we were concerned that the DX58SO was a bit light on features compared to the other boards.

For example, the DX58SO has only four memory slots rather than the six slots present on the competing boards. Because the X58 supports triple-channel memory, the Intel board is limited to one triple-channel memory bank versus two banks on competing boards. In practice, that means almost nothing, as the Intel board can be equipped with 12 GB of memory operating in triple-channel mode. We're unlikely ever to need more than 12 GB of memory on this system, so the additional memory slots are of no real benefit.

This system will have six drives installed—an SSD boot/system drive, four hard drives, and an optical drive—so we need at least six SATA ports. That turns out not to be an issue, as all of the candidate motherboards provide at least six SATA ports. We'd also like at least two eSATA ports for connecting external hard drives, which we'll use for daily backups. The Intel DX58SO includes two eSATA ports, as do two or three of the competing boards, but most include only one. We didn't rule out any boards on that basis, as it's easy enough to add eSATA ports by installing a $15 expansion card. Still, it would be nice to have them on-board.

Most of the motherboards in this price range have three, four, five, or even six PCI Express x16 slots, while the DX58SO has only two. We really need only one PCI Express 2.0 x16 slot, for the video adapter, but we'd like to have two, just in case we ever decide to install dual video adapters in CrossFireX mode to run graphics-intensive games.

Brian Bilbrey Comments

Ha! About the only game you run is Solitaire. More likely, you'll use the video cards as fast math coprocessors, as you mentioned previously.

Brian Bilbrey Comments

A SATA 6 Gb/s motherboard can be awfully nice when paired with an SSD that has similar bandwidth, like the 256 GB Crucial RealSSD C300 2.5" SATA 6Gb/s.

Dual-Channel Versus Triple-Channel Memory

But what about performance? Dual-channel memory is faster than single-channel memory, so triple-channel memory must be faster still, right? Wrong.

We did detailed benchmark testing and found no real performance differences between triple-channel mode and dual-channel mode. Triple-channel mode won about half the time, but only by a couple of percentage points. Dual-channel mode won the rest of the time, but again only by a couple of percentage points. It really doesn't matter which mode you use.

What About SATA 6 Gb/s?

It has a higher number, so it's easy to assume that SATA 6 Gb/s must be better than SATA 3 Gb/s. But the fastest current hard drives can barely saturate an obsolescent SATA 1.5 Gb/s interface, let alone swamp the 270+ MB/s data rate of a SATA 3 Gb/s interface. Right now, only fast enterprise-class (i.e., very expensive) solid-state drives can saturate a SATA 3 Gb/s interface, so in practical terms SATA 3 Gb/s is sufficient for even an extreme desktop system. If the price of very fast SSDs suddenly plummets, you can always install a PCI Express SATA 6 Gb/s adapter.

What About USB 3.0?

When we built the project systems for this book, a few motherboards with USB 3.0 support were just becoming available. We decided not to make USB 3.0 a checklist item, and in fact gave a downcheck to motherboards that included USB 3.0. Why? Early implementations of what is destined to become a widespread standard are often deficient in their support for that standard, sometimes in subtle ways. The first motherboards with USB 1.0 support later showed incompatibilities with later USB 1.0 devices, as did the first USB 1.1 and USB 2.0 motherboards with later devices built to those standards. We have no reason to believe the same will not be true of early USB 3.0 motherboards.

Fortunately, there's no real disadvantage to buying a motherboard that lacks USB 3.0 support. USB 2.0 is more than fast enough for all of our USB devices. For high-data-rate applications like external hard drives or HD camcorders, we use eSATA or FireWire. As devices that require USB 3.0 become more common, so will $15 PCI Express USB 3.0 adapter cards that fully support the standard. When (or if) we need USB 3.0 support, we'll install one of these cards. We recommend that you do the same.

For most people, including us, anything more than two x16 slots is just marketing hype, since they'll never be used. It is important that both slots are electrically full x16, though, which often isn't the case. A PCI Express 2.0 slot may be x16 physically, but only x8, x4, or even x1 electrically. Both x16 slots in the DX58SO are x16 electrically, so either (or both) can support even the fastest video adapters.

Then there was the matter of communications ports. This system will have a ton of peripherals connected to it: one or two printers, at least one scanner, a webcam, USB speakers, an inexpensive headset for Skype, good headphones for listening to audio or watching videos without disturbing Barbara, a high-quality noise-canceling microphone for overdubbing audio tracks on our videos, a USB microscope camera, and a partridge in a pear tree. We'll also need free USB ports to connect our MP3 players, digital voice recorder, digital SLRs, and the USB flash drives we use for quick backups during the working day. Most of the motherboards we looked at included four, six, or eight USB 2.0 ports. The Intel DX58SO provides 12 USB 2.0 ports. Of course, it's easy enough to add USB ports by installing an adapter card, but again, it's nice to have as many as you need already on-board.

Finally, we wanted two IEEE-1394 (FireWire) ports to connect our camcorders. (We could get by with one port, but switching cables gets old fast.) Most of the motherboards in our price range provide one FireWire port, if any; the Intel DX58SO and two of the GIGABYTE models provide two. Once again, we could add FireWire ports by installing an adapter card, but the presence of two FireWire ports on the Intel board gave us yet another nudge in its direction.

We settled on the Intel DX58SO, but of course your own priorities may make one of the competing models a better choice for you. The Intel board was ideal for us because it's on the low end of our price range, provides every feature we wanted, and offers Intel's usual rock-solid reliability and compatibility.

In the same $200 to $225 range as the Intel DX58SO, the GIGABYTE GA-X58A-UD3R is an excellent choice, as are the ASUS P6T or P6T SE and the ASUS P6X58D. If you need a μATX board, choose the ASUS Rampage II GENE. If you're willing to spend closer to $300 on your motherboard, look at the ASUS P6T Deluxe, P6TD Deluxe, or P6X58D Premium, or the GIGABYTE GA-X58A-UD5. If you don't want to spend even $200 on the motherboard, the standout choice among less expensive X58 models is the ASRock X58 Extreme. For an AMD processor, use the ASUS M4A89TD PRO or the GIGABYTE GA-890FXA-UD5.

Processor

Intel Core i7-980X (*http://www.intel.com*)

For most systems, we give some thought to which processor is the best match for our needs and budget. For our extreme system, there really wasn't much to think about. We wanted the fastest desktop processor available, and that was the Intel Core i7-980X. With its high clock speed and six multithreaded cores, the Core i7-980X simply blew away every competing processor, as well it should, given its $1,000 price tag. The Core i7-980X is 60% faster than AMD's best, the Phenom II X6 1090T—which was almost impossible to actually buy when we built this system—and 50% faster than Intel's next-fastest model, the Core i7-970.

Although plunking down a grand just for the processor may sound ridiculous in this day of perfectly usable complete systems that sell for $500, what's really important isn't cost so much as cost/benefit ratio. Robert typically works 7-day, 60+-hour weeks, most of it spent in front of his main office system. The difference in cost between the Core i7-980X and a less capable processor amounts to less than a dollar a day over the expected lifetime of the system. If, say, rendering a video clip or compiling a program takes 30 seconds on the $1,000 Core i7-980X and twice that long on a $300 processor, that may seem a trivial difference. It's not. That's an extra 30 seconds that Robert has to sit twiddling his thumbs, waiting on the processor. Every time. Multiply that 30 seconds by many such events per day—often many such events per *hour*—and paying that extra dollar a day for the Core i7-980X starts to sound like a real bargain.

Of course, not everyone uses a computer as heavily, or for such processor-intensive tasks. A system doesn't need a $1,000 processor to qualify as extreme. High-performance processors start at around $250 to $300, including the slower quad-core Intel Core i7 models and the fastest hex-core AMD Phenom II X6 models. For that price, you'll get a processor that's half as fast as the Core i7-980X, but still noticeably faster than a mainstream processor.

Memory

Crucial Ballistix BL3KIT25664BN1608 PC3-12800 6 GB kit (2GB×3)
(*http://www.crucial.com*)

When determining memory requirements, it's important to remember that a hex-core processor like our Intel Core i7-980X is effectively six individual processors. Each of those processors needs as much memory as a single-core processor does. We consider 1 GB per core the sweet spot, so we decided to install at least 6 GB of memory in our hex-core extreme system.

Of course, each of the six cores in the Intel Core i7-980X can run two threads, so we might have decided to install 1 GB per thread, for a total of 12 GB of system memory. However, based on previous experience with Robert's earlier extreme system—a four-core Intel Core2 Quad Q9650 running 32-bit Linux, with only 3 GB of the 4 GB installed visible to the operating system—we decided that 6 GB of total memory would probably suffice, even running a 64-bit OS. Memory prices were very high when we built this system, so we decided to install 6 GB initially with the intention of upgrading that to 12 GB, if necessary, once memory prices had decreased.

The Intel DX58SO motherboard supports several different memory bank configurations, but the fastest of those requires installing three matched PC3-12800 memory modules in banks A, B, and C. Those modules can be 2 GB DIMMs, for a total of 6 GB, or 4 GB DIMMs, for a total of 12 GB. We chose a fast, low-latency 6 GB Crucial memory kit, because in the 20 years we've been using Crucial memory we've never had a problem with it.

XMP

eXtreme Memory Profile (XMP) is an Intel-developed extension to JEDEC memory standards that allows premium DDR3 memory to run at timings faster than standard JEDEC values. XMP essentially automates the formerly manual process of tweaking memory to run faster than its nominal speed. Using XMP requires XMP support in both the system BIOS and the memory modules themselves.

A standard memory module includes a Serial Presence Detect (SPD) ROM, from which the system BIOS can read recommended timings for that module. These standard timings are generally quite conservative, and therefore provide slower (but safer) memory performance data than the module is actually capable of providing. XMP-enabled memory modules use an unallocated area in the SPD ROM to store additional memory timing settings—designated "enthusiast" and "extreme"—that

yield higher memory performance at the risk of compromising system stability. Gamers, overclockers, and other performance enthusiasts often enable XMP on their systems for the minor performance advantage it provides.

The Intel DX58SO and the Crucial Ballistix memory modules we used in our extreme system both support XMP, but by default run with standard memory settings. If you want to enable XMP, run BIOS Setup, choose the Enthusiast or Extreme profile, ignore all the Intel warnings, save the settings, and restart the system.

In case you're curious, we run our extreme system with standard JEDEC timings. The small performance advantage of XMP is more than offset by the risk of reduced system stability, at least to our way of thinking.

Video Adapter

ASUS EAH4350 SILENT/DI/512MD2(LP) (*http://www.asus.com*)

Choosing a video adapter (or adapters) for an extreme system can be anything from very simple to very complicated indeed. If 3D graphics performance is unimportant—as it is for our extreme system—you can simply use integrated video or install an inexpensive video adapter. If 3D graphics performance is critical—as it is for a gaming system—you'll have some decisions and trade-offs to make.

Nearly all desktop 3D graphics adapters are based on a chipset (*graphics processor unit*, or GPU) from one of two companies, ATI or NVIDIA. Each of these companies produces many chipsets in a wide range of prices and performance levels. Numerous companies produce video adapters based on these chipsets, at prices ranging from $20 or so up to $750 or more. As you might expect, more expensive cards are faster. At the low and middle ranges, price correlates pretty well with performance. For example, an $80 video adapter is much faster than a $40 adapter, and a $160 adapter is much faster than the $80 adapter.

Above $150 or $200, you rapidly enter the realm of decreasing returns. A $300 adapter may be only 25% faster than a $150 adapter, and a $600 adapter may be only 10% faster than a $300 adapter. Even a $75 adapter is fast enough to play all but the most recent graphics-intensive games at reasonable frame rates, although you may have to use something less than maximum resolution and make other tweaks to get smooth game play.

Advances in video chipsets occur in Internet time. If you buy the fastest video adapter available today, it'll have midrange performance in 12 to 18 months and entry-level performance in two to three years. That's why many serious gamers replace their video adapters every six months. If you're serious about PC gaming, we recommend you do the same. Otherwise, just choose a video adapter that fits your needs and budget, and drive it until it drops.

Several years ago, when PC gaming was at its peak, both NVIDIA and ATI introduced support for yoking together multiple video adapters to provide higher graphics performance. NVIDIA's method, called *Scalable Link Interface* (SLI), and ATI's *CrossFireX* are similar in concept and implementation, but incompatible with each other. Either allows you to install multiple video adapters that function as one faster adapter.

Initially, these technologies were used by serious gamers to get higher video performance than even the fastest single adapter could provide. It was (and still is) commonplace for serious gamers to install two (or more) super-high-end video adapters in one system. The resulting video performance isn't quite twice as fast as that of a single super-high-end card, but it comes close.

Later, many gamers realized that they could beat the diminishing bang-for-the-buck ratio of very expensive video adapters. Rather than installing one $600 adapter, they'd install two $300 adapters, which together were much faster than the single $600 adapter. You can use that same strategy to get much higher graphics performance in a lower price range. For example, two $150 adapters will typically significantly outperform one $300 adapter, and even two $75 adapters will probably outperform one $150 adapter.

We won't recommend specific video adapter models here, again because video adapters change in Internet time. If you need high-end 3D graphics video performance, do some online research before you buy. There are numerous websites devoted to gaming hardware, but two we have found to be reliable are AnandTech (*http://www.anandtech.com*) and Tom's Hardware (*http://www.tomshardware.com*).

Of course, 3D graphics performance is unimportant for our particular extreme system, so none of this applies. We could even have used integrated video, except that most extreme motherboards, including ours, don't include integrated video. So we went off in search of an inexpensive but reliable video adapter.

Any of several candidates would probably have served as well, but we chose the ASUS EAH4350 SILENT/DI/512MD2(LP), which NewEgg had on sale for $29.99, with free shipping and a $10 mail-in rebate. Our net cost was $19.99 plus the cost of a stamp.

The RADEON HD 4350 chipset is no barn-burner nowadays, but it's more than fast enough for our purposes. This is a low-profile, passively cooled, silent video adapter that's targeted at the media center/home theater market, but it's also a good fit for our needs. The card includes 512 MB of DDR2 memory and has enough horsepower to render full 1080p video smoothly, which is the most we'll ever ask of it.

Sound Adapter

Integrated

Integrated audio on most modern motherboards is excellent, so much so that standalone sound adapters are almost never needed nowadays. Even most serious audiophiles and gamers find integrated audio acceptable, and the integrated Intel HD audio on the DX58SO motherboard is certainly more than good enough to suit nearly anyone's needs.

If you plan to use a 5.1, 6.1, or 7.1 speaker system for gaming and you need EAX audio support for positional audio with your games, install a Creative Sound Blaster X-Fi XtremeGamer (PCI interface) or Sound Blaster X-Fi Titanium (PCI Express interface). But before you buy any sound adapter, test the integrated audio to see if it suits your needs.

Boot/System Drive

Crucial CT128M225 128 GB SSD (*http://www.crucial.com*)

We wish we could use a solid-state boot/system drive in every system we build. In fact, we wish we could use SSDs exclusively. That day isn't here yet, but it's rapidly drawing nearer as SSD capacities continue to increase and prices continue to decline. For the time being, unless you have an unlimited budget, you'll have to use rotating drives for bulk data storage. But on an extreme system, we can afford to devote some of the budget to buying an SSD large enough to store our system, temporary, and working files.

We decided to allocate $300 to $400 of our budget to the SSD. That left us with a major decision to make: should we choose a *single-level cell* (SLC) SSD of smaller capacity or a *multi-level cell* (MLC) SSD of larger capacity? SLC drives are usually faster and degrade more slowly than MLC drives, but they also cost about four times as much for a given capacity.

When we built this system, $300 to $400 was enough to buy a 32 GB SLC SSD or a 128 GB MLC SSD. Although we'd obviously have preferred to use an SLC drive for its performance and durability, 32 GB was simply too small for what we wanted to do with the drive. The next step up, a 64 GB SLC drive, would have cost $600 to $800, which was simply too large a chunk of the budget to devote to the SSD. And even with 64 GB, we'd have been cramped for space.

So, we reluctantly decided to limit our candidates to MLC models and look for a drive in the 128 GB range. We found about two dozen drives that met our budget and capacity requirements, from manufacturers like Corsair, Crucial, Kingston, OCZ, and Western Digital. (The Intel X25-M would also have been a serious candidate, but unfortunately the 80 GB model was too small for our needs and the 160 GB model was too expensive.)

Based on our universally good experiences with Crucial products over many years, we chose the Crucial CT128M225 SSD. With sustained 250 MB/s reads and 190 MB/s writes, the M225 is one of the fastest drives in its class. It's large enough and fast enough to do what we need it to do, and it does so at a reasonable price.

Data Drives

Seagate Barracuda XT ST32000641AS 2TB (four) (*http://www.seagate.com*)

We've used and recommended Seagate hard drives for many years, and have never had cause to regret it. Seagate Barracuda-series drives are fast, extremely reliable, quiet, and reasonably priced.

Of course, we didn't actually decide on Seagate drives without considering competing models from other manufacturers. Of the few 2 TB 7,200 RPM SATA drive models available, we ruled out the Hitachi models immediately, despite their low price, based on their small caches and short warranties. That left only two candidates, the Western Digital Caviar Black and the Seagate Barracuda XT, both of which sell for the same price.

Western Digital recently went through a bad patch of several years' duration, during which we refused to use or recommend WD drives. In the last couple of years, the reliability of WD drives seems to have improved dramatically, and we've returned them to our recommended list. The Caviar Black models are louder and run hotter than similar Barracuda models, but have excellent performance.

One major reason the Caviar Black drives are so popular is the widespread perception that they outperform competing models by significant margins. In fact, our benchmark tests showed that the performance of the Caviar Black and Barracuda XT is very similar overall, with the Caviar Black winning some tests and the Barracuda XT others. In every case, the margin of victory was at most a few percentage points.

Given the identical prices and similar performance, we gave the nod to the quieter and cooler-running Seagate Barracuda XT. We decided to install four of them in our extreme system, for a total of 8 TB of rotating storage. We considered configuring these four drives in a RAID 3 array to maximize long-block sequential read performance—which is ideal for video editing—but that would have required buying an expensive hardware RAID controller and would have given us only 6 TB of visible disk space. Since we have the very fast SSD available to our video work files, the additional speed of the RAID 3 wasn't really needed.

Backup Hardware

SYBA SD-ENC50020 eSATA Dual SATA Hard Drive Docking Station

At first glance, it might seem impossible to maintain adequate backups of this system without spending a fortune on a high-end tape changer. With as much as 8,000+ GB of storage to be backed up, there aren't many options.

A full backup with a DVD burner would fill a couple of thousand DVD+R discs—at a cost of several hundred dollars just for the discs—and would take a week or so to complete, even burning discs 24/7. And that doesn't count the time or cost required to replace the DVD burner several times. Blu-ray would be no better. A full backup would require more than three hundred 25 GB BD-R discs—again at a cost of several hundred dollars—and by the time it finished, your expensive Blu-ray burner might be on its last legs.

Fortunately, our situation isn't as dire as it appears, because most of our data is already backed up on the source video tapes, flash memory cards, optical discs, and internal hard disks that our camcorders and digital SLRs use for primary data storage. Original camcorder tapes and optical discs are cheap, so they simply go directly into the fire safe. Images that were originally recorded to flash memory cards and internal camcorder hard drives—very expensive forms of storage—can be transferred to inexpensive standard hard drives and placed in the fire safe. That accounts for the vast bulk of that 8,000 GB of data.

That leaves us with a relatively small amount of data that requires routine daily backup—email, configuration files, working video editing files, and so on. Even when we're actively working on a video project, our daily backup sets are seldom larger than 50 GB, and often much less.

External hard drives are the fastest and least costly way to do those backups, and are nearly as reliable as tape changers that sell for the price of a good used car. Even if you have to buy drives specifically for backing up, the cost is reasonable. Standard 7,200 RPM 3.5" SATA hard drives sell for as little as five cents per gigabyte. And you may not need to buy them. This is a good way to use older, smaller hard drives that have been retired from older systems—as long as they're not *too* old. We actually use a collection of Seagate Barracuda hard drives of 500 GB, 1 TB, and 1.5 TB capacity.

Some people use commercial or homemade external hard drives for this purpose, but there's a better way. Our problem with external hard drives is that we want to take them with us when we leave the house, and that's awkward. Each time, we have to disconnect the power and data cables, and the external enclosures themselves are bulky enough that they don't fit comfortably in Robert's Lands' End canvas attaché. (Yes, it has to be said, Robert carries a *purse*; just hope he doesn't hit you with it.)

On his old main system, Robert used a pair of Antec MX-1 external USB hard drive enclosures. Getting tired of hauling around those enclosures, he eventually just removed the lids to convert them from external hard drive enclosures to hard drive docking stations. That way, he could simply pull the hard drives out of the frames and take just the drives along.

Fortunately, we found a better way. We came across the SYBA SD-ENC50020 eSATA Dual SATA Hard Drive Docking Station one day when we were on the NewEgg website looking for other components, and immediately ordered one. At $25 (and with free shipping that day), it was a no-brainer. The SYBA unit, shown in Figure 5-4, was designed from the ground up to do what we'd been doing as a kludge with the Antec units.

The ENC50020 has two bays that accept standard 2.5" or 3.5" SATA hard drives, which just slide in and out and can be clamped into place. The construction is mostly plastic, but the unit appears quite durable. It connects to the computer via two eSATA cables, which are long enough to allow the unit to sit on a desk and still reach the bottom expansion slot of a case sitting on the floor.

Because this unit uses native eSATA rather than the bridged eSATA used by most competing units, its performance is exceptional, as fast as an internal hard drive. We'd gotten used to the USB interfaces on the Antec MX-1 enclosures,

Figure 5-4. *SYBA SD-ENC50020 hard drive docking station*

which provided sustained write throughput of only 25 to 30 MB/s. For our first test of the SYBA eSATA unit, we timed the transfer of a 33 GB archive file at 5:42, which translates to about 95 MB/s. We used Seagate Barracuda 7200.12 drives both internally and externally, and this transfer rate is typical of those drives when used internally. From that, we concluded that the transfer rate to the external SYBA unit really is bound by the performance of the hard drives rather than the interface.

With throughput of about 6 GB/min or 360 GB/hour (less with older, slower drives), the SYBA unit is a reasonable backup solution even if your backup sets are in the terabyte range. It, or something very like it, is the only reasonably priced solution for high-capacity backup on a home system.

Optical Drive(s)

Sony Optiarc AD-7260S-0B DVD burner (*http://www.sony-optiarc.us*)

Every system needs at least a DVD burner, if only for loading software, casual duping of optical discs, and so on. We have no need of reading, let alone writing, Blu-ray discs on our extreme system, so a simple DVD burner is all we need.

The current crop of DVD burners are all about as good as you might expect for their price, which is to say mediocre at best. Compared to premium drives of years past, current optical drives have relatively poor burn quality and are not very durable. Still, what can one expect for $25? Even Plextor burners, which were once absolutely superb and burned discs of higher quality than commercial pressed discs, are a pale shadow of what they once were, despite their current premium pricing.

We've had the best experience recently with units made by ASUS, LiteOn, and Samsung, which we consider pretty much interchangeable. But, despite the fact that we swore off Sony products after the root-kit fiasco, we decided it was time to look at a Sony optical drive. The Sony Optiarc drives are produced as a joint venture between Sony and the optical drive division of NEC, which no longer brands its own optical drives. We'd always had good experiences with NEC optical drives, so we decided to order a Sony Optiarc unit and run it through its paces. Short take: the Sony Optiarc drive produces reasonable-quality burns—comparable to the ASUS, LiteOn, and Samsung drives—and appears to have similar durability. In other words, nothing special. If we had it to do over again, we'd probably just order an ASUS, LiteOn, or Samsung burner.

If you need to read Blu-ray discs, install a read-only BD-ROM drive in addition to the DVD burner. (You can buy a hybrid drive that reads Blu-ray discs and reads/writes DVDs, but most of them are expensive and you'll wear them out reading and writing DVDs.) The best choices among BD-ROM drives are the LiteOn iHOS104 and the ASUS BR-04B2T. If you seldom write DVDs and want a single hybrid drive, the standout bang-for-the-buck choice is the Samsung SH-B083L/BSBP combo drive, which costs only $5 or $10 more than BD-ROM drives and also includes DVD burning support.

If you also need to write Blu-ray discs, be prepared to spend some money. BD-R/RE drives are expensive, as are the discs. The drive choices are relatively limited, but we think the best BD-R/RE burner is the Pioneer BDR-205BKS.

Ron Morse Comments

The current Pioneer burners are nice, but overpriced compared to the competition. They do better burns than the LG and Samsung drives I have here. Are they worth the extra money? Probably not.

Keyboard and Mouse

Microsoft SideWinder X6 keyboard (*http://www.microsoft.com*)

Microsoft SideWinder mouse

As always, the choice of keyboard and mouse is extremely personal. What we love, you may hate, and vice versa. Over the years, we've tried wired and wireless keyboards and mice from literally dozens of manufacturers, but we keep coming back to Microsoft and Logitech products. Both provide a huge range of options, and both provide value for money, even in their inexpensive lines.

With our extreme system budgeted at $3,500, we decided we could afford to devote more than usual to the keyboard and mouse. We ended up choosing Microsoft SideWinder models, which are intended for gamers but also have many features that are nice for general use. For example, the detachable numeric keypad on the SideWinder X6 can be repurposed as a macro pad. Robert never uses the numeric keypad anyway, so being able to define dedicated macro keys is very useful. The SideWinder mouse is available in various models with different resolutions. High-resolution pointing is important in many games, but it can be just as important for general use, including video editing. Besides which, how many other mice have an LCD display?

Ron Morse Comments

I have to put in a plug for the guys at Unicomp, who still make and sell the classic IBM Model "M" keyboards (http://pckeyboards.stores.yahoo. net/keyboards.html). There is no substitute. If you're building the highest-quality computer possible, you should use the highest-quality keyboard available. The Model "M" lasts forever…mine was made in 1994.

Speakers

Logitech Z-523 40 W 2.1 Speaker System (*http://www.logitech.com*)

Our extreme system needs a decent set of speakers. The extreme system will sit on or under Robert's desk and he doesn't game, so he prefers a 2.1 speaker system. He'll actually use his existing Logitech Z3 speaker set on the new system, but the Z3 set is no longer available.

Fortunately, Logitech has replaced the Z3 with the Z-523 2.1 set, which sells for under $100 and has equally excellent sound quality. If you want a 2.1 set with top-notch sound but more output power, the standout choice is the 200W Logitech Z-2300, which sells for half again as much as the Z-523.

If you don't want or need a subwoofer, you can choose among many excellent 2.0 speaker sets. In the $60 range, the best choices are the Behringer MS16, the Creative Inspire T10, and the Logitech Z-320. In the $100 range, we like the Behringer MS20 and the M-AUDIO Studiophile AV 30 sets. In the $150 range, the M-AUDIO Studiophile AV 40 set is the best choice.

In 5.1 speaker systems, the 70W Logitech X-540 sells for well under $100 and has excellent sound for the price. If you want the best 5.1 speaker system available and can afford the $400 price tag, buy the Logitech Z-5500 set. With four 62W RMS satellite speakers, a 69W center-channel speaker, and a 188W subwoofer, the Z-5500 produces a wall-rattling 505W RMS. You don't just *hear* the bass, you *feel* the bass vibrating your internal organs. The Z-5500 is the leading high-end choice among serious gamers, but at lower volume it's also excellent for anything from listening to background music to playing DVDs.

Display

ASUS VW266H 25.5" LCD display (*http://www.asus.com*)

It's obviously impossible to recommend any particular display absolutely, because your needs and budget may be very different from ours. Fortunately, nowadays it's pretty difficult to get a bad LCD display, as long as you stick with good brand names and avoid the least expensive models.

We'll use this system heavily for video editing, and we'll soon be getting into HD video, so it's essential to have a display with at least 1080p (1920×1080) resolution. WUXGA (1920×1200) or even WQXGA (2560×1600) resolution would be better still, because that would allow us to view the HD video at full resolution while still having a bit of screen real estate available to view the timeline.

Unfortunately, the smallest and least expensive WQXGA displays are 30" and $1,200, both of which are bigger numbers than we're prepared to deal with. So we looked at WUXGA displays, hoping to find something suitable in the $300 to $400 range. We found half a dozen candidates from good manufacturers, ranging in size from 24" to 28".

If you want a really large display, the 28" Hanns.G HH-281HPB offers a huge screen, good display quality, and reasonable features at a bargain price. Samsung offers two 24" models, the 2433BW near the lower end of our price range, and the 2443BW at the top end. Both provide excellent display quality, and either would be an excellent choice for many people.

It's hard to choose just one display from such a great group, but we finally decided to recommend the ASUS VW266H for the extreme system. At just under 26", the VW266H will "feel" huge to nearly anyone who's not used to a large display. Despite its size, at a normal working distance the VW266H provides a sharp, crisp image. It's priced near the middle of our range, and to get a noticeably better display you'd have to spend two to three times as much.

Component Summary

Table 5-1 summarizes our component choices for the extreme system.

Table 5-1. *Bill of materials for extreme system*

Component	Product
Case	Antec Dark Fleet DF-85
Power supply	Antec CP-850 850W power supply
Motherboard	Intel Extreme Series DX58SO
Processor	Intel Core i7-980X
CPU cooler	(Bundled with processor)
Memory	Crucial Ballistix BL3KIT25664BN1608 PC3-12800 6 GB kit (2GB×3)
Video adapter	ASUS EAH4350 RADEON HD 4350 PCI Express 2.0 x16
Sound adapter	(Integrated)
Boot/system drive	Crucial CT128M225 128 GB SSD

Table 5-1. Bill of materials for extreme system

Component	Product
Data drives	Seagate Barracuda XT ST32000641AS 2TB (four)
Optical drive	Sony Optiarc AD-7260S-OB DVD burner
Keyboard	Microsoft SideWinder X6 keyboard
Mouse	Microsoft SideWinder mouse
Speakers	Logitech Z-2300 200 W 2.1 Speaker System
Display	(See text)

Building the Extreme System

Figure 5-5 shows the major components of the extreme system. In the background, the Antec DF-85 case on the left is flanked by the Antec CP-850 power supply, with the Microsoft SideWinder X6 keyboard atop it. At left center is a stack of four Seagate Barracuda XT 2 TB hard drives, with the Crucial Ballistix 6 GB memory kit and the Crucial CT128M225 128 GB solid-state drive to their right. At the center is the SYBA hard drive docking station, with the ASUS EAH4350 Silent video adapter atop it. To the far right is the Microsoft Side-Winder mouse. In the foreground, the Intel DX58SO motherboard in the center is flanked on the left by the Intel Core i7-980X processor and on the right by the massive Intel CPU cooler.

Sequencing the Build

Although by necessity we describe building the system in a particular order, you don't need to follow that exact sequence when you build your own system. Some steps—for example, installing the processor and memory before installing the motherboard in the case—should be taken in the sequence we describe, because doing otherwise makes the task more difficult or risks damaging a component. Other steps, such as installing the video adapter after you install the motherboard in the case, must be taken in the order we describe, because completing one step is a prerequisite for completing another. But the exact sequence doesn't matter for most steps. As you build your system, it will be obvious when sequence matters.

Figure 5-5. *Extreme system components, awaiting construction*

Before you start building the system, verify that all components are present and accounted for. We always remind readers to do that, but for some reason we often forget to do it ourselves. In fact, you may have noticed that we forgot the optical drive in Figure 5-5. (We soon located it on the dining room table, buried under a pile of detritus from a system build we'd just completed.)

Chapter 5

Preparing the Case

To begin preparing the DF-85 case, place it upright on the work surface and remove the four thumbscrews, two per side, that secure the side panels, as shown in Figure 5-6. Note the protective film covering the side panels. Leave this film in place until you finish the build.

Swing the rear of the left side panel away from the case, as shown in Figure 5-7, and lift it free. Place the side panel aside, where it won't be scratched. Remove the right side panel as well. The thumbscrews are not captive, so to avoid misplacing them it's a good idea to tape them to the side panels or reinsert them in the screw holes on the chassis until they're needed.

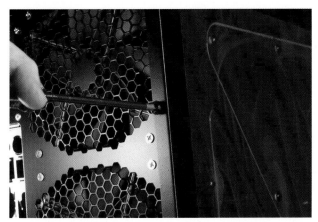

Figure 5-6. *Remove the thumbscrews that secure the side panels*

Figure 5-7. *Remove the side panels and set them aside*

The first thing you'll notice inside the case is a gigantic, inflexible wad of front-panel cables hanging down behind the drive bays, all bunched together by several twist-ties. That mess of cables will interfere with subsequent steps, so the first thing we did was remove the cable ties, as shown in Figure 5-8, straighten and sort the cables, and stuff them into a drive bay, as shown in Figure 5-9.

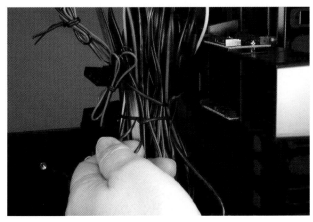

Figure 5-8. *Remove the twist ties that secure the cable bundle*

Figure 5-9. *Stuff the front-panel cables into a drive bay to get them out of the way for now*

The next step is to remove the stock I/O shield. To do so, use a tool handle to press in on the shield until it snaps out, as shown in Figure 5-10. You can discard or recycle the stock I/O shield.

Locate the custom I/O shield that was supplied with the motherboard. Verify that the I/O shield matches the motherboard rear-panel ports by aligning the I/O shield with the back-panel motherboard ports, as shown in Figure 5-11.

Figure 5-10. *Use a tool handle to snap out the stock I/O shield*

Figure 5-11. *Compare the custom I/O shield with the motherboard back-panel connectors*

Used Goods?

It doesn't happen often, but once or twice we've opened a shrink-wrapped box and found that the I/O shield in the box didn't match the motherboard. We can't believe the motherboard came from the factory that way. Our strong suspicion is that the vendor sold us used goods.

Motherboards are among the most commonly returned computer components. A less-than-honest vendor can simply re-shrinkwrap the returned board and sell it as new. If the original purchaser accidentally boxed up the motherboard with the generic I/O shield from the case instead of the I/O shield supplied by the motherboard, that explains how an incorrect I/O shield ended up in a sealed box.

When you unpack a motherboard, verify that the original seal is still present. If you find a broken or missing seal (and certainly if you find a mismatched I/O shield), we recommend returning the motherboard for refund or replacement.

Working from inside the case, orient the custom I/O shield properly and then press it until it snaps into place. Make sure that all four corners and edges are fully seated. I/O shields are made of thin metal with some sharp edges, so we generally use a tool handle, as shown in Figure 5-12. As you press on the I/O shield to seat it, apply counter-pressure with your fingers to the outside of the shield to avoid bending it.

With the I/O shield installed, the next step is to determine which positions require standoffs for the motherboard mounting screws. To do that, first hold the motherboard up to a bright light to count the number of mounting holes in the board. Then count the number of standoffs that are already installed in the case, if any. Lower the motherboard into position, as shown in Figure 5-13, and slide it into full contact with the I/O shield.

Figure 5-12. *Install the custom I/O shield supplied with the motherboard*

Figure 5-13. *Lower the motherboard into the case to determine which positions require stand-offs to be installed*

Look down through each motherboard mounting hole to determine if a standoff is already installed in the corresponding position. (Don't confuse CPU cooler mounting holes with motherboard mounting holes; our motherboard had four CPU cooler mounting holes.) Take note of how many and which of the preinstalled standoffs are in the proper positions, which positions have a standoff installed but no corresponding mounting hole, and which positions require a standoff to be installed.

In our case, the Antec DF-85 had six standoffs preinstalled, all of which corresponded to mounting holes in the motherboard. The motherboard has 10 mounting holes, so we needed to install four more standoffs. We counted out four standoffs from the parts bag, and installed them.

You can install standoffs with your fingers or by using a 5 mm nut driver, as shown in Figure 5-14. If you use a nut driver, be very careful not to overtorque the standoffs. They're made of soft brass and the motherboard tray is made of thin steel, so it's very easy to strip the threads by overtorquing. Just finger-tight plus perhaps a quarter turn is sufficient.

Measure Twice, Cut Once

Before you proceed, make absolutely certain that no "extra" standoffs are installed. That is, no standoff should be installed that doesn't correspond to a motherboard mounting hole. An extra standoff may contact the bottom of the motherboard, causing a short circuit. If this happens, at best the system may not boot. At worst, the short circuit may damage the motherboard or other components.

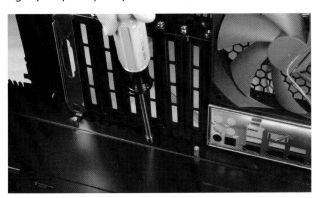

Figure 5-14. *Install standoffs at all required positions*

Installing the Power Supply

The next step is to install the power supply. We used an oversized Antec CPX form factor power supply. If you're using the Antec DF-85 case but with a standard ATX power supply, disregard the steps in this section that describe removing the ATX adapter plate.

To begin, remove the ATX adapter plate by removing the four screws that secure it, as shown in Figure 5-15.

Once you've removed the four screws, press in on the adapter plate until it releases and lift it free of the case, as shown in Figure 5-16.

Do not discard the ATX adapter plate. If you ever need to replace the power supply with an ATX unit, you'll need the adapter plate. We recommend taping the four screws to the adapter plate, as shown in Figure 5-17, and taping the adapter plate itself to the top of the power supply. The power supply will become warm while running, so we recommend using a heat-resistant tape. (We later replaced the transparent tape shown in Figure 5-17 with heat-resistant duct tape.) Tape the plate securely to prevent vibration.

The Antec CP-850 is a modular power supply. The following cables are permanently connected to the power supply:

- 1 24-pin (20+4) main ATX power cable
- 1 four-pin ATX12V (CPU) power cable
- 1 eight-pin EPS12V (CPU) power cable
- 2 eight-pin (6+2) PCI Express power cables
- 1 3xMolex + 1xFloppy drive power cable
- 1 3xSATA drive power cable

You can also connect up to four optional cables to the four jacks on the power supply. The six optional cables included with the power supply are:

- 2 six-pin single PCI Express power cables
- 2 3xMolex drive power cables
- 2 3xSATA drive power cables

This modularity allows you to connect only the cables you need, avoiding a tangle of unused cables, and also allows you to mix and match cables. For example, if (as in our system) you plan to install many hard drives but have no need of extra PCI Express power cables for multiple high-end video adapters, you can use all four of the available jacks to connect SATA drive power cables. (Only two such cables are included, but more can be purchased separately from Antec.)

Choose the optional power cables you need, and press the plug on each cable into one of the jacks on the power supply, as shown in Figure 5-18.

Once you've connected the optional cables you need, slide the power supply into the case, as shown in Figure 5-19.

Figure 5-15. *Remove the four screws that secure the ATX adapter plate*

Figure 5-16. *Remove the ATX adapter plate and set it aside*

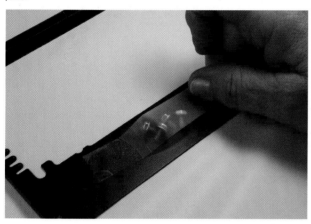

Figure 5-17. *Tape the screws to the ATX adapter plate and store them for possible later use*

Figure 5-18. *Connect the modular cables you need to the power supply jacks*

Finally, secure the power supply with the four provided screws, as shown in Figure 5-20.

Figure 5-19. *Slide the power supply into position*

Figure 5-20. *Secure the power supply to the chassis with the four provided screws*

Populating the Motherboard

It is always easier to populate the motherboard—i.e., install the processor and memory—while the motherboard is outside the case. In fact, sometimes you must do so, because installing the CPU cooler requires access to both sides of the motherboard. (Some cases, including the Antec DF-85, have a CPU cutout in the motherboard tray that gives access to the CPU cooler area on the bottom of the motherboard. With one of these cases, you can swap out the processor or replace the CPU cooler without removing the motherboard.)

Even if it is possible to populate the motherboard while it is installed in the case, we always recommend doing so with the motherboard outside the case and lying flat on the work surface. More than once, we've tried to save a few minutes by replacing the processor without removing the motherboard. Too often, the result has been a damaged motherboard and/or processor. (Most recently, Robert managed to pull out the CPU by its pins while attempting to remove the CPU cooler in Barbara's sister's old system. We ended up replacing that system with the budget system described earlier in this book.)

Installing the processor

First, and we can't emphasize this enough—particularly if you're installing a $1,000 processor—**always ground yourself** before touching the processor, motherboard, or other static-sensitive components. You can do that just by touching an exposed metal surface of the power supply or the case chassis. Even if the system is not plugged into a wall receptacle, the metal mass of the power supply and chassis provides an adequate sink to dissipate any static charge.

To begin, open the socket lever by pressing it down and away from the latch, as shown in Figure 5-21. The tension is quite high, so you have to apply significant pressure to release the lever.

Raise the socket lever to the fully vertical position, as shown in Figure 5-22.

Figure 5-21. *Open the socket lever by pressing it down and sliding it out from under the latch*

Figure 5-22. *Raise the socket lever to the fully vertical position*

Chapter 5

Lift the load plate to the fully open position, as shown in Figure 5-23.

Remove the black plastic socket cover from the socket by grasping the cover with your thumb and forefinger and pulling it out of the socket, as shown in Figure 5-24. With the cover removed, the fragile socket contacts are exposed. Do not touch the contacts or allow anything other than the processor to contact them. Store the socket cover for possible future use. If you ever remove the processor from the socket, always reinstall the socket cover immediately.

Figure 5-23. *Lift the load plate to the fully open position*

Figure 5-24. *Remove the socket cover*

Once again, ground yourself. (It does no harm to ground yourself frequently. Better too often than too seldom.) Open the processor box and locate the processor. Carefully open the hard plastic shell that contains the processor. Ground yourself again. Remove the processor from the shell and snap off the plastic cover on the pin side of the processor. Retain that cover for possible future use.

Hold the processor body between your thumb and forefinger, as shown in Figure 5-25. Locate the two notches in the processor circuit board (visible on the upper left and right edges of the processor circuit board in Figure 5-25) and the two corresponding posts on the inner edge of the processor socket. Align the processor over the socket, making sure the keying notches on the processor align with the posts in the socket. Bring the processor close to the socket and lower it straight down without tilting or sliding it in the socket. The processor should seat completely in the socket without any pressure whatsoever. If it does not, lift it gently, realign it, and drop it gently into the socket.

Lower the load plate back into closed position, as shown in Figure 5-26.

Press down on the load plate with one hand while you use the other to close and latch the processor lever, as shown in Figure 5-27. (Barbara moved her finger from the load plate for visibility in this image.) Make sure the cammed rod at the front of the socket engages the tab on the front of the load plate.

The surface of the processor should be completely clean. If there are any fingerprints, dust, skin oil, or similar contaminants on the processor surface, use a clean paper towel to polish the surface, as shown in Figure 5-28.

Figure 5-25. *Align the processor with the socket and drop it gently into place*

Figure 5-26. *Lower the load plate into closed position*

Figure 5-27. *Press the socket lever down and into locked position under the latching hook*

Figure 5-28. *If necessary, use a clean paper towel to polish the processor surface and remove contaminants*

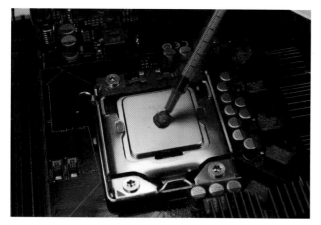

Figure 5-29. *Squirt the contents of the thermal compound syringe onto the center of the processor surface*

Intel provides a syringe with a premeasured amount of Dow thermal compound. Remove the cover from the tip of the syringe, place the tip at the center of the processor, and expel the entire contents of the syringe onto the processor surface, as shown in Figure 5-29.

If you ever replace the processor or CPU cooler, do not reuse the existing thermal compound. Remove the old thermal compound from the processor surface and heatsink base, and polish them clean. If the old thermal compound is tenacious, you can use a hair dryer to warm it slightly and rub it off. Replace it with new thermal compound. We use Antec Silver thermal compound, but any approved thermal compound will do.

Installing the CPU cooler

The stock Intel DBX-B CPU cooler supplied with the Core i7-980X processor is huge. With maximum power dissipation of 130W, it has to be. Because of its size and weight, this CPU cooler requires a supporting bracket on the underside of the motherboard. (If you use a different processor, the stock CPU cooler may mount via locking posts that don't require the support bracket.)

To begin installing the CPU cooler, loosen the four captive thumbscrews that secure it to the support bracket, as shown in Figure 5-30.

Remove the support bracket and set it aside for now. Invert the CPU cooler and peel off the protective plastic film that covers the heatsink base, as shown in Figure 5-31.

Figure 5-30. *Loosen the four captive thumbscrews that secure the CPU cooler to the support bracket*

Figure 5-31. *Peel off the protective plastic film that covers the heatsink base*

Lift the edge of the motherboard nearest the CPU socket, and slide the support bracket under the motherboard. Position it so that all four of the threaded hubs protrude though the mounting holes surrounding the processor socket. Carefully lower the motherboard and verify that all four of the threaded hubs are visible in the mounting holes. Position the CPU cooler over the threaded hubs, with each captive thumbscrew resting on a hub. Press down on each captive thumbscrew and tighten it, as shown in Figure 5-32. The thumbscrews are spring-loaded, so finger-tight is sufficient to secure them.

The last step is to connect the CPU fan power cable to the CPU fan power header pins on the motherboard, which are located near the rear-panel I/O connectors. Align the keyed cable connector with the keyed motherboard connector, and press the cable connector down until it fully seats on the motherboard header pins, as shown in Figure 5-33.

Figure 5-32. *Position the CPU cooler over the four threaded hubs in the support bracket and tighten the four thumbscrews to secure it*

Figure 5-33. *Connect the CPU fan power cable to the CPU fan power header pins*

Figure 5-34. *Set the CPU fan speed*

The stock Intel CPU fan has a tiny switch, shown in Figure 5-34. By default, this switch is set to Q (for quiet). With the switch in the P (for Performance) position, the CPU fan runs faster (and louder).

We didn't want to take any chances with a $1,000 processor, so we started testing with the switch in the P position. At idle, the indicated CPU temperature was 31° C (~88° F) with the switch set to P, and 32° C (~90° F) with it set to Q. Under full load, the CPU temperature was 61° C (~142° F) with the switch on P, and 67° C (~153° F) with it on Q. Those temperature differences are relatively insignificant, but the difference in fan noise was very noticeable. We suggest you try it both ways. If the noise doesn't bother you with the fan set to Performance mode, use it. Otherwise, you don't give up all that much cooling efficiency by going to Quiet mode.

Aftermarket Coolers?

Recent Intel stock coolers are generally quite good. They're usually not quite as efficient or as quiet as the best aftermarket coolers, but they're also usually not far behind. So we were curious to see how the stock Intel DBX-B cooler compared to a top-notch aftermarket cooler, the Thermalright Ultra-120 eXtreme.

As it turns out, Intel outdid itself with the DBX-B cooler. The Ultra-120 eXtreme beat the DBX-B cooler, but not by enough to justify its $60 price tag. At idle, the system actually reported that the Intel cooler won by one degree. (Idle temperatures reported by motherboard sensors are notoriously unreliable, so about the most we can conclude from this data is that either cooler does an excellent job of cooling the CPU under light loads.) At full load, the reported CPU temperature with the Thermalright cooler was 58° C (136.4° F), only three degrees cooler than the DBX-B managed.

Usually, you give something up by using the stock cooler from a retail-boxed processor. In this case, Intel's stock cooler proved to be a match for first-rate aftermarket coolers—and a lot less expensive.

Chapter 5

Installing memory

The next step is to install the memory modules. Once again, ground yourself to the power supply or chassis each time before you touch the motherboard or a memory module.

The Intel DX58SO motherboard has four memory sockets that accept 240-pin DDR3 memory modules (DIMMs). The black memory socket (nearest the processor) is Channel A, DIMM 1. Moving toward the front edge of the motherboard, the three blue sockets are Channel A, DIMM 0, Channel B, and Channel C, respectively.

If you have a set of three memory modules that are identical in speed and capacity, install them in the three blue memory slots. If you have two matched modules, install them in memory slots B and C. If you have only one memory module, install it in slot C.

To install a memory module, first ground yourself by touching the power supply or case chassis. Swing the pivoting latches open on both ends of the memory socket(s) you intend to use. Remove the module from its packaging, and position it as shown in Figure 5-35 with both edges of the module aligned with the slots in the memory socket.

Memory modules and sockets are keyed with a notch in the contact (bottom) edge of the memory module and a matching nub in the socket that prevent a memory module from being installed backward. Verify that the key is aligned properly on the module and socket, and then use both thumbs to press down firmly on the module, as shown in Figure 5-36, until the module seats completely in the socket.

Figure 5-35. *Align the memory module with the socket*

Figure 5-36. *Press down firmly to seat the memory module in the socket*

As the memory module seats in the socket, the pivoting latches at both ends of the socket should swing back up into the latched position, engaging the slots in the center of the edges of the module, as shown in Figure 5-37. If the pivoting latches don't move into latched position on their own, move them into place manually. (Note that the latch on the rear module in Figure 5-36 did not engage. We subsequently latched that one manually.)

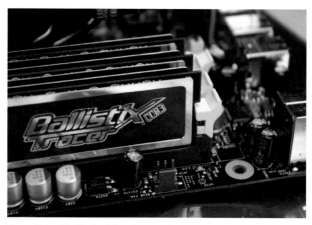

Figure 5-37. *Verify that the pivoting latches have locked each memory module into place*

Installing the Motherboard

Installing the motherboard is the most time-consuming step in building the system because there are so many cables to connect. It's important to get all of them connected right, so take your time and verify each connection before and after you make it.

Connecting drive cables

We'll install six drives in this system—the SSD boot drive on SATA port 0, four hard drives on SATA 1 through SATA 4, and an optical drive on SATA 5. The SSD will be installed in the removable drive bay, which has a captive black SATA data cable. We found a silver metallic SATA data cable to use with the optical drive. That leaves us with four standard red SATA data cables for the hard drives.

As you're building a system, it's pretty easy to determine which drive is connected to which port. After the cables are dressed, it's a lot less obvious. So, for example, if at some point our disk monitoring software tells us that the hard drive connected to SATA port 3 is failing, figuring out which physical drive needs to be replaced can be nontrivial.

The easy way to avoid having to tear down the system to figure out which drive is which is to label the SATA data cables, as shown in Figure 5-38. Use a felt-tip pen to draw lines on both sides of both ends of each SATA cable.

The SATA ports on most motherboards are vertical. The SATA ports on the Intel DX58SO motherboard are horizontal, facing the front of the board, so we decided it would be easier to connect the SATA data cables to the motherboard before installing the motherboard in the case. Connect the optical drive data cable and the four hard drive data cables, as shown in Figure 5-39.

Figure 5-38. *Labeling a SATA data cable that will connect to SATA port 2*

Figure 5-39. *Connecting the SATA data cables to the motherboard*

The SATA data cable for the 2.5" removable drive bay is a captive cable with a black sheath and connector. Locate it among the bundle of front-panel cables at the top front of the case, and connect it to SATA port 0, as shown in Figure 5-40.

Seating and securing the motherboard

To begin, slide the motherboard into the case, as shown in Figure 5-41. Carefully align the back-panel I/O connectors with the corresponding holes in the I/O template, and slide the motherboard toward the rear of the case until the motherboard mounting holes line up with the standoffs you installed earlier.

Figure 5-40. *Connect the captive black SATA data cable from the top 2.5" removable drive bay*

Figure 5-41. *Slide the motherboard into position, making sure the back-panel I/O connectors align with the holes in the I/O shield*

It's helpful to keep the front edge of the motherboard slightly raised as you slide the motherboard into position. As the back-panel I/O connectors on the motherboard come into contact with the back-panel I/O template, lower the

---

Chicken and Egg

It may be easier to connect the front-panel switch/indicator and port cables before you install the motherboard in the case. The trade-off is that if you install the motherboard first, you have plenty of cable length, but the pins you must connect those cables to are deep in the case and hard to get to. If you install the cables first, the pins are more easily accessible, but you have very little cable slack to work with, both when you connect the cables and when you slide the motherboard into the case. We generally install the motherboard first and worry later about getting all the cables connected.

---

front edge of the motherboard until it is level and then press gently to seat the back-panel ports in the template. In theory, at least, this prevents the metal grounding tabs on the I/O template from intruding into the ports.

Before you secure the motherboard, verify that the back-panel I/O connectors mate properly with the I/O template. Make sure none of the grounding tabs intrude into a port connector. An errant tab at best blocks the port, rendering it unusable, and at worst may short out the motherboard.

Less Is More (or Less)

When you install motherboard mounting screws, you're also putting torque on the standoffs. Tighten the motherboard screws gently, using a standard screwdriver. When you feel tension, stop turning the driver. If you overtorque the mounting screws, you're also overtorquing the standoffs, which may strip. Particularly if you're using an aluminum case, don't even think about using a power screwdriver.

After you position the motherboard and verify that the back-panel I/O connectors mate cleanly with the I/O template, insert a screw through one mounting hole into the corresponding standoff. You may need to apply pressure to keep the motherboard positioned properly until you have inserted two or three screws.

If you have trouble getting all the holes and standoffs aligned, insert two screws but don't tighten them completely. Use one hand to press the motherboard into alignment, with all holes matching the standoffs. Then insert one or two more screws and tighten them completely. Finish mounting the motherboard by inserting screws into all the standoffs and tightening them, as shown in Figure 5-42.

After you install all of the mounting screws, do a final check to ensure that none of the rear-panel I/O ports are fouled by grounding tabs on the I/O shield, as shown in Figure 5-43.

Figure 5-42. *Secure the motherboard by driving screws through the mounting holes into the standoffs*

Figure 5-43. *Verify that none of the back-panel I/O ports are fouled by the grounding tabs on the I/O shield*

At this point, you can clear up the cable clutter a bit by routing the free ends of SATA data cables 1 through 5 through the access cutout to the underside of the motherboard tray. We'll fish them back through other cutouts when we connect the drives.

Connecting power to the motherboard

The next step is to connect the main and supplemental power cables to the motherboard. To begin, locate the 24-pin main ATX power cable in the bundle coming out of the power supply. Route it out the right side of the chassis and then pass it back into the motherboard chamber via the cutout nearest the main ATX power connector on the front edge of the motherboard. The cable connector is keyed to the motherboard jack by a combination of square and rounded holes for each of the 24 pins. Orient the connector with the keys aligned and press the cable connector down firmly until it seats in the motherboard jack, as shown in Figure 5-44. Verify that the latch on the cable connector snaps into place over the tab on the side of the motherboard jack.

Most motherboards use the four-pin ATX12V connector to provide supplemental 12VDC current to the processor socket. Some motherboards that accept high-current processors, including the DX58SO, substitute the eight-pin EPS12V connector, which can provide twice as much 12VDC current and is really just two ATX12V connectors side by side.

Some power supplies, including the CP-850 we're using, provide both ATX12V and EPS12V connectors. Others do not provide an EPS12V connector, but provide two ATX12V connectors, which can both be plugged into a motherboard EPS12V connector to provide the necessary current. If your power supply provides only one ATX12V connector, it cannot be used with a motherboard that requires an EPS12V cable.

Locate the EPS12V cable in the bundle of cables coming out of the power supply. Route it out through the right side of the case and back into the motherboard chamber through the same cutout you used for the 24-pin main ATX power cable. The EPS12V motherboard jack and EPS12V cable connector are keyed. Align the keys properly and press the cable connector down firmly until it seats in the motherboard jack, as shown in Figure 5-45. Verify that the latch on the cable connector snaps into locked position over the tab on the side of the motherboard jack.

Figure 5-44. *Align the main ATX power cable connector with the motherboard jack and press down until it seats completely*

Figure 5-45. *Align the EPS12V power cable connector with the motherboard jack and press down until it seats completely*

Connecting front-panel ports, switches, and indicators

The next step is to connect the front-panel ports, switches, and indicators. Figure 5-46 shows the front-panel connector positions on the DX58SO motherboard.

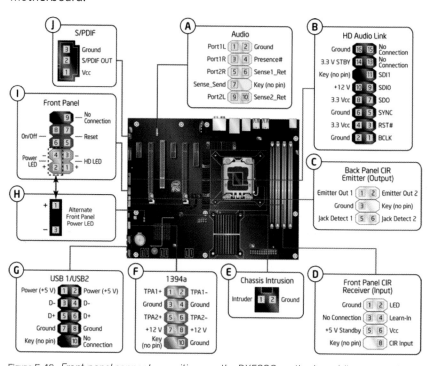

Figure 5-46. Front-panel connector positions on the DX58SO motherboard (image courtesy of Intel Corporation)

Note that the type and number of front-panel ports on a case seldom corresponds to the front-panel connectors available on a motherboard. For example, the DF-85 case provides three front-panel USB 2.0 ports, while the DX58SO motherboard provides six internal USB 2.0 connectors. The DX58SO also provides internal connectors for a front-panel FireWire and an IR emitter, for which the DF-85 has no front-panel ports. Conversely, the DF-85 provides a front-panel USB 3.0 port, for which the DX58SO provides no connector.

To begin connecting front-panel cables, locate the front-panel audio cable in the bundle of cables at the top front of the DF-85 case. That cable is double-ended, with connecting blocks for both HD audio and AC'97 audio. Locate the HD audio header-pin set on the DX58SO motherboard, near the expansion slot covers. That cable connector and the header-pin set are keyed with a blocked hole and missing pin, respectively. Orient the cable connector so that the missing pin and blocked hole are aligned, and then press the cable connector firmly onto the header-pin set, as shown in Figure 5-47.

The Intel DX58SO motherboard provides three internal USB 2.0 header-pin sets, each of which supports two USB 2.0 ports. The DF-85 case has three front-panel USB 2.0 ports, which connect to the motherboard via two USB 2.0 cables, one with a two-port 10-pin (2X5) connector and the other with a one-port 5-pin (1X5) connector.

Locate the dual-port USB 2.0 cable in the bundle of front-panel cables coming from the top front of the DF-85 case. Route that cable to one of the USB 2.0 header-pin sets on the motherboard. Orient the cable connector so that the blocked hole in the connector corresponds to the missing pin in the motherboard header-pin set. Press the cable connector onto the header pins until it seats completely, as shown in Figure 5-48.

Figure 5-47. *Connect the front-panel HD audio cable to the motherboard*

Figure 5-48. *Attach the front-panel dual-port USB 2.0 cable to a motherboard USB 2.0 header-pin set*

Locate the single-port USB 2.0 cable in the bundle of front-panel cables. Route that cable to a second motherboard USB 2.0 header-pin set. Orient the cable connector so that the blocked hole in the connector corresponds to the missing pin in the motherboard header-pin set. Press the cable connector onto the header pins until it seats completely, as shown in Figure 5-49.

The next step is to connect the power switch, reset switch, and hard drive activity LED, as shown in Figure 5-50. The two switches are not polarized and may be connected in either orientation. The HDD LED cable connector is polarized, with the black wire as ground and the red wire as positive. Orient the cable connector with the red wire corresponding to the HDD+ pin.

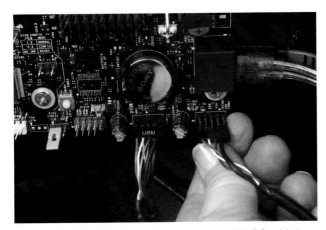

Figure 5-49. *Attach the front-panel single-port USB 2.0 cable to a motherboard USB 2.0 header-pin set*

Figure 5-50. *Connect the power switch, reset switch, and HDD LED cables*

Installing the Hard Drive(s)

The next step is to install the hard drives. The exact procedure for doing so differs according to the number of hard drives you are installing, which drive bays you install them in, and whether or not you want the hard drives to be hot-swappable.

The DF-85 case has three 3.5" hard drive cages, each of which has three drive bays, for a total of nine 3.5" hard drive bays. The DF-85 includes two Fleet-Swap brackets, each of which converts two adjacent standard drive bays to hot-swappable drive bays.

By default, the two Fleet-Swap brackets are installed in the top and bottom drive cages, but you can reposition them anywhere in the nine-bay hard drive area. To do so, remove the two screws that secure the Fleet-Swap bracket, as shown in Figure 5-51, and slide the Fleet-Swap bracket toward the side opposite those screws until it unhooks. Then lift it out.

The remaining five 3.5" hard drive bays function as standard nonremovable drive bays. Since we are installing four hard drives and the two Fleet-Swap brackets provide positions for four drives, we decided to use the Fleet-Swap brackets for all of our hard drives, thereby making them removable and hot-swappable.

Before we started installing hard drives, we decided to do something about the clutter of SATA data cables that was obstructing the rear of the hard drive bays. We fed the free end of each of the five non-captive SATA data cables through the cutout adjacent to the motherboard SATA ports, as shown in Figure 5-52. As we install the drives, we'll feed only as much cable as needed to reach the drive back through a cutout, leaving the excess cable length on the cable management area on the right side of the case.

> **Really Hot Swapping**
>
> *If you intend to hot-swap drives, don't forget to enable AHCI in BIOS Setup. Otherwise, you may corrupt data on the drives.*

Figure 5-51. *Removing a Fleet-Swap drive bracket*

Figure 5-52. *Route the SATA data cables through the cutout to the rear side of the motherboard tray*

Each of the three hard drive cages is covered by a swinging door that can be latched and unlatched by applying finger pressure to the left side of the door. There is also a locking lever inside the case, about midway up the left edge of the front bezel. When this locking lever is in the locked (down) position, the drive bay doors cannot be opened. To begin installing the hard drives, locate the locking lever and slide it up to the unlocked position, as shown in Figure 5-53.

With the locking lever in the unlocked position, press on the left edge of a drive bay door to release the latch and then swing the door open, as shown in Figure 5-54.

Figure 5-53. *Slide the drive bay door locking lever up to the unlocked position*

Figure 5-54. *Unlatch the drive bay door by pressing in on the left side, and then swing the door open*

The hard drives simply slide into position in the bays, where they are retained by spring tension and the closed drive bay door. Optionally, you can drive four screws directly through the sheet metal of the drive cage to secure the drive permanently, whether or not that drive connects to a Fleet-Swap bracket. (Obviously, if you secure a drive in a Fleet-Sway bay to the chassis with screws, it will no longer be removable.) Figure 5-55 shows Barbara sliding a hard drive into position, where it will mate with the Fleet-Swap bracket connectors visible behind the drive.

After you've installed the drive or drives in a drive cage, close and latch the drive bay door, as shown in Figure 5-56. If you want the hard drives to be removable, leave the drive bay cover locking lever in the upper position. Otherwise, you can slide it down to lock the drive bay covers.

The next step is to connect power to the hard drive(s). To do so, route a SATA power cable from the power supply chamber out through the right side of the case and then back into the motherboard chamber through an access cutout close to the rear of the drives.

We were able to power two hard drives in the top two bays and the optical drive from one three-position SATA power cable, although it was a very tight fit, as shown in Figure 5-57. If the hard drives had been mounted in a standard bay rather than a Fleet-Swap bay, we'd have had to allocate a separate power cable to the optical drive.

Continue routing SATA power cables and connecting them to drives until all of your hard drives have power. Then locate the SATA data cables in the mess of cables on the right side of the case, and feed them back through the access holes near the drives. Connect each SATA data cable to the corresponding hard drive, as shown in Figure 5-58.

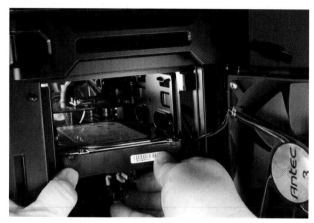

Figure 5-55. *Slide the hard drive into the drive bay*

Figure 5-56. *Close and latch the drive bay door*

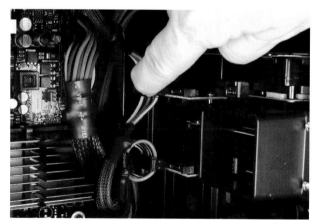

Figure 5-57. *Connect a SATA power cable to the power connector on the Fleet-Swap bracket*

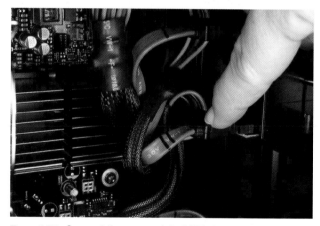

Figure 5-58. *Connect the appropriate SATA data cable to each of the hard drives*

Installing the Optical Drive

The next step is to install the optical drive in one of the 5.25" external drive bays at the top of the DF-85 case. Each of those is covered by a swinging door that looks like an open-end wrench. (We love it.) To begin, press in on the left side of the top door to release the catch and then swing the door open, as shown in Figure 5-59.

Working from inside the case, use your fingers or the end of a screwdriver to press out on the plastic drive bay bezel until it snaps out, as shown in Figure 5-60.

Figure 5-59. *Press in on the left side to release the catch, and then swing open the door covering the top 5.25" drive bay*

Figure 5-60. *Snap out the plastic drive bezel*

We intended to install our DVD writer in the top drive bay, but when we attempted to slide the drive into the bay we found that it was obstructed by the cables that feed the removable 2.5" drive bay on top of the case. Although we could have crammed the drive into that top bay, we decided to leave that bay unused and install our optical drive in the middle bay.

To remove the steel RF shielding plate from the middle drive bay, insert a screwdriver and twist the plate back and forth, as shown in Figure 5-61, until it snaps free. Be careful of the sharp burrs left on either side of the drive bay.

With the RF shielding plate removed, slide the optical drive into the bay, as shown in Figure 5-62.

Secure the optical drive with at least four screws, two per side, as shown in Figure 5-63.

We used the third SATA power connector from the cable we connected to the hard drives in the top two bays. If necessary, run a SATA power cable from the power supply chamber outside and along the right side of the case and up to the top drive bay area, and pass it into the main chamber through an access cutout near the optical drive. Align the L-shaped key on the power cable connector with the mating key on the drive power connector, and press the power cable connector firmly onto the drive connector, as shown in Figure 5-64.

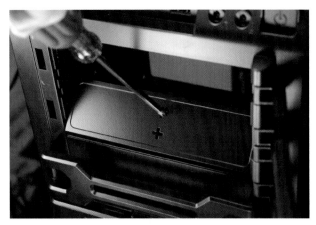

Figure 5-61. *Use a screwdriver to work the steel RF shielding plate back and forth until it snaps out*

Figure 5-62. *Slide the optical drive into the bay*

Figure 5-63. *Secure the optical drive with at least two screws per side*

Figure 5-64. *Connect power to the optical drive*

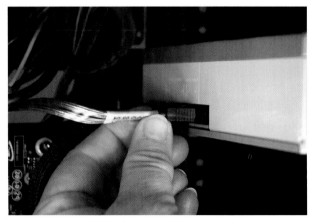

Figure 5-65. *Connect the SATA data cable to the optical drive*

Locate the free end of the SATA data cable for the optical drive in the mess of cables on the right side of the case, and route the connector end back into the main compartment through an access cutout near the optical drive. Align the L-shaped keys on the power cable connector and the drive connector, and press the data connector into place, as shown in Figure 5-65.

Installing the SSD Boot Drive

The next step is to install the SSD boot drive, which really just means sliding it into the 2.5" removable drive bay on top of the system. When we shot Figure 5-66, Robert had partially inserted the Crucial SSD into the drive bay and told Barbara to go ahead and slide it into place. Fortunately, Barbara is more observant than Robert. She noticed that the SATA connectors on the back of the drive and in the drive bay were not aligned.

So, as unintuitive as it seems, the Crucial SSD goes into the drive bay with the label facing down. Slide the drive partway into the drive bay, as shown in Figure 5-67. Make sure the SATA data and power connectors line up properly, and then slide the drive all the way into the bay until the connectors seat completely.

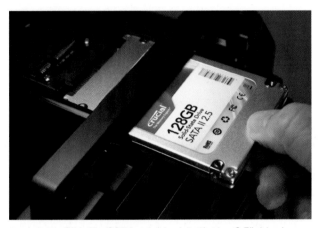

Figure 5-66. *Slide the SSD boot drive into the top 2.5" drive bay (but not this way)*

Figure 5-67. *Slide the SSD into the bay until the connectors mate completely*

If you've been paying attention, you may have noticed that while we connected the captive black SATA data cable from this drive bay to the motherboard earlier, we haven't yet connected power to the drive bay. We'll do that later, as we're connecting the system fans.

Installing the Video Adapter

The next step is to install the video adapter. If you're installing one video adapter, install it in the primary PCI Express x16 video adapter slot (the one located nearest the processor). Use the secondary video adapter slot only if you're installing a second video adapter, or for installing a non-video PCI Express expansion card.

To install the video adapter, first ground yourself to the frame or power supply and then remove the video adapter from its packaging. Hold the adapter up to the primary PCI Express x16 slot to determine which slot cover needs to be removed. Remove the screw that secures the expansion slot cover, as shown in Figure 5-68.

Grasp the expansion slot cover, tilt it slightly toward the case interior (as shown in Figure 5-69), and pull the slot cover free. Note that in some cases the screw that secures one expansion slot cover may overlap the edge of the adjacent slot cover. In that situation, you'll need to loosen the interfering screw before removing the slot cover.

Figure 5-68. *Remove the screw that secures the expansion slot cover*

Figure 5-69. *Remove the slot cover*

Position the video adapter vertically over the slot, as shown in Figure 5-70, and press down with both thumbs until the adapter seats completely in the slot. Depending on the motherboard and video adapter you use, this can require anything from very little pressure to significant pressure. In some cases, the required pressure was so high that we worried we'd crack the motherboard. If seating the adapter seems to require too much pressure, remove the adapter and make sure that everything is lined up properly and there are no obstructions. (In one case that Barbara will never let Robert forget, Robert tried to seat a video adapter in a slot that had an errant internal USB cable draped across it.)

Figure 5-70. *Position the video adapter over the slot and press down firmly with both thumbs to seat it*

Chapter 5

The PCI Express x16 video adapter slot has a latch that pivots up to seat in a slot on the bottom edge of the adapter. Make sure that latch is mated with the adapter, as shown in Figure 5-71. (Also make sure, if you remove the video adapter later, to unlatch it before you try to pull it from the slot.)

Once the video adapter is fully seated and latched into the slot, reinstall the screw to secure the video adapter bracket to the chassis, as shown in Figure 5-72. Make sure the card remains fully seated in the slot as you tighten the screw.

Figure 5-71. *Pivot the latch into position to lock the video adapter into the slot*

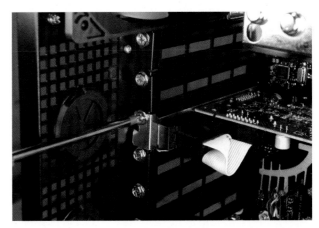

Figure 5-72. *Reinsert the screw to secure the video adapter to the chassis*

Video Card Power

We used a fanless video card that requires no supplemental power. However, most video adapters, particularly high-performance gaming adapters, require more power than the slot can provide. Supplemental power may be provided to the video adapter by connecting a six-pin or eight-pin PCI Express power cable. An adapter may have either or both of those connectors. Some video adapters that have eight-pin PCI Express sockets accept either a six- or eight-pin power cable, while others specifically require an eight-pin PCI Express power cable. Refer to your video adapter's manual for details.

Some video adapter fans are powered separately, by connecting a Molex power supply cable directly to a socket on the adapter. If your adapter uses such an arrangement, make sure to connect fan power or you may cook your video card in short order.

Ron Morse Comments

One or more.… My ATI HD5850 needs two six-pin PCI Express power connectors. Typically, the card vendor will provide four-pin Molex–to–six-pin PCI Express converter cables. If not, find a geek. He will be drowning in them. Or go to RadioShack. They're about $1 each.

Finishing Up

At this point, we're nearly finished. With the exception of a few stray fan power cables, not much cable dressing remains to be done in the main chamber, as shown in Figure 5-73.

All that remains to be done is to connect power to all seven case fans and the 2.5" removable drive bay, and then to neaten up the rats' nest of cables on the right side of the system before we reinstall the right side panel.

If you haven't done so already, route at least one Molex power cable from the power supply chamber to the cable management area on the right exterior of the case. Locate the power cables for all seven of the case fans and route them to the cable management area as well. Connect the fans and drive bay power cables to the cable from the power supply, as shown in Figure 5-74.

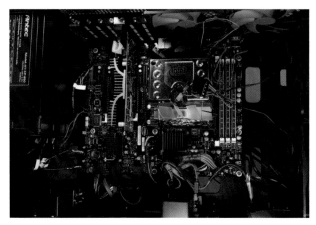

Figure 5-73. *The case interior before cleanup*

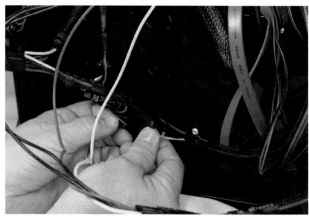

Figure 5-74. *Connect power to the case fans and the 2.5" removable drive bay*

Figure 5-75. *The cable management area, before dressing*

The fan power connectors are piggyback Molex connectors, with a female jack on one side of the connector and a male plug on the other. Fans draw little power, so you can connect several (or all) of them to one power supply Molex connector, just by piggybacking the fan power connectors together.

Once you've connected power to the fans and the 2.5" removable drive bay, you can sit back and admire the incredible mess of cables, shown in Figure 5-75. Organize the cables into bundles and use the cable wraps preinstalled on the back of the motherboard tray to tie off those bundles. After you do that, slide the right side panel back into place and secure it with the two thumbscrews you removed earlier.

Before you connect power to the system, verify the fan speed settings. The two top and two rear fans are dual-speed and are set by default to low speed. They are controlled by a block of four switches on the upper rear of the case. The three front fans have continuously variable speeds, from 1,000 RPM on the lowest setting to 2,000 RPM on the highest. Each front fan is controlled by the small knob at the lower-right corner of its drive bay cover. By default, the front fans are set to their lowest speed. Turn the knob clockwise to increase the speed, if necessary.

We found that the default low settings for all seven of the fans provided adequate cooling with a reasonable noise level. We suggest you increase the fan speed only if cooling is inadequate at the lower speed.

Zero RPM Fans

Some power supplies, including many Antec units, provide "Fan Only" Molex connectors. If you power one or more of the DF-85 fans with such a connector, set the fan speed to high. Otherwise, the reduced voltage available on the Fan Only Molex connector may be insufficient to start the fan spinning.

The Smoke Test

After you finish building the system, take a few minutes to double-check everything. Verify that all cables are connected properly, that all drives are secured, and that there's nothing loose inside the case. Check one last time that the power supply is set for the correct input voltage, if applicable, and the power switch is in the "off" position. It's a good idea to pick up the system and tilt it gently from side to side to make sure there are no loose screws or other items that could cause a short. Use the following checklist:

- ☐ Power supply set to proper input voltage (if applicable)
- ☐ No loose tools or screws (shake the case gently)
- ☐ Heatsink/fan unit properly mounted; CPU fan connected
- ☐ Memory modules fully seated and latched
- ☐ Front-panel switch and indicator cables connected properly
- ☐ Front-panel I/O cables connected properly
- ☐ Hard drive data cable(s) connected to drive(s) and motherboard
- ☐ Hard drive power cable(s) connected
- ☐ Optical drive data cable connected to drive and motherboard
- ☐ Optical drive power cable connected
- ☐ All drives secured to drive bay or chassis, as applicable
- ☐ Expansion cards fully seated and secured to chassis
- ☐ Video adapter power connected (if applicable)
- ☐ Main ATX power cable and ATX12V power cable connected
- ☐ Front, top, and rear case fans connected
- ☐ All cables dressed and tucked

Once you're certain that all is as it should be, it's time for the smoke test. Leave the left side panel off for now. Connect the power cable to the wall receptacle and then to the system unit. Unlike many power supplies, the Antec CP-850 has a separate rocker switch on the back that controls power to the power supply. By default, it's in the "0," or off, position, which means the power supply is not receiving power from the wall receptacle. Move that switch to the "1," or on, position. Press the main power button on the front of the case, and the system should start up. Check to make sure that the power supply fan, CPU fan, and case fans are spinning. You should also hear the hard drive spin up. At that point, everything should be working properly.

Once the system passes the smoke test, power it down and connect your keyboard, mouse, display, and any other external peripherals. Start the system and run BIOS Setup. Set the correct date and time. If you plan to hot-swap hard drives, make sure you've enabled AHCI. Once you complete BIOS Setup configuration, save your changes, shut the system down, and restart it with the operating system distribution disc in the optical drive. Install the OS, updated drivers, and your applications software, and you're ready to roll. Oh, and don't forget to replace the side panel.

Final Words

This system went together easily. Actual construction took about 90 minutes, as usual in our case spread out over several days as we photographed each step. If this is the first time you've built a system, leave yourself a full weekend to build it, install software, and so on.

We're quite pleased with the performance of this system. It "feels" at least twice as fast as Robert's former quad-core extreme system. That impression is borne out by this system's video-rendering performance. A video clip that required five minutes to render on Robert's old extreme system now renders in about two minutes.

The system is too loud to call a Quiet PC, but it's much quieter than some of the leaf-blower extreme systems we've built in the past. In a relatively quiet room, the hum of all those fans is clearly audible from across the room. In a typical office environment, particularly with the system under the desk, the noise level is acceptable, at least to us.

Building a Media Center System

We admit it. We're audio/video Luddites. When the receiver in our 15-year-old home audio system failed a few years ago, we didn't bother to replace it. We have a Panasonic 27″ analog television, basic $10/month analog cable TV service with only the broadcast channels, and no satellite receiver.

We rent movies and TV series from Netflix, borrow them from the public library or friends, or buy the DVD sets. (As we write this, we've just gotten around to renting *The Sopranos*. It's new to us....) We sometimes watch local TV news, sports, and weather in real time, but that's about it. We've even given up watching PBS because of the intrusive begging and increasingly common commercials.

If there's something we really want to see, we usually just buy the DVD set or wait until it's available from Netflix. A few times a year, when we don't want to wait for the DVD release, we record the program on our DVD recorder. The last time we watched a prime-time network television episode live was sometime in the 20th century. We've never bothered watching TV online, because the programs available on Hulu and the network websites contain embedded commercials that can't be skipped. If we can't watch something without commercials, we simply refuse to watch it.

So, why do we need a media center system? We don't, at least if you define a media center system as incorporating PVR/DVR (personal/digital video recorder) functions. In fact, we built a very capable PVR/DVR media center system for the first edition of this book. After we verified that everything worked as it should, we found that we never used the system to record programs. We turned it off. It gathered dust, and eventually we salvaged its parts for other systems. There was nothing wrong with that system, mind you. It worked perfectly. We simply had no need for its recording capabilities. For the second edition of this book, we built another capable PVR/DVR media center system, this one with multiple analog and digital tuner cards. Once again, we turned it on, tested it and found it did everything expected of it, and then turned it off when we realized that we weren't using it.

But there's much more to a media center system than just recording TV programs. The first sentence of Wikipedia's HTPC entry is a pretty good working definition:

Gotcha

One problem with depending on DVDs is that DVD releases are unpredictable. For example, we rented and watched season 1 of Crossing Jordan soon after the DVD set was released in 2008. Alas, we then learned that the remaining five seasons haven't been released on DVD and probably never will be because of music licensing issues. Oh, well.

We had a similar problem with the fine British comedy-drama Cold Feet, starring the delightful Helen Baxendale. After we'd rented and watched the first three series, we realized belatedly that Netflix didn't have series four and five. We immediately tried to buy those, only to learn that series four and five had never been released for the US market and were unavailable for purchase.

Amazon had one used copy of series four, but in Region 2 format, which is incompatible with our equipment. Arrrggggh. If we weren't law abiding, we might have installed a good BitTorrent client and visited Pirate Bay.

> A Home Theater PC (HTPC) or Media Center is a convergence device that combines a personal computer with a software application that supports video and music playback, and *sometimes digital video recorder functionality.*

The emphasis is ours. Sometimes, indeed. A couple of years ago, media center systems were all the rage. Best Buy featured several models in every Sunday supplement section. The Dell and HP home pages had media center systems splashed all over them. NewEgg carried a couple of dozen models. Even Sears sold media center systems. And the focus was always on recording TV programs.

Nowadays, things are very different. We searched the Best Buy website for "media center" and "HTPC" and got no results. The Dell site lists no media center systems, and only one third-party add-on box to provide media center functions when coupled to a standard PC. The HP website lists nothing, nor does the NewEgg site. You can still buy dedicated media center systems, but only from "boutique" vendors. What happened?

First and foremost, media center systems were simply much too expensive for what they do, ranging in price from perhaps $800 at the low end up to $2,500 or more. You could accomplish much the same things with a $150 DVD recorder or a $300 TiVo, or you could simply rent a PVR from your satellite or cable TV provider for a few bucks a month. Furthermore, TiVo, DVD recorders, and satellite/cable PVRs are reasonably reliable appliances; ordinarily, they Just Work. Media center PVR systems tended to crash, fail to record scheduled programs, and otherwise fall down on the job.

So, why bother to include a chapter on building a media center system? Because PVR functions were never anything more than a distraction from the real purpose of a media center system: centralizing your home media storage and making your media easy to access from anywhere in your home.

But what if you also want to record television programs? In that case, our best advice is:

- If your television service is delivered by digital cable or satellite and you want PVR functions, rent or purchase a PVR box from your cable or satellite provider. If your cable or satellite receiver provides dual outputs and your television has dual inputs, you can instead use a DVD recorder, with or without a hard drive for extended recording time. Current U.S. law mandates that any television device that includes a tuner must include an ATSC digital tuner, so a DVD recorder may have no tuner, only a digital tuner, or both analog and digital tuners.

- If you have analog cable TV service, you'll probably be happy with a DVD recorder, but those are becoming increasingly harder to find. Inexpensive cable/satellite PVR boxes are driving them from the market.

- If, like an increasing number of people, you have "cut the cable" and depend on over-the-air DTV, purchase a DVD recorder with an ATSC tuner.

Brian Bilbrey Comments

As long as the TV provider PVR works just fine. My wife Marcia hardly ever watches "live" TV, but has many hours of programming recorded each week that can be easily fast-forwarded through the mercantile segments of each program.

Determining Functional Requirements

For this third iteration, we were determined to design a media center system that fit our actual needs, rather than those of some hypothetical "average" reader. By following our thought process, you should be able to come up with a media center system configuration that fits your needs as well.

We've never really needed our media center system to include TV recording functions, and it's becoming increasingly obvious that many other people don't, either. So, we'll design this system to focus on pure media center functions. If we need to record TV programs, we'll use one of the methods we listed in the previous section, and we'll assume that you will, too.

Here's the list of requirements we came up with:

Video output requirements

Obviously, the low resolution of our current 27" analog television severely constrains what we can do with the system. It was about time to replace our old TV anyway, so we checked Costco to see what TVs were selling for nowadays. We were surprised to find that we could buy a pretty reasonable 42" HDTV with full 1080p support for $600, so for design purposes we assumed that would be our media center system display.

HDTV 1080p resolution is actually 1920×1080, so we'll need to make sure our video adapter can drive the display at that resolution. We'll also need to verify that the outputs on the media center system match the inputs on the TV, which are HDMI/HDCP times four for video, and SP/DIF digital optical plus stereo in for audio.

Watching DVD videos

We currently watch rental DVDs using a standard Panasonic DVD player, which the media center system will replace. We don't currently own or rent Blu-ray discs, but we want to make sure that our media center system can be easily upgraded to support Blu-ray in the future.

Rather than handling the physical discs, we want to rip our collection of purchased DVDs to the hard drive so that we can watch any of them just by pointing and clicking. That means we'll need plenty of disk space. We want sufficient storage for 500+ DVDs. Allowing additional capacity for music and other files means we'll want perhaps 4 TB of disk space in our media center system.

Watching web videos

We find ourselves spending increasingly more of our viewing time watching web videos on YouTube and similar services. We don't care about support for iTunes or other copy-protected video download services, but it's essential that this system make it easy to browse/watch unprotected web videos.

Listening to audio

We've already converted our collection of about 1,000 audio CDs to 320 kb/s VBR (variable bitrate) MP3 files, which Barbara listens to using MP3 players in her SUV and at the gym. It makes sense to use the media center system as the central storage location for these audio files, allowing them to be played back locally in the den or remotely on other systems in the house. We'd like the system to index our collection and offer the standard options for playback (full searchability by title/artist/genre, random shuffle, playlists, and so on). When we buy a new CD, we want to be able to pop it into the system and have the system automatically rip it, store it, and index it.

Viewing images

We have thousands of image files taken with our Pentax digital SLRs and stored in RAW (PEF) format. We'd like the system to store and index these files and make them readily searchable, viewable, and editable. It should also make it easy to produce hard copies, either by sending them to our color printer or by uploading them to the Walgreens website, which we use for most of our photo printing.

Video editing/production

Robert shoots a lot of videos for his YouTube channel, TheHomeScientist. Currently, he edits them on his main office system, but it would be nice to be able to do at least preliminary rough-cut editing while kicking back and relaxing on the sofa. Essentially, that means we'll need a faster processor, more memory, and a faster hard drive than we might otherwise use. We transfer videos from the camcorder to Robert's main office system, so FireWire support isn't necessary.

Web browsing

We want instant access to the Web. For example, while we're watching a DVD, we might want to pause the video and pop up a browser window to look up a cast member in the Internet Movie Database. Or, if we've just gotten back from walking the dog, we might want to check our email to see if our VoIP telephone service has emailed us a new voicemail message notification with an encapsulated audio file.

Interface

Our first thought was to use a standard media center "10-foot interface" with large text and icons and a handheld remote control for navigation. Then we realized that with a 42" display running at 1920×1080 resolution, we didn't need that; we could simply use a standard desktop interface, which will be easily readable at that size and distance. That means we won't need a handheld remote and receiver for the media center system. Instead, we can just use a wireless keyboard/mouse with sufficient range to reach across the room.

Hardware Design Criteria

With the functional requirements determined, the next step was to establish design criteria for the media center system hardware. Here are the relative priorities we assigned for our media center system.

Here's the breakdown:

Price	★★☆☆☆
Reliability	★★★☆☆
Size	★★☆☆☆
Noise level	★★★★☆
Expandability	★★☆☆☆
Processor performance	★★★☆☆
Video performance	★★☆☆☆
Disk capacity/performance	★★★☆☆

Price

> Price is a consideration, but only in the sense that we don't want to waste money. This media center system will be our shared den PC, and we spend a lot of time in the den. Accordingly, we'll use only first-rate components in this system, and if spending a few extra dollars buys us additional performance, reliability, or functionality, we'll spend the extra money.

Reliability

> Reliability is moderately important for this system, but primarily because this system will run 24/7/365, and we don't want to have to stop what we're doing to fix it in the middle of an evening's viewing. Although the system will store as much as 4 TB of data, we won't use RAID. We'll keep copies of our audio and video collections on network or external hard drives, and if worse comes to horrible we can simply re-rip our audio CD and DVD collections.

Brian Bilbrey Comments

That's just awful, IMO. Your time is far more valuable than a few terabytes of disk. I'd reconsider RAID, or have the system auto-rsync to an equivalent amount of disk in some system at the other end of the house each night, overnight.

Size

> Size is a consideration for this system only in that it must fit the area available for it. We do want it to look like a standard home theater component rather than a computer. So, rather than using the smallest available case, we decided to choose from among cases designed for home theater use.

In Our Defense

Well, as we said, we do keep copies of our audio and video data on network or external drives (actually, we keep copies on multiple network and external drives). Worse would really have to come to horrible before we had to re-rip anything at all.

Clearances Matter (and So Does Cooling)

If your system will reside in an entertainment center, make sure that the case you choose fits. In particular, if your entertainment center has an enclosed back, make sure the case is not too deep. Allow room for video and power cables. Also, many media center cases exhaust warm air through side or top vents, so it's important to maintain an inch or more of clearance near those vents to prevent overheating.

Even if the clearances are adequate, you also need to consider cooling. Even a cool-running PC produces much more heat than a typical A/V component, and is often left running 24/7. Before you run your media center system for any extended period in an A/V rack, verify that the ventilation and cooling are sufficient to protect the system from overheating.

Noise level

> Noise level is moderately important for this system. On one hand, when the system is being used to view a movie or listen to music, system noise is swamped by the sound coming from the speakers. On the other hand, because this system is always running, it must be reasonably quiet to avoid interfering with other uses of the room. On the gripping hand, it's

across the room from where we sit, so minor system noise is acceptable. Accordingly, we decided to use quiet standard components, but not go to extremes to minimize system noise.

Expandability

Expandability is relatively unimportant. Any new component we install will likely replace an old component, so we have no real need for spare drive bays, expansion slots, and so on. We want provision for at least one optical drive and two hard drives. We'll choose a motherboard with integrated everything, so we could actually get along with no expansion slots at all. We do want to make provision for adding unrelated functions to the system, such as controlling a home weather station or functioning as an automated attendant and voicemail controller for our telephone system, but we can accommodate that requirement with at most one or two available expansion slots and an available USB port or two.

Processor performance

Processor performance is moderately important for our configuration, mainly because we'll be doing some video editing on this system. (The same would be true if we were using this system for PC gaming, which we won't, but you may.) That means we'll need a mainstream processor in this system. Otherwise, we'd have chosen a budget processor like the AMD Athlon II X2 240 Regor, which is sufficient for 1080p video playback, at half the price.

Video performance

Video performance is relatively unimportant for our configuration. Integrated video is sufficient for everything we'll do with this system, including video editing. We'll choose a motherboard that provides integrated video but also includes a PCI Express x16 slot, just in case at some point we decide to add a standalone video adapter. If you'll use your system for 3D gaming, you'll want at least one PCI Express x16 expansion slot, and you'll want to make sure that the case and power supply you choose are adequate to support the video card(s).

Disk capacity/performance

Disk capacity and performance are moderately important, capacity more so than performance. We estimated our disk storage requirements to be 4 TB. At the time we built this system, 2 TB drives were the largest available, so a pair of those fit our requirements nicely. Standard 7,200 RPM SATA hard drives are more than fast enough to keep up with anything we're likely to demand of this system. If after a couple of years we find ourselves a bit cramped for storage space, we'll simply swap out the pair of 2 TB drives for a pair of 4 TB drives, or whatever size drives are then available.

Component Considerations

With our design criteria in mind, we set out to choose the best components for the media center system. The following sections describe the components we chose, and why we chose them.

Display

Sharp LC-42SB48UT (*http://www.sharpusa.com*)

The most prominent component of any media center system is, of course, the display. Our old analog 27" television obviously wasn't going to cut it as a media center display, so with some trepidation we visited the Costco website. Our two primary criteria were full HDTV 1080p support (1920×1080 resolution) and a 40" to 42" screen (about the largest we have room for). We expected the model we'd want would cost $1,500 or so.

We were pleasantly surprised to find that 1080p support is now almost universal, and that 42" models were quite affordable. After carefully checking specifications and reviews, we settled on the Sharp LC-42SB48UT, the least expensive 42" 1080p model that Costco offered. The price was only $600.

The LC-42SB48UT lacks some of the bells-and-whistles features of more expensive models—LED backlighting, picture-in-picture, picture-outside-picture, and so on—but it's more than adequate for our needs. The image quality is excellent, and the unit provides a plethora of I/O connectors, including no fewer than four HDMI/HDCP ports. At 6.5 ms, the response time is fast enough even for most gaming.

Obviously, you needn't buy a display if you already have a 1080p HDTV with the necessary inputs. If you have a 720p HDTV, make sure the video out on the motherboard or video adapter you choose supports 720p resolution.

Case and Power Supply

Antec NSK-2480 (*http://www.antec.com*)

Antec Fusion Remote (*http://www.antec.com*)

If appearance doesn't matter, you can, of course, build your media center system in a standard computer case. But for many people, the critical *Spousal-Unit Approval* (SUA) criterion (otherwise known as, "You're not putting *that* in my den!") demands a case that matches standard home-audio components in size and appearance as closely as possible. Barbara has a sense of humor about these things. Many spouses do not, so it's worth checking before you purchase a case.

When we were designing our media center system, we visited NewEgg to see which media center cases they offered. There were 77 media center cases available, ranging from $40 to $60 no-name units we wouldn't use on a bet to a $600 Zalman unit that we wouldn't pay for on a bet.

Decide first if you need a front-panel display and, if so, which type. Many media center cases use LED or LCD displays, which we think are less than ideally suited for that purpose. Some media center cases use a *vacuum-fluorescent display* (VFD), which we prefer. Particularly if you intend to include PVR functionality in your media center system and will use a 10-foot interface rather than a standard PC desktop interface, the display *may* be worth having. Otherwise, we consider it a distraction, and an expensive one at that.

Silver Cases

The one thing we don't like about the NSK 2480 case is the silver/aluminum front panel, which is actually plastic. The problem is that it's impossible to match that front panel with the front bezel of any optical drive we've ever seen. We have three or four older optical drives with different "silver" bezels, but none of them are an exact match with any silver case we've ever seen. Apparently, others came to the same conclusion, because optical drives with silver bezels are now almost impossible to find. Actually, anything but black is now almost impossible to find, including the formerly common beige and somewhat less common white.

The problem is that an "almost-match" looks hideous. It's worse looking than a complete mismatch, such as using a black optical drive in a silver case. The Antec Fusion case doesn't have this problem, because it has a flip-up optical drive cover that conceals the front bezel of the optical drive. Alas, the NSK 2480 is available only in silver. If Antec offered a black version, that's what we'd have chosen. This system is going to sit in our den, so we'll probably remove the front panel of the case and spray-paint it matte black or a dark charcoal gray. If necessary, we can also spray-paint the front bezel of the optical drive to match exactly.

Most media center cases that include a front-panel display also include a remote-control module (an IR receiver and remote control). These are useful if you intend to use a 10-foot interface, but not needed if you use a standard PC desktop interface. Even if you want a remote control module, don't rule out an otherwise desirable case simply because it doesn't include one. You can purchase a remote control and IR receiver separately that you may actually prefer.

Although you can pay upward of $600 for a media center case, we set an arbitrary $200 limit, including the power supply. Although we'd prefer to pay less, neither do we want something cheap and cheesy-looking in our den. Fortunately, that price range includes numerous attractive models from Antec, Apex, Ark, Lian-Li, nMEDIAPC, Silverstone, Zalman, and other manufacturers.

Antec has been the bang-for-the-buck leader in PC cases for a long time, so we weren't surprised as we culled down the field to find that our two finalists were both Antec cases.

For a case with a front-panel display, our pick is the Antec Fusion Remote, which is available in either silver or black. This is essentially the same case we used in the second edition of this book. Sometimes, oldies really are goodies. The only real difference between the original Antec Fusion case and the version sold today is that the original version included a power supply and the current model does not. Adding a $40 Antec EarthWatts 380W power supply brings the total cost to about $175, well within our price range.

For a case without a front-panel display, our pick is the $110 Antec NSK-2480, which is available only in silver, unfortunately. This is essentially the same product as the Fusion Remote, but with a 380W EarthWatts power supply included and the front-panel display, remote-control module, and front-panel FireWire port removed. The absence of the front-panel display frees up a second 5.25" external drive bay, which can be used for a second optical drive (such as a Blu-ray reader) or for a third hard drive.

Black Isn't Black

You may assume that you could avoid this problem just by buying a black case and using an optical drive with a black bezel. Alas, black isn't black, at least when it comes to consumer products. "Black" comes in a huge variety of shades, from dark gray to truly black. There are warm blacks, cool blacks, and neutral blacks. Then there's the matter of texture. Even if their blacks are very similar, a matte drive looks odd in a semi-matte case, and vice versa. Chances are small that your optical drive bezel will match the front panel of your case, and even a slight mismatch is glaringly obvious.

If you want your case and bezel to match, you're going to have to spray paint both of them. (We chose a very dark neutral charcoal gray in semi-matte finish.) So, as it turns out, the only real advantage to starting with a black case rather than an aluminum or silver model is that it's easier to cover with the paint (and scratches don't show up as well).

If you plan to run Windows 7 rather than Linux on your media center system, either of these cases is suitable for a light- to medium-duty gaming rig. You'll want to choose a video adapter that doesn't draw much current or produce much heat or noise, but numerous low- to midrange video adapters meet those criteria.

Processor

Intel Core i3-530 (*http://www.intel.com*)

Most of the core functions of a media center system require relatively little processing power. For playing back audio and video, even a dual-core Intel Atom processor would suffice, although it might be marginal if we later upgrade our media center system to Blu-ray. Also, the A/V output options on Atom processor/motherboard combos are too limited for a media center system. Finally, because we want our media center system to function as a general-purpose PC, we decided we needed at least a low-end mainstream processor.

In that range, the Intel Core i3-530 is the obvious choice. It costs only $50 or so more than a budget CPU, and its performance approaches that of more expensive mainstream units. Because we intend to do some light video editing on this system, we actually considered using a Core i5 processor, but we concluded that would be overkill. The video editing we'll do on this system will be just that—editing—rather than rendering, which is the real horsepower pig.

> **Drive It Until It Drops**
>
> *A subtle point is that a media center system is likely to be upgraded much less frequently than a desktop PC. Once a media center system is built, configured, connected, and tested, it should reasonably be expected to live quietly in the home-audio rack for several years between upgrades. Accordingly, when the choice is between "just enough" and "more than I'll ever need," we suggest you choose the latter.*

Motherboard

Intel BOXDH55TC (*http://www.intel.com*)

Our choice of the Antec Fusion case dictates a microATX motherboard. For our Core i3-530 processor, we wanted a Socket LGA 1156 motherboard with support for at least 8 GB (and, preferably, 16 GB) of dual-channel DDR3 memory. We'd prefer four memory slots rather than two. That way, if we install only two memory modules initially, we can upgrade the memory simply by adding a pair of DIMMs rather than removing existing memory. Support for Core i3 and Core i5 processors would be nice, just for future-proofing, although it's unlikely we'll ever upgrade the processor in this system.

Expansion slots aren't critical, because we want a board with integrated everything. We'd like a PCI Express 2.X x16 expansion slot in case we ever need to install a separate video adapter. It would be nice to have at least one PCI expansion slot and one or two PCI Express x1 slots, in case we ever decide to add an expansion card or two to support ancillary functions such as home control, a weather station, or a PC-based telephone system.

We need at least three SATA connectors, one for the optical drive and two for the hard drives. SATA 6 Gb/s would be nice for future-proofing, but SATA 3 Gb/s is all we really need. We'd also like at least one and preferably two eSATA ports, just in case at some point we decide to expand disk storage with external hard drives.

USB 3.0 support would be nice, but in practical terms USB 3.0 peripherals are still thin on the ground. USB 2.0 is sufficient for our current needs and likely to remain so for the foreseeable future. If at some point we find a gotta-have USB 3.0 peripheral, we'll simply install a USB 3.0 expansion card. Because we transfer camcorder videos on Robert's main office system, a FireWire port isn't necessary.

In terms of A/V outputs, it's essential that the motherboard provide at least an HDMI connector with HDCP support, and we'd like to have a dual-channel DVI-D connector as well. Standard 5.1 audio out is required, and we'd like to have a digital audio out as well.

Entering all of these requirements into the NewEgg filtering system returned nine suitable boards, including models from ASUS, eVGA, GIGABYTE, Intel, and MSI. Any of those would be suitable, but we have a strong preference based on experience for motherboards from ASUS, GIGABYTE, and Intel. Over the years, we've come to use ASUS and GIGABYTE motherboards almost exclusively for AMD-based systems. For Intel processors, we've found Intel motherboards to be rock-solid reliable, so for this system we chose the retail-boxed Intel DH55TC motherboard.

Memory

Crucial Ballistix CT2KIT25664BN1337 4 GB Kit (2 GB×2)

(*http://www.crucial.com*)

The Intel DH55TC has four DDR3 memory slots and supports dual-channel memory operation with PC3-8500 or PC3-10600 modules in capacities up to 4 GB per slot. Our original rule of thumb was 1 GB of RAM per processor. With the advent of multi-core processors, we modified that rule to 1 GB per core. Nowadays, with multi-core processors running multiple threads per core, our current rule is 1 GB per thread. On that basis, we decided to install 4 GB of system memory.

When we checked the Crucial memory configurator to find modules compatible with the DH55TC motherboard, we found that four 1 GB modules cost more than two 2 GB modules, so we chose a 4 GB kit with two 2 GB PC3-10600 modules. Using only two DIMMs means we leave two memory slots free for future expansion.

At the time we ordered, Crucial offered three PC3-10600 4 GB memory kits, one with its standard modules with CL9 memory timing, and the other with its high-performance Ballistix modules at CL7 or CL6 timings. The CL6 Ballistix kit cost 50% more than the standard kit, but the CL7 Ballistix kit was only $8 more. We chose the CL7 Ballistix kit for its superior cooling and additional safety margin over the standard modules. (We'd probably have chosen the same memory for the mainstream system, but when we built that system the CL7 Ballistix modules were selling at a significantly higher premium.)

Video Adapter

Integrated

Video output requirements for our media center system are relatively undemanding. We need a video adapter that can output 1920×1080 full HDTV resolution and that has an output connector compatible with our HDTV. The Intel integrated video provided by the DH55TC motherboard and Core i3-530 processor meets both requirements, with power to spare.

We'll connect our media center system to our HDTV using the *High-Definition Multimedia Interface* (HDMI) connector on the rear panel of the motherboard. That HDMI connector also supports *High-Bandwidth Digital Content Protection* (HDCP), an Intel DRM technology. Ordinarily, we'd have no truck with any DRM technology, but having HDCP support may come in handy in the future if we want to implement Blu-ray or another technology with embedded DRM that requires HDCP.

The Intel DH55TC motherboard also provides a dual-link *Digital Visual Interface-Digital* (DVI-D) connector. DVI-D is essentially an older version of HDMI that is electrically compatible but uses physically incompatible connectors. Most HDTV units that predate HDMI use DVI connectors, and DVI-to-HDMI adapter cables are readily available.

Having that DVI-D connector also keeps our options open. It will be useful, for example, when we're building the media center system and installing software, because we can use any DVI-compatible flat-panel display in our workroom. Also, although we may be a bit paranoid, if we ever have conflicts or compatibility problems with the HDCP DRM on the HDMI output, we can simply disable it and use the DVI-D output to connect to our HDTV, using an inexpensive adapter cable.

We'll run Linux on our media center system, but if we were running Windows 7 and wanted to use the system for gaming, we'd install a separate video adapter. The days when serious gaming demanded a $500 video card (or cards) that drew 120W are long gone (although some devoted PC gamers still install multiple high-end video adapters). Nowadays, you can play all but the most demanding 3D games at reasonable frame rates with a $75 to $125 video adapter. As of summer 2010, the best choice is a passively cooled (for minimum noise) ATI RADEON HD 4670 or 4850 adapter. Obviously, make sure the card you choose has an HDMI output.

Wireless Networking Adapter

ASUS PCE-N13 802.11 b/g/n PCI Express wireless adapter
(*http://www.asus.com*)

Although we plan eventually to connect the media center system to our 1000BaseT (gigabit) wired Ethernet network, there's currently no Ethernet jack near the television. Running that cable will be a major project, because the television sits against an insulated exterior wall with no access above the ceiling or below the floor. So, for the time being, we decided to install a wireless networking card in the media center system and simply make it a client on our wireless network.

If we intended to use a wireless network adapter as a permanent solution, we'd install an ASUS PCE-N13 802.11 b/g/n PCI Express wireless adapter, which sells for under $30, is very fast, and provides full WPA2 security. However, because we'll use wireless networking only until we have time to install an Ethernet cable, we fished around in our spare parts closet and came up with an old D-Link DWL-G520 AirPlusXtremeG 802.11 b/g/g+ PCI wireless adapter. With nominal data rates up to 108 Mb/s and WPA support, it's both fast enough and secure enough for our temporary needs. And it didn't cost anything.

Of course, as Barbara will tell you, Robert's "temporary" solutions have a way of becoming permanent, so perhaps we should have installed the ASUS 802.11n adapter. Oh, well. That'll be easy enough to fix later.

Hard Disk Drive(s)

Seagate Barracuda XT ST32000641AS 2TB (two) (*http://www.seagate.com*)

You'll have some decisions to make when you choose a hard drive or drives for your media center system. If you're not storing much video (or if your video is stored remotely on a home server system), you can probably get by with one $50 mainstream desktop hard drive. At the other extreme, if you have a large DVD collection that you want to rip and store locally on your media center system, as we do, you'll need all the hard drive capacity you can get.

When we were building our media center system, the largest drives available were 2 TB drives, the most expensive of which cost more than twice as much as the least expensive models. Why the large difference? Speed, amount of cache, and interface. The least expensive 2 TB drives run at 5,400 RPM, have 8 MB, 16 MB, or 32 MB of cache, and use the SATA 3.0 Gb/s interface. Those that cost twice as much run at 7,200 RPM, have 64 MB of cache, and use the SATA 6.0 Gb/s interface.

At this point, the SATA 6.0 Gb/s interface is just marketing hype. Even the fastest current hard drives can't saturate the SATA 3.0 Gb/s interface, so doubling that interface speed is meaningless. But rotation speed and cache size are real issues, ones that may affect the performance of the media center system.

For simple media playback, a 5,400 RPM drive is fast enough, and it has the advantages of being quieter and cooler-running than most 7,200 RPM drives. In this class, the standout choices are the Samsung SpinPoint and EcoGreen series drives and the Western Digital Caviar Green series drives.

If you're doing more than just media playback on your media center system, or if it will also multitask—for example, serving multiple audio/video streams to other systems in your home—7,200 RPM drives are a better choice. They're more expensive, run hotter, and make more noise than 5,400 RPM models, but they're fast enough for disk-intensive tasks like serving multiple video streams or editing video.

The two real competitors in the high-performance 7,200 RPM segment are the Seagate Barracuda 7200.12 and Barracuda XT series and the Western Digital Caviar Black series. Performance-wise, they're very similar. The Seagate drives win some benchmark tests and the WD drives others. The Barracudas generally outperform the Caviars in sequential read/write performance, which is more important than random read/write performance for a media center system. The Barracudas also run noticeably cooler and quieter than the Caviars, both of which are important for a media center system.

So, which drives would we go for? For a media center system with moderate storage requirements, choose a Seagate Barracuda 7200.12 drive of moderate capacity. If you need massive storage capacity but 5,400 RPM performance is sufficient, install one or two 2 GB Samsung SpinPoint drives. If you need both massive capacity and high performance, install one or two 2 TB Seagate Barracuda XT drives.

What About Backup?

Backing up a system with gobs of disk space is problematic. Optical discs don't hold enough data, and tape drives are very expensive. External hard drives are often the only realistic option.

At first glance, backup may seem to be unimportant for a typical media center system. After all, we're already backed up in the sense that all of the music and videos that we've ripped to our media center system are still on the original discs and all of our camcorder video is still on the original tapes. If a hard drive fails, we haven't actually lost any data.

On the other hand, the thought of having to re-rip all those discs gives us pause. It takes only a few minutes to rip an audio CD or a DVD, but multiply that by a thousand discs and you're looking at a serious time investment. So we decided to spring for a couple of extra 2 TB Barracuda XT drives, install them in external drive enclosures, run a full data backup set from the media center system, and then periodically back up any new or changed files on the media center system.

Brian Bilbrey Comments

OK. That makes me feel better. But detach them from the system and put them elsewhere, except for during the once-a-month/week refresh cycle.

Optical Drive

LiteOn iHAS424-98 DVD writer (*http://us.liteonit.com/us/*)

At $25 or so, DVD writers are pretty much commodities nowadays, although over the last couple of years we've had the best experience with units made by ASUS, LiteOn, and Samsung. The day we ordered components for this system NewEgg offered free shipping on the LiteOn drive but not on the similar ASUS and Samsung units, so we ordered the LiteOn.

Interestingly, the drive we ordered was retail-boxed. NewEgg also had the bare drive, but that day it was charging a dollar *more* for the bare drive than the retail-boxed model. Hmmm.

Retail-Boxed Versus Bare Drives

Ordinarily, a retail-boxed optical drive costs a few bucks more than a bare drive. For that extra money, you usually get mounting screws (be still, our throbbing hearts), a cheap SATA cable, and an OEM software disc. That software may include some Windows utilities (such as LightScribe support for burning labels on LightScribe discs or a disc-quality scanner) and may or may not include a "Lite" version of Nero Burning ROM or some other disc burning software.

If you run Windows and don't have disc burning software, or if you happen to need a SATA cable to install the drive, the retail-boxed version may be a good deal. Otherwise, unless the price difference is tiny, buy the OEM (bare) drive.

Backup Hardware

Antec Easy SATA (*http://www.antec.com*)

SYBA SD-ENC50020 (*http://www.syba.com*)

Seagate 3 TB FreeAgent GoFlex Desk (*http://www.seagate.com*)

We actually installed no backup hardware in our media center system, because what little backup it requires can be done across our network. If you do need backup hardware for your media center system, there are three obvious alternatives: an internal hard drive docking station (like the Antec Easy SATA), an external hard drive docking station (like the SYBA SD-ENC50020), or a standard external hard drive (like the Seagate FreeAgent).

Installing the Antec Easy SATA or a similar internal docking station requires a second 5.25" external drive bay, which is available with the Antec NSK-2480 (and many other media center cases), but not with the Antec Fusion Remote. If you have an available 5.25" external drive bay, the Antec Easy SATA is both the cleanest and least expensive solution. It allows you to recycle older SATA hard drives, and its eSATA transfers are very fast.

The SYBA SD-ENC50020 external hard drive docking station offers the same performance as the Antec Easy SATA for about the same price, but it supports two hard drives simultaneously at the expense of additional clutter. However, neither of the cases we recommend has an external eSATA port, let alone the two eSATA ports required by the SYBA unit to support dual drives. You can, of course, substitute a case (or motherboard) that does provide external eSATA connectors, but it's easy enough to solve the problem with the components we used.

The SYBA unit includes two long eSATA cables, which have a standard SATA connector on one end and the special eSATA connector on the other. These cables can't be used on this system, because it has no eSATA connectors. The solution is simple. Just order an extra pair of standard SATA cables 18" to 24" long. Connect one end of each cable to a motherboard SATA port, run the cables out the back of the case, and connect them to the SYBA unit. Problem solved.

If you prefer a standard external hard drive, any of the Seagate FreeAgent models is a good choice. In particular, we're looking forward to seeing the 3 TB Seagate FreeAgent GoFlex Desk, which had been announced but was not yet available when we were building this system. Obviously, we can recommend it only provisionally, since we haven't actually seen it yet, but the specifications and suggested retail pricing indicate that this external drive will offer a lot of bang for the buck.

There is one obvious problem, though, at least for our chosen media center configuration. The 3 TB Seagate external unit can use any of three interfaces: USB 2.0, USB 3.0, and FireWire 800. We don't have either of the latter two on our media center system (although you may choose a motherboard that provides one or both of those), and USB 2.0 is simply too slow. Filling a 3 TB drive at a typical USB 2.0 data rate of 25 to 30 MB/s would require more than a full day.

If your own media center configuration has USB 3.0 or FireWire available, the GoFlex 3 TB unit is a practical backup choice. Of course, you can also choose an external hard drive that uses an eSATA interface and run one or two SATA cables out the back of the case, as we recommended for the SYBA unit.

Keyboard and Mouse

Microsoft Wireless Desktop 3000 (*http://www.microsoft.com*)

The primary requirement here is a wireless keyboard/mouse combo that works reliably at across-the-room distances. Most wireless keyboards and mice designed for desktop use have a range of a meter (40") or so at most. Among the units with sufficient range, we think the standout choice is the Microsoft Wireless Desktop 3000. At a street price of around $60, the Wireless Desktop 3000 is inexpensive, well built, and has a rated range of 30 feet. It uses alkaline batteries rather a rechargeable battery, but battery life is rated at eight months.

Speakers

Home audio speakers:

Logitech Z-5500 speaker system (*http://www.logitech.com*)

Logitech X-540 speaker system

Most people who build a media center system install it in their home entertainment center and connect the PC audio outputs to an existing receiver or amplifier. Obviously, if you already have a good receiver and speakers, you might as well use them.

Of course, not everyone has a suitable receiver and speaker set. When we built the home theater PC system for the first edition of this book, we'd just decided to move our elderly JVC receiver and speakers to the downstairs guest suite and replace them with a high-powered PC speaker system. At that time, the best PC speaker set available was the Logitech Z-680 5.1 speaker system, which we used then and still use now.

Several years ago, Logitech replaced the Z-680 with the Z-5500, which has similar specifications and equal sound quality. The street price of the Z-5500 is $375 or so, considerably less than the price of a traditional home audio receiver and speakers with comparable power and sound quality. The Z-5500 incorporates four satellite speakers for left/right and front/rear audio, a center-channel speaker, and a low-frequency emitter (LFE) subwoofer. The satellite speakers are rated at 62W RMS each, the center-channel speaker at 69W RMS, and the LFE at a massive 188W RMS, for a total RMS output of 505W.

> **Peak Versus RMS**
>
> *Two methods are commonly used to specify the output power of amplifiers. Peak power is often specified for computer speakers, particularly inexpensive ones, but is essentially meaningless. Peak power indicates the maximum instantaneous power an amplifier can deliver, but it says nothing about how much power it can deliver continuously. The root mean square (RMS) power rating is more useful because it specifies how much power the amplifier can deliver continuously.*

The Z-5500 speaker system includes Dolby Digital & DTS hardware decoding and is THX certified. We confess that we don't understand what all that means, but our audiophile friends tell us those are Good Things. And, although admitting it may label us as audio barbarians, we have to say that the audio from our older Z-680 speaker system still sounds as good to us as anything else we've listened to, and the Z-5500 audio quality is just as good.

If the Z-5500 speaker set is a bit expensive for your budget, consider the Logitech X-540, which costs about $90, provides 70W RMS total power, and has very good sound quality for the price. Or you can, of course, simply use the speakers built into your HDTV.

Component Summary

Table 6-1 summarizes our component choices for the media center system.

Table 6-1. Bill of materials for media center system

Component	Product
Display	Sharp LC-42SB48UT 42" 1080p HDTV
Case	Antec Fusion Remote or Antec NSK-2480
Power supply	Antec EarthWatts 380
Processor	Intel Core i3-530
Motherboard	Intel DH55TC
Memory	Crucial Ballistix CT2KIT25664BN1337 4 GB Kit (2 GB×2)
Video adapter	Integrated or RADEON HD 4670/4850
Wireless network adapter	ASUS PCE-N13 802.11 b/g/n wireless adapter (see text)
Hard drives	Seagate Barracuda XT ST32000641AS 2TB (two)
Optical drive	LiteOn iHAS424-98 DVD writer
Backup hardware	Antec Easy SATA hard drive docking station (see text) Seagate 3 TB FreeAgent GoFlex Desk (see text) SYBA SD-ENC50020 Hard Drive Docking Station (see text)
Keyboard and mouse	Microsoft Wireless Desktop 3000
Speakers	Home audio speakers or Logitech Z-5500 speaker system
HDMI cable	Nippon Labs Premium High Performance HDMI1.3-6
Remote control	Logitech 915-000132 Universal Harmony 300 Remote

Building the Media Center System

Figure 6-1 shows the core components of the media center system. At the top left of the image, the Antec Fusion Remote media center case sits atop the Antec NSK-2480 media center case. (When we shot this image, we still hadn't decided which case to use.) On the left are the Crucial Ballistix 4 GB memory kit and Nippon Labs HDMI cable, with a pair of 2 TB Seagate Barracuda XT hard drives to their right. The LiteOn optical drive and the Intel Core i3-530 processor sit atop the Intel DH55TC motherboard, with the Logitech Universal Harmony 300 remote in front of them. The Sharp 42" 1080p HDTV we bought for our media center display wouldn't fit in the picture.

Figure 6-1. *Core media center system components, awaiting construction*

Before you proceed, verify that you have all of the necessary components. Open each box and confirm that all items on the packing list are present.

Preparing the Case

To begin preparing the Antec NSK-2480 case, place it on a flat surface and remove the single thumbscrew at the top rear, as shown in Figure 6-2. Then slide the top panel to the rear and lift it off, as shown in Figure 6-3.

Avoid Fireworks

Before you do anything else, make sure that the power supply is set to the correct input voltage. Some power supplies, including the EarthWatts 380 unit bundled with the Antec NSK-2480 case, autodetect input voltage and set themselves automatically. Other power supplies require moving a slide switch to indicate the correct input voltage.

If your mains voltage is 115V and the power supply is set for 230V, no damage occurs. The system simply won't start. However, if your mains voltage is 230V and the power supply expects 115V, you will see a very short and expensive fireworks show the first time you plug in your new system. The motherboard, processor, memory, expansion cards, and drives will all be burnt to a crisp within a fraction of a second.

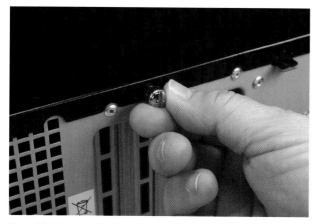

Figure 6-2. *Remove the thumbscrew that secures the top panel*

Figure 6-3. *Slide the top panel to the rear and lift it off*

Remove the optical drive bay by sliding it toward the rear of the case, pivoting it upward, and then lifting it free of the chassis, as shown in Figure 6-4.

With the optical drive bay removed, you have access to the bundle of cables from the power supply. Remove the AC power cord and set it aside. Remove the cable wraps that bundle the power supply cables, as shown in Figure 6-5, and straighten out the various cables.

Figure 6-4. *Remove the optical drive bay*

Figure 6-5. *Remove the cable tie that secures the bundle of cables from the power supply*

Like most cases, the Antec NSK-2480 comes with a generic rear-panel I/O shield. Generic I/O shields don't fit any motherboard we've ever used, so we're not sure why case makers bother to include them. Removing the generic I/O shield simply adds one more task.

To remove the generic I/O shield, press gently inward on it with a screwdriver handle, as shown in Figure 6-6. Don't worry about bending the I/O shield, because you'll discard it anyway. Do take care not to bend the cutout area of the case, which would make it very difficult to install the proper I/O shield. Support the edge of the cutout area with your fingers, and press on the generic I/O shield until it snaps out.

Chapter 6

Every motherboard comes with a custom I/O shield that matches the ports on its rear I/O panel. The included I/O shield is nearly always correct, but we have on occasion received a motherboard with an incorrect I/O shield. Before you install the custom I/O shield supplied with the motherboard, compare it against the motherboard I/O panel, as shown in Figure 6-7. If you received the wrong I/O shield, contact the motherboard manufacturer to request a replacement.

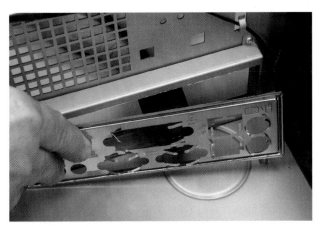

Figure 6-6. *Press gently on the generic I/O shield until it snaps out*

Figure 6-7. *Compare the custom I/O shield with the I/O panel of the motherboard*

To install the custom I/O shield, first make sure that it's oriented properly relative to the back-panel motherboard ports. Working from inside the case, align the I/O shield with the cutout. Using a screwdriver handle, start at one corner, as shown in Figure 6-8, and press gently until the I/O shield snaps into place. Run the screwdriver handle around the edges and corners of the I/O shield to ensure that it's fully seated.

After seating the I/O shield, hold the motherboard aligned in position directly over the case. Compare the positions of the motherboard mounting holes with the standoff mounting positions in the case. The Intel DH55TC has eight mounting holes. The Antec NSK-2480 case has six standoffs preinstalled, all of which correspond to mounting hole positions in the motherboard. Locate and note the two positions that require standoffs to be installed.

Install a brass standoff in each required position, and then use the motherboard again to verify that a standoff is installed at each of the required eight positions. Although you can screw in the standoffs using just your fingers, it's much easier and faster to use a 5 mm nut driver, as shown in Figure 6-9. Be careful not to overtorque the standoffs as you install them. The standoffs are made of soft brass, and the motherboard tray, although steel, is relatively thin. Applying too much torque can strip the standoff or the screw hole. Finger-tight is good enough, plus maybe an extra quarter turn or so.

Better Safe Than Sorry

Make absolutely sure that every standoff installed corresponds to a motherboard mounting hole. An extra standoff can contact the bottom of the motherboard, causing it to short and possibly damaging or destroying the motherboard and other components.

Figure 6-8. *Press gently to seat the custom I/O shield*

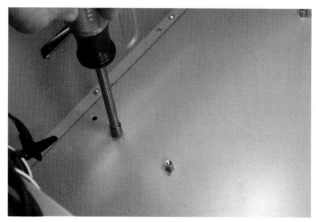

Figure 6-9. *Install a standoff in each position that corresponds to a motherboard mounting hole*

Preparing the Motherboard

The next step is to prepare the motherboard by installing the processor, CPU cooler, and memory. Although some case and motherboard manuals suggest installing these components after the motherboard has been installed in the case, it's easier and often safer for the motherboard to mount the processor, cooler, and memory first.

Installing the processor

To begin, locate the processor socket. Ground yourself by touching the chassis, and then release the metal socket lever by pressing it down and away from the socket body. Once the catch releases, lift the lever until it's fully vertical. Lifting the lever raises the load plate and exposes the socket. Snap out the black plastic socket cover and set it aside. Don't discard the socket cover. If you ever remove the processor from the socket, you should replace the socket cover to protect the socket until another processor is installed.

Ground yourself to the power supply or chassis frame, and then open the processor package. Snap off the black plastic processor cover and set it aside. Once again, store the processor cover in case you ever need to remove the processor.

The processor and socket are keyed to prevent the processor from being inserted backward into the socket. The gold triangle visible in Figure 6-10 on the left corner of the processor matches a beveled corner on the processor socket. The processor and socket are also keyed with two notches on the edge of the processor that mate with two protruding nubs on the inside edge of the socket. Make sure the processor and socket are aligned properly and then drop the processor straight into the socket, as shown in Figure 6-10. The processor should seat completely without you needing to apply any pressure. If it doesn't, lift the processor from the socket, recheck the alignment, and try again.

With the socket lever still vertical, lower the load plate, as shown in Figure 6-11.

Figure 6-10. *Align the processor with the socket and then drop the processor into the socket*

Figure 6-11. *Lower the load plate into the closed position*

Lower the processor lever to cam the load plate into locked position. Make sure the notch at the front of the load plate latches under the shoulder screw cap, as shown in Figure 6-12.

Press the processor lever flush with the motherboard and snap it into place under the load plate latch, as shown in Figure 6-13.

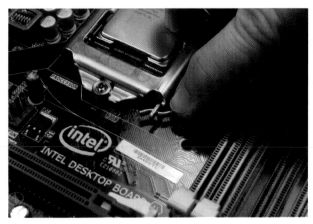

Figure 6-12. *Lower the processor lever to cam the load plate into locked position*

Figure 6-13. *Press the processor lever flush with the motherboard and snap it into the load plate latch*

Examine the surface of the processor for fingerprints, dust, or other contaminants. If any are present, polish the surface of the processor with a clean paper towel before you proceed to installing the CPU cooler. (If you're reinstalling the CPU cooler, make sure to remove all of the old thermal compound. You can use a hair dryer to soften it and make it easier to rub off.)

Installing the CPU cooler

Remove the CPU cooler from its packaging and look at the bottom of the cooler. The gray patches on the copper bearing surface of the cooler, visible in Figure 6-14, are thermal compound. This thermal compound melts each time the processor warms up, filling the voids between the surfaces of the processor and the base of the heatsink to ensure good heat transfer. If any of those patches are damaged, carefully rub off any remaining thermal compound, polish the surface of the heatsink base, and apply an approved thermal paste.

The CPU cooler mounts to the motherboard using four posts that protrude through matching holes in the motherboard. Because the posts and holes are in a square pattern, you can install the CPU cooler in any of four orientations. It doesn't matter which you use, so we generally install the CPU cooler so that the CPU fan power lead has just enough slack to reach the CPU fan power header pins on the motherboard.

You can't install the CPU cooler with the motherboard on a hard surface because, when seated, the posts protrude slightly on the back side of the motherboard. Placing the motherboard on a soft surface (such as packing foam) allows the posts to penetrate the motherboard and lock into position. If you use foam, make sure to keep the antistatic bag the motherboard was packaged in between the motherboard and the foam. Or, you can do what we usually do, which is to support the motherboard at a slight angle to provide clearance for the posts as we press the posts into place.

To install the CPU cooler, align the tips of its four posts with the four mounting holes in the motherboard. Once all four posts are aligned, press down firmly on one post, as shown in Figure 6-15, until you feel it snap into place.

Figure 6-14. *Verify that the thermal compound on the copper heatsink base is undamaged*

Figure 6-15. *Align each CPU cooler post with a mounting hole and press down until it snaps into place*

After you seat the posts, use a flat-blade screwdriver to turn the top of each post in the direction of the arrow to lock it into position, as shown in Figure 6-16.

Finally, connect the CPU fan power cable to the CPU fan power header pins on the edge of the motherboard, as shown in Figure 6-17. This connector is keyed. Make sure the slot in the cable connector aligns with the projecting tab on the motherboard header-pin set, and then slide the cable connector onto the pins until it seats.

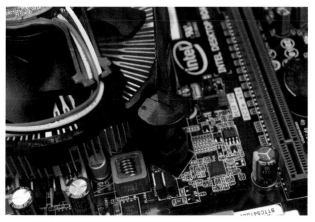

Figure 6-16. *Lock each CPU cooler post by turning the head in the direction of the arrow*

Figure 6-17. *Connect the CPU fan power cable to the CPU fan power header pins*

Installing memory

The next step is to install the memory modules. The DH55TC motherboard accepts 240-pin DDR3 memory modules. Installing memory modules in pairs enables dual-channel memory operation for faster memory performance.

If you are installing two identical memory modules, install them in the two blue slots. If you are installing two matched pairs of memory modules that differ in capacity, install the higher-capacity pair in the two blue slots and the lower-capacity pair in the black slots. Although it will reduce overall memory performance, you can install three memory modules if two of them are a matched pair. In that case, install the matched pair in the two blue slots, and the third module in either black slot.

In any case, fill the slots nearest the processor first and work forward toward the edge of the board. Ground yourself by touching the power supply or chassis frame before you handle a memory module. To install the first module, position it vertically over the appropriate slot. Align both edges of the module with the slots in the vertical posts on the sides of the slot. DDR3 DIMMs are keyed with an off-center notch on the contact edge of the DIMM. Make sure this notch aligns with the corresponding post in the slot, and then slide the DIMM into position, as shown in Figure 6-18.

After you've aligned the module properly, place one thumb on each side of the module and press down firmly until it snaps into place, as shown in Figure 6-19. Repeat this procedure to install any remaining DIMMs.

Figure 6-18. *Position the memory module with the notch aligned with the socket tab*

Figure 6-19. *Press straight down with both thumbs until the module snaps into place*

Installing the Motherboard

Installing the motherboard is the most time-consuming part of the build, because there are so many cables to be connected. Take your time during this phase, because it's important that all of the cables be connected properly.

Connecting front-panel switch and indicator cables

Ron Morse Comments

I like to use a thick towel or something that's larger than the motherboard just in case it moves around a bit. The little component lead stubs on the back of a motherboard can do a number on the paint finish on the exposed edge of the case.

Ordinarily, we install the motherboard in the case before connecting cables to it, but this combination of motherboard and case has so little clearance that we decided to connect the cables first. If you're using the Intel DH55TC motherboard and Antec NSK-2480 case, we recommend you do the same. To do so, route the front-panel switch, indicator, and port cables into the motherboard chamber and out the top of the case. Place the protective plastic bag that contained the motherboard on top of the chassis over the motherboard chamber, and balance the motherboard on top of the chassis.

The only essential front-panel connector is the power switch, which must be connected before you can start the system. You'll probably also want to connect the reset switch and the hard disk activity LED (shown in Figure 6-20). If you are using a different case, it may have front-panel cables for which there are no corresponding header-pin sets on the motherboard. Conversely, a motherboard may have header-pin sets for which the case has no corresponding cables. For example, the Intel DH55TC motherboard has pins for a power LED, for which the Antec NSK-2480 case does not provide a cable. (The NSK-2480 power LED connects directly to a Molex connector from the power supply. When the system is turned on, the power LED is illuminated.)

Figure 6-20. *Connect the front-panel switch and indicator cables*

Before you begin connecting front-panel cables, examine the connectors. Each should be labeled descriptively (POWER SW, RESET SW, HDD LED, and so on). Match those descriptions with the front-panel connector header pins on the motherboard to make sure you connect the correct cables to the appropriate pins. The power and reset switch cables are not polarized and may be connected either way. LED cables may or may not be polarized, but if you connect a polarized LED cable backward the worst that happens is that the LED won't light up. Most Antec cases use white wires for ground and colored wires for signal. Some cases use black wires for ground, and a few use green.

When you're connecting front-panel cables, try to get it right the first time, but don't worry too much about getting it wrong. Other than the power switch cable, which must be connected properly for the system to start, none of the other front-panel switch and indicator cables are essential, and connecting them incorrectly won't damage the system.

Bright Lights

The NSK-2480 power LED and HDD LED are quite bright. They're not intrusive in a normally lit room or if you're not looking directly at the system, but in a typical home theater setup the lights are often dimmed and the media center system is usually quite close to the television. Under those conditions, you may find the power and HDD LEDs distracting. For that reason, some builders don't bother to connect them. The only downside to doing that is that if you later decide you want those indicators working, you may have some difficulty getting the cables connected. We suggest that you connect the power and HDD LEDs initially. If you decide they're too bright, you can disconnect them easily.

Connecting front-panel audio

The NSK-2480 front-panel audio cable terminates in two connectors, one labeled HD AUDIO and the other FP'97. The motherboard HD audio front-panel audio connector is located near the PCI expansion slot and is keyed with a missing pin. The audio cable HD audio connector has a corresponding blocked hole, to prevent the connector from being installed backward. Align the HD audio cable connector over the HD audio header-pin set on the motherboard, and press the cable connector straight down until it seats completely, as shown in Figure 6-21.

Figure 6-21. *Connect the front-panel audio cable to the motherboard HD audio connector*

Connecting front-panel USB ports

The Antec NSK-2480 case provides two front-panel USB ports with cables that terminate in one Intel-standard dual-USB connector. Locate that cable, which is labeled USB, and connect it to one of the three dual-USB motherboard connectors located near the left front edge of the motherboard near the SATA ports, as shown in Figure 6-22. The motherboard connector is keyed with a missing pin that corresponds to a blocked hole on the cable connector, so it's difficult to connect the cable incorrectly. (However, it *is* possible to offset the cable connector against the motherboard connector and still seat the connector.) Note that we chose to use the FP USB 2 header-pin set, which can instead be used to connect an internal Intel SSD. We have no plans to install such a drive, and this header-pin set is perfectly usable for a standard USB front-panel connection.

Figure 6-22. *Connect the front-panel USB cable to a motherboard dual-USB connector*

Seating and securing the motherboard

To begin, lower the motherboard into the case, as shown in Figure 6-23, with the front edge of the motherboard slightly raised. Carefully align the back-panel I/O connectors with the corresponding holes in the I/O shield, and slide the motherboard toward the rear of the case as you lower the motherboard to horizontal. This process is hard to describe, but easy to do. The goal is to get the back-panel ports on the motherboard low enough that they come into contact with the I/O shield grounding tabs, without those tabs intruding into the ports themselves. (The Ethernet grounding tab is usually the problem; we've been known to bend that tab slightly upward to facilitate installing the motherboard and then bend it back down into contact afterward.)

Maintain slight rearward pressure on the motherboard to keep it in contact with the I/O shield. Examine the rear I/O panel to make sure that none of the I/O shield grounding tabs intrude into a port connector. More than once,

Chapter 6

we've mounted a motherboard, inserted all the screws, and connected all the cables before we noticed that there was a metal tab sticking into one of our USB or LAN ports. Before you secure the motherboard in place, verify that the back-panel I/O connectors are mated cleanly with the I/O shield, as shown in Figure 6-24. A bright flashlight can be very helpful here.

Figure 6-23. *Slide the motherboard into position*

Figure 6-24. *Make sure the back-panel connectors mate cleanly with the I/O shield*

Once the motherboard is positioned properly and you have verified that the back-panel I/O port connectors are mated cleanly with the I/O shield, insert a screw through each motherboard mounting hole into the corresponding standoff, as shown in Figure 6-25. For the first two or three screws, you may have to apply pressure with one hand to keep the holes and standoffs aligned while driving the screw with the other.

Figure 6-25. *Securing the motherboard*

At times it's difficult to get all the holes and standoffs aligned. If that occurs, insert two screws into easily accessible positions, but don't tighten the screws completely. You should then be able to force the motherboard into complete alignment, with all holes matching the standoffs. At that point, insert one or two more screws into standoffs and tighten them completely. Finish mounting the motherboard by inserting screws into all the standoffs and tightening them. Don't put excessive force on the screws, or you may crack the motherboard. Finger-tight is plenty, plus at most a quarter turn.

Screwed

Although the problem is more common with cheap motherboards and cases, even if you're using high-quality components it can be difficult, if not impossible, to get all of the mounting holes aligned with the standoffs. There simply isn't much slack to work with. With high-quality components, everything usually lines up perfectly (although it may take some pressure). But if you find yourself unable to insert all of the motherboard mounting screws, don't despair. We like to get all the screws installed, both for physical support and to make sure all of the grounding points on the motherboard are grounded, but getting most of them installed—say six or seven of the eight—is normally good enough.

If you are unable to install all of the screws, take the time to remove the brass standoffs where no screw will be installed. A misaligned standoff may short something out. In situations where we couldn't use all of the brass standoffs because of alignment issues, we have been known to trim double chopsticks to length and install them as substitute standoffs. They're the right thickness to support the motherboard and are made of non-conducting wood.

It's particularly important to provide some support for the motherboard near the expansion slots, where significant pressure may be applied when installing cards. If the motherboard is unsupported, pressing down on it may crack it.

Playing Both Ends Against the Middle

Both ends of a SATA cable are identical in terms of pin assignments and keying, so it usually doesn't matter which end you connect to the motherboard and which to the drive. Many SATA cables have simple plastic connectors on both ends, but some, including those supplied with some Intel motherboards, have metal latching connectors on one or both ends that are designed to lock the cable to the connector.

If you subsequently remove such a cable, make sure to press the latch to disconnect it before you pull the cable, or you may damage the motherboard connector and/or the cable. Back in the days when latching SATA connectors were still very uncommon, we once pulled a SATA cable from a motherboard without watching what we were doing. We heard a loud cracking noise. Fortunately, it was the cable we damaged rather than the motherboard, but it might easily have been otherwise.

Connecting SATA data cables

The next step is to connect the SATA data cables for the hard drives and the optical drive. The Intel DH55TC motherboard provides a cluster of six SATA connectors near the left front corner of the motherboard. Four of these, color-coded black, are standard SATA data connectors. Two, color-coded red, are eSATA connectors, which may be used to connect standard SATA devices as well as eSATA devices. Intel properly labels the four standard connectors SATA 0 through SATA 3. (Some motherboards begin numbering at SATA 1.) We'll connect our two hard drives to SATA ports 0 and 1, and our optical drive to SATA port 2.

Locate three SATA data cables, which may be supplied with the motherboard, the drives, or both. Connect those SATA data cables to SATA ports 0, 1, and 2, as shown in Figure 6-26. Align the cable connector with the motherboard connector, making sure that the L-shaped keys on both connectors are oriented properly, and then press the cable connector straight down until it seats in the motherboard connector. (As a close examination of Figure 6-26 shows, we actually used three different SATA cables; they just happened to be the first three we pulled from our supplies closet.)

The two hard drive SATA data cables can remain in the motherboard chamber for now, but we need to route the optical drive SATA data cable through the bulkhead and into the chamber that contains the power supply and optical drive. To do so, loosen the screw that secures the sliding access panel in the bulkhead, as shown in Figure 6-27, and slide the panel fully open.

Figure 6-26. *Connect the SATA data cables to the motherboard ports*

Figure 6-27. *Loosen the screw that secures the access panel*

Pass the free end of the optical drive SATA data cable through the access door and into the chamber that contains the optical drive bay, as shown in Figure 6-28.

Figure 6-28. *Pass the SATA data cable for the optical drive into the power supply chamber*

Routing and connecting power to the motherboard

The next step is to route the main ATX power cable and the ATX12V (CPU) power cable from the power supply chamber to the motherboard chamber and connect those cables. To begin, pass the 24-pin main ATX power cable from the power supply chamber into the motherboard chamber, as shown in Figure 6-29.

Align the 24-pin main ATX power cable connector with the motherboard socket, as shown in Figure 6-30, and press down firmly until it snaps into place. Examine the connection visually to verify that the connectors are fully mated and that the latch has engaged. A partially seated main ATX power connector can cause subtle problems that are very difficult to troubleshoot.

Figure 6-29. *Route the main ATX power cable from the power supply chamber into the main chamber*

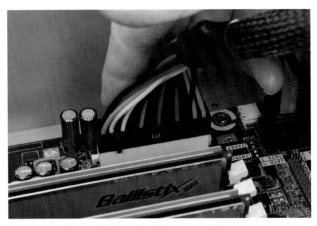

Figure 6-30. *Connect the main ATX power cable*

The next step is to route and connect the ATX12V power cable, as shown in Figures 6-31 and 6-32. The ATX12V motherboard connector is located between the CPU socket and the rear I/O panel. Orient the ATX12V cable properly, and press down firmly until it snaps into place. Examine the connection to make sure that the latch is engaged.

Figure 6-31. *Route the ATX12V power cable from the power supply chamber into the main chamber*

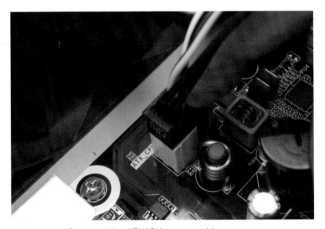

Figure 6-32. *Connect the ATX12V power cable*

Installing the Optical Drive

The next step is to install the optical drive. The Antec NSK-2480 case provides two external 5.25" drive bays, either or both of which can be used for optical drives or other 5.25" devices, such as the Antec Easy SATA hard drive docking station. To begin installing the optical drive, press the inside of the plastic bezel until it snaps out, as shown in Figure 6-33.

Chapter 6

Locate the optical drive cage that you set aside earlier. Slide the optical drive into the cage and use four or more of the provided screws to secure it, as shown in Figure 6-34. Make sure to orient and position the optical drive as shown. It needs to protrude from the front of the drive cage if you want the optical drive bezel to be flush with the case bezel.

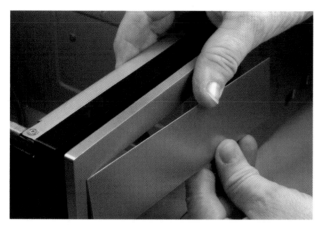

Figure 6-33. *Snap out the plastic bezel from a 5.25" external drive bay*

Figure 6-34. *Secure the optical drive to the bay with four screws*

Slide the optical drive cage into the case with the front tilted downward, as shown in Figure 6-35.

Lower the rear of the optical drive cage, making sure that the projecting nubs on the cage frame fit into the cutouts on the chassis, and then slide the optical drive cage into the locked position, as shown in Figure 6-36.

Figure 6-35. *Slide the optical drive cage into the case*

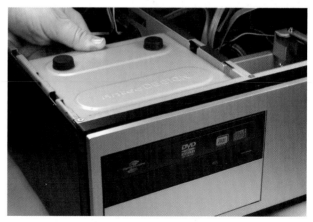

Figure 6-36. *Slide the optical drive cage into the chassis*

Locate an available SATA power cable from the power supply and connect it to the optical drive power connector, as shown in Figure 6-37. (We used the SATA power cable with the P5 connector.) Make sure the L-shaped keys on the cable connector and drive connector are aligned properly, and then press the cable connector onto the drive connector until it seats completely.

Locate the SATA data cable that you previously fed through from the motherboard chamber to the power supply chamber, and connect that SATA data cable to the optical drive, as shown in Figure 6-38. Make sure the keying on the drive and cable connectors is aligned properly, and then press the connector into place until it's fully seated.

Figure 6-37. *Connect a SATA power cable to the optical drive*

Figure 6-38. *Connect the SATA data cable to the optical drive*

Routing Drive Power Cables to the Motherboard Chamber

The next step is to route power cables for the hard drives, fan, and power LED from the power supply chamber into the motherboard chamber. We'll need Molex power connectors for the power LED and both case fans, and two SATA power connectors for the hard drives. Depending on your configuration, it can be important which cables you choose to route. Obviously, you need the right number and type of power connectors for the devices you need to connect. Less obviously, depending on your power supply, some cables may be longer or shorter than others, or may have the wrong type of connector in the right place, or vice versa. We routed the P2 cable (shown in Figure 6-39) and the P10 cable (shown in Figure 6-40) into the motherboard chamber. That combination works for the configuration we used, but again, check your own configuration to be sure.

Draw sufficient length of each cable into the motherboard chamber to reach the devices you need to connect. Don't forget to allow some slack for cable dressing. Once you've done that, you can slide the bulkhead access door closed, as shown in Figure 6-41, and tighten the screw that secures it.

Figure 6-39. *Routing the P2 cable into the motherboard chamber*

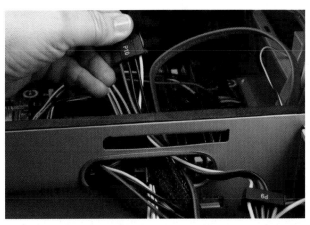

Figure 6-40. *Routing the P10 cable into the motherboard chamber*

Figure 6-41. *Slide the bulkhead access door closed*

Installing the Hard Drive(s)

The next step is to install the hard drive(s), a task that's considerably more involved with the NSK-2480 than it is with most cases. The NSK-2480 mounts one or two hard drives vertically in a separate chamber at the front of the case. In most cases, you can install hard drives and connect the power and data cables without much regard for sequence. In the NSK-2480, the sequence is important because access to the drive connectors is restricted after you've inserted them in the cage. To begin, remove the four screws that secure the top plate of the hard drive chamber, as shown in Figure 6-42, and then remove the top plate, as shown in Figure 6-43, and set it aside.

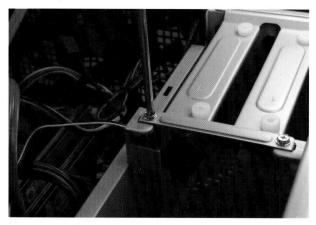

Figure 6-42. *Remove the four screws that secure the top plate of the hard drive chamber*

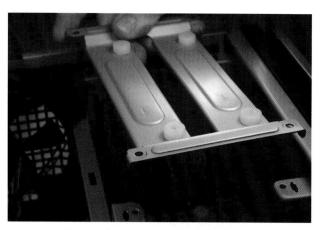

Figure 6-43. *Remove the top plate from the hard drive chamber*

Connect an available SATA power cable to the first hard drive, as shown in Figure 6-44. We used the P9 connector.

Connect a SATA data cable to the first hard drive, as shown in Figure 6-45.

Figure 6-44. *Connect a SATA power cable to the first hard drive*

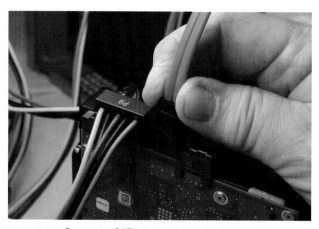

Figure 6-45. *Connect a SATA data cable to the first hard drive*

P9 or P6?

We mentioned the connector by number not because of function or power provisioning, but simply to indicate which connector we found most convenient to use because of cable length, connector positioning, and so on.

Slide the first hard drive into the hard drive chamber, oriented as shown in Figure 6-46.

Hard drives can be secured with two screws driven through the top plate and (optionally, according to Antec) with two more screws driven through the bottom of the case. Rather than having our hard drives hanging like bats, suspended from the top plate and free-floating on the bottom, we prefer to secure our drives with four screws as usual. To do that, turn the case on its side, while supporting the hard drive to make sure it doesn't fall out. Use one hand to wiggle the hard drive back and forth until the grommeted screw holes in the bottom of the case align with the drive screw holes. Drive in two screws, as shown in Figure 6-47, to secure the drive to the bottom of the case.

To install the second hard drive, connect a SATA data cable and a SATA power cable, as shown in Figures 6-48 and 6-49.

Figure 6-46. *Slide the first hard drive into the hard drive chamber*

Figure 6-47. *Secure the first hard drive with two screws through the bottom of the case*

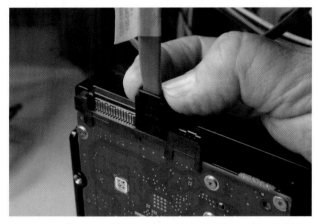

Figure 6-48. *Connect a SATA data cable to the second hard drive*

Figure 6-49. *Connect a SATA power cable to the second hard drive*

Slide the second hard drive into the hard drive bay, wiggle it back and forth until the screw holes in the drive align with those in the chassis, and secure the drive to the chassis by driving in two hard drive mounting screws, as shown in Figure 6-50.

Figure 6-51 shows both hard drives properly mounted.

The next step is to replace the top plate on the hard drive bay and secure each hard drive by driving two hard drive mounting screws through the plate and into the drive, as shown in Figure 6-52.

Figure 6-50. *Secure the second hard drive to the chassis by driving two hard drive mounting screws through the bottom of the case and into the drive*

Figure 6-51. *Both hard drives properly mounted*

The final step in installing the hard drives is to reinstall the four screws that secure the top plate to the hard drive bay, as shown in Figure 6-53.

Figure 6-52. *Secure both hard drives to the top plate of the hard drive bay by driving two hard drive mounting screws into each drive*

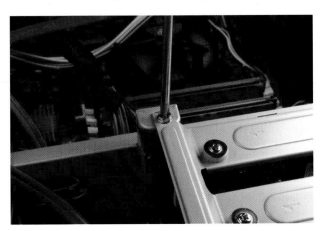

Figure 6-53. *Secure the top plate to the hard drive bay by driving in four screws*

Installing the Expansion Cards

If you have a video adapter or expansion cards to install, now is the time to do it. We had only a half-height PCI wireless networking card to install, and we actually installed it earlier in the build. Then, as we were writing this section, we realized that we should shift this step to very late in the build. The potential problem is that a full-length, full-height expansion card may block the sliding access plate in the bulkhead, making it difficult to route cables from the power supply chamber to the motherboard chamber.

To begin installing your expansion card(s), determine which card(s) will occupy which slot(s), and therefore which expansion slot covers you need to remove. You can do that by holding the card in position against the appropriate motherboard slot and determining which expansion slot cover that card's expansion bracket covers. Once you've determined that, remove the screw that secures the expansion slot cover, as shown in Figure 6-54.

With the screw removed, tilt the expansion slot cover slightly toward the front of the case, as shown in Figure 6-55, and pull straight up to remove it.

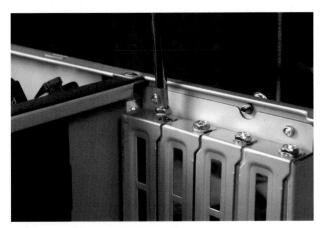

Figure 6-54. *Remove the screw that secures the expansion slot cover*

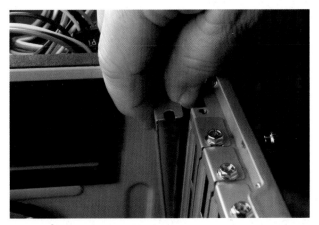

Figure 6-55. *Tilt the expansion slot cover toward the inside of the case and pull it free*

Align the contact edge of the expansion card with the slot and press down firmly to seat the card, as shown in Figure 6-56. Verify visually that the card is fully seated. Video adapters are particularly problematic. The video adapter may appear to seat. You may even feel it snap into place. That doesn't guarantee that it's completely seated. Always examine the slot carefully to make sure that the card is fully seated and level in the slot, with the top edge of the card contacts flush with the top edge of the slot. After you seat each expansion card, reinsert the screw to secure the bracket to the chassis. After you tighten the screw in the retaining bracket, double-check to make sure the card is completely seated in its slot. (Sometimes, driving the screw into the bracket can twist the card up and out of the slot slightly; in that situation, you're better off omitting the screw entirely.)

Check the Latch, Both Ways

A plastic retention mechanism is used to secure a PCI Express video adapter in the slot. When you install a video adapter, make sure the retention mechanism latches. When you remove a video adapter, make sure to unlatch the retention mechanism before you attempt to remove the card from the slot.

If the expansion card has any sort of external dongle, antenna, or other connector, hook it up now. For example, Figure 6-57 shows Barbara attaching the antenna to the WiFi card.

Figure 6-56. *Align the expansion card with the slot and press down firmly to seat it*

Figure 6-57. *Connect the WiFi antenna to the back of the card*

Finishing Up

We're in the home stretch now. All that remains is to connect power to the case fans and the power LED (if you choose to do that), and a few minor cleanup tasks. Figures 6-58, 6-59, and 6-60 show Barbara connecting power for the power LED, using connector P10, and to the case fans using the P2/P3 connectors.

Figure 6-61 shows our media center system at this point in the build. Obviously, we can't leave that rats' nest of cables flopping around in there where they might foul a fan, so the next task is to dress the cables.

> **Nobody's Perfect**
>
> *One of our tech reviewers asked if the SATA data cables should have been routed through the cutout between the motherboard chamber and the hard drive chamber, and whether there was sufficient clearance for the cover with the SATA cables run over the top edge of the bulkhead (as it isn't clear in the image). The answer to both of those questions is yes. We should have routed the SATA cables through the cutout, but we didn't notice that until after we'd finished building the system. And there is sufficient clearance between the top edge of the bulkhead and the case cover, so we elected to leave the cables as they were and simply tie them off to the chassis frame.*

As Figure 6-62 shows, even at full extension the ATX12V cable wasn't long enough to route along an edge of the motherboard, so we did the best we could. We tried it both ways, running it along the back of the motherboard as well as the front. We got the fan power cables secured away from the blades and used the cable wraps to tie the cable bundles to the chassis. While we were at it, we rerouted the SATA data cables to run them through the chassis cutout visible underneath them in the preceding image.

Figure 8-58. *Connect power to the power LED*

Figure 8-59. *Connect power to the first case fan*

Figure 8-60. *Connect power to the second case fan*

Figure 8-61. *Our media center system, before cleanup*

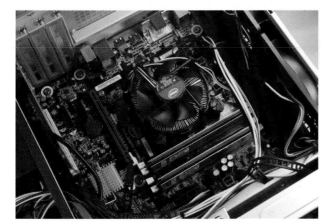

Figure 8-62. *The final system, with cables dressed*

Only the Good Die Young

When you turn on the rear power switch, the system will come to life momentarily and then die. That's perfectly normal behavior. When the power supply receives power, it begins to start up. It quickly notices that the motherboard hasn't told it to start, though, so it shuts down again. All you need to do is press the front-panel power switch and the system will start normally.

Ron Morse Comments

Robert makes a good case for preferring the eSATA interface over the slower USB connection for removable, "hot-pluggable" storage devices, but there's a potential gotcha: it only works if both the SATA disk controller on the motherboard and the operating system support it.

You won't have a problem if you follow Robert's recommendations for the hardware and use Linux, Windows Vista, or Windows 7 as your operating system, but Windows XP doesn't support AHCI—at least, not without a complicated and error-prone modification to the system software. If for some reason you find yourself using Windows XP as the operating system on your media center PC, leave the BIOS setting for the SATA controller in default IDE mode and make do with the USB interface for external storage

The CPU fan cable was obnoxious. It was too short to route and dress the way we wanted to, and too long to leave flopping loose. We finally looped it over one of the CPU cooler posts and declared the job done. (Until we powered up the system for the smoke test and quickly realized that the CPU fan cable had fouled the CPU fan.)

Once you have the cables dressed, take a few minutes to double-check everything one last time before you apply power to the system. Use the following checklist:

☐ No loose tools or screws (shake the case gently)

☐ CPU cooler properly mounted; CPU fan connected

☐ Memory modules fully seated and latched

☐ Front-panel switch and indicator cables connected properly

☐ Front-panel I/O cables connected properly

☐ Hard drive data cables connected to drive and motherboard

☐ Hard drive power cables connected

☐ Optical drive data cable connected to drive and motherboard

☐ Optical drive power cable connected

☐ All drives secured to drive bay or chassis, as applicable

☐ Expansion cards fully seated and secured to chassis

☐ Main ATX power cable and ATX12V power cable connected

☐ All cables dressed and tucked

Once you're certain that all is as it should be, it's time for the smoke test. Leave the cover off for now. Connect the power cable to the wall receptacle and then to the system unit. Flip the rear power switch from 0 to 1. Press the main power button on the front of the case, and the system should start up. Check to make sure that the power supply fan and CPU fan are spinning. You should also hear the hard drives spin up. At that point, everything should be working properly.

After the system passes the smoke test, turn it off and connect the keyboard, mouse, display, and any other external peripherals. When the BIOS Setup screen appears, run BIOS Setup and verify that all hardware is recognized and that the date and time are set correctly. Verify that the optical drive is first in the boot sequence screen. If you've installed a removable or eSATA hard drive, make sure to configure the IDE/ATA options to enable AHCI. Once BIOS Setup is the way you want it, save your changes and exit. Put your operating system disc in the optical drive and turn the system off. Restart it and install the operating system.

Installing Software

Now that we've built the system, it's time to install the software we need. For each of the first two editions of this book, we spent a couple of weeks installing and testing scads of media center applications, everything from Windows Media Center Edition to third-party Windows PVR apps to half a dozen Linux media center apps. We played around with numerous handheld remotes and IR receivers and spent time tweaking various software plug-ins to do things like convert recorded TV programs to DVD format or send commands to a cable box to turn it on and change channels.

We started to do the same thing this time, looking at Windows 7, Mythbuntu, LinuxMCE, and many other media center apps. Then it finally hit us. If we won't use our media center system to record TV programs, we don't need any of this specialized software. With an HDTV, we don't need a low-resolution 10-foot interface and a handheld remote to control the system. We can do everything we need to do with Windows 7 or a standard Linux distribution with a standard wireless keyboard and mouse, and you probably can, too.

Windows certainly has some very nice features, and for many people it will be the perfect media center operating system. But Linux also has some very nice features, and since we run Linux on all of our other systems, we decided to make our media center system Linux-based as well. Even if you're a Windows or OS X household, you may well find that Linux is the best choice for your media center system. If nothing else, Linux and all of the applications we feature in this section cost nothing, which can save you several hundred dollars on your new media center system.

Of course, you may decide to run Windows 7 on your media center system, either because you're just more comfortable with it or because you intend to use the system for gaming, or both. (Linux positively suX0rz for gaming. If we decide to run games, we'll buy an xBox, PS3, or Wii console.)

Operating System

Ubuntu Linux (*http://www.ubuntu.com*)

We chose Ubuntu Linux for our media center system, mainly because it's what we run on all of our other PCs. Ubuntu is the most popular desktop Linux distribution, and for good reason. It's newbie-friendly, well maintained, and has a huge selection of freely downloadable software available in its repositories. Nearly any Linux application you might want to use is likely to be available in a version for Ubuntu. If you're already comfortable with another Linux distribution, use it. But if you're new to Linux, Ubuntu is an excellent way to get started.

To install Ubuntu, visit the website and download the ISO file. Burn that file to a CD in ISO mode. (That is, burn the downloaded ISO file as a disc image rather than as an individual file.) If you're downloading the Linux ISO to a Windows system and don't have disc-burning software that can burn ISO image files, download and install ImgBurn (*http://www.imgburn.com*).

Make sure you've set up the BIOS to boot from the optical drive, insert the disc in the drive, start the system, and follow the prompts to install Ubuntu. (If during installation you have no clue about which options to select, just accept the defaults.) As soon as the installation is complete and the system reboots, click the System menu, choose Update Manager, and allow Ubuntu to download and install all updates.

The standard Ubuntu distribution includes by default most of the general-purpose applications you might need—things like OpenOffice.org for word processing and spreadsheets, Firefox for web browsing, and so on. But there's tons more stuff available, and all at no cost. Anything we might need for our media center system is available for Linux. Those Linux applications are usually at least as capable as similar apps available for Windows, and often more so.

Windows users are invariably surprised when they see how easy it is to install Linux apps. In Ubuntu, you can simply click Add/Remove from the Applications menu, select the application or applications you want to install, and click Apply Changes. Linux automatically downloads and installs the new application(s). If a new application requires supporting files that aren't already installed on your system, those additional files are automatically downloaded and installed as well. Figure 6-63 shows the Ubuntu Add/Remove dialog just after we installed LAME (the consensus best MP3 encoder), which is included in the Ubuntu Restricted Extras package.

Mythbuntu for TV Recording

If you did install a TV tuner card or cards in your media center system, you can make things a lot easier by installing Mythbuntu (http://mythbuntu.org) rather than the standard Ubuntu distribution. Mythbuntu is a modified version of Ubuntu that has MythTV preinstalled and preconfigured. By default, Mythbuntu uses the minimalist XFCE user interface and does not install the general-purpose applications that are bundled with the Ubuntu distribution, but Mythbuntu is actually Ubuntu under the hood. You can have the capabilities of both Ubuntu and Mythbuntu simply by installing Mythbuntu and then using the Control Centre to install the ubuntu-desktop package and any other packages you need.

If you do decide to install Mythbuntu for PVR functions, we strongly recommend you check their supported hardware list and hew rigorously to it. During a back-channel conversation between Robert and our tech reviewers, Ron Morse—who's forgotten more about Linux than Robert ever learned—commented

that, despite playing with it extensively, he'd never been able to get Mythbuntu to work. Robert replied that he'd installed Mythbuntu (and earlier versions of MythPC) on several systems, as far back as 2004, and had never had a problem getting it to work.

The reason for that difference became clear as the conversation continued: Robert had used only the exact components that appeared on the supported hardware list. Ron had tried to use some components that were very similar to supported components (e.g., a different model of tuner card, but one based on the same chipset as a supported tuner card). Close doesn't cut it with Mythbuntu. If you're going to try it, do it right. Make sure every component you use is explicitly listed as supported.

Or, as Ron suggests, install a version of Windows 7 that includes Media Center and have done with it.

Figure 6-63. *The Ubuntu Add/Remove Applications dialog*

Audio CD Ripping and Encoding

K3b + LAME (Ubuntu repositories)

Ripping a CD is the process of extracting the original music tracks from an original audio CD as WAV files. *Encoding* is the process of converting those WAV files to some other audio format, such as MP3. There are dozens of audio CD rippers available for Linux, but the one we find ourselves coming back to every time we try something different is K3b (KDE Burn, Baby, Burn), shown in Figure 6-64, which is also the best disc burning application available for Linux. To install K3b, click the Ubuntu Applications menu and choose Add/Remove. When the Add/Remove Applications dialog appears, type "K3b" in the search box. Mark the K3b checkbox, and click the Apply Changes button.

Like the gold-standard Windows application Exact Audio Copy, K3b performs extremely accurate rips. It's also very convenient to use, particularly if you have a huge stack of audio CDs to rip. As you insert each audio CD, K3b automatically looks up the CDDB track information, rips the audio data to WAV files (which can be deleted automatically as processing for each CD is complete), and encodes those WAV files as MP3 files or in another format you specify. All you have to do is insert a new audio CD each time K3b finishes processing the last one and ejects it.

Some years ago, we ripped our entire collection of audio CDs to uncompressed WAV files, because we wanted the best possible audio quality. Unfortunately, a typical audio CD contains about 600 MB of WAV files, so our collection of several hundred CDs occupied about 500 GB of disk space. As it turned out, that was overkill.

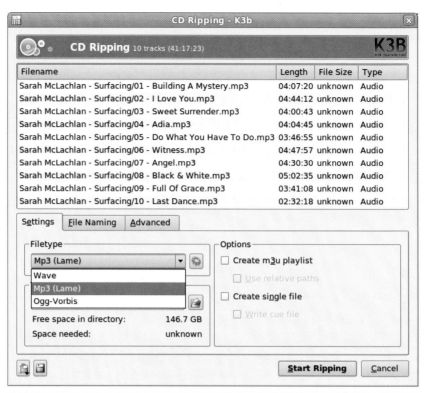

Figure 6-64. *Ripping and encoding an audio CD with K3b and LAME*

We did some listening comparison tests, putting the original WAV files up against MP3 files compressed with the LAME encoder set to use the "insane" preset, which encodes MP3 audio at 320 kb/s VBR (variable bit rate). Listening with a high-quality receiver and speakers, we couldn't tell any difference at all between the uncompressed files and the MP3 files. So we re-encoded all of those tracks to MP3 files, reducing our storage requirements from 500 GB to about 125 GB and at the same time quadrupling the number of tracks that fit on Barbara's MP3 players.

If you decide to rip and encode your audio CD collection, we strongly recommend that you encode your tracks as MP3 files for maximum compatibility with portable players and so on. And, if you decide to encode to MP3, don't even think about using any encoder other than LAME. Nothing else comes close to LAME in audio quality. Use the LAME "insane" preset for the best possible audio quality.

Unfortunately, installing K3b does not install the LAME encoder by default. To get LAME, click on the Ubuntu Applications menu and run Add/Remove Applications to install the Ubuntu Restricted Extras package, as described previously. Once LAME is installed, put an audio CD in the drive, run K3b, and choose Rip Audio CD from the Tools menu. When the CD Ripping dialog appears, click the gear tool next to the Filetype drop-down list, and configure LAME to your preferences. Figure 6-65 shows the LAME command-line options we use.

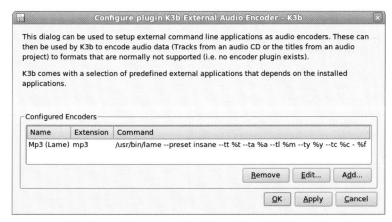

Figure 6-65. *The External Audio Encoder dialog, where LAME is configured*

Music Management

Rhythmbox Music Player (default)

Amarok (Ubuntu repositories)

If your CD collection is anything near the size of ours, you'll end up with an MP3 directory that contains hundreds of subdirectories, which in turn contain thousands to tens of thousands of MP3 files. Just double-clicking any of those MP3 files will start it playing, but that's obviously not an ideal way to manage your music collection. Fortunately, there are at least two good Linux applications available to manage your music files.

By default, Ubuntu installs the Rhythmbox music player, shown in Figure 6-66. Rhythmbox is essentially a partial clone of the iTunes application, except that it points to free music stores rather than the commercial Apple iTunes service. Rhythmbox provides all of the basic music management/player features, along with some nice extras such as smart playlists and the ability to burn a playlist to CD. Rhythmbox is a bit light on features for our tastes, but it's extremely popular and may be all you need.

To start using Rhythmbox, open the Ubuntu Applications menu, choose the Sound & Video submenu, and click Rhythmbox Music Player. Open the Rhythmbox Edit menu, choose Preferences, point it to your MP3 directory, and set up Rhythmbox the way you want it. It will scan and index your audio collection automatically, a process that took less than half an hour when run against our 125 GB music directory. Once the indexing completes, you're ready to roll.

The other standout choice among Linux music managers is Amarok, shown in Figure 6-67. Amarok supports every music management/player feature we can imagine, and then some. It's not included in the standard Ubuntu distribution, so if you want to use it you'll have to add it manually. To do so, click the Ubuntu Applications menu and choose Add/Remove. When the Add/Remove Applications dialog appears, type "Amarok" in the search box. Mark the Amarok checkbox, and click the Apply Changes button.

Figure 6-66. The Rhythmbox music player main screen

Figure 6-67. The Amarok music player main screen

Once Amarok is installed, open the Settings menu and choose Configure Amarok to display the Configure – Amarok dialog shown in Figure 6-68. Point Amarok to your MP3 directory or directories, make any other changes you wish, apply the changes, and dismiss the dialog.

Like Rhythmbox, Amarok automatically scans and indexes your music files. Unlike Rhythmbox, Amarok takes a lonnnnngggg time to index a sizable collection. When we started Amarok indexing our 125 GB MP3 directory, we figured it'd take maybe half an hour. Four hours later, it finally finished indexing, having hammered the hard drive the whole time. Still, we think the additional features of Amarok are worth waiting a few hours for.

Figure 8-88. *The Amarok music player configuration screen*

Once Amarok finishes indexing, you can leave it active as an icon in the system tray. Accessing your music files and playlists requires only one click on the icon.

DVD Ripping

DVD Shrink (search the Web to find it)

DVDFab (*http://www.dvdfab.com*)

DVD rippers extract the program content from DVD-Video discs while removing copy protection, region coding, and other DRM measures. They may output the unprotected audio and video data as individual directories and files, or as a single ISO file ready to be burned to a DVD. Some DVD rippers offer you the option of producing discrete files or a single *ISO* file.

Because burnable dual-layer DVDs are relatively expensive and of questionable reliability, many DVD ripping applications offer you the option of compressing the original DVD material to fit an inexpensive standard 4.4 GB DVD±R(W) disc. The quality of the compression varies widely from one ripper to another and with the configuration of the ripper. Depending on the amount of data on a particular DVD-Video disc, the best rippers may produce compressed rips that are nearly indistinguishable from the original DVDs, even when viewed on an HDTV. Some rippers offer a high-quality mode, which does deep analysis of the data before compressing it for maximum quality, and a fast mode, which compresses the data as quickly as possible but with lower quality.

DVD rippers are commonly used in two ways.

First, and probably most common, is *rent-rip-and-return* (RRR), where the user rents a DVD-Video disc from Netflix, Blockbuster, or Redbox (or borrows it from the local public library), rips a copy of the video for his own collection, and returns the original disc. RRR drives the MPAA nuts, but there's not much they can do about it. The more charitable term for RRR is time-shifting.

Second, many people rip their purchased DVD-Video discs to place-shift or format-shift the content. For example, they may rip videos to lower-resolution, highly compressed files that match the screen resolution and storage capacity of their cell phones. Or, as in our case, they may rip their DVD-Video discs to the hard drives of their media center systems.

Although there are several DVD ripping apps available for Linux, such as K9copy, none of them are as good as the corresponding Windows applications. Fortunately, that's not a problem, because the best Windows DVD ripping applications install and run perfectly well under Ubuntu Linux.

The great-granddaddy of DVD rippers is DVD Shrink 3.2.0.15, shown in Figure 6-69, which was last updated in July 2004, just before the MPAA attack lawyers shut it down. Despite its age, DVD Shrink is still many people's first choice of DVD rippers. It does what it does quickly and well. When set to use deep analysis for maximum quality, the resulting videos are often indistinguishable from the originals.

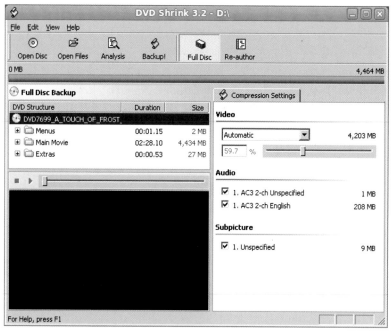

Figure 6-69. *The DVD Shrink main screen*

DVD Shrink is extremely easy to use. After you install it and configure it as you wish, you can simply put a protected DVD-Video disc in the drive and click Open Disc. DVD Shrink runs a quick preliminary analysis and then returns to the main screen. If you want to back up the DVD without any changes, simply click the Backup button and let 'er rip. If you want, for example, just the movie, you can click Re-author and eliminate unwanted structure elements.

You can also make some minor changes that may have major quality benefits. For example, you can opt to eliminate the soundtrack in alternate languages, rip only stereo sound rather than stereo plus 5.1 sound, or eliminate the director's comments audio track. You can also choose to replace some useless video content (for example, coming attractions) with a simple placeholder image, which frees up space for the content you want to keep.

To install DVD Shrink under Ubuntu Linux, you must first install WINE (Wine Is Not an Emulator), a Linux package that allows many Windows programs to run under Linux. To do so, open the Ubuntu Applications menu and choose Add/Remove. In the Add/Remove Applications dialog, search for WINE. Mark the checkbox and click the Apply Changes button.

We can't give you a URL to download DVD Shrink, but a quick Google search will turn up numerous download sites. Save the installer executable to your hard drive and double-click it to fire up the WINE installer. You can accept all the WINE installer defaults, except that we recommend you set the Windows type to Windows XP. When the installation finishes, you'll be prompted to restart your system (which actually does a virtual Windows restart rather than restarting the Linux system). After the restart, DVD Shrink will appear in the Applications→WINE→Programs submenu. If you requested it during installation, there'll also be a program icon on your desktop.

Although DVD Shrink works with nearly all DVD-Video discs, a few discs that were created after the final release of DVD Shrink use altered copy-protection methods that DVD Shrink can't handle. The usual symptom is a "disc read error" message during the preliminary scan or the analysis pass. If that occurs, DVD Shrink can't rip that DVD (although it can still be used to compress files ripped by a more recent ripper). You'll need to rip the disc with a different ripper, such as DVDFab, shown in Figure 6-70.

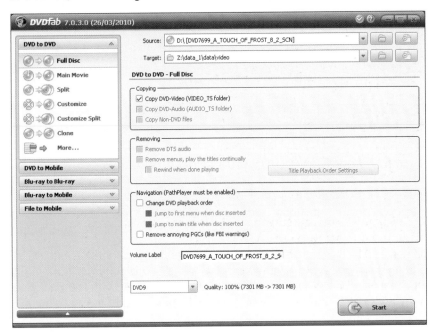

Figure 6-70. The DVDFab main screen

The most recent free version of DVDFab will almost certainly be able to rip any DVD-Video disc that DVD Shrink chokes on. (The pay version of DVDFab has many additional capabilities and is well worth considering.)

The free version of DVDFab operates only in file mode, ripping the contents of a DVD-Video disc to directories and files rather than to an ISO image file. Although the free version can compress these files to fit a 4.4 GB writable DVD, we've found that it's better to rip the files uncompressed (using the 100% or DVD9 setting) and then run DVD Shrink against those files to produce a compressed ISO image file for later burning to disc.

To install DVDFab, download the latest installer from the website and save it to the hard drive. Double-click the installer file to fire up the WINE installer, and proceed as described for installing DVD Shrink.

Video Playback

VLC Media Player (Ubuntu repositories)

For watching videos, we need an application to turn our HDTV computer monitor back into an HDTV, without distracting elements like the task bar, menu, or mouse pointer visible. We also need all of the controls present on a DVD player—play, pause, next/previous chapter, and so on.

There are many video playback applications available for Linux, but for our purposes the VLC Media Player is the standout choice. Figure 6-71 shows the VLC control panel, which offers every control imaginable for playing back DVD and other video content.

Figure 6-71. *The VLC control panel*

Ubuntu does not install VLC by default. To install it, first make sure that you've installed the Ubuntu Restricted Extras package, which includes several of the codecs needed to display video in various formats. Then click the Ubuntu Applications menu and choose Add/Remove. When the Add/Remove Applications dialog appears, type "VLC" in the search box. Mark the VLC checkbox in the packages list and click Apply Changes to install VLC.

With one exception, the default configuration of VLC will probably be suitable. To modify VLC settings, click Tools on the VLC control panel and choose Preferences to display the Preferences dialog shown in Figure 6-72. About the only change you may want to make is to mark the Fullscreen checkbox to cause VLC to come up in full-screen mode by default for watching videos.

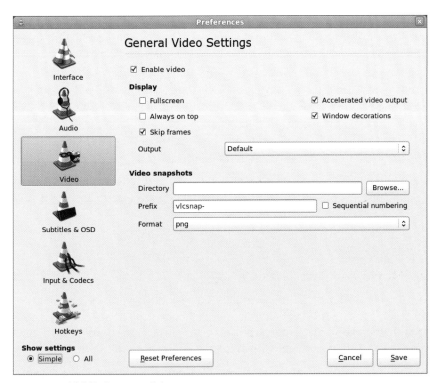

Figure 6-72. *VLC Preferences dialog*

Unless you change preferences, VLC displays video in windowed mode, as shown in Figure 6-73. You can toggle VLC output to full-screen mode from the VLC control panel Video menu. From full-screen mode, press the Escape key to return to the windowed display.

Figure 6-73. *VLC windowed display output*

Image Management and Editing

digiKam (Ubuntu repositories)

There are many image management and editing applications available for Linux, but we think digiKam (Figure 6-74) is the best choice. We use it primarily to index, annotate, manipulate, and edit our collection of thousands of digital camera images, but it's also useful to manage and edit other images in nearly any format. (For example, we used it to manage the TIFF screen captures used in this chapter.)

Figure 6-74. *digiKam splash screen*

Ubuntu doesn't install digiKam by default. To install digiKam, click the Ubuntu Applications menu and choose Add/Remove. When the Add/Remove Applications dialog appears, type "digiKam" in the search box. Mark the digiKam checkbox in the packages list and click Apply Changes.

When you fire up digiKam for the first time, the splash screen shown in Figure 6-74 appears, and persists until the program has finished scanning your hard drives. In our case, that took more than an hour, with the hard drives banging away the whole time. Of course, if you don't have 12 TB of disk space and tens of thousands of image files, your wait will be shorter.

Once indexing completes, you can use digiKam to organize your images into albums, attach captions, tags, and ratings to each image, and so on. Figure 6-75 shows the main screen of digiKam as we began to attach captions and tags to some recently shot images.

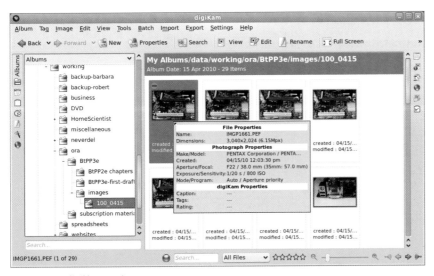

Figure 6-75. *digiKam main screen*

Indexing, annotating, and viewing image files is essential, but we also need the ability to edit and convert those image files. For example, as Robert was working on this section, Barbara handed him the DSLR she'd used to shoot images on a recent trip and asked him to download the RAW format image files she'd shot and convert them to JPEGs that she could have printed at Walgreens. No problem. For image editing, digiKam includes the professional-grade showFoto image editor, shown in Figure 6-76.

Figure 6-76. *showFoto main screen*

We've used a lot of image editors, and nothing else we've used comes close to the capabilities of showFoto. Like many well-designed applications, showFoto can be used on many levels, from easy cleanup and format/resolution conversions to very complex bit-level functions that we don't completely understand. (OK, that we don't understand at all.)

Camcorder Capture

Kino (Ubuntu repositories)

Transferring your camcorder video to the media center system may be as simple as connecting the camcorder to a USB port. If the camcorder is a USB mass storage device, Linux pops up a File Browser window that lists the video files on the camcorder. From there, just copy the files to the video directory on your hard drive. If your camcorder captures video to an optical disc, insert the disc into the optical drive and copy the files from File Browser to your hard drive.

If your DV camcorder uses the IEEE 1394 (FireWire) interface, you'll need a separate program to transfer your video files. The best one we've found is Kino, shown in Figure 6-77. That's Robert in our home lab, shooting an intro segment for one of his YouTube Home Scientist videos (*http://www.youtube.com/user/TheHomeScientist*).

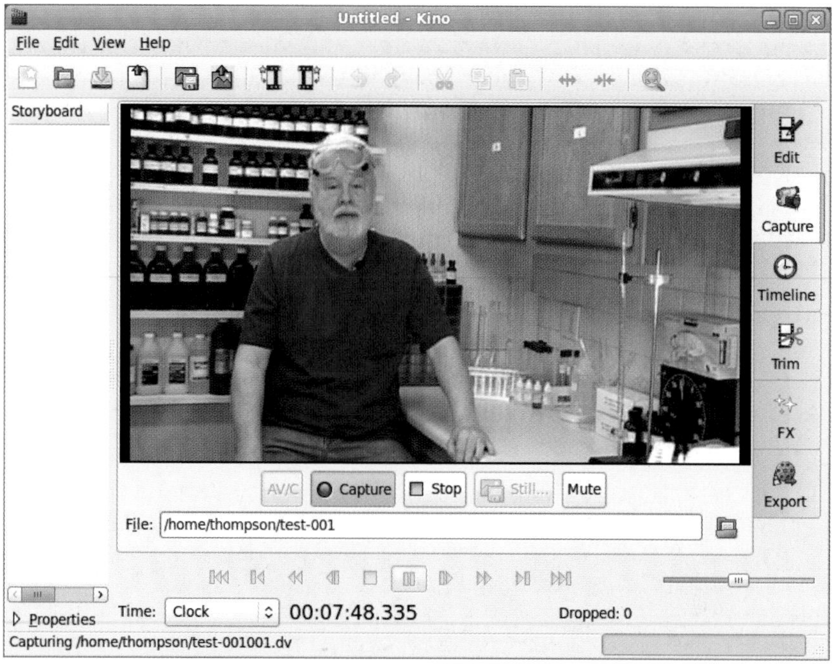

Figure 6-77. *Kino capturing video footage from our DV camcorder*

> **FireWire if You Need It**
>
> *The Intel DH55TC motherboard does not provide a FireWire interface. We captured that screen on Robert's main system, where he does all the video transfers and heavy lifting. If you want FireWire support on your media center system, choose an ASUS, GIGABYTE, or Intel motherboard that provides it, or simply install an inexpensive FireWire adapter card.*

Kino requires FireWire support, which is not installed in Ubuntu by default. To install Kino and FireWire support, from the Ubuntu main menu choose System→Administration→Synaptic Package Manager. Search for "raw1394". When the list of packages that contain that string appears, mark the checkbox for the *libraw1394* library item and select it for installation. Then search for "Kino" and mark it for installation. Click the Apply button to install Kino and 1394 support. When the packages are installed, close Synaptic.

You may encounter the same problem we do with 1394 support. If you run Kino and attempt to capture DV footage, it may tell you that the file */dev/raw1394* is not available. The problem is that accessing that file requires root access. You can fix that problem as follows:

1. Close Kino.

2. Open a terminal window (Applications→Accessories→Terminal).

3. At the prompt, type `cd /dev` and press Enter.

4. At the prompt, type `sudo chmod 777 raw1394` and press Enter (and type your password if prompted).

5. Close the terminal window and restart Kino.

The *raw1394* library will be available until the system is rebooted. (Yes, this is a kludge, and there's probably a better way to do it. If so, we don't know what that is.)

Camcorder Video Editing

Cinelerra (*http://cvs.cinelerra.org*)

When we started shooting YouTube videos, we spent a long time checking out various Linux video editors. Kino includes video editing functions, but they're limited and crude. We looked at several other editors, all of which had one or another fatal problem. Several friends and associates recommended we buy a Mac. Fortunately, we borrowed one first and played around with iMovie. We found that package so feature-poor that we considered it unusable, and the commercial alternatives for OS X or Windows cost much more than we were willing to pay.

Finally, we came across Cinelerra, shown in Figure 6-78. Cinelerra is a professional-grade video-editing program that's similar in power and features to Adobe's Premiere Pro or Apple's Final Cut Pro but on a basic level is about as easy to use as Apple's iMovie. After playing around with Cinelerra for an hour or two, we were able to do everything we could do with iMovie, and a lot more.

> **Easy Does It**
>
> *Ubuntu recently added the video editor PiTiVi as a standard package. It's considerably less powerful than Cinelerra, but it's also easier to learn and may be all you need. Look for PiTiVi under the Applications→Sound & Video menu.*

Figure 6-78. *Using Cinelerra to edit one of Robert's YouTube videos*

The good news about Cinelerra is that it's free, incredibly powerful, and (relatively) easy to learn to use. The bad news is that its interface is, uh, unusual. But you'll get used to that quickly enough. The other bad news is that you'll have to get your hands dirty to install it. It's not included in Ubuntu, and it's not available in the Ubuntu repositories. Cinelerra does, however, maintain its own repository, and it provides packages for current and recent Ubuntu releases.

For complete instructions on installing Cinelerra, point your web browser to *http://cvs.cinelerra.org/getting_cinelerra.php#ubuntu*.

Final Words

Now that we've finally done it, we can't believe we waited this long to build a real media center system and connect it to an HDTV. For relatively little money, we now have all of our audio and video content centralized and easily accessible, not just in the den, but from anywhere in the house, and we no longer have to swap discs in and out.

Barbara has instant access to the Web and her email. (Robert still has a separate den system, so he can browse the Web or check email while Barbara watches a video.) Robert can kick back on the sofa and edit videos on a big screen with high-quality audio. In fact, all of the functionality of a general-purpose PC is always available, just one click away.

Of course, we seldom leave well enough alone. Here are some possible future upgrades we're considering:

Security video

> Among our planned projects is implementing a complete home video security system with TCP/IP webcams and Linux security video management software. We'll set up webcams to monitor the exterior doors, home interior, and yard, and run monitoring and video stream recording software on the media center system. When someone rings the doorbell, one click will display the front-door webcam video/audio on the HDTV. We can even implement motion activation in software. When something changes significantly in a camera's field of view, recording kicks in automatically.

> We'll set up a *cron* job to transfer video still sequences via our broadband connection to an off-site server in case we're burgled and the media center system is stolen. To guard against a burglar smart enough to cut our cable, we'll also set up cooperative arrangements with neighbors to transfer video still sequences by WiFi to their systems, and vice versa.

Home control

> We played around years ago with X10 home control but found it to be unreliable. We may try again with a later technology, such as INSTEON or Universal Powerline Bus. If we do, the media center system will be an ideal central control system.

Weather station

Barbara is a weather junkie. We have a standalone weather station with remote sensors for temperature, rainfall, and so on. It records things like maximum/minimum temperature since the last reset, but what Barbara would really like is a logging system that tracks and records temperatures and other data very accurately and with fine granularity. The media center system is an ideal control center for this project.

Recording TV programs

Yeah, we know. After arguing that there are much better alternatives for recording television programs, here we are talking about maybe adding PVR functions in the future. For now, we'll continue using our DVD recorder when we infrequently want to record OTA programs. But everything dies sooner or later, and when our current DVD recorder goes to that great electronics warehouse in the sky, we may decide it makes more sense to add a tuner card and PVR software to our media center system than to replace the DVD recorder.

These are just a few upgrade ideas. We'll probably think of many more uses for our media center system, and we suspect those of you who build your own media center systems will do the same.

Building an Appliance/ Nettop System

7

In a strict sense, we define an *appliance system* as a small, quiet computer that is dedicated to one task or a group of related tasks, such as a home server, a *network-attached storage* (NAS) box, a media center front-end, or a home-automation controller. In a broader sense, an appliance system may be a general-purpose computer that is particularly small, quiet, and unobtrusive. By that definition, the archetypal appliance systems are the Mac mini and the many models of ASUS Eee nettop systems and all-in-ones.

But we don't have to buy a Mac Mini or ASUS Eee. We can build our own system based on a 6.7" square Mini-ITX motherboard with an AMD or Intel processor and run Windows 7 or Linux on it. Because we're designing and building it ourselves, we can optimize our system for our own needs and budget.

For example, we can build an inexpensive, nearly silent appliance system with moderate performance around an Intel Atom motherboard and processor, or we can build a system with mainstream desktop performance around an Intel Core i3 or Core i5 processor. If we want both silence and high storage performance at the expense of storage capacity, we can install a fast, silent solid-state drive (SSD). If our priorities are low noise and high storage capacity at the expense of disk performance, we can install a quiet, high-capacity 5,400 RPM laptop drive. Or we can strike a happy compromise between noise level, capacity, and performance by installing a 7,200 RPM or faster laptop hard drive. Those aren't options with the Mac mini or the ASUS Eee.

The point is, we can have it our way, and so can you. In this chapter, we'll design and build the perfect appliance system for our needs. But your priorities may differ from ours, so we'll also point out alternatives all along the way.

Determining Functional Requirements

The problem with determining functional requirements for an appliance system is that the appliance umbrella covers a huge range of systems. For example, we found 18 ASUS Eee models, ranging from a $230 nettop with a single-core Intel Atom CPU and no display to an $1,100 all-in-one model with a Core2 Duo processor and a 21" LCD display.

We can't build an all-in-one system—one that embeds the motherboard and drives in the display—but that's all to the good. With an all-in-one system, if one thing breaks, the whole computer is unusable while you ship it off for repair and wait for its return. With a separate system unit and display, it's easy to repair or swap out the faulty component and have the system back up and running quickly.

By necessity, we had to choose specific components for our own appliance system. That allowed us to optimize it for our own requirements, but obviously your own priorities may differ. Accordingly, we specify numerous alternative choices, indicating the components that we might have used if we had been designing the appliance system for a different purpose.

We set our price goal at $350 without the display, external peripherals, or software—the same as for our budget system. The two systems are very different in their emphases, though. The appliance system makes small size and low noise the priorities at the expense of performance; the budget system emphasizes bang for the buck.

When we sat down to think through our own requirements for an appliance system, here's what we came up with:

Size

> We plan to use a Mini-ITX motherboard, so we looked at Mini-ITX cases in the 7-liter range (roughly the dimensions of a letter-sized sheet of paper, by about 4" high). That gives us room for a slim optical drive, one 2.5" hard drive bay with a spare bay for future expansion, and one or two half-height PCI and/or PCI Express expansion cards. A 7-liter case is about two-thirds larger in every dimension than a Mac mini case—about five times the volume—but still small enough to be unobtrusive.

Reliability

> One of the major characteristics of any appliance is that it Just Works. When you click the button on the remote control, you expect your television or DVD player to power up every time, day after day, year after year. That's a bit much to expect from any computer system, so our goal is reasonably high reliability.

> Of course, the trade-off here is between reliability on the one hand and performance and cost on the other. We could design a system with extreme reliability by eliminating moving parts entirely—leave out the optical drive, use a passively cooled processor and power supply, use an SSD drive(s) rather than mechanical hard drives, and so on. By doing that, though, we'd also significantly increase costs, or decrease functionality and performance, or both. We decided to strike a happy medium here, shooting for high reliability without needlessly increasing costs or sacrificing performance and functionality.

Performance

> We don't expect our appliance system to be anywhere near as fast as a mainstream desktop system, but we do want enough horsepower to browse the Web, check email, watch YouTube videos, and so on—all without any noticeable sluggishness. In fact, a system with even half the processor and disk performance of the budget system would be more than

adequate for our needs, both now and for the next few years. This system won't have the performance needed for even undemanding 3D games, so integrated video will suffice.

Noise level

We want our appliance system to be unobtrusive, but that requires more than just small size. A small system that sounds like a leaf blower is an epic fail. Building a completely silent system is possible, but it involves too many cost, performance, and reliability trade-offs. We decided to aim for a system that was extremely quiet, but not completely silent. If system noise is not noticeable from two or three feet away, that's sufficient.

Hardware Design Criteria

With the functional requirements determined, the next step was to establish design criteria for the appliance PC hardware. Here are the relative priorities we assigned for our appliance PC. Your priorities may, of course, differ.

Our appliance system configuration is heavily skewed toward reliability, size, and noise level, with other elements taking a backseat. Here's the breakdown:

Price	★★★☆☆
Reliability	★★★★☆
Size	★★★★☆
Noise level	★★★★☆
Expandability	★☆☆☆☆
Processor performance	★★☆☆☆
Video performance	★☆☆☆☆
Disk capacity/performance	★★☆☆☆

Price

Price is moderately important for this system, as we'll use it only as a supplemental system. We're willing to spend about the same amount we did for the higher-performance budget system. Obviously, if this were to be a primary system, we'd boost the budget significantly.

Reliability

Reliability ties for top importance with size and noise level. We'll make minor compromises in cost, performance, or features to make this system as reliable as possible without taking any of the extreme measures described in the preceding section.

Size

Size is another high priority. We don't need a truly tiny system, but we want something that will fit comfortably and unobtrusively on Robert's end table, either nestled in under the LCD display's bezel or perhaps sitting under its base.

Noise level

Noise level is as important as reliability and size. That means we'll need a passively cooled processor and a notebook hard drive. If the system has any fans, we'll want them to run at very low speed while still providing adequate cooling.

Expandability

Expandability is unimportant for our appliance system. We may at some point want to make some minor system upgrades, such as adding an expansion card or more memory and perhaps a second hard drive, if we have a free bay. To the extent that we can provide for such future expansion without compromising higher-priority considerations, we'll do so. But we consider expandability as tied with video performance for dead last in priority.

Processor performance

Processor performance is relatively unimportant for our appliance system. Minimizing noise in a small case just about requires a passively cooled processor, like some of the Intel Atom models. We'd like a dual-core processor with a CPU Mark score of 500 or higher, but we wouldn't rule out a single-core unit if it meets our needs better than the available dual-core models.

Video performance

Video performance is tied with expandability for the lowest priority. We want integrated video good enough to drive the display we choose at its optimum resolution. Other than that, we'll make no demands of the video subsystem.

Disk capacity/performance

Disk capacity and performance are relatively unimportant, in the same category as processor performance. Size and noise constraints mean we'll have to use a 2.5" notebook hard drive rather than a 3.5" desktop unit. We'd like a 1 TB 7,200 RPM drive, but that's not an option in this size range. We'll choose a higher-capacity 5,400 RPM drive rather than a small-capacity 7,200 RPM unit. The extra speed would be nice, but the higher capacity is a bigger priority for us.

Brian Bilbrey Comments

If this system has a home server to pull files from, a smaller, faster drive might be much better, or even a small, inexpensive SSD just for the OS, with all data stored on the server.

Component Considerations

If you've ever built a standard PC, you'll probably be surprised when you first see just how small all the components for an appliance system are. Mini-ITX motherboards are much smaller than what you'll be used to. Drives look like they've shrunk in the dryer. The largest Mini-ITX cases are small, and the smallest are tiny.

All of this may have a major impact on your system design and build. You'll have to verify, for example, that your optical drive fits your case. You'll probably use a slim (quarter-height) optical drive, but you may find that not just any slim drive will do. The depth of a particular slim optical drive may be greater than the case will accommodate.

Similarly, the motherboard layout may assume much more significance than it has in an ATX or even μATX system. For example, the main ATX power cable from your power supply may be too short to reach the connector on the motherboard, or parts of the case frame may block access to motherboard connectors. The standard CPU cooler you planned to use may be too tall to fit the case, and so on.

Sometimes, there'll be an easy solution. You may, for example, be able to connect a front-panel USB cable to a different set of motherboard USB header pins than you planned to use, or you may be able to bend something just slightly, enough to give you clearance to plug in a cable or drive in a screw. But sometimes a particular component just can't be made to work in a particular case, which is why it's important to do your homework.

Before you actually order any component, check the website for detailed specifications—things like component height or mounting hole positions. Study a high-resolution image of the motherboard and match it up against the case you intend to use. You may find that an essential motherboard connector is blocked by the bottom of the power supply or that some of the components near the edge of the motherboard are too tall to fit under the edge of an intruding part of the case frame.

In short, you have to take much more care in choosing components for a Mini-ITX system than you do with larger systems. (We actually built our appliance system using the components we recommend, but we didn't build systems around our suggested alternatives, so you'll need to check carefully for yourself.)

Even if you're careful to choose only components that fit the case, you may find that building the system is more involved than you expected. With larger systems, you can usually install components in nearly any order that makes sense to you. With a Mini-ITX system, you may have to install components in one particular order, because installing one component may block the access you need to install another component.

If you use components other than those we actually used to build the system illustrated here, don't be surprised if you have one or two false starts. That happens to us more often than not when we build a tiny system with components that we haven't used before.

Worst case, you may get the whole system assembled before you realize that you forgot to install a cable whose motherboard connector is no longer accessible. So you remove the drives and bays, disconnect everything until you have access to the hidden connector, connect that cable in the proper sequence, and rebuild the rest of the system. You may spend an extra half-hour building the system and curse yourself for not getting it right in the first place, but that's just part of building tiny systems.

With those cautions kept firmly in mind, here are the components we chose for our own appliance system.

Case and Power Supply

Antec ISK 300 Mini-ITX case (*http://www.antec.com*)

When we wrote the preceding edition, Mini-ITX products were available but had not yet become mainstream. In particular, the selection of suitable Mini-ITX cases was extremely limited. But Mini-ITX "arrived" in 2009, and a wide selection of Mini-ITX motherboards and cases is now readily available.

Mini-ITX cases range in volume from about 1.8 liters (a smidgen larger than a Mac mini) to 15 liters (a bit smaller than a basketball). Most mainstream Mini-ITX cases are either flat ("book-style") or cubic, but models are also available for rack-mounting or installing in vehicles.

Some Mini-ITX cases, such as the Antec 300-150, have a built-in power supply that connects to a standard AC wall receptacle. The power supply provides the usual power cables for the motherboard and drives, just as in a standard ATX system. Other Mini-ITX cases, such as the Antec 300-65, use an external power brick that provides low-voltage DC current to a jack on the case. That jack connects to a circuit board inside the case, which provides the usual power cables for the motherboard and drives.

Cases with an internal power supply (usually) have higher output, and may be necessary if you use a relatively fast processor (such as an Intel Core 2 Duo or 45W AMD Athlon) rather than an Intel Atom—or if you install a high-current video adapter or multiple 3.5" hard drives. Conversely, cases that use an external power brick are (usually) cooler-running and quieter overall and may provide an extra drive bay without increasing the case volume. They are also usually somewhat less expensive.

Book-style cases are generally less obtrusive and more space-efficient, particularly if you intend to use a passively cooled processor such as an Intel Atom. The greater height of a cube or shoebox case may be required if your processor requires active cooling or if you intend to install a full-size video adapter. Another benefit of these somewhat larger cases is that many accept standard-size optical drives and 3.5" hard drives, which broadens your options and cuts your costs.

Among the book-style cases, our first choice is the **Antec ISK 300**, which is available with a 150W internal power supply or a 65W power brick. The only minor fault we noticed with these cases is that the side cooling fan is noisier than we'd like. Even with the fan running at low speed, the hum is audible to us if the system is less than a meter away. Most people probably wouldn't consider the fan noise objectionable, but if you do you can easily replace the case fan with a $10 aftermarket fan that's much quieter.

If you're building a Mini-ITX home theater system, you may prefer the **Thermaltake RSI H SD100**. If you want to use a mainstream processor and standard-size optical and hard drives, our pick is the **Thermaltake Element Q VL52021N2U**, which includes a 200W SFX power supply. If we were building a "pocket battleship" Mini-ITX system with a fast processor and high-performance graphics card, we'd choose the **Silverstone Sugo SG05-B**, which includes a 300W power supply and can accept a RADEON HD 4850 graphics card.

Processor, CPU Cooler, and Motherboard

Intel D510MO (*http://www.intel.com*)

Depending on the processor you choose, the CPU performance of your appliance system may vary by an order of magnitude or more. At one extreme, you can build your appliance system around a processor like the Intel Core i5 and achieve performance that matches that of all but the fastest desktop systems. At the other extreme, you can choose a processor like the dual-core Intel Atom D510, which is much slower but also much less expensive and much cooler-running.

The Intel D510 Atom is slow only in comparison to more expensive recent processors, though. To put the performance of the D510 Atom in perspective, it's faster than high-performance processors from just a few years ago, such as the AMD Athlon 64 4000+ and the 3.8 GHz Intel Pentium 4. Millions of people still use systems with those older, slower processors and are perfectly content with their performance.

Before you decide on a processor, decide just how much performance you really need. It's tempting to build a faster appliance system than you really need, but the downsides of doing that are that your fast appliance system will be larger, noisier, and more expensive.

For a typical appliance system, we think the best choice is an Intel Atom D510 processor on an Intel D510MO motherboard. That combination is fast enough to handle routine tasks under Linux or Windows. The integrated Intel Graphics Media Accelerator 3150 (GMA 3150) video is not fast enough for full-HD video playback, but it is fast enough for SD video and has excellent display quality for typical general computing tasks. (We do wish the D510MO included a DVI or HDMI output rather than just analog VGA, but that's acceptable for our purposes.) The processor and video together draw a maximum of only 13W, which means the system can use passive cooling. The motherboard meets Intel's usual quality, compatibility, and reliability standards, which are extremely high. And the whole shebang—motherboard with processor installed—costs well under $100.

Other than the analog-only video port, our only criticism of the D510MO is that it includes only two SATA connectors, which limits us to one hard drive and one optical drive. Or so it seems at first glance. In fact, we could install an optical drive just long enough to install the operating system and then remove it and substitute a second hard drive. Alternatively, we could install a half-height PCI or PCI Express expansion card to get additional SATA ports.

The **GIGABYTE GA-D510UD** is another excellent choice. It's very similar to the Intel D510MO, but costs $10 or so more. For that extra money, you get an added standard ATA port and two more SATA ports. GIGABYTE (along with ASUS) makes first-rate motherboards, and we might actually have chosen this board if it had been the same price as Intel's offering or if it had included a DVI/HDMI video output. But in our experience it's tough to beat Intel motherboards for quality, stability, and reliability, so we happily selected the Intel D510MO.

Of course, you may need more horsepower—CPU, video, or both—than the D510MO provides. Here are some options:

- If processor performance is adequate but you need better video performance, choose an ASUS or GIGABYTE D510 Atom motherboard that uses embedded NVIDIA 8xxx/9xxx-series or ION video. Those boards are more expensive than the D510MO, but their embedded video is more than adequate to handle full-HD video streams, such as for Blu-ray playback. Alternatively, look for an ASUS or GIGABYTE Atom motherboard that includes a PCI Express x16 expansion slot and install a standalone video adapter. Of course, that means you'll probably also need a larger case and power supply.

- If you need better processor performance, buy the **Intel DH57JG**, which supports fast Intel Core i3 and Core i5 processors, includes integrated Intel HD graphics, and provides a PCI Express x16 expansion slot. Once again, you'll probably want to choose a cube- or shoebox-style case with an internal power supply of 200W or more.

Why no AMD products? In our opinion, the Intel platforms are simply a much better choice for any appliance system, and we don't see that changing any time soon.

Memory

Crucial CT2KIT12864AA800 PC2-6400 Kit (2 GB×2)
(*http://www.crucial.com*)

The Intel D510MO motherboard has two DDR2 memory slots and supports dual-channel memory operation with PC2-5300 or PC2-6400 modules in capacities up to 2 GB, for a maximum of 4 GB. At the time we built this system, PC2-6400 CL6 modules sold for the same price as PC2-5300 CL5 modules. Even with one extra wait-state, the PC2-6400 memory is slightly faster, so that's what we installed.

We might have gotten away with installing only 2 GB of memory in this system, but the 4 GB memory kit cost only about $40 more than the 2 GB kit. We decided that a system with a low-power processor and 5,400 RPM hard drive could really use a bit of extra help, so we decided to install a 4 GB memory kit. We chose a compatible 4 GB memory kit from Crucial because we've never had a problem with Crucial memory.

Video Adapter

Integrated Video

The Intel D510MO motherboard includes integrated GMA 3150 video, which is sufficient for our needs. If we required more integrated graphics power, we'd have chosen an Atom motherboard that included integrated NVIDIA 8xxx/9xxx-series or ION video. If we required still more graphics horsepower, we'd have chosen an Atom motherboard with a PCI Express x16 slot and installed a midrange video adapter, such as an ATI RADEON HD 4xxx-series card.

Primary Storage

Seagate Momentus 5400 ST9640320AS (640GB) (*http://www.seagate.com*)

This section was originally titled "Hard Drive," but an appliance system doesn't necessarily use a traditional 3.5" hard drive, or even a 2.5" laptop hard drive. Nowadays, a *solid-state drive* (SSD) is an affordable option. Each of those three types has advantages and disadvantages.

A typical 3.5" 7,200 RPM desktop hard drive can have a capacity of 2 TB or more and, at roughly $0.10/GB, has by far the lowest cost per gigabyte of any of these drive types. Read and write speeds are both high, as is reliability. Most book-style Mini-ITX cases are too small to have a 3.5" drive bay, and we rejected those few that did for other reasons. Some cube-style Mini-ITX cases provide one 3.5" drive bay, and a few provide two or more. If the case you choose has a 3.5" drive bay and you require significant storage capacity, installing a quiet desktop 3.5" hard drive is by far the most cost-effective decision.

Nearly all Mini-ITX cases include one or more 2.5" drive bays. Mainstream 2.5" laptop hard drives are available with capacities up to 1 TB and rotation rates from 4,200 to 7,200 RPM. A few 10,000 and 15,000 RPM models are available, but their prices are outrageous, their capacities small, and their heat production and noise prodigious. The price, capacity, and performance of laptop hard drives are closely interrelated: the largest drives are expensive and slow, the fastest drives are expensive and small, and the least expensive drives are small and slow.

A typical laptop 2.5" hard drive has half the capacity of a 3.5" desktop hard drive that costs the same, and runs at 5,400 rather than 7,200 RPM. You pay that premium for the smaller physical size and lower power consumption. Read and write speeds are closely matched and vary from moderate to high depending on the type of drive. Laptop hard drives have a reputation for unreliability compared to desktop hard drives, but in all fairness that's probably because they are typically used in poorly ventilated laptop systems that are much more likely than desktops to be dropped or shocked. If the case you choose does not accept a 3.5" hard drive, the most cost-effective choice is a 2.5" hard drive in whatever combination of capacity, performance, and price is best for your needs.

Solid-state drives debuted in consumer systems as very expensive options for high-end notebook systems, but they are becoming increasingly common in Mini-ITX systems. Their advantages are obvious: high performance, low power consumption (and heat production), and completely silent operation. SSDs are available in many form factors, including some units that can be installed in a PCI slot, leaving a drive bay available for another drive.

With the exception of their very high price per gigabyte, the disadvantages of SSDs are less obvious, but worth considering. First and foremost, SSDs wear out as they are used. Consumer-grade multi-level cell (MLC) SSDs are generally rated for one to two million write cycles (1,000 to 10,000 writes per cell) and professional-grade single-level cell (SLC) SSDs for about five million write cycles (100,000 writes per cell). Even with wear-leveling enabled and a large allocation of spare sectors, the capacity of any SSD gradually decreases with use as more individual cells become unusable.

The performance of SSDs is a mixed bag. Excluding the least expensive models, a new SSD generally offers noticeably faster read performance than a hard drive. In particular, random reads are much faster because there are no heads to be moved and zero latency. Writes are much slower than reads, however, and write performance declines as the drive ages, even if the operating system fully supports TRIM (as do Windows 7 and recent Linux releases). In some cases, write performance may degrade sufficiently to cause the system to appear to hang for a second or more while a write is completed.

Finally, although it's not an issue for most people, it's impossible to securely wipe an SSD. Well, at least if you expect the drive to be usable after it's wiped.

Balancing all of these factors, we decided that a 2.5" laptop hard drive was the best choice for our appliance system. We'd budgeted about $100 for primary storage. That would have bought us a 1 TB or larger 7,200 RPM 3.5" desktop hard drive, but alas, we had no room for a 3.5" drive. For $100 we could have purchased a 32 GB MLC SSD, but that was simply too little storage space. So we looked at 2.5" laptop hard drives. The 5,400 RPM 640 GB Seagate ST9640320AS Momentus was selling for about $90, and the 7,200 RPM 320 GB Seagate ST-903203N3A1AS Momentus for $20 more. We decided on the larger, slower model, but on another day we might just as easily have chosen the smaller 7,200 RPM drive.

Optical Drive

LiteOn DS-8A4S Slim Internal DVD Burner (*http://www.liteonit.com*)

One of the drawbacks of using a small Mini-ITX case is that few of them, including the one we chose, have room for standard optical drives. That meant we needed a "slim" DVD burner. Compared to standard units, the selection of such drives is quite limited, the prices are higher, and the durability is lower. Still, the only alternative would have been to use a different case, and that we didn't want to do.

Slim internal DVD burners are available in slot-load and tray-load models. Our experience with slot-load drives from numerous manufacturers has been uniformly terrible. (We once had to tear down a system and remove and disassemble the optical drive to reclaim the DVD it had eaten, which was a friend's only backup copy.) Ruling out slot-load models left us with several tray-load models to consider. Of those, we ruled out Sony and LG models because our experience with slim drives from those manufacturers has been less than good. That left us with the LiteOn DS-8A4S drive, which we purchased.

External Peripherals

We're going to wimp out here. It's not that we don't want to list recommended external peripherals for the appliance system. It's that we can't, because the best external peripherals for our appliance system probably won't be the best for your system. Accordingly, all we can recommend is that you choose external peripherals according to your budget and the purpose of your system.

Our appliance system will replace Robert's current den system, a mini-tower unit. Yes, we also have a media center system with a 42" HDTV display in the den, but Robert may want to do something else while Barbara re-watches *Brideshead Revisited*. Of course, Barbara may want to do something else while Robert watches *Firefly* or *Buffy the Vampire Slayer* (for the fourth or fifth time), but she doesn't want a computer and display on her end table.

Component Summary

Table 7-1 summarizes our component choices for our appliance system.

Table 7-1. *Bill of materials for appliance system*

Component	Product
Case	Antec ISK 300-150 Mini-ITX case w/150W power supply
Motherboard	Intel D510MO
Processor	Intel D510 Atom (installed on motherboard)
CPU cooler	(Installed on motherboard)
Memory	Crucial CT2KIT25664AA800 PC2-6400 4 GB Kit (2 GB×2)
Video adapter	(Integrated)
Hard disk drive	Seagate ST9640320AS Momentus 5400 (640 GB)
Optical drive	LiteOn DS-8A4S Slim Internal DVD Burner

Building the Appliance System

Figure 7-1 shows the internal components of the appliance system. (Yep, that's the same image we used on the cover.) The Intel D510MO motherboard sits atop the Antec ISK300-65 case, with the Crucial 4 GB memory kit to its left. At the bottom right are the LiteOn slimline DVD writer and the Seagate Momentus 2.5" hard drive. That's everything. Not many components, but that's all it takes to build our appliance system.

Figure 7-1. *Appliance system components, awaiting construction*

> **What's Wrong with This Picture?**
>
> *OK, we admit it. We compromised our technical integrity to get a prettier cover image. We figured we'd better 'fess up now, before one of our sharp-eyed readers noticed the glaring mistake in this image and called us to account. Yes, that's a 7 mm Sears Craftsman nut driver, which we chose for its pretty orange handle. We've used cases that require a 5 mm or 6 mm nut driver, but never a 7 mm one. And we didn't actually need a nut driver for this system, anyway.*

If this is your first system build, it might take you an hour or so. If you've built systems before, you'll probably have it ready to boot up in only 10 or 15 minutes. Before you proceed, make sure you have everything you need. Open each box and verify the contents against the packing list. Make sure the I/O shield and all driver discs, cables, screws, and other small components are present.

Order Is Important

When you build a standard desktop or tower PC, the exact component installation sequence usually doesn't matter much. With an appliance system, that's often not true. The small case means there's little room to work in. One component may be inaccessible after you've installed another component. If you forget to connect a cable to the motherboard, for example, you may later have to partially disassemble the system to get to it.

The Antec ISK300 case is much better than most small cases in this respect. The integrated top and side panels slide off as a unit, which means the interior is quite accessible, albeit a bit cramped in places. If you're using a different case, it's worth spending some time thinking through the installation order before you actually start connecting things. Otherwise, you may have to tear everything down and start again.

As you build your system, pay particular attention to cable routing. As you connect cables, make sure you route them along and around frame components so that it will be possible to dress and tie off the cables neatly to avoid restricting air flow or fouling the fan.

Preparing the Case

To begin preparing the Antec ISK300-65 case, remove the three thumbscrews that secure the cover, as shown in Figure 7-2. (On our case, the thumbscrews were tight enough that we needed a screwdriver to loosen them.)

After you remove the thumbscrews, slide the cover back about a third of the way and then lift the cover straight off, as shown in Figure 7-3.

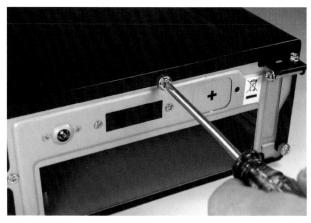

Figure 7-2. *Remove the three thumbscrews that secure the cover*

Figure 7-3. *Slide the cover back about a third of the way and lift it off*

The next step is to remove the drive tray assembly. To do so, remove the three Phillips screws—one at the center rear and one each at the left and right front—that secure it to the chassis frame, as shown in Figure 7-4. Grip the middle of the tray, as shown in Figure 7-5, and slide the tray toward the rear of the chassis until it comes free. Lift the drive tray clear of the chassis and put it aside.

Figure 7-4. *Remove the three Phillips screws that secure the drive tray to the frame*

Figure 7-5. *Slide the drive tray back and lift it off*

With the drive tray removed, the inside of the case is visible. If you've spent any time inside a PC before, the first thing you'll probably notice is that there are lots of power supply wires, but no power supply. That circuit board at the lower front of the case accepts 19VDC from the power brick and converts it to the voltages needed by the system components.

You'll also notice a thin metal I/O shield, which you can put aside for later disposal. Nearly every case we've used, including the Antec ISK300-65, includes a generic I/O shield whose holes never seem to match the port arrangement on any motherboard ever manufactured on planet Earth. We're not sure why case manufacturers include these worthless bits of metal.

But we do need to install an I/O shield, both to block dust from entering the large hole that would otherwise be present and to make sure the case provides proper ventilation to the processor and chipset. Open the motherboard box and locate the I/O shield provided with the motherboard. Before you proceed, place that I/O shield against the back panel of the motherboard, as shown in Figure 7-6, to verify that the holes in the template match the ports on the motherboard. (You might think the template and motherboard are guaranteed to match, since they came in the same box. Not always. We've found mismatched I/O shields supplied with more than one motherboard, including some from first-tier manufacturers.)

Once you've done that, install the custom I/O shield. Working from inside the case, align the bottom, right, and left edges of the I/O shield with the matching case cutout. When the I/O shield is positioned properly, begin on one corner and press gently along the edges to seat it in the cutout, as shown in Figure 7-7.

You Can't Get There from Here

If you're using the Antec ISK300-65 case and Intel D510MO motherboard, jump forward and read the section on seating and securing the motherboard before you actually install the I/O shield.

Figure 7-6. *Verify that the I/O shield matches the motherboard rear-panel ports*

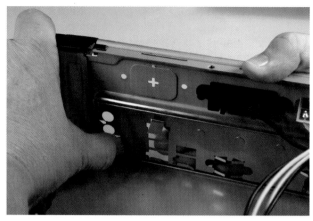

Figure 7-7. *Position the I/O shield and snap it into place*

The I/O shield should snap into place, although getting it to seat properly sometimes requires several attempts. As you apply pressure from inside the case against the template, use your finger to apply offsetting pressure on the outside of the template to avoid bending it. If you can't get it to snap into place using finger pressure alone, use the handle of your screwdriver to press along the edges until you feel it seat.

Be careful not to bend the I/O shield when you seat it. The template holes need to line up with the external port connectors on the motherboard I/O panel. If the template is bent even slightly it may be difficult to seat the motherboard properly. After you seat the I/O shield, temporarily place the motherboard in position to verify that the back-panel I/O ports on the motherboard align properly with the corresponding holes in the I/O shield.

Once you're sure the I/O shield is installed and aligned properly, hold the motherboard over the case, aligned and positioned as it will be when it is installed in the case. Look down through each motherboard mounting hole to locate the mounting positions on the base of the case. The goals are to make sure that there is a standoff installed that corresponds to each motherboard mounting hole, and that no extra standoffs are installed.

If necessary, install and/or remove standoffs until each motherboard mounting hole has a standoff and each standoff has a motherboard mounting hole. You'll probably be able to use your fingers to install or remove standoffs. If the fit is too tight for finger pressure alone, use needlenose pliers.

Once you've installed and/or removed the standoffs required to match the motherboard mounting hole configuration, do a final check to verify that (a) each motherboard mounting hole has a corresponding standoff, and (b) no standoffs are installed that don't correspond to a motherboard mounting hole.

The Intel D510MO motherboard has four mounting holes. The Antec ISK300-65, like many cases, ships with several standoffs preinstalled. All four of the standoffs preinstalled in the ISK300-65 corresponded with mounting holes on the D510MO motherboard, so we didn't need to install or remove any standoffs.

Place the prepared case aside for now.

Installing Memory

The D510MO motherboard comes with the Atom processor and CPU cooler preinstalled, so all we need to do to prepare the motherboard is install the memory modules.

Installing memory in the Intel D510MO motherboard is straightforward. We have two memory modules to install, and two memory slots available.

To begin, ground yourself. Place the antistatic wrapper from the D510MO motherboard on a flat surface, and place the motherboard atop the wrapper. Pivot the white plastic locking tabs on both sides of both DIMM sockets outward to prepare the slots to receive DIMMs, as shown in Figure 7-8.

Orient the first DIMM with the notch in the contact area of the DIMM aligned with the raised plastic tab in the DIMM socket and slide it into place, as shown in Figure 7-9.

Avoid Static Shock

Before handling memory modules or other static-sensitive components, first touch the chassis frame to ground yourself.

Figure 7-8. *Pivot the DIMM slot locking tabs outward to prepare the slot to accept a DIMM*

Figure 7-9. *Orient the DIMM with the notch aligned properly with the socket*

With the DIMM properly aligned with the slot and oriented vertically relative to the slot, use both thumbs to press down on the DIMM until it snaps into place. The locking tabs should automatically pivot back up into the locked position, as shown in Figure 7-10, when the DIMM snaps into place. If they don't, close them manually to lock the DIMM into the socket, as shown in Figure 7-11.

Repeat this procedure for the second DIMM. With the memory installed, you're almost ready to install the motherboard in the case. Before you do that, check the motherboard documentation to determine if any configuration jumpers need to be set. The Intel D510MO has only one jumper, the BIOS Setup configuration jumper, which sets operating mode. On our motherboard, that jumper was set correctly to Normal (pins 1 and 2 jumpered) by default, so we proceeded to the next step.

Figure 7-10. *Seat the DIMM by pressing firmly until it snaps into place*

Figure 7-11. *Make sure the latches engage the notches on the DIMM to lock the DIMM into place*

Neatness Counts

Before you install the motherboard, tie off the front-panel and other cables to keep them out of the way. The limited working space inside a small case makes it easy to lose track of a cable and later find that it's caught underneath the mounted motherboard and can't be pulled free because the connector jams it in place.

Installing the Motherboard

Installing the motherboard is the most time-consuming step in building the system because there are so many cables to connect. It's important to get all of them connected right, so take your time and verify each connection before and after you make it. Figure 7-12 shows the positions of the major components and connectors on the Intel D510MO motherboard. Refer to this diagram as you install the motherboard and connect the cables.

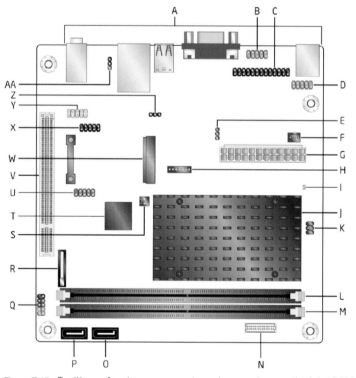

Figure 7-12. *Positions of major components and connectors on the Intel D510MO motherboard (image courtesy of Intel Corporation)*

Chapter 7

Here's the key:

A – Back-panel connectors

B – Serial port header (COM1)

C – Parallel port header

D – Serial port header (COM2)

E – LVDS inverter power voltage selection jumper (optional)

F – Chassis fan header

G – Power connector (2×12)

H – LVDS inverter power connector (optional)

I – Standby power LED

J – Intel Atom processor

K – LVDS inverter voltage selection header (optional)

L – DIMM channel A socket, DIMM 0

M – DIMM channel A socket, DIMM 1

N – LVDS panel connector (optional)

O – SATA connector 1

P – SATA connector 0

Q – Front-panel header

R – Battery

S – Front-panel wireless activity LED header

T – Intel NM10 Express Chipset

U – Front-panel USB header (with Intel Z-U130 USB Solid-State

Drive (or compatible device) support

V – PCI conventional bus connector

W – PCI Express x1 Mini Card connector

X – USB front-panel header

Y – Front-panel audio header

Z – BIOS setup configuration jumper block

AA – S/PDIF header

Seating and securing the motherboard

Particularly with Mini-ITX cases, clearances may vary from adequate to tiny to nonexistent. You may find it's simply impossible to get everything assembled without making a minor case mod or two, temporary or permanent. With various small cases and motherboards, we've had to do everything from temporarily bending something out of the way to enlarging an access hole with our Dremel Moto-Tool to supergluing the I/O shield to the back of the case.

We encountered just such a situation with the Antec ISK300-65 case and the Intel D510MO motherboard. We should emphasize that the problem was really neither Antec's nor Intel's fault. Although the Mini-ITX specification is well defined, when you're working in three dimensions with small clearances, there's enough slop in the specification to allow some problems to occur.

A different Mini-ITX motherboard might have fit the ISK300-65 case with no problems; the D510MO motherboard might have fit a different Mini-ITX case without problems. Unfortunately, the only way to know for sure if a particular combination of motherboard and case will go together smoothly or require minor case mods is to try it.

In our situation, the problem was a lack of clearance caused by a combination of the metal port enclosure (labeled H949d in Figure 7-13) on the D510MO motherboard that contains the keyboard and mouse PS/2 ports, and a projecting black plastic expansion connector that joins part of the ISK300-65 case to the frame, just to the right of the H949d enclosure.

With the I/O shield in place, there was simply no way to slide the motherboard into position, because we couldn't slide the H949d enclosure past that protruding expansion connector. We considered temporarily removing the assembly secured by the expansion connector and then reinstalling it after the motherboard was in place, but that looked to be more work than it was worth.

So we decided to use our butt nippers to nibble off excess plastic from the offending expansion connector, as shown in Figure 7-14. That, of course, required removing the I/O shield.

> **Don't Cut Too Much**
>
> *Remove only excess protruding plastic; leave enough of the connector to keep the subassembly secured. If you don't have butt nippers, you can use a sharp knife or single-edge razor blade to remove the excess plastic.*

Figure 7-13. *Motherboard installation blocked by a protruding connector*

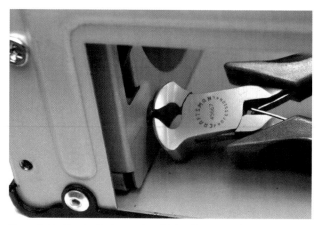

Figure 7-14. *Use butt nippers to nibble off excess plastic from the offending projection*

Slide the motherboard into position, carefully aligning the back-panel I/O connectors with the corresponding holes in the I/O shield. Once the motherboard is in position, examine the rear I/O panel carefully to make sure that none of the grounding tabs are protruding into jacks.

Chapter 7

Keep pressure on the motherboard to align the standoffs with the corresponding mounting holes, and drive screws into all four standoffs to secure the motherboard in place, as shown in Figure 7-15. Tighten the screws finger-tight, plus at most a quarter turn. Overtorquing the screws may crack the motherboard or make it difficult to remove later. After you secure the motherboard, verify once again that the back-panel I/O connectors mate properly with the I/O shield.

Figure 7-15. *Secure the motherboard by driving screws into all four standoffs*

Connecting motherboard cables

The final steps required to install the motherboard are to connect the various signal, data, and power cables. It doesn't much matter in what order you connect these cables, but make sure to get all of them connected. Figure 7-16 shows the positions and pinouts of the connectors on the Intel D510MO motherboard. Refer to this diagram as you connect the cables.

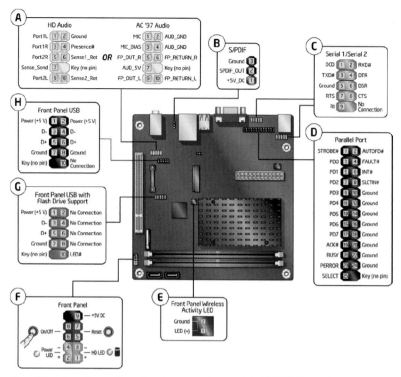

Figure 7-18. *Locations of header-pin connectors on Intel D510MO motherboard (image courtesy of Intel Corporation)*

To begin, locate the 2×12 main ATX power connector (item G on the diagram) on the motherboard and the corresponding power cable in the bundle of cables coming from the circuit board in the ISK300-65 case. The main ATX power cable in the ISK300-65 case is long enough to reach the socket on the D510MO motherboard, but only just. Get as much slack in that cable bundle as possible by separating unrelated cables from the main ATX power cable bundle.

Because it's so short, you'll have to route that cable bundle directly across the processor heatsink (the black multi-pronged assembly in the middle of the motherboard). Don't be concerned about heat affecting the wires; the Intel Atom processor consumes very little power and produces very little heat. The tips of the heatsink prongs don't become hot enough to melt the insulation on the wires.

Align the main ATX power cable connector as shown in Figure 7-17. Press it firmly into place until the latch on the cable connector snaps into place over the lip on the motherboard jack. Make absolutely sure that the latch snaps into place. A poorly seated ATX main power cable can cause many subtle and intermittent problems.

Next, locate one of the SATA data cables supplied with the motherboard (another good reason to buy a retail-boxed motherboard). Both ends of these cables have the same connectors, and either end can be used to connect to the motherboard or a drive. Note that each connector has a locking latch that mates with the connectors on the motherboard and drives. Make sure this latch snaps into the locked position when you connect a cable to either the motherboard or a drive. (Not all SATA cables have these latches; if you use a cable without a latch, simply make sure it's fully seated in the socket.)

Use a permanent marker to draw a single line on each end of one cable, as shown in Figure 7-18. Although it may be obvious when you're building the system which cable connects which motherboard SATA port to which drive, it will be less so with the cables bundled and dressed months later, when you want to upgrade or replace a drive. If your system uses more than two SATA ports, label the remaining cables as well: no lines for port 0, one line for port 1, two lines for port 2, and so on.

Figure 7-17. *Align the main ATX power connector and press it firmly into place*

Figure 7-18. *Label both ends of one SATA cable with one stripe for SATA port 1*

Next, locate the Slimline SATA adapter in the Antec parts bundle. One end of this adapter has a single connector that fits both the SATA power and SATA data connectors on the slimline SATA optical drive. The other end of the adapter branches into a power cable with a Molex jack that connects to a Molex plug from the power supply board and a standard SATA data cable that connects to a motherboard SATA port. Connect the Slimline SATA adapter SATA data cable to motherboard SATA port 0 and one end of the standard SATA data cable to motherboard SATA port 1, as shown in Figure 7-19.

The next step is to connect the front-panel switch and indicator cables, as shown in Figure 7-20. Refer to section F on the diagram in Figure 7-16 for the pinouts. Each of the front-panel switch and indicator cables is labeled descriptively, e.g., "Power," "Reset," and "HDD LED." Match those descriptions with the front-panel connector pins on the motherboard to make sure you connect the correct cables to the appropriate pins.

The power switch and reset switch connectors are unpolarized, so they may be connected in either orientation, as long as you connect each cable to the correct pair of pins. The HDD activity LED cable is polarized and should be connected with the correct polarity. (If you get it wrong, though, the worst that happens is that the LED fails to illuminate.)

Figure 7-19. *Connect one end of each SATA cable to the corresponding motherboard SATA port*

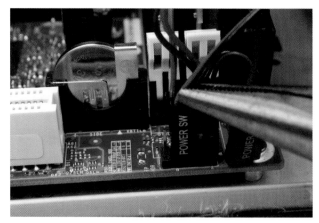

Figure 7-20. *Connect the front-panel switch and indicator cables*

The next step is to connect one of the front-panel audio cables to the audio header pins, which are located at the left rear of the motherboard, near the PCI expansion slot. The ISK300-65 case provides two monolithic front-panel audio cables—HD audio and AC'97—that are keyed with a blocked hole that corresponds with a missing pin on the motherboard connector. Align the HD audio cable connector as shown in Figure 7-21, and press firmly to seat it.

The final step in installing the motherboard is to connect the front-panel USB ports to the motherboard. The Antec ISK300-65 case provides a monolithic 10-pin (5×2) dual-port USB connector that matches the standard Intel USB pin assignments.

The Intel D510MO motherboard provides two internal USB 2.0 header-pin sets, but they are not identical. One set of USB header pins, labeled H in Figure 7-16, provides standard connections for two USB ports. That's the one to which we'll connect the front-panel USB cable. The second set of USB header pins actually provides only one standard USB port, plus an LED signal pin. That set of header pins is intended to be used to connect an internal SSD drive. We'll leave that set of header pins unused, at least for now.

The Antec front-panel USB cable connector is keyed with one blocked hole that corresponds to the one missing pin in the Intel USB header-pin group. Orient the cable connector properly and slide it onto the header pins, as shown in Figure 7-22. If your case uses front-panel USB cables with individual connectors for each wire (or a different connector block pinout), refer to the pin assignment shown in Figure 7-16 to get those individual wires connected correctly.

Do what you can to bundle and tie off the cables and tuck them out of the way. Use the black plastic cable ties included in the ISK300-65 parts bundle.

Figure 7-21. *Connect the front-panel HD audio cable to the front-panel audio connector pins*

Figure 7-22. *Connect the front-panel USB cable to the mother-board USB header pins*

Installing the Drives

The Antec ISK300-65 has one external 5.25" drive bay for a slimline optical drive and two internal 2.5" drive bays for hard drives. Our motherboard provides only two SATA ports, which we'll use to connect one optical drive and one hard drive.

The first step is to install the hard drive in the HDD tray. To do so, recover the drive tray assembly you set aside earlier. Remove the thumbscrew that secures the HDD tray to the drive tray assembly, as shown in Figure 7-23.

Slide the HDD tray back slightly to free the locking hinges, and lift the HDD tray away from the drive tray assembly, as shown in Figure 7-24.

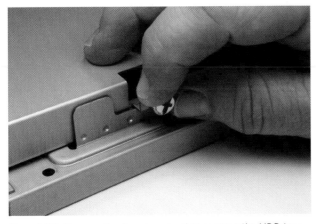

Figure 7-23. *Remove the thumbscrew that secures the HDD tray to the drive tray assembly*

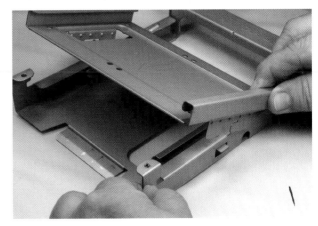

Figure 7-24. *Lift the HDD tray free of the drive tray assembly*

Slide the hard drive into the HDD tray, as shown in Figure 7-25, with one side of the drive under the retaining lip of the HDD tray. The rear (connector side) of the hard drive should be toward the rear of the tray, and overhanging slightly.

Hold the hard drive in position with your thumb, invert the tray, and place it on a flat surface. If necessary, move the drive until the drive screw holes align with the mounting holes in the HDD tray and insert the first screw. Drive that screw partially in, but leave enough slack that the drive can still move freely. Insert the remaining three screws and tighten all four screws finger-tight plus a quarter turn or so, as shown in Figure 7-26.

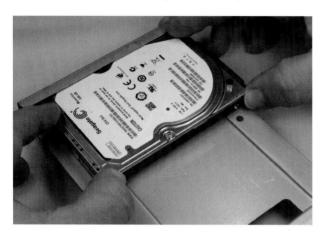

Figure 7-25. *Orient the hard drive correctly, and slide it into the HDD tray*

Figure 7-26. *Holding the hard drive and tray inverted, partially drive one screw*

At this point, following Antec's instructions, we reattached the HDD tray to the drive tray assembly and reinserted the thumbscrew to secure the HDD tray to the drive tray assembly, as shown in Figure 7-27.

Although with the hard drive in place we were able to install the optical drive and connect the power and data cables to the hard drive and optical drive, in retrospect it would have been easier to replace the HDD tray in the drive tray assembly after we'd installed the optical drive and connected its data and power cables.

The next step is to install the optical drive. With the front of the case facing you, first strip the protective tape from the drive bezel.

Press gently on the upper-right corner of the optical drive bezel, as shown in Figure 7-28, and release the pressure to open the bezel, as shown in Figure 7-29.

Working from inside the case, use gentle finger pressure to pop the drive bay face plate free of the bezel, as shown in Figure 7-30.

Working from the rear of the assembly, slide the optical drive into position, as shown in Figure 7-31.

Locate the optical drive screw in the Antec parts bundle (it's the tiniest screw there). Slide the optical drive back and forth until the screw hole in the optical drive is visible through the mounting hole just behind the HDD tray mounting thumbscrew in the drive assembly tray. Insert and tighten the optical drive screw to secure the optical drive, as shown in Figure 7-32.

Figure 7-27. *Reattach the HDD tray to the drive tray assembly*

Figure 7-28. *Press gently on the optical drive bezel to unlatch it*

Figure 7-29. *Release the optical drive bezel and allow it to pivot down*

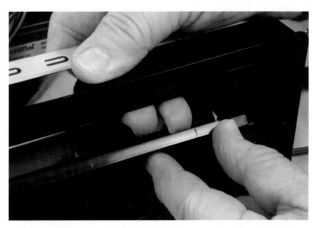

Figure 7-30. *Press gently from inside the case to pop out the drive bay face plate*

Figure 7-31. *Slide the optical drive into the bay*

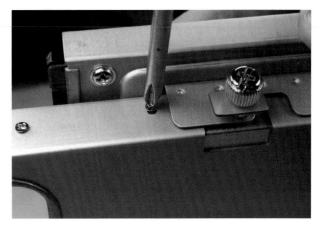

Figure 7-32. *Insert the optical drive screw to secure the optical drive*

Before you reinstall the drive tray assembly, you need to connect the case fan power cable and the Slimline SATA power cable. Locate the fan power cable and a Molex power cable from the power supply circuit board, and connect them, as shown in Figure 7-33.

After you connect the case fan power cable, set the fan speed switch on the top rear of the case. By default, it's set to low. We recommend setting fan speed to high initially for better cooling. Only if you find the fan makes too much noise on high should you consider setting it to medium or low.

Locate another available Molex connector from the power supply, and connect the power jack from the Slimline SATA adapter to it.

The next step is to connect the Slimline SATA adapter to the optical drive, as shown in Figure 7-34. If necessary, you can remove the HDD tray temporarily and replace it after you connect the Slimline SATA adapter (as we did to shoot this image).

Figure 7-33. *Connect the case fan power cable*

Figure 7-34. *Connect the Slimline SATA adapter to the optical drive*

We're about to make things much less accessible, so before you proceed, do a final check of the interior of the case:

- ☐ No loose tools or screws (shake the case gently)
- ☐ I/O shield not fouled
- ☐ Memory modules fully seated and latched
- ☐ Main ATX power cable connected and latched
- ☐ SATA data cables for hard drive and optical drive connected to motherboard
- ☐ Front-panel switch and indicator cables connected properly
- ☐ Front-panel audio and USB cables connected properly
- ☐ Power connected to case fan and Slimline SATA adapter
- ☐ Hard drive and optical drive secured to drive assembly tray
- ☐ Slimline SATA adapter connected to optical drive
- ☐ All cables dressed and tucked out of the way (insofar as possible)

Once you've completed the checklist, the next step is to reinstall the drive tray assembly. Slide it into position and secure it with three screws (one rear and two front), as shown in Figure 7-35.

Fish the SATA data and power cables for the hard drive up through the frame of the drive tray assembly and connect them to the hard drive, as shown in Figure 7-36.

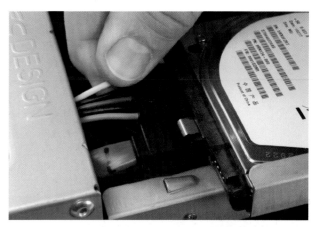

Figure 7-35. *Reinstall the drive tray assembly and secure it with three screws*

Figure 7-36. *Connect the SATA data and power cables to the hard drive*

Final Assembly Steps

Congratulations! You're almost finished building the system. About all that re-mains is to reinstall the cover and fire up the system. Make one final check to verify that the cables are tucked away, the case fan is not fouled, and so on.

Once you're satisfied that everything is correct, it's time for the smoke test. Leave the cover off for now. Connect the AC power cable to the power brick, plug the AC cable into a wall receptacle, and then connect the DC cable from the power brick to the system unit. Press the main power button on the front of the case, and the system should start up. Check to make sure that the case fan is spinning. You should also hear the hard drive spin up. At that point, ev-erything should be working properly.

Turn the system off and disconnect the DC power cable from the case. Before you reinstall the cover, locate the sticky labels in the motherboard box and ap-ply them to the inside of the cover, making sure not to cover up any ventilation holes. Slide the cover back onto the case and reinsert the three thumbscrews at the rear of the case to secure the cover.

Move the system to the location where you plan to use it. Connect the key-board, mouse, display, and Ethernet. Plug the AC cable from the power brick into a wall receptacle and the DC cable from the power brick into the jack on the rear of the case. Power up the display and turn on the system.

When the boot screen appears, enter BIOS Setup and verify that everything is as it should be (the full amount of memory recognized, time and date cor-rect, and so on). Set the boot sequence to attempt booting from the optical drive first and the hard drive second. Save the BIOS settings and allow the system to reboot. Insert your Windows or Linux distribution disc in the optical drive, close the tray, and turn off the system. Restart the system, and follow the prompts to install Windows or Linux.

Final Words

Our appliance system failed the smoke test. (No, it didn't erupt in a shower of sparks and gouts of smoke.) When we connected power to it, the green power LED on the motherboard lit, but nothing happened when we pressed the power button. Hmmm. So we went back and re-rechecked all the cable connections, and we found that the 24-pin main ATX power connector wasn't completely seated. Pressing that down until the connector clicked into place solved the problem, and the system started normally.

We hit a home run with this system. It's everything we hoped for, and more. Although the benchmarks say the dual-core Atom processor is only half the speed of the Athlon II X2 240 processor we used in the budget system and the server system, this system "feels" reasonably responsive running Windows 7 and even more so running Ubuntu 10.4 Linux. It's obviously not suited to heavy multitasking—nor was it ever intended to be—but for web browsing, checking email, editing documents, and so on, it's more than fast enough.

The system is very quiet if the case fan is running at low speed. At the default high speed, the case fan produces a whine that's audible from across the room. Set to medium speed, the case fan is quiet enough to be inaudible from more than a couple of feet away. (It would be more noticeable in a quiet environment, but our den is about as noisy as most.) When Robert hooked up this system next to the sofa in the den and powered it up with the case fan set to low, he first thought the system wasn't running. At low fan speed, which seems adequate to cool this system, you have to have your ear right next to the system to hear anything at all. The Seagate Momentus notebook drive is inaudible other than during heavy seeks, when a subdued clicking noise is barely audible.

We decided to push the limits of this system a bit, so we connected it temporarily to our HDTV and ran some video. SD (DVD) video rendered perfectly, so we decided to run a 1080p HD video clip from the hard drive to see how well the Atom processor and 5,400 RPM hard drive could keep up. Here we ran into the hardware limitations of this system. We're not sure if the bottleneck was the Atom processor or the hard drive, but dropped frames and other artifacts were pretty obvious. Not that that mattered, because we didn't design this system for media center use. The 2D video quality, running on Robert's 22" LCD display, is excellent.

What would we change? Not a thing, except maybe the hard drive. The 5,400 RPM 640 GB Seagate Momentus 2.5" notebook hard drive provides high capacity and decent performance at a reasonable price, but a 5,400 RPM drive just isn't as snappy as a 7,200 RPM drive. If we had been willing to trade off lower capacity against higher performance at the same price point, we'd have installed a 7,200 RPM 320 GB Seagate Momentus hard drive. But, on balance, we're just as happy with the larger 5,400 RPM drive. Programs load a bit more slowly, it's true, but then with 4 GB of memory we tend to keep our most-used programs loaded all the time anyway.

Building a Home Server

A *home server* is a computer located in a private residence that is dedicated to providing file sharing and other centralized services to other computers within that residence. A home server may also provide *virtual private network* (VPN) service or password-controlled access to allow authorized people to access server resources remotely via the Internet. Some home servers are configured as public-facing Internet hosts that run web servers, mail servers, or other services open to the Internet at large.

> **Media Center System Versus Home Server**
>
> *Although they appear superficially similar, there are significant differences between a media center system and a home server. Both store files, but there the similarity ends.*
>
> *A media center system sits front and center in the den or living room and is used interactively in much the same way as a desktop system, albeit usually from across the room. Size, noise level, and appearance are important, and disk storage is typically fairly limited.*
>
> *A home server usually sits in a closet or buried under a desk somewhere, and is seldom if ever used interactively. Size, noise level, and appearance are generally less important for a server, and the amount of disk storage it supports is massive. For example, our media center system has two hard drives, for a total of 4 TB of disk space; our home server will eventually host eight hard drives, with a total of 24 TB of disk space. It may also host several eSATA external hard drives for even more disk space.*
>
> *You can, of course, combine the functions of these two systems, building a media center system with lots of disk space, and also using it as a general-purpose home server. The drawback is that you'll need to use a much larger (and likely louder) case, which many people would find unacceptable in their dens or living rooms.*

By the mid to late '90s, all the necessary pieces were in place for home networking to take off. Many households had two or more computers (and wanted to share their printers and other expensive peripherals), networking hardware had become affordable, and Windows 95 and 98 made it easy to set up a home network. Finally, always-on DSL or cable broadband Internet access was becoming common, and many people wanted to share that fast Internet connection with all of the computers in the house.

These early home networks were almost invariably peer-to-peer. All or most of the computers in a home network shared disk storage and other resources with all of their peers. Almost no one used a dedicated server, because PCs were still relatively expensive and setting up a server-based network was much more complicated than simply sharing resources on a peer network.

That started to change, almost by accident, as more and more people bought new PCs to replace older models. Some people donated their old computers to charities or simply discarded them, of course, but many decided to run those old systems as dedicated home servers, perhaps installing larger hard drives to provide more shared disk space.

Even today, a repurposed older system is by far the most common type of home server. That's unfortunate, because an old system is about the worst possible choice for a home server. Granted, a typical home server doesn't require much processor horsepower, but that's about the only way an older system is suited to be a home server.

Think about it. You'll probably load up your home server with gobs of data that really matter to you: irreplaceable digital camera images and home video footage, your pr0n collection, all of your documents, your old tax returns and business records, and so on. Do you really want all of that precious information residing on a system that's near the end of its design life, with a five-year-old motherboard and power supply? That's a disaster waiting to happen.

Fortunately, it doesn't cost much to build a new home server, one that uses new components and is designed for reliability. You don't need much in the way of processor performance, so even a budget processor will suffice. You don't need a motherboard with high performance or a lot of features, so again even a budget model is suitable. You don't need much memory. You don't need a fancy case—in fact you can even recycle that old case (but not the power supply). You don't even need a display, keyboard, and mouse, because you can run your new server headless (without a keyboard, mouse, or display). Even an optical drive is optional.

You will need to spend some money on the important stuff: a good power supply, an extra case fan (or two or three...), a large hard drive or two (or three or four...), and a good *backup power supply* (BPS) or *uninterruptible power supply* (UPS). You may also need to spend some money on backup hardware. But in return you'll get a rock-solid reliable data repository that you can trust to keep your priceless data safe.

Determining Functional Requirements

We began by sitting down to think through our requirements for a home server. Here's the list of functional requirements we came up with:

Reliability

> First and foremost, the home server must be reliable. Our server will run 24/7/365, and yours probably will, too. Other than periodic downtime to blow out the dust, upgrade hardware, and so on, we expect our server to Just Work without us having to think about it.

Massive storage capacity

In the past, we routinely used lossy compression formats like JPEG and MPEG to cut down file sizes. The problem with lossy compression is that, by definition, it loses data relative to the original source format. We want to store our digital camera images as RAW files, our camcorder video as DV files, and our scans of old photographs as lossless TIFFs. Some of those source formats are themselves compressed with lossy algorithms, so the last thing we want to do is lose still more data by converting them to something lossier still.

Modern digital AV devices produce a huge amount of data. For example, we accumulated more than 20 GB of data just shooting RAW digital camera images for this book. Our SD DV camcorder records about 13.5 GB/hour. We intend to upgrade to an HD camcorder, which boosts storage requirements to about 40 GB/hour. (Raw HD footage can be captured at about 185 MB/ *second*, if you have a drive array fast enough to keep up.) We have hundreds of family photographic prints, some dating from the mid to late 19th century. Scanning just one of those at high resolution may require 50 MB or more of disk space, as may scanning just one of our 35 mm color slides or negatives at 4,000 DPI, even using lossless compression.

And then there's our collection of ripped CD-Audio and DVD-Video discs. All of them are stored on our media center system and we also have the original discs, so at first glance it might seem wasteful to store copies on our home server. But that ignores the time and effort we put in ripping all those discs in the first place. We *really* don't want to have to re-rip hundreds and hundreds of discs if a hard drive fails in our media center system.

In short, we have a ton of data, so we need a ton of disk space on our server. We decided that 6 TB (6,000 GB) would suffice, at least to get started. You might not have as much data as we do, but you probably have a lot more than you think. Consider your own current and future storage requirements carefully before you configure your home server.

Data safety

We've never lost any data other than by our own stupidity, and we want to keep it that way. Accordingly, you might expect that we'd configure our home server with RAID storage. We didn't. Here's why.

Using RAID can increase storage performance on a heavily loaded server, and it allows data to be recovered if a hard drive fails. Although it may sound odd, neither of those benefits is particularly important to us. A modern SATA hard drive is fast enough to saturate our 1000BaseT (gigabit) Ethernet network all by itself, so we don't need higher disk performance. And hard drive failures are so rare that it's simply not worth worrying about them.

Because RAID doesn't protect against the more common causes of data loss—accidental deletion, data being corrupted by a virus or malfunctioning hardware, or catastrophic loss caused by theft or fire—we'd still need to maintain backups even if we had a full RAID storage system. Given that we back up frequently—when we're actively creating new data, we often do differential backups several times a day—the only thing that using RAID would buy us is a very limited protection against losing a very small amount of un-backed-up data, and that only in the event of a hard drive failure.

Ultimately, we decided that the small benefits weren't worth the additional cost and complexity of installing RAID. We decided to use nonredundant SATA hard drives in our home server. By giving up the small additional safety factor provided by RAID, we'll gain more available hard disk space and free up at least a couple of drive bays that can be used for later expansion.

Flexibility

Initially, our home server will be almost exclusively a file server. It will run Linux, though, so at some point we may decide to add other functions to the home server. To allow for that possibility with minimum disruption, we'll configure the server initially with enough processor and memory to allow adding functions incrementally without upgrading the hardware.

Expandability

When we set out to design our new home server, we considered building it as an appliance system with an Intel Atom Mini-ITX board in a tiny case. There are advantages to such a server. It's small and can be put anywhere, and it doesn't consume much power, produces little heat, and doesn't make much noise.

But we soon realized that for us the lack of flexibility inherent in a small system outweighed its advantages. Looking back on how our last server had grown and changed over the years made it clear that we wanted a larger form factor for our new server.

Our last server was built in 2006, and originally had four 500 GB drives installed, for a total of 2 TB of disk storage. We reached that storage limit within a year, a lot faster than we'd expected. As a stopgap, we installed a 750 GB drive, for a total of five drives and 2.75 TB. As drive prices continued to fall, we replaced or added drives until we eventually ended up with four 1 TB drives installed, and a total of 4 TB of storage. (We recycled the 500 and 750 GB drives as external hard drives for backups.)

That was where things stood when we set out to design and build our new server. With 4 TB, we still had some available space, but the trend was clear. The largest available hard drives when we designed our new server were 2 TB, so we decided to start with three of those, for a total of 6 TB. But we knew our storage requirements would continue to grow, so we wanted a system that we could expand to at least six or eight hard drives. With 3 TB drives on the near horizon, that means we can eventually expand this server to a capacity of between 18 TB and 24 TB, which should hold us for a while. (We're sure that in a few years we'll look back with amusement on the days when we thought 24 TB was a lot of disk space.)

Networking

Of course, a server is useless if you can't get data into and out of it, so we need fast, reliable networking support. Our current home network is a mix of 100BaseT (100 Mb/s) and 1000BaseT (1,000 Mb/s, "gigabit") Ethernet devices that we're currently in the process of upgrading to exclusively

1000BaseT. We've complained elsewhere about the 25 MB/s throughput of USB 2.0, and, at about 10 MB/s, 100BaseT is even worse. A 1000BaseT network transfers data at about 100 MB/s, or about the same rate as a fast hard drive. That's acceptably fast for our purposes, so we'll choose a motherboard that supports 1000BaseT Ethernet.

Hardware Design Criteria

With the functional requirements determined, the next step was to establish design criteria for the home server hardware. Here are the relative priorities we assigned for our home server. Your priorities may, of course, differ.

Price	★★★☆☆
Reliability	★★★★☆
Size	★★☆☆☆
Noise level	★★★☆☆
Expandability	★★★☆☆
Processor performance	★★☆☆☆
Video performance	☆☆☆☆☆
Disk capacity/performance	★★★★☆

Here's the breakdown:

Price

> Price is moderately important for this system. We don't want to spend money needlessly, but we will spend what it takes to meet our other criteria.

Reliability

> Reliability is the single most important consideration. If this system goes down, we're out of action until we can get it running again. We didn't award this category five stars because we don't have the budget to build a professional-grade server with expensive features like dual-failover motherboards or redundant power supplies.

Size

> Size is relatively unimportant. Our home server will reside under the desk in Robert's office, which has enough room for a mid-tower system. (A full tower would be pushing it.)

Noise level

> Noise level is unimportant for a server that sits in a server room, but in a residence it may be critical. Because the home server will be installed in Robert's office, it's important to keep the noise level relatively low. We'll choose quiet standard components, but not expensive "Quiet PC" technologies.

Expandability

> Expandability is moderately important. Our server will initially have four hard drives installed, but we may want to expand the storage subsystem later. Similarly, although we'll use the integrated SATA and network interfaces initially, we may eventually install additional disk adapters, network interfaces, and so on.

Processor performance

> Processor performance is relatively unimportant. Our home server will run Linux for file sharing, which places little demand on the CPU. However, the server may eventually run some server-based applications. The incremental cost of installing a budget dual-core processor and sufficient memory to support those possible software upgrades is small enough that we'll do it now and have done with it.

Video performance

Video performance is of literally zero importance, because we'll run our home server headless. That is, we'll temporarily install a monitor while we install and configure Linux, but we'll subsequently manage the server from a desktop system elsewhere on the network. We'll either use a motherboard with integrated video, or install a video card for just long enough to get Linux installed and working.

Disk capacity/performance

Disk capacity and performance are very important. Our home server will have only one or two simultaneous users, so standard 7,200 RPM SATA hard drives will provide more than adequate performance. Capacity is the more important consideration for our server. We want 6 TB of hard disk space initially, and we'd like to be able to expand that to 12 TB or more without making major changes to the case or the existing drive subsystem. That means we'll need to use relatively few high-capacity hard drives instead of many lower-capacity drives.

RAID is NOT Backup

We can't say it often enough. RAID does not substitute for backing up. RAID protects against data loss as a result of a drive failure, and may increase performance. But RAID does not and cannot protect against data loss or corruption caused by viruses, accidental or malicious deletions, or catastrophic events such as a fire, flood, or theft of your server.

Brian Bilbrey Comments

RAID 6 is actually more than just RAID 5 with another parity stripe. It's usually configured with a different checksum algorithm, to protect against algorithmic weakness. In addition, with the real possibility of a bit error during a rebuild following drive loss, I'd consider RAID 6 to be required when individual drives of 750 GB or larger are used.

RAID for Home Servers

Although we elected not to use RAID on our home server, that doesn't mean RAID isn't right for your home server. *RAID* is an acronym for *Redundant Array of Inexpensive Disks*. A RAID stores data on two or more physical hard drives, thereby reducing the risk of losing data when a drive fails. Some types of RAID also increase read and/or write performance relative to a single drive.

Five levels of RAID are formally defined, RAID 1 through RAID 5. (Some manufacturers sell proprietary arrays that they describe as RAID 1.5, RAID 5E, RAID 5EE, RAID 6, RAID 7, RAID DP, RAID K, RAID S, RAID Z, and so on, but those are merely enhanced versions of one of the standard RAID levels.)

RAID levels are optimized to have different strengths, including level of redundancy, optimum file size, random versus sequential read performance, and random versus sequential write performance. RAID 1 and RAID 5 are commonly used in PC servers. RAID 3 is used rarely (generally for streaming video). RAID 2 and RAID 4 are almost never used. The RAID levels typically used on home servers are:

RAID 1

RAID 1 uses two drives that contain exactly the same data. Every time the system writes to the array, it writes identical data to each drive. If one drive fails, the data can be read from the surviving drive. Because data must be written twice, RAID 1 writes are a bit slower than writes to a single drive. Because data can be read from either drive in a RAID 1, reads are somewhat faster. RAID 1 is also called *mirroring*, if both drives share one controller, or *duplexing*, if each drive has its own controller.

RAID 1 provides very high redundancy, but it is the least efficient of the RAID levels in terms of hard drive usage. For example, with two 2 TB hard drives in a RAID 1 array, only 2 TB of total disk space is visible to the system. RAID 1 may be implemented with a physical RAID 1 controller or in software by the operating system.

Chapter 8

RAID 5

RAID 5 uses three or more physical hard drives. The RAID 5 controller divides data that is to be written to the array into blocks and calculates parity blocks for the data. Data blocks and parity blocks are interleaved on each physical drive, so each of the three or more drives in the array contains both data blocks and parity blocks. If any one drive in the RAID 5 fails, the data blocks contained on the failed drive can be re-created from the parity data stored on the surviving drives.

RAID 5 is optimized for the type of disk usage common in an office environment—many random reads and fewer random writes of relatively small files. RAID 5 reads are faster than those from a single drive, because RAID 5 has three or more spindles spinning and delivering data simultaneously. RAID 5 writes are typically a bit faster than single-drive writes. RAID 5 uses hard drive space more efficiently than RAID 1.

In effect, although RAID 5 uses distributed parity, a RAID 5 array can be thought of as dedicating one of its physical drives to parity data. For example, with three 2 TB drives in a RAID 5 array, 4 TB—the capacity of two of the three drives—is visible to the system. With RAID 5 and four 2 TB drives, 6 TB—the capacity of three of the four drives—is visible to the system. RAID 5 may be implemented with a physical RAID 5 controller or in software by the operating system. Few motherboards have embedded RAID 5 support.

RAID 3

RAID 3 uses three or more physical hard drives. One drive is dedicated to storing parity data, with user data distributed among the other drives in the array. RAID 3 is the least common RAID level used for PC servers, because its characteristics are not optimal for the disk usage patterns typical of small office LANs. RAID 3 is optimized for sequential reads of very large files, so it is used primarily for applications such as streaming video.

Then there is the so-called RAID 0, which isn't really RAID at all because it provides no redundancy:

RAID 0

RAID 0, also called *striping*, uses two physical hard drives. Data written to the array is divided into blocks, which are written alternately to each drive. For example, if you write a 1 MB file to a RAID 0 that uses 256 KB blocks, the first 256 KB block may be written to the first drive in the array. The second 256 KB block is written to the second drive, the third 256 KB block to the first drive, and the final 256 KB block to the second drive. The file itself exists only as fragments distributed across both physical drives, so if either drive fails all the data on the array is lost. That means data stored on a RAID 0 is more at risk than data stored on a single drive, so in that sense a RAID 0 can actually be thought of as less redundant than the zero redundancy of a single drive. RAID 0 is used because it provides the fastest possible disk performance. Reads and writes are very fast, because they can use the combined bandwidth of two drives. RAID 0 is a poor choice for desktops and workstations, which typically do not load the disk subsystem heavily enough to make RAID 0 worth using. Heavily loaded servers, however, can benefit from RAID 0 (although few servers use bare RAID 0 because of the risk to the data stored on a RAID 0 array).

Finally, there is *stacked RAID*, which is an "array of arrays" rather than an array of disks. Stacked RAID can be thought of as an array that replaces individual physical disks with subarrays. The advantage of stacked RAID is that it combines the advantages of two RAID levels. The disadvantage is that it requires a lot of physical hard drives:

Stacked RAID

The most common stacked RAID used in PC servers is referred to as RAID 0+1, RAID 1+0, or RAID 10. A RAID 0+1 uses four physical drives arranged as two RAID 1 arrays of two drives each. Each RAID 1 array would normally appear to the system as a single drive, but RAID 0+1 takes things a step further by creating a RAID 0 array from the two RAID 1 arrays. For example, a RAID 0+1 with four 2 TB drives comprises two RAID 1 arrays, each with two 2 TB drives. Each RAID 1 is visible to the system as a single 2 TB drive. Those two RAID 1 arrays are then combined into one RAID 0 array, which is visible to the system as a single 4 TB RAID 0. Because the system "sees" a RAID 0, performance is very high. And because the RAID 0 components are actually RAID 1 arrays, the data are very well protected. If any single drive in the RAID 0+1 array fails, the array continues to function, although redundancy is lost until the drive is replaced and the array is rebuilt.

Until a few years ago RAID 0+1 was uncommon on small servers because it required SCSI drives and host adapters, and therefore cost thousands of dollars to implement. Nowadays, thanks to inexpensive SATA drives, the incremental cost of RAID 0+1 is very small. Instead of buying one $200 hard drive for your small server, you can buy four $100 hard drives and a $50 RAID adapter. You may not even need to buy the RAID adapter, because some motherboards include native RAID 0+1 support. Data protection doesn't come much cheaper than that.

RAID 1 Versus RAID 0+1

If your storage subsystem has four hard drives, there is no point to using RAID 1 rather than RAID 0+1, assuming that your motherboard or RAID adapter supports RAID 0+1. A RAID 1 uses two of the four drives for redundancy, as does the RAID 0+1, so you might just as well configure the drives as a RAID 0+1 and get the higher performance of RAID 0+1. Either RAID level protects your data equally well.

Hardware Versus Software Versus Hybrid RAID

RAID can be implemented purely in hardware, by adding an expansion card that contains a dedicated RAID controller, processor, and cache memory. Hardware RAID, if properly implemented, offers the highest performance and reliability and places the fewest demands on the main system processor, but is also the most costly alternative. True hardware RAID adapters cost several hundred dollars and up, and are generally supplied with drivers for major operating systems (including Windows and Linux).

Software RAID requires only standard ATA or SATA interfaces, and uses software drivers to perform RAID functions. In general, software RAID is a bit slower and less reliable than hardware RAID and places more demands on the main system processor. Most modern operating systems, including Windows and

Linux, support software RAID—usually RAID 0, RAID 1, and RAID 5—and may also support RAID 0+1. We believe that well-implemented software RAID is more than sufficient for a typical home server, if indeed RAID is desirable at all.

Hybrid RAID combines hardware and software RAID. Hybrid RAID hardware does not contain the expensive dedicated RAID processor and cache memory. Inexpensive RAID adapters have limited or no onboard processing, and instead depend on the main system processor to do most or all of the work. With very few exceptions, motherboards that feature onboard RAID support, such as Intel models, use hybrid RAID, although it is sometimes incorrectly called hardware RAID. If you choose a hybrid RAID solution, make certain that drivers are available for your operating system.

And what if you choose not to use any form of RAID, as we did? We decided to install three 2 TB drives in our home server, configured as a *JBOD* (Just a Bunch of Drives). All three drives function independently as ordinary drives, and we get the full 6 TB combined capacity of the three drives. If we installed a fourth 2 TB drive, we could choose any of the following disk configurations without making any hardware changes:

JBOD

All four drives operate independently. With four 2 TB drives, the operating system "sees" 8 TB of disk capacity. Performance and data safety are determined by the performance and reliability of the individual drives. Note that a drive failure is four times as likely to occur with four drives spinning than it is when only one drive is spinning. If a drive fails, you lose whatever data was stored on that drive, but the data on other drives is not affected.

RAID 5

All four drives are assigned to the RAID 5. The operating system sees 6 TB of disk capacity. (The equivalent of one drive's capacity is used to store parity data, although that data is actually distributed across all four drives.) Read and write performance for small files is the same or slightly faster than with individual drives. Read and write performance for large files is slightly slower than with individual drives. RAID 5 offers moderate redundancy. Any one drive may fail without loss of data. If two drives fail simultaneously, all data on the array will be lost.

RAID 10

All four drives are assigned to the RAID 10, as in effect a RAID 0 pair of RAID 1 mirrored drives. The operating system sees 4 TB of disk capacity. Read performance for any size file is noticeably faster than with JBOD or RAID 5, particularly when the drives are heavily loaded. Write performance is also faster. RAID 10 offers very high redundancy. Any two drives may fail without loss of data, as long as they are not both members of the same RAID 1. If both drives in a RAID 1 fail simultaneously, all data on the array will be lost.

With the hardware configuration we detail later in this chapter, you can choose any of these disk configurations during setup. You don't even need to pop the lid or move any cables. But give some serious thought to which configuration to use. If you change your mind later, you can reconfigure the disk subsystem, but you'll need to back up all of your data and restore it after you set up the new configuration.

Component Considerations

With our design criteria in mind, we set out to choose the best components for our home server system. The following sections describe the components we chose, and why we chose them.

Brian Jepson Comments

I'd argue that the likelihood is some (probably small) value greater than four times more likely, given that additional drives add heat and vibration. I'm reminded of Brendan Gregg's experiment in the effect of noise on JBOD arrays: http://blogs. sun.com/brendan/entry/unusual_ disk_latency.

My favorite moment comes at 0:59 when he looks like he's about to say something and then goes right back to the array.

Brian Bilbrey Comments

Given the time needed to repopulate the data after acquiring another drive, I'd almost certainly put five or six 2 TB drives in a RAID 6 configuration, rather than just using JBOD. My time has value, too.

If I were optimizing a server for write performance, I'd mirror RAID 0 arrays of two or three drives each to yield maximum performance with mirroring protection, but without the parity calculation overhead.

Note that I'm running 3Ware (now LSI) hardware RAID without a battery backup in my home server/ workstation today. I'm currently undecided about the next generation. This chapter should help inform my decision.

Case and Power Supply

Antec Atlas 550 Server Case (*http://www.antec.com*)

A home server can be built in anything from a tower case specifically designed to house servers down to the smallest of small form factor cases. True server cases are usually large, heavy, and expensive—overkill for a typical home server. Very small cases may be suitable for some home servers, but their lack of drive bays and low-output power supplies often rule them out.

For our home server, the ideal case must be reasonably priced, be equipped with a top-quality power supply of 500W or more, have at least six or eight drive bays—ideally, with provisions to soft-mount hard drives for higher reliability—and have enough fans (or fan positions that we can populate) to provide high cooling efficiency. We'd also like the case to be attractive and reasonably quiet.

The key considerations for a home server case are the number of drive bays it provides and its cooling efficiency. In a residential environment, noise level and appearance may also be important. For us, all four of those factors were important. We wanted at least half a dozen hard drive bays to accommodate our initial disk configuration while leaving drive bays available for future expansion. Effective cooling is critical for obvious reasons. Noise level is important because this server will live in Robert's office, which already has several computers contributing to the noise level. Appearance is important because Robert doesn't want an ugly box sitting in his office.

We budgeted $140 to $160 for the case and power supply, because a top-quality 500W or better power supply costs at least $80 and a suitable case at least $60. That ruled out several otherwise suitable server cases from Intel and Super Micro that were priced considerably higher. If our budget could have extended to $200 or more, we'd have seriously considered models like the **Antec Titan 650**, the **Intel SC5299UPNA**, and the **Super Micro CSE-733i-645**.

In the $150 price range, the **Antec Atlas 550** is the standout choice, so much so that we couldn't find any comparable cases at anything close to its price. Despite its mini-tower form factor, the Atlas 550 provides a total of eight drive bays—four external 5.25" bays and four internal 3.5" bays—and accepts full ATX (although not extended ATX) motherboards. Only the four internal bays have shock mounts for the hard drives, but if we want to install drives in the external bays we can use silicone washers from the hardware store.

In stock form, the Atlas 550 has very good cooling. In addition to the power supply fan, a three-speed 120 mm rear fan is standard. There are also three open fan positions, for one 80 mm fan on the side panel and two front 92 mm fans to cool the hard drives. Frankly, we're not sure why Antec didn't just include those two 92 mm fans as a standard feature.

The Atlas 550 is a reasonably quiet case, particularly if you run the case fans at less than full speed. The TruPower power supply is nearly inaudible, particularly running lightly loaded. Appearance is obviously a matter of taste, but we think the Atlas 550 is a very attractive case. We wouldn't hesitate to use it in our den, library, or living room, let alone our offices.

Motherboard and Processor

ASRock K10N78M Pro (*http://www.asrock.com*)

AMD Athlon II X2 240 (*http://www.amd.com*)

Most home servers spend most of their time reading, writing, transmitting, and receiving files, none of which places much burden on a processor. Other than stability and reliability, the only requirements for the motherboard are that it supports at least a couple of gigabytes of memory, provides ports for connecting at least the three SATA hard drives we plan to install initially, and provides at least one fast, reliable Ethernet port. Of course, even a motherboard that lacks those ports can be expanded by adding PCI or PCI Express adapter cards to increase the port count.

In fact, we seriously considered using an inexpensive Intel Atom motherboard/processor combo for our home server. We decided not to, but only because Atom motherboards are short of both ports and expansion slots. Instead, we decided to use the same processor and motherboard we used in the budget system. (Why reinvent the wheel?) That boosted our cost for the motherboard and processor from $80 or so for the Intel Atom motherboard/processor to $120 or so for the budget motherboard/processor, less the cost of the $15 expansion card we'd have had to add to provide more SATA ports.

That $25 or so extra was well worth spending. Rather than a tiny motherboard with very limited expansion capabilities, we ended up with a µATX motherboard with four SATA ports, a PCI Express x1 expansion slot, and two PCI expansion slots. We also ended up with a processor that's several times faster than the Atom, giving us some headroom if we later decide to add other functions to the server.

We used the ASRock motherboard and Athlon II X2 processor because we'd used them to build (and torture-test) the budget system and knew they were both inexpensive and reliable. With the light burden a home server system places on the processor and motherboard, just about any AMD or Intel budget processor in any other ASRock, ASUS, GIGABYTE, or Intel motherboard would have done as well.

In fact, if we hadn't needed to use all-new components for our server for the purpose of this book, we might well have recycled the processor and motherboard from one of our existing systems. A two-year-old system that was built

You Want a Cable with That Drive?

Most retail-boxed motherboards and retail-boxed hard drives come with drive cables, but if you plan to install multiple drives it's worth checking the detailed motherboard and drive specifications to see what's included in the box. The ASRock K10N78M Pro, for example, includes only one standard ATA/IDE cable and one SATA cable. We ordered OEM (bare) hard drives, so no cables were included with the drives. We have spare SATA cables all over the place, so it wasn't an issue for us, but it may be for you. When you order your components, order extra cables if there aren't enough included with the motherboard and drives.

Another problem you may encounter, particularly with µATX and Mini-ITX motherboards, is that the cables supplied with the motherboard may not be long enough for some larger cases. Very few motherboard makers specify their products to that level of detail, so about the best you can do is hope, unless you want to order some long cables just to be sure.

If you do find yourself needing to buy longer cables, don't visit the local big-box stores. They may carry the cables you need, but the price will probably be outrageous. Instead, look for a local system builder, who probably has hundreds of the things in a back room and will probably be willing to sell you a couple cheap.

with high-quality components is, in our experience, just finishing an extended burn-in, and is probably good for several more years. About the only change we'd make to such recycled components would be to replace the CPU cooler (or at least its fan) and to remove the memory modules, polish the contacts, and reinstall them. Alas, none of this is true for typical mass-market systems, many of which are built with the cheapest possible third- and fourth-tier motherboards, cheap memory, and so on.

Memory

Crucial CT2KIT25664AA800 PC2-6400 4 GB kit (2 GB×2)

(*http://www.crucial.com*)

The ASRock K10N78M Pro motherboard has two memory slots that support a maximum of 8 GB of memory. Our normal practice for 32-bit operating systems is to install 1 GB of memory per core (or per thread, for multithreaded processors). On that basis, a pair of 1 GB memory modules for a total of 2 GB of system memory would probably have sufficed. A 32-bit OS recognizes at most 3 to 3.5 GB of memory, so installing more than 4 GB would be pointless.

However, in our 20 years of dealing with servers, we've never heard anyone complain that a server had too much memory. It's possible that at some point we'll install a 64-bit operating system on this server, which would effectively double the memory requirements to 4 GB. A pair of 2 GB memory modules didn't cost all that much more than a pair of 1 GB modules, so we decided to install 4 GB of memory initially. We considered installing a pair of 4 GB modules to max out system memory at 8 GB, but at the time we built this system 4 GB modules were selling for more than twice as much per gigabyte as 2 GB modules, so that would have been a waste of money.

We chose a Crucial 4 GB (2 GB×2) memory kit, using the online Crucial product selector to ensure compatibility with our motherboard. The motherboard supports DDR2-533 (PC2-4200), DDR2-667 (PC2-5300), DDR2-800 (PC2-6400), and DDR2-1066 (PC2-8500) memory modules. Although Crucial offered PC2-4200 and PC2-5300 modules for this motherboard, those modules were priced the same as PC2-6400 modules, so there was no reason to choose the slower modules. The PC2-8500 modules were considerably more expensive than the PC2-6400 modules and would have provided no noticeable performance benefit, so we settled on the PC2-6400 kit.

Hard Disk Drives

Seagate Barracuda XT ST32000641AS 2TB (three)

(*http://www.seagate.com*)

The disk subsystem of our home server must be capacious, fast, and reliable: capacious because this server will store all of the data we want to keep online, which is currently nearly 4 TB and growing; fast because when we retrieve a file we don't want the server slowing things down; and reliable, well, for obvious reasons. Here are our recommendations:

Capacity

Our target for capacity was 6 TB (6,000 GB). The largest hard drives available when we built this system held 2 TB, so using three of those hits our target while leaving five free drive bays for later expansion.

We considered using 1.5 TB drives, which when we built this system had the lowest price per unit storage—about $0.07/GB versus about $0.10/GB for the 2 TB models—but we decided that we'd rather pay slightly more per gigabyte than use an extra drive bay. Installing four 1.5 TB drives would also have maxed out our motherboard's four SATA connectors, so we'd need to use an ATAPI optical drive. If (when) we wanted to add a hard drive, we'd need to buy and install a SATA expansion card.

> **Brian Bilbrey Comments**
>
> *I buy the ES (or whatever they're calling the Enterprise-grade) drives, generally at a 50% premium over the equivalent-sized consumer spindle. I figure the sleep I gain from improved drive reliability is worth every penny.*

Performance

High-capacity SATA hard drives are available in 7,200 RPM mainstream models and 5,400 or 5,900 RPM economy models. We seriously considered using the slower drives, which would have reduced drive costs significantly. For example, when we built this system, 2 TB 5,900 RPM drives were selling for literally half the price of 7,200 RPM models. As tempting as it was to cut our drive costs by half, we decided that the performance penalty was too high a price to pay, particularly since we intend to use this server for years to come.

Reliability

There are different kinds of reliability. First, of course, is the inherent reliability of the hardware itself. Seagate Barracuda SATA drives are extremely reliable, as any data recovery firm knows. We have had fewer failures with Seagate drives than with any other brand, and many of our readers report similar experiences. A clean, well-ventilated system with reliable power protection contributes further to drive reliability. And, although we could nearly eliminate the small risk of data loss caused by a drive failure by configuring our four drives in a RAID 5, that would cost us a quarter of our available storage.

Which brings up the final type of reliability: procedural reliability. Our procedures replicate our data, both manually and automatically, to multiple systems on our network. For example, our audio/video data will reside both on this server and on our media center system, Barbara's scans of family photographs will reside both on this server and on her main system, and our raw camcorder video will reside both on this server and on Robert's main system.

A failed hard drive on the server might cost us at most a few minutes' work, depending on which drive failed. Chances are that a drive failure will lose us no work at all, and all we'll have to do is replace the failed drive and restore the data to it from a backup. We can live with that.

Obviously, the best storage configuration for your needs may differ significantly from our configuration. Not everyone needs a 6 TB server, and many people will happily accept the slower performance of 5,400 RPM or 5,900 RPM drives in exchange for cutting their drive costs significantly.

Strength in Numbers

One of the advantages of having several hard drives installed is that it provides a great deal of flexibility. With three 2 TB drives, for example, you can configure your disk subsystem as a 6 TB JBOD or a 4 TB RAID 5. With four 2 TB drives, you can set up an 8 TB JBOD, a 6 TB RAID 5, or a 4 TB RAID 10.

We actually borrowed a fourth 2 TB Barracuda XT from one of the other project systems long enough to test a RAID 10 configuration. When we tested hard drive performance locally, RAID 5 and particularly RAID 10 were faster than JBOD in some benchmarks, as we expected. But for accessing files over the network—which is all that really matters—our 1000BaseT

network was the bottleneck. Network file reads and writes were no faster with RAID 10 than with JBOD, again as we expected.

We concluded that using RAID with 7,200 RPM drives in the server was pointless. But, although we didn't have enough 5,400 or 5,900 RPM drives to test our hypothesis, we would expect a server using those slower drives in a JBOD to be disk-bound rather than network-bound. In that case, we'd probably buy an extra drive or drives and configure them as a RAID 10. When 10000BaseT network components become affordable, we'll revisit the RAID issue.

Of course, you needn't fill all or even most of your drive bays initially. You can start small and expand as needed. For example, you might start with just one or two drives, and simply add another drive each time your data approaches maximum disk capacity. This is particularly easy to do with a JBOD; with a RAID you may have some backing up and restoring and reconfiguring to do each time you install a new drive or drives.

Ad Hoc Backups

Don't overlook the opportunity to use new drives for ad hoc backups when you expand your system. For example, one of our readers started with a pair of 7,200 RPM 1 TB drives set up as a RAID 1. Then she got into shooting HD video and decided to add a pair of 5400 RPM 1.5 TB drives for bulk data storage and to convert the RAID 1 to a JBOD to give her additional fast hard drive capacity.

That took her from a 1 TB RAID 1 configuration to a 5 TB JBOD, and of course she ran two full backups to eSATA external hard drives before doing anything else. Then she realized she could

use the two new hard drives to make two more full backups. So she put the two new hard drives in her eSATA dock, formatted them, copied the contents of the RAID 1 to both of them, shut down the system, and disconnected the drives.

She said she'd have been very uncomfortable having only one full backup before breaking and reformatting the RAID 1, and at least slightly uncomfortable having only two backups. But, as she said, with four full backups there was more chance that she'd be struck by lightning than that she'd lose all her data during the upgrade.

The Big 3-0

As we wrote this, 2 TB drives were the largest available, but Seagate has announced plans to ship a 3 TB model in late 2010. No doubt Samsung, Western Digital, and other drive makers will follow Seagate's lead and introduce similar models.

Unfortunately, the BIOSs on nearly all current motherboards do not support booting from drives larger than 2 TB. This is a hard limitation. There's no way to get around it, short of replacing the motherboard with a model that uses a Unified Extensible Firmware Interface (UEFI) BIOS.

Fortunately, this limitation applies only to the boot drive. As long as you boot the system from a 2 TB or smaller drive, and as long as your operating system, HDD device drivers, and/or HBAs or RAID controllers support drives larger than 2 TB, you can install as many 3 TB drives as you have SATA ports available for them.

With three 2 TB drives and five spare drive bays, we have room to expand our own server to a total of 21 TB without replacing any drives. That should suffice for the expected life of the server.

Backup Hardware

None

Easy SATA (*http://www.antec.com*)

SYBA SD-ENC50020 Hard Drive Docking Station (*http://www.syba.com*)

Backing up a multi-terabyte server is a real challenge. Optical discs just don't cut it. A full backup of a 6 TB server fills more than 1,300 DVD+R discs. Blu-ray isn't much better; a 6 TB backup fills 240 BD-R discs. And you'd have to sit there around the clock for several days swapping discs. Tape backup would be nice, but even an 800 GB LTO Ultrium tape drive runs $1,500 or more, and a tape changer with enough capacity that's fast enough for backing up a multi-terabyte server overnight costs as much as a decent used car. And then there's the cost of the tapes.

That leaves hard drives as the only practical solution. They're inexpensive, fast, easy to use, and reasonably rugged. A USB 2.0 external hard drive transfers data at about 30 MB/second, or about 108 GB/hour, so backing up 1 TB of data would take close to 10 hours. That's much too slow, unless your server has a relatively small amount of data that needs routine backup. An eSATA external hard drive or a removable SATA hard drive is much faster than USB 2.0, because backup throughput is limited by the speed of the hard drives themselves rather than the interface. In our tests, a Seagate 7,200 RPM hard drive transferred data via eSATA at a sustained rate of more than 100 MB/s, or close to 400 GB/hour.

We listed our first choice of backup hardware as "none" because we didn't actually install any backup hardware in our home server (well, we did, but only for the purpose of shooting images for this chapter). Our server runs headless and is backed up across the network to removable hard drives in Robert's main desktop system, but many home servers require local backup hardware.

If you need to back up your server locally, our first choice would be either an Antec Easy SATA, which allows you to install or remove a bare SATA hard drive simply by sliding it into or out of the frame, or a SYBA hard drive docking station. The SYBA unit holds two hard drives, but requires an eSATA port for each. Since we have only four SATA ports available in this system, three of which are devoted to hard drives, we decided to install an Antec Easy SATA frame and allocate the fourth SATA port to it.

Data to Go

At $20 or so, the Antec Easy SATA units are inexpensive enough that you might want to consider purchasing one or more of them for each of your systems. If you install all of your hard drives in these frames, you can simply slide out the drives and take them with you when you leave the house. You can also install an empty Easy SATA frame in each of your systems and use two or three hard drives as a rotating backup set for all of your systems.

Of course, carrying bare hard drives around risks damaging them. There are several possible solutions to that problem. First, some hard drives come packaged in resealable hard plastic blister packs, which are excellent for transporting and storing drives. If you don't have those, you can purchase padded hard drive wallets for each of your drives. Alternatively, if the drives you purchase are shipped in protective bubble wrap, you can simply reuse that bubble wrap.

Optical Drive

None

Our home server runs headless, so it doesn't really need an optical drive, except for installing the operating system. The ASRock motherboard has four SATA ports, three of which are devoted to hard drives, leaving one available for a SATA optical drive (or adding another hard drive later). The motherboard also provides one ATA/133 port, so we *could* install an ATAPI optical drive on the ATA port, but that drive would simply sit there collecting dust for months on end. It would also occupy a drive bay that we might need later for an additional hard drive.

The usual reason for installing an optical drive on a server—making backups—doesn't apply to this system, either. It will be backed up across the network. Our home server will sit in Robert's office in the far back corner under Robert's desk (a 3′ solid-core door mounted to the wall studs). This will be very much an out-of-sight-out-of mind system. In fact, Robert put entries in his calendar so he wouldn't forget to vacuum out the dust bunnies every few months.

Of course, your situation may be different. If you need a DVD writer in your server, install one of the ASUS, LiteOn, or Samsung models mentioned in one of the other system chapters. If you intend to use Blu-ray BD-R/RE for backup, install the Pioneer Blu-ray writer. Of course, if you intend to install several hard drives in your server and also intend to leave an optical drive installed permanently, you may need to use a different motherboard that provides additional ATA and/or SATA ports.

We elected to conserve both ports and bays by connecting an optical drive only long enough to install the operating system. As it happened, we had an old ATAPI DVD available, so we connected it temporarily to the ATA port on the motherboard. We could also have connected a SATA optical drive temporarily, or even used one of our USB external optical drives.

Keyboard, Mouse, and Display

Because this home server runs Linux, we need a keyboard, mouse, and display only for initial installation and configuration. Once the server is running, we can manage it remotely from one of our desktop systems.

UPS

Falcon Electric SG or SSG Series On-Line UPS (*http://www.falconups.com*)

Running a server without a UPS is foolish. Even a momentary power glitch can corrupt open databases, trash open documents, and crash server-based apps, wiping out the work of everyone connected to the server. A UPS may literally pay for itself the first time the power fails.

We used and recommended APC UPSs for many years. Then, after we experienced several premature failures of APC units and received numerous messages from readers about their increasingly frequent problems with APC units, we decided to look elsewhere. On the advice of our friend and colleague Jerry

Pournelle, we looked at Falcon Electric UPSs, which turned out to be as good as Jerry said they were. (Years ago, an earthquake rattled Chaos Manor, knocking over everything in the server room. All of Jerry's equipment failed, except the Falcon Electric UPS, which just kept running, lying on its side amidst the debris of his computer room.) We've now used Falcon Electric units exclusively for about five years, without so much as a hiccough.

Falcon Electric units are built to industrial standards, and priced accordingly. You won't find Falcon UPSs at online resellers or big-box stores, but they are readily available from numerous distributors. Check the Falcon Electric website for details.

Our server connects to a 2 kVA Falcon Electric SG Series On-Line UPS that was already located in Robert's office, protecting his desktop system. That unit has plenty of reserve capacity to protect the server as well, so there was no need to install a separate UPS for the server.

We think it's worth spending the extra time, effort, and money to get a Falcon Electric UPS. They really are better-built and more reliable than consumer-grade models. If the Falcon Electric units are out of your price range, we think the APC Smart-UPS units remain the best of the mass-market UPSs, despite the problems we and our readers have had with them from time to time. (We've had more problems with other brands.) If you're on an even tighter budget, the APC Back-UPS units are reasonable choices.

If you've decided to forego a UPS entirely, we suggest you think again. Any power protection is better than none at all. Even the inexpensive units that look like fat outlet strips are better than nothing. Their run-time is very short, but even a few seconds of backup power is often sufficient. If you buy one of these inexpensive units, just make sure that the VA rating is high enough to support the draw of your server. Also be aware that the built-in surge and spike suppression in these units is often very poor, so it's worthwhile to install a good surge protector between the power receptacle and the UPS.

Component Summary

Table 8-1 summarizes our component choices for the home server system.

Table 8-1. Bill of materials for home server

Component	Product
Case	Antec Atlas 550 Server Case
Power supply	(Bundled 550 W)
Motherboard	ASRock K10N78M Pro
Processor	AMD Athlon II X2 240 (retail boxed)
CPU cooler	(Bundled with processor)
Memory	Crucial CT2KIT25664AA800 PC2-6400 4 GB kit (2 GB×2)
Video adapter	(Integrated)
Sound adapter	(Integrated)
Hard drives	Seagate Barracuda XT ST32000641AS 2TB (three)

Table 8-1. Bill of materials for home server

Component	Product
Backup hardware	(See text)
Optical drive	(None; see text)
Keyboard	(None; see text)
Mouse	(None; see text)
Speakers	(None; see text)
Display	(None; see text)
UPS	Falcon Electric SG or SSG Series On-Line UPS

Building the Home Server

Figure 8-1 shows the major components of the home server. Well, except for the Falcon Electric UPS—it weighs a ton, and we didn't feel like hauling it from Robert's office into the kitchen and lifting it up onto the table.

The AMD Athlon II X2 240 Regor processor is visible at left center, with a Crucial 4 GB memory kit sitting atop it, leaning against the Antec Atlas 550 case. To the right is the Antec Easy SATA drive caddy, with the ASRock K10N78M Pro motherboard front and center. The three Seagate Barracuda XT 2 TB hard drives are visible at the lower left. That's everything we need to build our server, other than the optical drive, display, keyboard, and mouse that we'll connect just long enough to get the software installed and configured.

Figure 8-1. Home server components, awaiting construction

> **He Got Up, Got Dressed, and Took a Shower**
>
> *As always, you needn't follow the exact sequence of steps we describe when you build your own home server. Always install the processor and memory before you install the motherboard in the case, because doing otherwise risks damaging the processor, memory, or motherboard. The exact sequence doesn't matter for most other steps, though. Some steps must be taken in the order we describe, because completing one step is required for completing the next, but as you build your system it will be obvious when sequence matters.*

Make sure you have everything you need before you start building the system. Open each box and verify the contents against the packing list.

Building the Home Server

Preparing the Case

The first step in preparing any case that has an installed power supply is to look for an input-voltage selector switch on the rear of the power supply.

If that switch is present, make sure it's set to the correct input voltage. If the switch is set for 230VAC and you connect the system to a 115VAC receptacle, nothing bad happens. The power supply provides only half the voltage the motherboard and other components expect, and the system simply doesn't power up. However, if the input voltage is set to 115VAC and you connect the power supply to a 230VAC receptacle, the system will receive twice the voltage it's designed to accept, and you'll get a nice (and expensive) fireworks show.

The Antec TruePower Trio 550 power supply in the Atlas 550 is autosensing, which means it detects the input voltage and adjusts itself automatically. No switch necessary, and nothing to worry about. But if you're using some other case and power supply, make sure to check.

To begin preparing the Antec Atlas 550 case, place it upright on a flat surface. Loosen both of the captive thumbscrews that secure the side panel, as shown in Figure 8-2, and then swing the panel out and remove it from the case, as shown in Figure 8-3.

Figure 8-3. *Swing the side panel out and remove it from the case*

Figure 8-2. *Loosen both captive thumbscrews on the rear of the left side panel*

The front bezel is secured by three black plastic latching tabs at the left front edge of the chassis. Press the top tab gently to release the tension and pull outward very gently on the top of the front bezel to prevent that tab from snapping back into place. Repeat this procedure for the middle tab, as shown in Figure 8-4, and the tab located near the bottom of the chassis frame.

After you release all three latching tabs, swing the front bezel out about 45°, as shown in Figure 8-5. Lift the front bezel straight up an inch or so, remove it, and place it aside.

With the front bezel removed, the hard drive cage cover, shown in Figure 8-5, is visible. Loosen the two thumbscrews, top and bottom, that secure the drive cage cover, as shown in Figure 8-6.

Figure 8-4. *Release the three latching tabs that secure the front bezel to the chassis frame*

Figure 8-5. *Swing the front bezel out to about 45°, lift it clear, and set it aside*

Figure 8-7. *Swing the drive cage cover open*

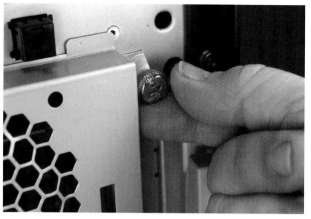

Figure 8-6. *Loosen the two thumbscrews that secure the hard drive cage cover*

Swing the drive cage cover open, as shown in Figure 8-7. Lift it straight up to remove it, as shown in Figure 8-8, and set it aside.

The drive cage contains four hard drive mounting trays, each of which is retained by a pair of spring-metal clips. Remove as many drive trays as you have hard drives to install by squeezing both clips and pulling the tray straight out of the chassis, as shown in Figure 8-9. Set the drive tray(s) aside for now.

For the best cooling, provide as much space as possible between the hard drives. If you're installing two hard drives, remove the top and bottom drive trays. If you're installing three hard drives, as we did, leave one of the middle two drive trays unused.

The plastic bag that contains screws and other components is located in one of the external drive bays at the top of the chassis. Use your dykes (diagonal cutters), as shown in Figure 8-10, to cut the plastic cable tie that secures the parts bag to the chassis. If you don't have dykes, carefully use a sharp knife or similar tool. Set the parts bag aside.

Figure 8-8. *Lift the drive cage cover slightly to release it, and set it aside*

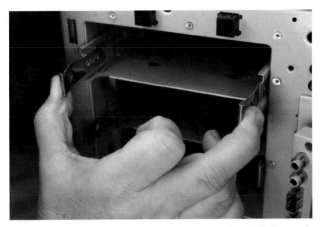

Figure 8-9. *Remove drive trays by squeezing both metal clips and pulling the drive tray straight out of the chassis*

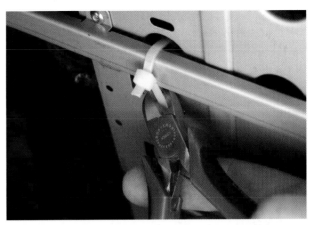

Figure 8-10. *Cut the cable tie that secures the parts bag to the chassis*

Installing the Hard Drive(s)

The next step is to install the hard drive(s). To begin, place the hard drive inverted (circuit board–side up) on a flat surface and position a drive tray on top of it, as shown in Figure 8-11. Make sure the drive and drive tray are oriented correctly, with the front of the hard drive on the side of the drive tray that has the metal clips. The rear of the hard drive, with the power and data connectors, should protrude from the rear of the tray, as shown in Figure 8-11.

Locate four of the special hard drive mounting screws in the parts bag. (One of these screws is shown at the bottom left of Figure 8-11.) Align the holes in the rubber grommets on the drive mounting tray with the screw holes in the bottom of the hard drive, and secure the hard drive by driving in the four screws. Tighten the screws finger-tight plus a quarter turn or so, but be careful not to overtighten them. Overtightening eliminates the noise- and vibration-damping benefits of the grommets. Repeat this procedure for each of your hard drives.

Locate as many SATA data cables as you have hard drives. The SATA ports on your motherboard may be numbered starting with 0 or 1. (The ASRock motherboard we used uses both numbering methods.) Use a felt-tip pen to label each SATA data cable on both ends with the number of the drive/port you'll use it with, as shown in Figure 8-12. Label both sides of each cable to make sure the label will be visible after the cables are installed.

Connect a SATA data cable to each of your hard drives, as shown in Figure 8-13. The connector is keyed with an L-shaped socket and plug. Make sure the cable connector and drive connector are aligned properly and then press the cable connector straight in until it seats. Avoid placing any lateral pressure or torque on the connectors, which are relatively fragile. Install the other SATA data cables on the remaining hard drive(s), if any.

> **Flat Versus Phillips**
>
> *Yes, we used a flat-blade screwdriver to secure the hard drives. The special hard-drive mounting screws Antec supplies have a combination straight/Phillips head, but the Phillips portion is so shallow that we were able to get a better grip with the flat-blade screwdriver.*

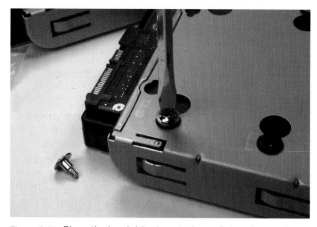

Figure 8-11. *Place the hard drive inverted on a flat surface and use four of the special drive-mounting screws to secure it to the drive tray*

Figure 8-12. *Label each of your SATA data cables with the drive/port number you'll use them with*

Feed the free end of the SATA data cable through the drive bay and into the interior of the case. Align the drive tray with the chassis and slide the tray into the chassis, as shown in Figure 8-14. Press the drive tray until the spring clips snap into place, securing the hard drive. Repeat this procedure for each of the remaining hard drives, if any. When you've finished, check all of the SATA data cables to make sure they're still fully seated.

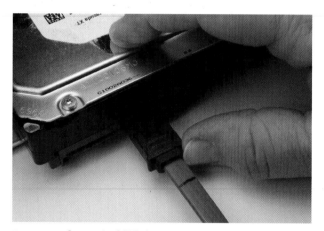

Figure 8-13. *Connect a SATA data cable to the hard drive*

Figure 8-14. *Slide the drive tray back into the chassis and press firmly until the spring clips snap into place*

To reinstall the hard drive bay cover, align the pins on the left side of the drive bay cover with the sockets on the chassis, and lower the drive bay cover back into place, as shown in Figure 8-15. Swing the drive bay cover closed and tighten both thumbscrews to secure it, as shown in Figure 8-16.

Chapter 8

Hard Drive Fans

If you want to install one or two 92 mm supplemental cooling fans for the hard drive bay, now is the time to do so. You can use any standard 92 mm case fan.

If you install one or both of these fans, make certain that they are oriented to push air into the case rather than draw air out of it. Look for an arrow on the body of the fan, which indicates the direction of the air flow.

To mount a fan, simply install the four mounting screws or expansion connectors supplied with the fan in the four holes surrounding the fan grill on the hard drive bay cover. Run the fan power cable into the interior of the case, and connect it to an available power connector.

If you install a fan or fans that have switchable speeds, decide how much noise you're willing to tolerate. If the server is in an area where noise is not an issue, set the fans to run on high. Otherwise, start by setting them on low and increase the speed later if you need more cooling.

Different fans have different power connectors. The most common is a standard Molex (old-style hard drive) power connector. If your power supply has one or more Molex connectors labeled Fan-Only, you can use those to allow the power supply to control fan speed. If you do that, set the fan power switch to high. If you set it to medium or low, the voltage supplied by the Fan-Only power connector may not be sufficient to spin up the fan. If your fan has a three- or four-pin header-pin connector, it's designed to be connected to the motherboard. Locate a header-pin connector on the motherboard labeled Aux Fan or Case Fan and connect the fan power cable to that set of header pins. Once again, if the fan has a speed switch, set it to high.

We decided not to install any hard drive fans in our server, at least initially. We'll keep an eye on hard drive temperatures, and install a fan or fans later if necessary.

Figure 8-15. *Align the pins on the drive bay cover with the sockets in the chassis and lower the drive bay cover back into place*

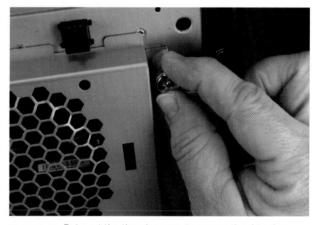

Figure 8-16. *Reinsert the thumbscrews to secure the drive bay cover*

Preparing the Motherboard

With the hard drives installed, the next step is to prepare the motherboard by installing the processor, CPU cooler, and memory. Some manuals suggest installing the motherboard in the chassis before installing the processor and memory, but after nearly cracking a motherboard by doing it that way, we decided it was much safer to install the processor and memory first.

To begin, locate the metal cam lever on the side of the processor socket. Press the cam lever slightly outward (away from the socket) to release it from the plastic latches that secure it, and then lift the lever, as shown in Figure 8-17.

Figure 8-17. *Release the cam lever from the processor socket and lift it up*

Open the outer box of the processor and remove the hard plastic shell that contains the processor. Open that package carefully. Touch the chassis or power supply to ground yourself before you touch the processor itself. Remove the processor from the antistatic foam bed on which it rests. Align and orient the processor carefully with the processor socket. The socket and processor are keyed, with an arrow on one corner of the processor and a corresponding key on one corner of the processor socket.

When you have the processor and socket aligned, simply drop the processor into the socket, as shown in Figure 8-18. The processor should seat fully with no pressure whatsoever. **Do not apply any pressure**; doing so risks bending the fragile contact pins. If the processor doesn't drop into the socket freely, it's not aligned properly. Realign it and try again until it drops easily into the socket and seats completely.

Once the processor is seated properly, swing down the metal cam lever and snap it into place under the plastic locking tab on the socket, as shown in Figure 8-19. You should feel slight resistance on the cam lever as the cam clamps the socket onto the processor pins. If the resistance is anything more than slight, back up and start over.

Figure 8-18. *Orient and align the processor properly with the socket and then drop it into place*

Figure 8-19. *Press the cam lever down and snap it into place under the plastic locking tab on the processor socket*

With the processor seated and clamped into place, the next step is to install the CPU cooler. Before you install the cooler, examine the bottom of the heat-sink to verify that the patch of thermal compound is present and undamaged.

The CPU cooler mounts to the processor socket using two shiny metal latches on the CPU cooler that fit over two black plastic tabs on the processor socket. One of those latches is free-floating, and the other has a camming lever that allows the CPU cooler to be locked into place. The CPU cooler can be oriented so that either latch fits over either tab, but it's more convenient to use the free-floating latch toward the interior of the motherboard (where there is less clearance) and the cammed latch on the edge of the motherboard.

Examine the CPU cooler and locate the side with the free-floating latch. Tilt the opposite side of the CPU cooler up slightly, and hook the free-floating metal latch over the black plastic tab on the side of the processor socket near the passive heatsink, as shown in Figure 8-20.

Pivot the CPU cooler down and into full contact with the processor, making sure that the first latch remains connected. Maintaining finger pressure to keep the CPU cooler in position, press the second (cammed) latch into posi-tion over the second black plastic tab, as shown in Figure 8-21.

> **When Recycling Is Bad**
>
> *If you ever remove and replace the processor, don't attempt to reuse the thermal compound. Rub off any compound present on the processor surface and the heatsink base—if it's tenacious, you can warm it slightly with a hair dryer—and then polish both the processor surface and the heatsink base with a clean paper towel to remove all traces of the old compound. Apply new thermal compound according to the instruc-tions supplied with it. (We generally use Antec Silver thermal compound, which is inexpensive and effective.)*

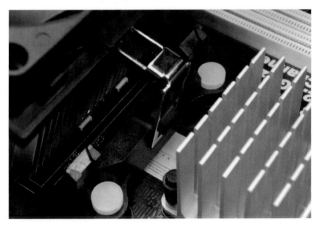

Figure 8-20. *Hook the free-floating metal latch over the black plastic tab on the processor socket*

Figure 8-21. *Press the cammed latch into position over the second tab*

Verify that both latches are secured over both tabs, and then press the black plastic cam lever down until it latches to lock the CPU cooler to the processor socket, as shown in Figure 8-22.

Ordinarily, the next step would be to connect the CPU cooler fan power cable to the motherboard CPU fan header pins. In this case, though, the position of the CPU fan header pins made it more convenient to install the memory be-fore we connected the CPU fan.

With the processor installed, the next step is to install the memory modules. To begin, swing open the DIMM locking tabs on both sides of both memory sockets, as shown in Figure 8-23.

Figure 8-22. *Press the black plastic cam lever on the CPU cooler down until it latches to secure the CPU cooler to the processor socket*

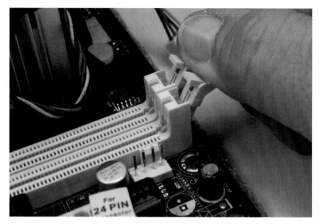

Figure 8-23. *Open the DIMM locking tabs on both sides of both memory sockets*

Before handling the memory modules, touch the chassis or power supply to ground yourself. Align the first DIMM with a memory socket, as shown in Figure 8-24. Make sure the keying notch on the contact edge of the memory module aligns with the keying tab in the socket and that the two sides of the memory module fit into the slots on the vertical sides of the memory slot.

Make sure that the memory module and slot are lined up properly, with the memory module vertical relative to the slot. Using one thumb on each side of the memory module, press straight down until the memory module snaps into place, as shown in Figure 8-25.

Figure 8-24. *Align the memory module with the socket*

Figure 8-25. *Press straight down on both sides of the memory module until it seats completely in the socket*

After you seat the memory module, make sure the plastic latching tabs on the memory socket have snapped into place to latch the module into position, as shown in Figure 8-26. If the latching tabs are not seated in the notches on the memory module, it's possible that the module is not seated completely. The metal contacts on the base of the module should be concealed by the memory socket. If any are visible, the module is not fully seated.

Repeat this process with the additional memory module(s).

With the memory installed, you can now connect power to the CPU fan, as shown in Figure 8-27.

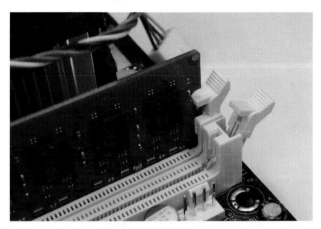 

Figure 8-26. *Verify that the memory module is latched into position*

Figure 8-27. *Connect the CPU fan power cable to the CPU fan header pins*

The motherboard is now prepared. Place it aside for now. Use the antistatic foam under the motherboard to make sure it's not damaged by static electricity.

Final Case Preparation

Next, we'll complete a few final case-preparation steps to ready the case to receive the motherboard. To begin, remove the I/O shield installed in the Antec Atlas 550 case. The easiest way to do that is to press on the outside of the I/O shield with a tool handle, as shown in Figure 8-28, until the I/O shield pops loose. You can discard this I/O shield.

Locate the I/O shield in the motherboard box and hold it up to the rear I/O panel of the motherboard, as shown in Figure 8-29, to make sure that the holes in the I/O shield correspond to the ports on the motherboard rear I/O panel.

Working from inside the case, position the I/O shield and use a tool handle to press gently on it until it snaps into position, as shown in Figure 8-30. Be careful not to bend the thin metal of the I/O shield. If necessary, use your fingers on the outside of the I/O shield to support it while you're pressing it into position.

With the custom I/O shield installed, the next step is to determine the proper number and location of the motherboard mounting standoffs. The ASRock motherboard has six mounting holes. The Atlas 550 case comes with four brass standoffs installed, only two of which are in the proper positions for the motherboard. (The remaining two are located off to one side where they can't contact the motherboard; you can leave those standoffs installed or remove them, as you like.)

Locate the motherboard mounting hole positions by holding the motherboard up to a bright light. Slide the motherboard temporarily into position in the case to determine which of the holes in the chassis need to have standoffs installed. We used a felt-tip pen to mark the holes in the chassis that needed standoffs to be installed, as shown in Figure 8-31.

Figure 8-28. *Use a tool handle to press on the outside of the I/O shield until it pops free*

Figure 8-29. *Verify that the custom I/O shield supplied with the motherboard in fact matches the rear I/O panel of the motherboard*

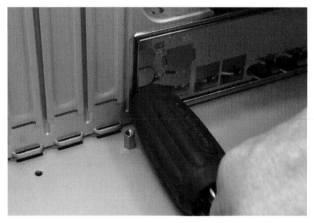

Figure 8-30. *Position the I/O shield and press gently until it snaps into position*

Figure 8-31. *Mark the chassis holes that need standoffs to be installed*

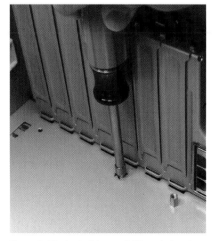

Figure 8-32. *Install four additional stand-offs in the marked mounting holes*

After you locate and mark the four additional mounting holes that require standoffs, hold the motherboard directly over the case and look straight down through each mounting hole in the motherboard to verify that you've marked the correct holes. Then locate the four additional standoffs in the parts bag and install them, as shown in Figure 8-32. You can use your fingers to install and tighten the standoffs, but we found it easier to use our 5 mm nut driver. Do not overtighten the standoffs, or you risk stripping the threads.

Installing the Motherboard

Slide the motherboard into position. Before you begin driving in screws to secure the motherboard, examine the back panel carefully to make sure that none of the grounding tabs on the I/O shield intrude into the motherboard port connectors, as shown in Figure 8-33. A bright flashlight is helpful here.

When you're sure the motherboard is properly positioned relative to the I/O shield, install one screw through the motherboard and into a standoff, as shown in Figure 8-34. Tighten that screw only partially.

Chapter 8

Figure 8-33. *Verify that none of the grounding tabs on the I/O shield have fouled motherboard I/O port connectors*

Figure 8-34. *Drive screws through the motherboard mounting holes and into their corresponding standoffs*

You'll need to apply some pressure against the springiness of the I/O shield to align the motherboard mounting holes with the standoffs. Get a second mounting hole aligned with its standoff and install a second screw. Once you've driven in the second screw, all of the mounting holes should align properly with their corresponding standoffs. Tighten all six motherboard mounting screws finger-tight, plus at most a quarter turn. Do not overtighten them, which risks cracking the motherboard.

Remove the cable tie that secures the bundle of cables from the power supply. Locate the ATX12V power cable, and route it to the ATX12V socket on the motherboard, located between the processor socket and the rear I/O panel. The ATX12V socket and plug are keyed. Orient the plug properly with the socket and press the connector into place, as shown in Figure 8-35.

Locate the 24-pin main ATX power cable in the power supply cable bundle, and route it to the front edge of the motherboard, just in front of the memory slots. The plug and jack are keyed. Orient the cable connector properly relative to the motherboard socket and press the cable connector into place, as shown in Figure 8-36. Make certain that the latch on the cable connector snaps into place over the tab on the motherboard connector to lock the cable into place.

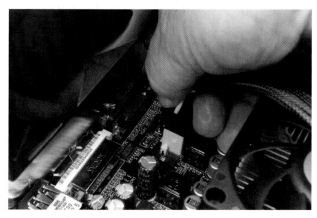

Figure 8-35. *Connect the ATX12V power cable from the power supply to the motherboard*

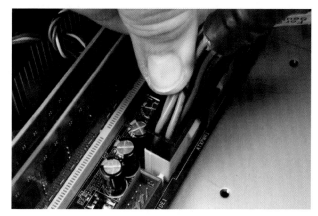

Figure 8-36. *Connect the 24-pin main ATX power cable from the power supply to the motherboard*

Connecting Front-Panel Ports and Indicators

With the case still on its side, it's now a good time to install the various front-panel connectors. To begin, locate the front-panel audio cable in the bundle of cables coiled up near the front of the case. This cable has two connectors, one for AC'97 audio and the other for HD audio. Locate the front-panel audio header-pin set in the back corner of the motherboard, which is keyed with a missing pin that corresponds to a blocked hole on the HD audio cable. Orient the HD audio cable connector properly relative to the header pins and press it onto those pins, as shown in Figure 8-37.

In addition to the six rear-panel USB ports, the ASRock motherboard includes two sets of USB header pins located near the front corner of the motherboard, each of which provides two USB ports. Locate the front-panel USB cable and route it to the USB header-pin set's location. Like the front-panel audio cable, the USB cable and motherboard connector are keyed with a missing pin and blocked hole. Orient the USB cable connector properly relative to the header-pin set, and press the connector onto the header pins, as shown in Figure 8-38.

The Atlas 550 also provides a front-panel IEEE1394 (FireWire) port, but our motherboard provides no connector for it. If your motherboard provides a set of FireWire header pins, connect that cable to those pins, but first verify that the pinouts on the cable connector and the header-pin set correspond properly. The motherboard manual and the case manual should both specify the pinouts used; if these do not match exactly, re-pin the cable connector using the instructions provided in the case manual.

With all of the front-panel ports connected, it's time to connect the front-panel switch and LED indicator cables. The two-pin switch connectors—the power switch and reset switch—are not polarized. They can be connected either way and will still work. Connect the reset switch and power switch by pressing their connectors onto the proper pairs of header pins, as shown in Figure 8-39.

LED connectors are polarized. If you connect one backward, the LED won't illuminate, but no damage is done. By convention, ground on these two pin connectors is the side with the white or black wire, and positive (+) is the side with a colored wire. Most motherboards have the proper polarity silkscreened onto the board near the connection, but this ASRock motherboard does not. Fortunately, the only LED cable we need to connect is the hard drive activity indicator, visible in Figure 8-39 behind and to the right of the POWER SW connector. That connector is oriented properly in the image, with the red wire toward the USB connector to its right.

With all of the front-panel cables connected, the next step is to connect the SATA data cables to the motherboard SATA ports. The ASRock motherboard provides four SATA ports, labeled SATAII_1 (Port 0) through SATAII_4 (Port 3). We have three hard drives to connect, and it doesn't really matter which drive we connect to which port. But we like to be as organized as possible, so by habit we connect the first hard drive to Port 0, the second to Port 1, and so on. To connect a SATA data cable, verify that the L-shaped key in the cable connector is oriented properly relative to the key in the motherboard SATA port, slide

Frying Peripherals

Years ago, we found out the hard way that just because a front-panel IEEE1394 cable connector fits an IEEE1394 header-pin set doesn't mean the connection is wired properly. We connected a camcorder to a miswired front-panel IEEE1394 port and promptly blew the circuitry on the camcorder. That was an expensive lesson, but one we'll never make again.

We Hate It When That Happens...

The power LED connector on the ASRock motherboard is two adjacent header pins. The Atlas 550 Power LED cable also uses two pins, but on a three-pin connector, with the middle position empty. This sort of mismatch is pretty common, particularly with the power LED and speaker connectors.

Unfortunately, there's no convenient way to solve the problem, unless the motherboard provides both sorts of connector (some do, but not this one). We actually decided to leave the power LED unconnected, because our server will sit under Robert's desk, where the power LED wouldn't be visible anyway.

If you want your power LED to work, you'll have to do some minor surgery. Use your dykes or a sharp knife to cut the three-pin power LED cable connector in half, leaving you with each of the two wires on separate connectors, and then connect those two wires individually to the appropriate motherboard header pins.

the connector into the port body, and press straight down until the connector fully seats, as shown in Figure 8-40. After you connect the hard drives, verify that all of the SATA data cables are securely seated on both ends.

Figure 8-37. *Connect the front-panel HD audio cable to the HD audio header pin set*

Figure 8-38. *Connect the front-panel USB cable to the USB header-pin set*

Figure 8-39. *Connect the front-panel switch and indicator cables*

Figure 8-40. *Connect the SATA data cables to the motherboard SATA ports*

With three hard drives installed, our configuration leaves one of the motherboard SATA ports free. We'll actually leave that port unused for now, but we may use it later to add a fourth hard drive. Depending on your hard drive configuration, you may have one or more ports free. You can use one of those for an optical drive or for the Antec Easy SATA hard drive docking station, which we'll talk about shortly.

Connecting Power to the Hard Drives and Fan

With the SATA data cables connected, it's time to connect power to the hard drives and case fan. Lest we forget, let's get the case fan connected first. In the bundle of cables coming from the power supply, locate the connector labeled FAN ONLY. Connect that cable to the power cable from the rear case fan, as shown in Figure 8-41. If you installed one or two 92 mm supplemental fans to cool the hard drive cage and didn't connect power to them at the time, connect them now as well.

The next step is to connect power to the hard drives. It pays to do a little bit of planning here, both to make sure you can dress all the cables neatly after you finish assembling the system and to make sure your SATA power cables can reach all of your SATA devices. If you're using only hard drives in your server, and if they're all located in the lower 3.5" hard drive cage, you won't have any problem. If you're installing SATA devices in the top (5.25") drive bays, getting power to all the SATA devices may be a stretch, literally.

To connect a SATA power cable to a drive, first ensure that the L-shaped key on the power cable and the corresponding key on the drive connector are oriented properly. Then slide the SATA power cable connector onto the drive power connector and press until it seats, as shown in Figure 8-42.

Fried Drives

Large hard drives aren't cheap. Although we connected the data and power cables to all three of the 2 TB drives in the sequence we describe here, we did that only to preroute the cables, to make it easier to dress them.

Before we powered up the system for the first time (the "smoke test"), we disconnected the power and data cables from all three of the 2 TB drives and temporarily connected an old 160 GB SATA drive. That way, if the power supply or motherboard turned out to be catastrophically defective, we'd fry only the old, small hard drive. Once we were satisfied that the system worked normally, we shut it down and reconnected the three real system hard drives.

In all of the systems we've built over the last 20 years, we've had only one catastrophic smoke test. That was enough to teach us caution. If you don't have an expendable spare hard drive, you can do the first boot with no drives connected or connect just an optical drive.

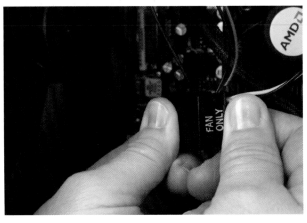

Figure 8-41. *Connect the case fan to a FAN ONLY power connector*

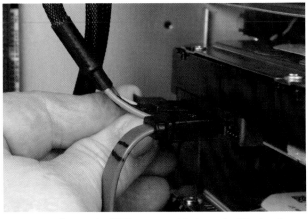

Figure 8-42. *Connect a SATA power cable to each of the hard drives*

Chapter 8

Installing an Optical Drive and/or Hard Drive Docking Station

At this point, we're nearly finished building the system. All that remains to be done is installing the optical drive or hard drive docking station—temporarily, in our case, but perhaps permanently in yours—and completing a few other final tasks.

Until now, we've been working with the case on its side. It's easier to install drives in the 5.25" drive bays if the case is sitting normally, so stand it up on your work surface. If you don't intend to leave an optical drive installed permanently, there's no point to installing it in the case. Instead, just set it on top of the case, as shown in Figure 8-43, and temporarily connect the SATA data and power cables to it.

Note the Antec Atlas 550 pamphlet between the optical drive and the Atlas 550 case. Although an optical drive is unlikely to short out even with the bottom of the drive in direct contact with the metal chassis frame, after once shorting out a hard drive we've gotten in the habit of using insulating material between the drive and the metal case.

If you're installing an optical drive permanently, locate two drive rails and the parts bag with the mounting screws. Position one drive rail as shown in Figure 8-44. With the drive rail in this position, the optical drive will protrude just far enough out of the chassis that its bezel is flush with the front case bezel.

Figure 8-43. *An optical drive connected temporarily*

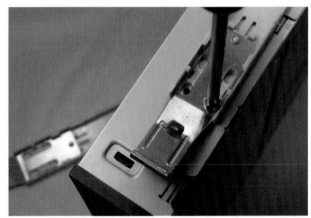

Figure 8-44. *Install drive rails on both sides of the optical drive*

There are four screw holes in the mounting rail and the drive, but we've never found it necessary to use more than two screws per drive rail, one at the bottom front and one at the top rear. Locate four drive mounting screws, and test one to make sure it matches the screw holes in the drive. Once you're sure you have the correct screws, secure both rails to the drive, using two screws for each. Connect a SATA data cable to the drive, feed that cable through the drive bay into the case, and then slide the optical drive into the case, as shown in Figure 8-45. Use both thumbs to press the drive into position until you hear the spring-metal tabs latch into place. Working from inside the case, connect a SATA power cable to the power connector on the rear of the drive.

If you're installing an Antec Easy SATA hard drive docking station instead of or in addition to the DVD writer, the procedure is the same: attach drive rails to both sides of the Easy SATA frame, slide the frame into the chassis, as shown in Figure 8-46, and connect SATA data and power cables.

Figure 8-45. *Slide the drive into the chassis and press until it latches*

Figure 8-46. *Installing an Antec Easy SATA hard drive docking station*

The Easy SATA docking station also provides an eSATA connector, visible in Figure 8-46 just to the left of Barbara's right thumb. If your motherboard has a spare SATA port and you want to make this eSATA port live, connect the captive cable inside the Easy SATA unit to that free SATA port. Note that this connector provides only SATA data, not power, so any external drive you connect to it must be powered separately.

Configuring and Using the Antec Easy SATA

To enable hot-swapping, the Antec Easy SATA docking station requires Advanced Host Controller Interface (AHCI) support. Before you install the operating system, enter BIOS Setup and locate the SATA configuration screen. If SATA is already set to use AHCI, you need make no changes. If SATA is set to IDE, change the setting to AHCI, save your settings, exit BIOS Setup, and restart the system.

If Windows Vista or Windows 7 is already installed, changing the SATA setting from IDE to AHCI will render the system unbootable, so exit BIOS Setup without making any changes. Visit http://support.microsoft.com/kb/922976 and follow the instructions there to enable AHCI on your system. If you have a recent Linux version installed, use your package manager to verify that the AHCI driver is installed, use BIOS Setup to enable AHCI, save the settings, and restart the system.

To install a hard drive in the Antec Easy SATA hard drive docking station, press the button on the left front of the docking station to release the latch, and slide the drive—with the circuit board side down and the SATA connectors facing the case—into the bay until you feel it seat. (When fully seated, the front of the

drive protrudes from the Easy SATA bay, which allows you to grip the drive to remove it.)

As soon as the drive connectors make contact, the drive should spin up. After a few seconds, as it reaches operating speed, a drive icon will appear automatically under Windows or Linux. (The drive icon may not appear automatically under Windows 7; if it doesn't, refresh [F5] your drives list and it should appear.) At that point, you can read from and write to the drive just as you would any internal hard drive.

To remove the drive, ensure that it is not in use and that all cached data has been flushed to the drive. (Right-click on the drive icon and choose "Remove Drive Safely," "Unmount," or a similarly worded option.) Press the button on the front of the Easy SATA bay to unlock the drive and then pull the drive far enough out of the bay to break the power connection. Allow several seconds for the drive to spin down and the heads to lock, and then pull the drive completely out of the bay. (If you simply pull the drive straight out of the bay without allowing it to spin down, the spinning platters act as a gyroscopic stabilizer, which is disconcerting. The first time we did that, we nearly dropped the drive.)

Finishing Up

At this point, the new system is just about ready to roll. Before you power it up, though, take a few minutes to do a few final tweaks.

First, if your server looks anything like ours did, there's a rats' nest of cables running hither and yon. Your new system will look better, be easier to trouble-shoot, and be more reliable if you dress those cables and tuck them out of the way. To dress the cables, organize them into bundles and route them as far away from the motherboard and other components—particularly fans—as possible. If necessary, disconnect cables temporarily to untangle them and reroute them as necessary. Use the cable ties supplied with the case to secure the bundles, and don't hesitate to tuck the cables under or tie them to chassis components to get them out of the way. (If you need more cable ties, the yellow plastic ties supplied with lawn bags work well.)

After you finish dressing the cables, do a final check to make sure everything is correct:

☐ Power supply input voltage set correctly (if applicable)
☐ No loose tools or screws (shake the case gently)
☐ CPU cooler properly mounted; CPU fan connected
☐ Memory modules fully seated and latched
☐ Front-panel switch and indicator cables connected properly
☐ Front-panel I/O cables connected properly
☐ Hard drive data cables connected to drives and motherboard
☐ Hard drive power cables connected
☐ Optical drive data cable connected to drive and motherboard
☐ Optical drive power cable connected
☐ All drives secured to drive bay or chassis, as applicable
☐ Expansion card(s) (if any) fully seated and secured to chassis
☐ Main ATX power cable and ATX12V power cable connected
☐ Case fan(s) installed and connected
☐ No unused cables flopping around

Once you're certain that all is as it should be, it's time for the smoke test. (As we mentioned earlier, you may want to do the smoke test with a minimal configuration to avoid risking all of your expensive hard drives.) Connect a keyboard, mouse, and display, and turn on the display.

Connect the power cable to the wall receptacle and then to the system unit. The Antec power supply has a separate rocker switch on the back that controls power to the power supply. By default, it's in the "0," or off, position, which means the power supply is not receiving power from the wall receptacle. Move that switch to the "1," or on, position. Press the main power button on the front of the case, and the system should start up. Check to make sure that all fans are spinning. You should also hear the hard drive(s) spin up. At that point, everything should be working properly.

False Starts

When you turn on the rear power switch, the system will come to life momentarily and then die. That's perfectly normal behavior. When the power supply receives power, it begins to start up. It quickly notices that the motherboard hasn't told it to start, though, so it shuts down again. All you need to do is press the front-panel power switch and the system will start normally.

If you did the smoke test with a minimal configuration, turn off the system now and reconnect the hard drives and any other components you'd left disconnected. After verifying that all connections are correct, turn the system back on and wait for the POST screen to display. Press F2 to enter BIOS Setup.

In BIOS Setup, verify that all of your devices are detected, including the full amount of memory, and set the correct date and time. Refer to your operating system documentation to determine if any other changes are necessary in BIOS Setup. Make any required changes, save those changes, and restart the system. At this point, you're ready to install your operating system and applications.

Final Words

This system went together smoothly and worked perfectly when we turned it on. Server hardware is useless without the software to run it, though, so we spent some time looking at various alternatives.

Choosing the operating system for a home server involves several trade-offs. We considered the following operating systems for our own home server:

Microsoft Windows Home Server

> Originally available only from hardware OEMs bundled with server hardware, Windows Home Server (WHS) can now be purchased separately for about $100. Early releases of WHS had an impressive feature set—not surprising, considering that WHS is essentially a cut-down version of Windows Server 2003 SP2—but suffered some serious problems, notably a severe data corruption bug that went unpatched for far too long. The current V1 release supports Windows 7 clients and is reliable.

> Microsoft plans to release WHS V2, a major upgrade, sometime in 2010. WHS V2 is based on Windows Server 2008 and requires a 64-bit processor, which obviously rules out upgrades for those running 32-bit systems. The WHS V2 feature set has not been announced as we write this, but we expect WHS V2 to include several major new features as well as significant upgrades to existing features.

> We ruled out WHS for our server because it would make no sense to buy and install the dated WHS V1 with WHS V2 so close to release. If WHS V2 includes features we want—and they are worth the (presumably) $100 price tag—it will be easy enough to buy and install it later. For now, we can do what we need to do (and do it well) using free software.

Desktop Windows

> We have numerous unused licenses lying around for versions of desktop Windows from Windows 7 all the way back to Windows NT 4. (Somehow we missed out on Vista.) We considered installing one of these—probably Windows XP—on our home server and simply setting up workgroup shares on the server. The problem with doing that is that desktop Windows is not designed to run headless, so we'd have to leave a display, keyboard, and

mouse connected to the server. We have plenty of spares lying around, but leaving those peripherals connected would make it difficult to tuck the server away under Robert's desk as we planned.

Ubuntu Server

Ubuntu Server is free-as-in-beer and free-as-in-speech. It uses text-based installation and maintenance, so it's unlikely to be suitable for anyone who's not comfortable with command-line Linux. On the other hand, this is serious server software. It's stripped down to essentials, hence the absence of a default GUI, and it's far faster than any of the other products we considered. One wonderful feature of Ubuntu Server is its scripted setup of a LAMP (Linux, Apache, MySQL, PHP/Perl/Python) server. Setting up a LAMP server manually may take a newbie hours (or an experienced Linux administrator maybe 20 minutes). With Ubuntu Server, setting up a LAMP server is a single menu option. Frankly, we think Ubuntu Server is a pretty good choice for a small office server, provided you're already a moderately experienced command-line-savvy Linux administrator (or have access to a Linux guru for advice and assistance). But it really is overkill for most home servers, which typically don't need to run web servers, mail servers, and so on.

A desktop Linux distribution

If your functional requirements are modest, don't rule out using a standard desktop Linux distribution like Ubuntu on your server. In theory, there are a lot of disadvantages to doing that, but in practice many of those objections disappear. For example, a desktop Linux distribution is usually slower than a purpose-built server distribution. So what? We'll never notice any tiny performance difference that may exist. A desktop distribution may not support software RAID. Again, we don't care, because we plan to run a JBOD on our home server. Desktop Linux distributions also have advantages relative to server distributions. The biggest advantage for most people is that the desktop distro uses a familiar graphic interface. Setting up a shared disk volume or printer is usually a matter of a few clicks. And most desktop Linux distributions are set up to allow remote management by default, or can easily be configured to do so.

A NAS package

There are several Linux- or FreeBSD-based *network-attached storage* (NAS) distributions that are optimized to function as servers rather than workstations. They do nothing that any other Linux or FreeBSD distribution can't do, but the advantage is that they're preconfigured to provide NAS functions with a standard installation. You could spend hours or days getting a desktop Linux or FreeBSD distribution set up to do the same things.

Among the most popular of these NAS packages are FreeNAS (*http://freenas.org*), NASLite (*http://www.serverelements.com*), and TurnKey Linux (*http://www.turnkeylinux.org*). All run on standard x86 systems and can be configured and managed from a web browser running on a network client. We also looked at NexentaStor (*http://www.nexenta.org*), which is an industrial-strength NAS environment based on OpenSolaris. The main

Nexenta product is commercial, but the community edition NexentaStor is freely downloadable and has only minor restrictions. (For example, the free version is limited to 12 TB of disk space in use.)

We looked at all of these alternatives except Windows Home Server, which we didn't have and didn't want to buy (for the reasons cited). We suggest you do the same before you decide on the OS for your server.

We first ruled out Windows Home Server, desktop Windows, and Ubuntu Server, for the reasons listed above. That left us with either desktop Linux or one of the NAS environments. We looked at several of the latter and decided that, as nice as some of them are, they really didn't do anything we needed to do that we couldn't do ourselves about as easily with a general Linux distro.

We ended up installing Ubuntu 10.04, mainly because it was familiar to us and we already knew how to do everything we needed to do to configure it as a remotely managed server. We run Ubuntu on all of our other computers, so using it on the server has the advantage of not requiring us to learn the ins and outs of a different operating system or distribution. Also, Ubuntu 10.04 is a long-term support (LTS) release, so we won't have to upgrade the OS until the next LTS release, 12.04, due in April 2012.

Alas, the best-laid plans sometimes go awry. Nothing we tried, including manually editing the *xorg.conf* file, allowed headless booting to work under Ubuntu 10.04. After beating our heads against the wall for several hours, we finally decided to punt. We installed Ubuntu 9.10, which worked perfectly.

Setting up headless booting, file sharing, and remote management in Ubuntu 9.10 took us all of 15 minutes, most of which we spent installing and configuring the Samba server, creating home directories and accounts, and setting permissions. When we finished setting up the server, we shut it down and disconnected the display, keyboard, and mouse. We then removed the optical drive, reinstalled the cover, moved the system under Robert's desk, connected it to the UPS and Ethernet, and pushed the start button. The system came up as expected and was visible to our network clients.

So we now have a stable server with gobs of disk space, which, after all, is what we set out to build.

Index

Symbols and Numbers

A

Mini-ITX PCs, 16–17
  recommended, 267–268
  SSD drives for, 271
mirroring (RAID 1), 296
MLC (multi-level cell) memory, 64
MLC (multi-level cell) SSD drive, 170
modular power cables, 45
Molex power connector, 44
monitors. *See* displays
Morse, Ron (contributor), xviii–xix
  classic IBM Model "M" keyboard,
      79, 174
  converter cables, 4-pin Molex to
      6-pin PCIe, 201
  cost of SSDs, 64
  CPU coolers, connecting to
      motherboard, 142
  degradation of optical drives, 66
  eSATA interface for removable
      storage, 244
  first time PC builders, advice for, 20
  protecting case from scratches by
      motherboard, 228
  SSDs for Windows 64-bit version,
      63
motherboards
  BIOS compatibility, 54
  cables included with, 301
  choosing, considerations for, 52–58
  communications ports on, 57–58
  compatibility with other
      components, 1
  configuration errors with, 25, 29
  cost of, 49–51
  CPU socket for, 52–54
  documentation for, 58
  expandability of, 8
  expansion slots of, 56–57
  form factor of, 55
  installing, alignment problems
      with, 232
  memory slots of, 55–56
  passive heatsink for, 16
  processor compatibility with, 54
  recommended, 59
    for appliance/nettop system,
        268–270
    for budget PC, 94–95
    for extreme PC, 164–166
    for home server, 301–302

for mainstream PC, 123–124
    for media center PC, 213–214
  standoffs for. *See* standoffs
  temperature sensors in, 14
  VRM compatibility, 54
movies. *See* DVDs; TV programs,
    recording
multi-level cell (MLC) memory, 64
multi-level cell (MLC) SSD drive, 170
Mushkin memory modules, 59
music CDs, ripping, 247–249
music management software,
    249–251
Mythbuntu Linux, 246

N

NAS (network-attached storage)
    package, 327–328
NEC displays, 76
needle-nose pliers, 21
nettop system. *See* appliance/nettop
    system
network-attached storage (NAS)
    package, 327–328
networking, for home server,
    291–292, 294–295
NewEgg, online vendor, 85–86
NexentaStor package, 327–328
noise level
  case affecting, 12
  case fans affecting, 15
  CPU cooler affecting, 13–14, 52
  dBs (deciBels) measurement for, 12
  of hard drives, 16
  mat underneath PC reducing, 15
  motherboard passive heatsink
      reducing, 16
  power supply affecting, 12–13
  priority of, 8
    for appliance/nettop system, 265
    for budget PC, 90, 91
    for extreme PC, 161
    for appliance/nettop system, 265
    for home server, 295
    for mainstream PC, 120, 121
    for media center PC, 209–210
  processor affecting, 11
  of small PCs, 17

sources of noise, 11
  video adapter passive heatsink
      reducing, 16
nut driver, 21
NVIDIA integrated video adapters, 72
  NVIDIA GeForce 8200, 94, 96
NVIDIA Scalable Link Interface (SLI),
    169
Nylon cable ties, 22

O

OEM packaging, 82
OEM Windows license, 4
operating system. *See also* Linux;
      Mac OS X; Windows
  distribution discs for, 22
  for media center PC, 245–246
  Missing Operating System error, 30
optical discs, 67
optical drives
  ATAPI compared to SATA, 306
  Blu-ray writers, 65
  choosing, considerations for, 64–66
  external, 66
  failure to boot from, 30–31
  recommended, 66–67
    for appliance/nettop system, 272
    for budget PC, 97
    for extreme PC, 173
    for mainstream PC, 127
    for media center PC, 217
    retail-boxed comapred to OEM
        version, 217
  USB portable optical drive, 306
OptiQuest monitors, 35

P

Parallel ATA (PATA) hard drives, 10, 61
passive heatsinks
  motherboard using, 16
  power supplies using, 13
  processors using, 13
  video adapter using, 16
PATA (Parallel ATA) hard drives, 10, 61
PCIe power connector, 43
PCI Express (PCIe) slots, 56
PCI slots, 56

PC Power & Cooling power supplies, 47
peak power rating, 219
performance
  balanced design affecting, 10
  benchmarks for, 33
  brand names related to, 34–35
  of hard drive, 10, 61
  priority of
    for appliance/nettop system, 266
    for budget PC, 90, 91–92
    for extreme PC, 160, 161–162
    for home server, 295–296
    for mainstream PC, 120
    for media center PC, 210
  of processor, 9
  of video, 9
peripheral power connectors, 43–44
personal/digital video recorder (PVR/DVR), 205–206. See also media center PC
PFC (power factor correction), 46–47
Phillips screwdrivers, 21
photo management and editing software, 256–257
Pioneer optical drives, 67
  Pioneer BDR-205BKS Blu-ray disc burner, 173
place-shifting DVDs, 252
Plextor optical drives, 66–67
pliers, 21
Pournelle, Jerry (columnist)
  experiences building a PC, 3
  Falcon Electric UPS, earthquake experience with, 306–307
  foreword by, ix–xii
power factor correction (PFC), 46–47
powering up
  checks to perform before, 19
  disconnecting hard drives before, 322
  high-pitched noise during, 31
  minimal configuration for, 20
  not working, 26–27
  two-tone siren sound after, 31
  working only briefly, 28, 117
power supplies
  80 PLUS initiative for, 13
  adequacy of, 28

autosensing, 134, 180, 309
brand name significance for, 35
bundled with cases, 39
choosing, considerations for, 41–47
compatibility with receptacle, 100
efficiency of, 13, 45–46
expandability supported by, 8
form factor of, 41
input voltage switch, 180, 221
main power connector for, 42
manufacturer of, 44–45
modular power cables for, 45
noise from, minimizing, 12–13
not opening, 1
PCIe power connector for, 43
peripheral power connectors for, 43–44
power factor correction (PFC) for, 46–47
recommended, 47
  for appliance/nettop system, 267–268
  for budget PC, 92
  for extreme PC, 163–164
  for home server, 300–301
  for mainstream PC, 122–123
  for media center PC, 211–213
supplemental power connector for, 42–43
troubleshooting, 26
wattage rating for, 41–42
pre-built PCs. See manufactured PCs
price
  of cases, 38
  of components
    shipping and taxes affecting, 81
    spending too much on, 10
    volume affecting, 2
  ESP (estimated selling price), 81
  of manufactured PCs, 2
  of memory modules, 60
  of motherboards, 49–51
  price comparison sites, 82
  priority of, 6
    for appliance/nettop system, 264, 265
    for budget PC, 91
    for extreme PC, 160

for home server, 295
for mainstream PC, 120
for media center PC, 209
of processors, 9, 34, 49–50
quality related to, 34
SRP (suggested retail price), 81
of SSDs, 63, 64
"sweet spot" for, 34
taxes on component purchases, 81
of USB flash drives, 68
of video adapters, 9
problems. See troubleshooting
processors (CPUs)
  bundled with CPU cooler, 51
  choosing, considerations for, 47–51
  cooling. See CPU coolers
  cost of, 34, 49–50
  embedded, 49
  motherboard compatibility with, 54
  performance of
    for appliance/nettop system, 264–265, 266
    for budget PC, 91
    comparisons of, 93–94
    for extreme PC, 160, 161
    for home server, 295
    for mainstream PC, 121
    measuring, 93
    priority of, 9
  power consumption of, noise and, 11, 13–14
  recommended, 51
    for appliance/nettop system, 268–270
    for budget PC, 93–94
    for extreme PC, 166–167
    for home server, 301–302
    for mainstream PC, 124–125
    for media center PC, 213
  temperature of, monitoring, 14
  troubleshooting, 27
product recommendations. See recommended products
product reviews, 36
PVR/DVR (personal/digital video recorder), 205–206. See also media center PC

Colophon

The heading and cover font are BentonSans, the text font is Myriad Pro, and the code font is TheSansMonoCondensed.

About the Authors

Robert Bruce Thompson is the author or coauthor of numerous books and online training courses about computers. Robert built his first computer in 1976 from discrete chips. It had 256 *bytes* of memory, used toggle switches and LEDs for I/O, ran at less than 1 MHz, and had no operating system. In the more than 30 years since he built that first system, Robert has bought, built, upgraded, and repaired hundreds of PCs for himself, employers, customers, friends, and clients. Robert also writes about science—including astronomy, chemistry, biology, forensics, earth science, physics, and other disciplines—and practices what he preaches in his home laboratory. You can watch Robert's Home Scientist video series at *http://www.youtube.com/TheHomeScientist*.

Barbara Fritchman Thompson worked for 20 years as a librarian before starting her own home-based consulting practice, Research Solutions (*http://www. researchsolutions.net*), and is also a researcher for the law firm Womble Carlyle Sandridge & Rice, PLLC. Barbara, who has been a PC power user for more than 20 years, researched and tested much of the hardware reviewed for this book. During her leisure hours, Barbara reads, works out, plays golf, and, like Robert, is an avid amateur astronomer.

Related Titles from O'Reilly

Hardware

BlackBerry Hacks

Building Extreme PCs

Building the Perfect PC, *2nd Edition*

Car PC Hacks

Craft: The Second Year

Designing Embedded Hardware, *2nd Edition*

Eccentric Cubicle

Fashioning Technology

Hardware Hacking Projects for Geeks

Home Hacking Projects for Geeks

Makers: All Kinds of People Making Amazing Things
  in Their Backyard, Basement or Garage

Make Magazine: The Fourth Year

Make Projects: Small Form Factor PCs

Making Things Talk

Nokia Smartphones Hacks

Palm and Treo Hacks

PC Hacks

PC Hardware Annoyances

PC Hardware Buyer's Guide

PCs: The Missing Manual

Repairing and Upgrading Your PC

Smart Home Hacks

Talk Is Cheap

The Best of Instructables, *Volume I*

The Best of Make

Treo Fan Book

Wireless Hacks, *2nd Edition*

Our books are available at most retail and online bookstores.
To order direct: 1-800-998-9938 • *order@oreilly.com* • *www.oreilly.com*
Online editions of most O'Reilly titles are available by subscription at *safari.oreilly.com*

Get even more for your money.

Join the O'Reilly Community, and register the O'Reilly books you own. It's free, and you'll get:

- $4.99 ebook upgrade offer
- 40% upgrade offer on O'Reilly print books
- Membership discounts on books and events
- Free lifetime updates to ebooks and videos
- Multiple ebook formats, DRM FREE
- Participation in the O'Reilly community
- Newsletters
- Account management
- 100% Satisfaction Guarantee

Signing up is easy:

1. Go to: oreilly.com/go/register
2. Create an O'Reilly login.
3. Provide your address.
4. Register your books.

Note: English-language books only

To order books online:

oreilly.com/store

For questions about products or an order:

orders@oreilly.com

To sign up to get topic-specific email announcements and/or news about upcoming books, conferences, special offers, and new technologies:

elists@oreilly.com

For technical questions about book content:

booktech@oreilly.com

To submit new book proposals to our editors:

proposals@oreilly.com

O'Reilly books are available in multiple DRM-free ebook formats. For more information:

oreilly.com/ebooks

Spreading the knowledge of innovators   oreilly.com

Buy this book and get access to the online edition for 45 days—for free!